POLITICAL CHANGE AND THE RISE
OF LABOUR IN COMPARATIVE PERSPECTIVE

Political Change
and the Rise of Labour
in Comparative Perspective

Britain and Sweden 1890–1920

Mary Hilson

NORDIC ACADEMIC PRESS

Nordic Academic Press
Box 1206, 221 05 Lund, Sweden
info@nordicacademicpress.com
www.nordicacademicpress.com

© Nordic Academic Press and the Author 2006
Typesetting: Stilbildarna i Mölle, Frederic Täckström
Cover design: Anette Rasmusson
Cover image: Labour-day demonstration 1903, Stortorget in Karlskrona.
Photograph from Blekinge museum's archives
Printrun: 1 2 3 4 5 6 7 8 9 10
Printed by Preses Nams, Riga 2006
ISBN 10: 91-89116-71-2
ISBN 13: 978-91-89116-71-9

Contents

Acknowledgements

Some parts of this book began life as a doctoral thesis on labour politics in Plymouth, and I would like to thank my supervisors at the University of Exeter, Joseph Melling, Helen Rogers and Andrew Thorpe, for their help and advice then and since. The opportunity to undertake a comparative study came with the award of a Study Abroad Studentship from the Leverhulme Trust, which gave me the chance to spend two years in Sweden between 1998 and 2000. The generous terms of the award were invaluable, not only in that they allowed me to undertake the primary research for this book, but also provided an opportunity to immerse myself thoroughly in Swedish historical research and academic life. I am also very grateful to the Department of Economic History at Uppsala University, which generously accommodated me as a visiting researcher, and provided me with excellent facilities during the whole time I was in Sweden. I have benefited from the advice of many colleagues in Uppsala, especially Maths Isacson, Alf Johansson, Göran Rydén and Göran Salmonsson. The Department of Scandinavian Studies, University College London, allowed me a term's sabbatical leave to complete the writing of this book as well as contributing towards the costs of several research trips to Sweden, and for this I also received financial support from the Dean's Travel Fund, Faculty of Arts and Humanities, and the Graduate School at UCL. At UCL I would like to thank in particular David Kirby and Thomas Munch-Petersen, both of whom read and commented on proposals for this book.

Many people have generously read and commented on drafts of chapters, including David Harvey, Hanna Hodacs, Pernilla Jonsson, Nick McGhee, Silke Neunsinger and Melly Barrett. I would like to thank Elisabeth Elgán, Katarina Friberg and Natasha Vall, who shared a session on Anglo-Swedish comparative history at the European Social Science History Conference (2004) in Berlin with me, along with many others who have commented on my work in this respect. Barbara Rosborg has been a generous source of advice on translating obscure terms from Swedish. Any errors or omissions which remain are of course my own responsibility.

Sweden has archive facilities for historical research which historians coming from Britain can only dream about. I would like to thank Ylva Lindström, Manne Dunge and staff at the Karlskrona Maritime Museum in Karlskrona; Per Lundin at the Folkrörelsearkiv at Bräkne-Hoby, Blekinge and Björn Gäfvert at the Krigsarkiv in Stockholm. In Britain, special thanks to Gill Tombs and the staff of the Member Relations Department, Plymouth and South Devon Co-operative Society for allowing me to use the co-operative archives – it is to be hoped that it will soon be possible to make this extremely valuable resource, currently locked away in store, available to historians again.

I would like to thank my editor at Nordic Academic Press, Annika Olsson, for her patience and helpfulness. The maps were drawn by Catherine D'alton in the Drawing Office, Department of Geography at UCL. The publication costs were supported by a grant from the Swedish Research Council.

Finally, my warmest personal thanks go to my parents, Frances and Michael Hilson, to my partner David Harvey, and to all my friends in Uppsala and beyond for helping to make my frequent trips to Sweden so enjoyable.

A Note on the Translation
of Swedish Terms

All the translations in the text are my own, unless otherwise stated. Many words were difficult to translate, and to avoid confusion I have, where possible, also given the Swedish equivalent in the text.

In writing about Karlskrona dockyard, I have preferred as far as possible to provide more or less literal translations of the Swedish shipbuilding trades, rather than adopting the most obvious English equivalent. This is partly because the demarcation of work was, inevitably, slightly different in Karlskrona to that in the British dockyards, or indeed in the private British shipbuilding industry. These translations are only approximate, however, and what follows is a short discussion of some of this terminology in more detail. In each case I have indicated the English term which I have used in the text with an asterisk.

The largest trade in shipbuilding were the *plåtslagare* (*platers). They were responsible for producing and hanging the large iron or steel plates which formed part the ship's hull; in other words they were responsible for the bulk of the heavy construction. Their work was more or less equivalent to the shipwrights' in the British naval dockyards. Although many Swedish shipbuilding workers were considered to have generic heavy engineering skills, the *plåtslagare* were one trade with skills specific to shipbuilding.

In private shipyards in Sweden, *plåtslagare* could be assisted in their work by a variety of other trades, including *spantbockare* (frame benders), *nitare* (riveters), *mothållare* (holders up) and *diktare* (caulkers). None of these trades were specified in the dockyard, implying that they were probably performed by *plåtslagarehantlangare* (*platers' helpers).

The *filare* (*fitters) were concerned with assembling the ships' engines; also repairing motors and machines, and assembling different parts of machines. Unlike *plåtslagare*, their skills were not specific to shipbuilding. Associated trades could include *maskinuppsättare* (lit: machine installer), *bänkarbetare: hopsättare* (machine bench worker: fitter), and *bänkarbetare: provare* (machine bench worker: tester).

Maskinarbetare (*machinists) could be translated as 'mechanics' though for the sake of clarity I have avoided this term, since it was sometimes used generically to describe all apprenticed craftsmen in Devonport dockyard. Associated trades included *svarvare* (*lathe turners) and *borrare* (*drillers) – in other words, those who used precision machine tools.

Metalworking traders included *smeder* (*blacksmiths), *kopparlagare* (*coppersmiths), *bleckslagare* (*tinsmiths), *gjutare* (*foundrymen) and *pannmakare* (*boilermakers).

Woodworking trades included *timmermän* (*carpenters) and *snickare* (*woodworkers). Both terms could in fact be translated as 'carpenters', but their work was different. *Timmermän* were employed to carry out the heavier wooden construction, and often worked on the keel and ribs of a new ship. Before the advent of metal shipbuilding, this group was the equivalent to the English shipwrights. *Snickare* carried out the finer woodwork. *Modellsnickare* were equivalent to *patternmakers.

Part I

Rethinking Comparative
Labour History

CHAPTER I

Introduction – Exceptionalism in Comparative Labour History

This book is a study of political change and the emergence of a working-class political movement in two naval dockyard towns, Plymouth
in Britain and Karlskrona in Sweden. Naval dockyard towns, where
a large proportion of the adult male population was employed in the
direct service of the state, and where the early twentieth century agitation for 'big navy' politics seemed to have a particular resonance,
have often been thought of as difficult territory for the labour movement, and for that reason have been largely ignored by labour historians. One of the main concerns of the study, therefore, is to explore
the politics of naval defence in the local context, and the particular
challenges which this presented to the emergent labour movement.
Through a detailed exploration of the conditions of dockyard work,
of everyday life and municipal politics at the local level, I hope to show
that the politics of the dockyard town in were in fact far more complex and interesting than they are sometimes assumed to be.

The study has a wider ambition though, and that is to investigate
a broad comparative question, namely, why did social democratic
labour parties emerge in most European countries during the late nineteenth century? A major problem of cross-national comparison is that
the historian is usually required to make huge generalisations, thus
ignoring the internal variations and complexities of a particular case
and presenting it in monolithic, over-simplified terms.[1] The preferred
methods of many labour historians – local and microscopic – do not
seem to lend themselves readily to international comparisons, especially where such comparisons have a tendency to over-exaggerate the
differences between states and nations at the expense of equally
important variations at local or regional level.[2] One of the aims of the
present study is to demonstrate that cross-national comparisons are

indeed compatible with local studies. It is argued that to be successful, cross-national comparisons have to be based on a more pluralist
understanding of the complex processes and regional patterns and variations which make up a national case. In recent years there have been
a number of calls for international comparative histories which move
beyond the nation state, but, as yet, not more than a handful of studies which has actually done this.[3] Moreover, much comparative labour
history continues to be informed by the influential thesis of exceptionalism, in particular the assumption that Britain was fundamentally different to the 'continental' labour parties. The difficulties with
this approach are explored in the first two chapters of the book, comparing the British case with Sweden. One of the advantages of a cross-
national comparative study is that it requires the historian to develop a familiarity with two separate historiographical traditions, thus
exposing sometimes long-held assumptions to new questions and
approaches.

I

The British labour movement has been described as "the most anomalous left in Europe".[4] Scholars have consistently regarded the British
left as fundamentally different from its continental counterparts,
exceptional in its historical development. The thesis of British exceptionalism has deep historical roots. Egon Wertheimer, observing the
British labour movement at first hand during the 1920s, noted the 'wide
difference' between the Labour Party and the socialist movement in
his native Germany. Continental socialist parties were dogmatic and
disciplined, homogenous and uniform in spirit, structure, organisation, vocabulary and leadership. In contrast,

> How different is the Labour Party! Without a past that sets it in
> opposition to State and society, it reflects the national character-
> istics of the English people, undeterred and untroubled by the oth-
> er Labour parties of the world. It is more British than German
> social democracy is German, Polish Socialism Polish.[5]

Two characteristics in particular seemed to set the British Labour Party apart from the rest of Europe: the limited influence of socialism
and the party's organisational structure, especially its relationship with
the trade unions. Following the defeat of Chartism in the mid-nine-

teenth century, so the argument went, the British working class had turned its back on revolutionary politics, embracing instead 'purely economic' trade union action to defend their interests. Rather than being united by class consciousness, British working-class politics was fragmented and sectional, steered by the pragmatism of the trade unions, and the alliance between labour interests and radical Liberalism.[6] The failure of Marxism to make more of an impact on the British working class could be explained by a number of anomalies within British social and political development: the social and geographical fragmentation of the working class; the apolitical nature of working-class associational culture in Britain; the extent to which the working class was integrated into existing political arrangements; and the lack of intellectual ideological leaders in the British labour movement.[7] For these reasons, class loyalty and cohesiveness, not socialist doctrine, became the unifying principle of the Labour Party. As one influential historian of the party suggested,

> One of the most highly class-conscious working-classes in the world produced a Party whose appeal was specifically intended to be classless. Accepting the Labour Party meant accepting not socialism but an intricate network of loyalties… This was a trade-union code of behaviour; so were the political aims of the Labour Party essentially trade-union ones.[8]

The exceptionalism of the British labour movement has to be seen within a wider tradition of historical writing which has set Britain's historical development apart from that of the rest of Europe, especially in its constitutional development.[9] This tradition pervades even the most critical accounts of national history. For Perry Anderson and Tom Nairn, the failure of the English working class to develop a revolutionary consciousness was attributed not so much to the specific conditions generated by late nineteenth century political and social developments, but to the 'cumulative fundamental moments of modern English history.'[10] The 'least pure' bourgeois revolution in Europe resulted in the emergence of a bourgeois capitalist class which was 'fragmentary and incomplete', while the experience of the world's first industrial revolution allowed the formation of an industrial proletariat which predated the development of socialist theory. This allowed the ruling class to inflict a comprehensive defeat on the English working class as early as the 1840s. By the 1880s, 'the world had moved on.

In consciousness and combativity, the English working-class had been overtaken by almost all its continental opposites... In France, in Germany, in Italy, Marxism swept the working-class. In England everything was against it.'[11] Thus, even though Anderson and Nairn's account was deeply critical of the trajectory of English history, it nonetheless remained indebted to the classic Whig interpretation – the evolution and continuity of English institutions, and the wholesale rejection of revolutionary change – to explain why the politics of the English working class differed from those of its continental counterparts.

The British Labour Party is not alone in having been described as exceptional. The absence of a European-style socialist party in the USA has been attributed to supposed American exceptionalism, especially those historical circumstances which worked in favour of individualism and against class consciousness in a country which was 'born modern'.[12] The development of the nineteenth century French labour movement was seen as paradoxical, in that a deep sense of class hostility and militancy on the shop floor failed to produce strong trade unions or socialist parties. Historians have cited the French path to industrialisation and the specificity of French political culture, among other causes, to explain this distinctiveness.[13] Meanwhile, the highly centralised structure of the German Social Democratic Party (SPD), and the influence of dogmatic Marxism on its ideology, have often been explained with reference to the German *Sonderweg*.[14] Germany's rapid and traumatic 'path to modernity' in the nineteenth century imposed socio-economic modernisation onto a state that remained relatively backward in political terms, which explained why bourgeois liberalism remained weak, and why it never collaborated with the working-class movement. This, together with the authoritarian reaction of the state to the German labour movement, forced the SPD into a state of isolation, and left it helpless to respond to the crises of the Weimar Republic.

With few exceptions, therefore, cross-national comparative studies in labour history have generally been individualising, to use Tilly's term; that is, they have attempted to identify and explain the differences between labour movements in different national contexts.[15] That this should be the case appears rather paradoxical, given the internationalist aspirations of the European labour movement. Marx and Engels had, in a famous passage from *The Communist Manifesto*, expressed their confident belief that international capitalism was undermining national differences among European workers.

> Modern industrial labour, modern subjection to capital, the same in England as in France, in America as in Germany, has stripped [the proletarian] of every trace of national character... National differences and antagonisms between peoples are daily more and more vanishing, owing to the development of the bourgeoisie, to freedom of commerce, to the world market, to uniformity in the mode of production and in the conditions of life corresponding thereto.[16]

The first edition of the *Manifesto* was published simultaneously in six European languages to underline the point that, as an international phenomenon, capitalism could only be challenged by a movement that was truly international in its scope. The views expressed in it were echoed throughout the late nineteenth century labour movement. 'The foundations, aims and methods of the proletarian class struggle are everywhere growing more similar,' declared Karl Kautsky in 1892.[17] Most socialists recognised that the socialist challenge would probably be modified to reflect varying conditions in different parts of Europe, but equally they retained their belief in the universal appeal of their movement, and its ability to transgress national boundaries. The leader of the Swedish Social Democratic Party, Hjalmar Branting, distinguished three main strands within the European labour movement: the 'scientific' socialism of the SPD; the French passion for *liberté, égalité* and *fraternité*; and the empiricism and pragmatism of English socialism.[18] According to Branting, however, the universalism of the socialist struggle transcended any purely national characteristics. Writing the foreword to the Swedish edition of Blatchford's *Merrie England*, which appeared in 1896, Branting emphasised the relevance of the English socialist tradition for Swedish social democracy:

> Both capitalism, and socialism its heir, have far too much of international humanity in their blood to be tied into national particularities. The Swedish worker, [when he] reads of contemporary England and of 'Merrie England'... will recognise himself in all essential respects, his own life of slavery, his own wretched uncertain existence... What does it then mean if one or another detail is different, if proletarianisation is in some cases even more acute [*skärande*] in England [than in Sweden]...?[19]

By the beginning of the twentieth century, however, and especially after the demise of the Second International, it was becoming clear that there were important national differences between the European labour movements. As political parties, labour movements were concerned with gaining control over the apparatus of the nation state, and their struggles to do this were thought to be shaped primarily by the peculiar conditions of the state of which they were a part. The principal concern of researchers in the years after 1918, therefore, was to explain why working-class politics varied in different parts of the continent.[20] The influence of the social sciences on historical research from the 1960s generated a new interest in the comparative method as the means by which hypotheses could be subjected to a rigorous quasi-scientific test, and causal variables could be isolated.[21] Indeed, as several comparative historians have pointed out, there was little point in a comparative history that attempted merely to describe differences or similarities between two cases; the main value of the comparative method lay in its ability to provide explanations for these differences and similarities.[22] International comparative labour history thus became concerned with the search for the variable, or the set of variables, which could best explain differences between two or more cases. Very briefly, these explanations could be divided into two groups. Early studies were concerned mostly with the timing and experience of industrialisation, and its implications for class formation. For example, Edvard Bull's 1922 comparison of the three Scandinavian countries sought to explain the apparently divergent path of Bull's own Norwegian Labour Party (DNA), which was the only pre-war social democratic party to join Comintern in 1919, with reference to Norwegian industrialisation. Bull found that Norwegian industrial development took place later and more rapidly than in the rest of Scandinavia, which led to a greater concentration of industry, and an industrial working class which had experienced much more traumatic social upheaval during its formation.[23] Bull's theory was later taken up by the American scholar Walter Galenson, whose own comparative studies helped to develop the thesis of a positive connection between rapid industrialisation and political radicalism.[24] According to the so-called Bull-Galenson thesis, the Danish experience of slow and piecemeal industrialisation, producing mostly for the home market, meant that farm labourers and urban artisans were gradually incorporated into the industrial working class. These groups were used to the discipline of working for an employer, and improvements in living standards meant that they were unlikely to turn to political extremism. The Danish case was diametrically opposed to that of Norway, therefore, where industrialisation was an 'explosive' force, shattering existing social bonds. Caught up in the upheavals and uncertainties of the process, and uprooted more thoroughly from the pre-industrial past, formerly independent peasants found themselves catapulted into industrial waged labour and exposed to a massive drop in living standards, which made them strongly susceptible to the appeal of political radicalism. Radicalism appealed most strongly to the rootless construction workers, who tended to migrate between workplaces, and came to form the main group behind the radical 'Tranmæl current' which gained ascendancy in the Norwegian Labour Party after 1918. Sweden, meanwhile, lay between these two extreme cases. Here, industrialisation was more rapid than in Denmark, but less of a brutal upheaval than in Norway, and the labour movement was consequently more moderate in its politics.

From the 1970s, a new generation of scholars declared themselves dissatisfied with economic explanations for labour movement difference, and attention was instead directed towards the structure of the state, and its willingness or otherwise to accommodate the demands of the working class.[25] The timing of democratisation had long been held to be important, but more systematic approaches to comparing state structures drew on a broader definition of the state, understood as, 'the continuous administrative, legal, bureaucratic and coercive systems that attempt not only to structure relationships between civil society and public authority in a polity, but also to structure many crucial relationships within civil society as well.'[26] Attention was turned therefore to the relationship between the working and ruling classes, and in particular, the response of economic and political élites to the demands of workers. Where the working class was denied full economic and political citizenship – as it was in Sweden, Finland, Austria and Germany – workers were more likely to turn towards revolutionary movements.[27] In Germany, the ties between the dominant *Junker* class and the state provoked direct antagonism with the labour movement, and turned it towards a centralised and tightly disciplined Marxist social democratic organisation. This contrasted with France, where the separation of dominant class and state resulted in a labour movement for which anarcho-syndicalism was the most attractive option, and with Britain, where a weak, fragmented state gave rise to a fractured labour movement which did not go to war with the state, but instead negotiated with individual employers to improve living standards. Labour movements, in other words, were organised in the image of the state which they hoped to conquer.[28] In more recent years, the concern with élite responses to working-class demands has been broadened to include industrial relations, and also the relationship between working-class and bourgeois liberal movements.[29] Gregory Luebbert's ambitious study of inter-war politics across Europe suggests that the possibilities for forging cross-class alliances between working-class movements, bourgeois liberal parties and the peasantry was key in determining whether inter-war regimes followed the path of liberal democracy, social democracy or fascism.[30]

Despite its continued influence, the exceptionalist thesis is problematic in several important respects. First, it often seems to imply the existence of an abstract model or ideal type against which other cases may be compared.[31] E P Thompson wrote a famous critique of the Andersen/Nairn thesis in these terms, in his essay 'The Peculiarities of the English', pointing out that their account of English history rested on an attempt to apply a continental model, derived from the French experience, to England.[32] The problem with this approach was that it ignored actual historical realities in favour of assumptions of what it 'should' have been like. Seen in its proper historical context, Thompson argued, the emergence of a bourgeois capitalist class in Britain was not 'incomplete', it was merely 'unusual':

> It arose, like <u>every</u> real historical situation, from a particular equilibrium of forces; it was only one of the seemingly infinite number of social mutations... which actual history provides in such profusion... It happened in one way in France, in another way in England. I am not disputing the importance of the difference – and of the different traditions which ensued – but the notion of typicality.[33]

At one level, therefore, Thompson's essay could be read as an argument for national specificity, against the abstract nature of overarching theories such as Marxism.[34] Nineteenth century industrialisation could not be understood as a monolithic and universal process, which had similar consequences and produced similar reactions across the continent. Rather, the political responses to industrialisation were always fragmented and widely varied, and had to be understood, therefore, in terms of 'unique processes', not only of industrialisation, but also of class formation and the role of the state. However, historical peculiarity should not be confused with historical exceptionalism. Indeed, Thompson's essay provides an important critique of the exceptionalist approach, which has been echoed by other scholars. Attempts to explain deviations from a supposed model or pattern were problematic in that they accounted for historical phenomena in terms of failure or absence, rather than what actually happened. The German *Sonderweg* was for example attributable to the 'failure' of liberalism, American exceptionalism to the 'absence' of a feudal past.[35] The main problem with this approach was that it often rested on very different assumptions about what was 'normal' within different historiographical traditions, and thus what required explanation as a deviation.[36] For some British historians, it was the strength of 'lib-labism' during the mid-Victorian period which seemed to be the anomaly, while their colleagues in Germany were equally concerned with accounting for the opposite: why did broad-based, cross-class liberalism fail in Germany during the same period?[37] Moreover, as the range of comparative studies proves, it has been impossible to agree on a standard case which could be taken as a 'normal' or model example against which other cases might be compared. If the real question underlying a comparative study is 'Why wasn't Britain France?' then it might also be asked, 'Why wasn't France Germany?' or 'Why wasn't Germany England?' As David Blackbourn and Geoff Eley pointed out in their critique of the *Sonderweg* theory, Anglo-American or French developments usually formed the 'ideal type' against which Germany was measured, and found wanting, by *Sonderweg* historians. The problem with this approach was that not only was Germany not England; England was not England either. Instead, German historians had persistently misunderstood British political and constitutional practice, and were operating with an imagined notion of a model liberal democracy which would have been unrecognisable to many English historians.[38] Such explanations may prove even more unsustainable when a third case is brought into the comparison.[39] As several recent comparative studies have pointed out, the German case has become distorted by constant comparisons with Britain. If Germany is instead compared to Sweden, the comparison helps not so much to confirm the *Sonderweg* theory, but also to contradict it. At the beginning of the twentieth century Sweden shared several characteristics with Germany, including the experience of rapid industrialisation and a strong bureaucratic state. The Swedish bourgeoisie was, if anything, weaker and more fragmented than its German counterpart, yet even so, Sweden was able to democratise more rapidly and less traumatically than Germany.[40]

A further problem with the exceptionalist thesis is that it helps to reinforce teleological assumptions about the inevitability of a pre-ordained national path.[41] Historical phenomena such as the emergence of a labour movement are explained in relation to a nation's 'path to modernity': the nature of pre-industrial society, and the measure of upheaval with which the transition to modernity was accomplished, are understood as the inevitable determinants of the forms which popular politics would take in the nineteenth century. Taken to its logical conclusion, this suggests that the reformism of the British labour movement could have been determined as long ago as the English Civil War in the seventeenth century. The defeat of Chartism in the 1840s merely sealed the fate of the British working class and confirmed its unstoppable course towards the rejection of socialism. Similarly, there have been recent attempts to understand the so-called 'Swedish model' of politics and social policy in the twentieth century in terms of a Swedish historical *Sonderweg* stretching back to the Enlightenment and even earlier.[42] In this way, therefore, supposedly objective historical accounts contribute to the foundational myths of modern European states, and have had a 'key political importance… in promoting a certain version of the nation's historical mission, its national myths about the past and its role and identity in the present.'[43]

II

One of the main advantages of the comparative approach over a single-nation study is that, by exposing national assumptions to the questions of a different historiographical tradition, it may compel a re-examination of long-held national assumptions, and ultimately, therefore, help to undermine the link between history-writing and nation-building.[44] Phenomena which may be taken for granted in the context of one case may begin to look much less inevitable when examined in the light of another; long-held assumptions may appear to be problematic. By examining the British case in the light of a comparison with Sweden, this study aims to reassess the thesis of British exceptionalism. The ongoing debate over European integration, and Britain's relationship to both Europe and America, suggests that such a reassessment is timely. Not only that, but the renewed attention in recent years to the international aspects of the capitalist economy – so-called globalisation – and the emergence of a international movement in opposition to it, serves as a reminder that the nineteenth century labour movement was also internationalist in outlook, and that the nation state might not be the most appropriate framework for its examination.

Recent methodological developments in social history, namely the criticism of materialist or structural explanations for political change, and interest instead in the language and ideology of popular politics, have also had important implications for cross-national comparison, and provoke a reassessment of the exceptionalist thesis.[45] Some historians have questioned the value of comparing historical phenomena across national boundaries, and turned instead to analysing processes of cross-national cultural transfer.[46] Attention has been directed to the spread of ideas across Europe and beyond, and relatively new fields of enquiry have been developed. The emphasis on the written word, through for example the translation and reception of important texts, has opened up the possibilities for an interdisciplinary approach. Most importantly, rather than reinforcing a sense of national specificity, attention to cultural transfer can help to reveal the complex, open and hybrid nature of different societies, deny exceptionalism and disrupt nationalist teleologies.[47] The emergence of so-called 'new British history' in recent years, with its focus on the relationships and exchanges between the four nations which make up Britain, as well as the impact of post-colonial scholarship on British history, has been extremely influential in this respect. However, as David Armitage has pointed out, in some respects this new focus has amounted to an extreme 'Euro-scepticism', which has isolated British history from European or 'continental' developments. Europe is hardly conceived as 'other', more likely as simply irrelevant to British history.[48]

The problem with the cultural transfer approach, and indeed with the methodological shift which underpins it, is that even though it undermines the notion that national histories developed in isolation, it can offer little satisfactory explanation for why large-scale historical phenomena should have developed in similar ways across national boundaries. Cultural transfer alone cannot explain the fundamental question which forms the starting point for this study: *why* did social democratic labour parties emerge in most European countries during the late nineteenth century? Why did groups of people, who for the most part had little direct knowledge of the existence of similar groups of people in other parts of Europe, engage in broadly similar types of political action at more or less the same time? It is here that a truly comparative approach would seem to be more fruitful. As Marc Bloch suggested, in what must be regarded as one of the founding texts of comparative history, the main value of the comparative method lies in its ability to explain phenomena which might otherwise be taken for granted.[49] For this reason, there have been several calls for more comparative labour history as a means of revitalising the field in recent years, although it might also be added that such studies remain regrettably rare, and that few would disagree with the observation that international comparative labour history remains 'a theory without much practice'.[50] There have, however, been some signs that comparative historians have consciously turned away from individualising comparisons which stress the exceptionalism of particular cases. John Horne's comparison of the French and British labour movements during the First World War is based on the assumption that, 'despite the deeply individualistic features imparted to labour movements by the national contexts in which they evolve, the essentially transnational processes which create them result in certain similarities.'[51] In particular, the experience of total war exhibited similar features in different settings, as did associated reformulation and acceleration in economic growth, the 'second wind' of industrialisation, which occurred during the same period. This is not to deny the existence of important variations, not least in the relationship between the industrial and political organisation of labour in the two countries, but these should not obscure the similar impact of the war and the changing role of the state during the period 1900–1914. In both countries, 'war moved the frontier between state and society', with important consequences for the labour movement.[52] Admittedly Horne is concerned with one single aspect of the European labour movement during its formative years, although that is a very important one. A more systematic comparison is provided by Stefan Berger's study of the British Labour Party and the German Social Democrats during the period 1900–31, which at times is almost polemical in its insistence on the importance of similarities over differences between the two cases. Berger undertakes a direct comparison of the two parties from a number of angles: the integration of the parties into their respective societies, party organisation, associational culture, and ideology. In both cases, his conclusion is that the similarities between the two cases outweighed the obvious differences. The main value of his approach lies in his willingness to compare developments across time, rather than presenting the more usual static picture. For example, rejecting the stereotyped view of a 'haphazard and amateurish' Labour Party organisation, contrasted with the efficient party machinery of the SPD, Berger describes the gradual and at times contested evolution of a central bureaucracy and branch organisation in both parties. This is not to deny that there were important differences between the SPD and the Labour Party. In organisation, 'the German party mirrored the federal German Reich, [while] the Labour Party in its organisation mirrored the centralised London-based system of government in Britain.'[53] Acknowledgement of these differences, however, should not obscure our recognition of the universal dynamic processes involved in the shaping of mass membership, social democratic parties. Thus Berger concludes that, 'it [may] be more appropriate to speak of a European labour movement including both the Labour Party and the SPD,' than to pursue *Sonderweg* or exceptionalist notions in the history of the labour movement.[54]

Overall, Berger presents a convincing refutation of exceptionalism in either the British or German cases. He is less concerned, however, with explaining the problem of formation: *why* did these labour movements emerge at more or less the same time and in similar ways? His basic theoretical assumption – that the emergence of independent labour movements is linked to the formation of an industrial working class – is given little space for discussion, and may seem rather problematic in the light of recent trends within the British historiography at least.[55] Although Berger's study remains an extremely valuable account, and indeed pioneering in its insistence on the need for universalising comparative labour history, there remains a need for comparative studies which consider more closely the common dynamic processes behind the emergence of social democratic parties in late nineteenth century Europe. Most importantly, such studies should also engage directly with important historical debates within the national historiography, treating the comparative method as a means to shed new light on such debates, rather than as a discrete field in its own right. Given the traditional focus of much labour history, such an approach must move beyond the nation state as the basic unit of comparison.[56] Attempting to link the study of a particular region, town, workplace or community with the demands of a cross-national comparison is not easy, but may be extremely fruitful, not least in that it challenges the dominance of national history from two different levels.[57] In this respect, it is worth noting that there have been some studies in recent years dealing with distinctive occupational communities, such as coalminers, dockers and shipyard workers.[58] In some cases these studies have also implied comparison of towns or regions within the framework of a cross-national study.[59] As Frank Broeze has pointed out, however, relatively few of these studies have moved beyond industrial sociology to explore the implications for labour ideology, party organisation and political behaviour.[60] Cross-national regional comparisons remain very rare, although examples from outside the field of labour history indicate the gains to be made from such an approach.[61]

For the purposes of the present study I have chosen to compare two naval dockyard towns: Plymouth in Britain and Karlskrona in Sweden. In part, therefore, this is a study of two occupational communities, which are considered to possess some degree of similarity by virtue of the nature of the work they performed – constructing warships – and the unusual conditions, as civilians in the direct employment of the state, in which they performed it. The literature relating specifically to the occupational culture and industrial relations of these workers, in Britain, Sweden and beyond, is discussed in chapter 3. In each case, however, the more ambitious aim was also to examine the implications of dockyard work and industrial relations for political changes in a local and national context. Naval dockyard towns have frequently been considered as 'exceptional' in their own right, difficult territory for an organised labour movement which was nominally, at least, committed to internationalism and disarmament. For this reason, perhaps, both Plymouth and Karlskrona have been largely ignored by labour historians. One of the main concerns of the study, therefore, is to explore the complexities of naval politics in the local context, at a time of heightened interest and debate in the role of the navy in both countries, and to examine the particular challenges which this presented to the organised labour movement. National politics was always important in determining the local possibilities for political action, but equally so was the need to defend local interests against the control and influence exercised from the centre. This dynamic tension between national and local, at a time when nation states became established as the main arena for political activity, is one of the central themes of the book.

The local studies form the core of the book, and are presented in chapters 4 and 5 (Plymouth) and chapters 6 and 7 (Karlskrona). First, however, it is necessary to establish the national contexts for the local studies and the cross-national comparison. Chapter 2 examines in detail the 'rise of labour' debate in both Britain and Sweden. Despite the very different contexts – Social Democratic success in Sweden and Labour weakness in Britain – the research agenda of labour historians in both countries have been remarkably similar, with debates about the formation of an industrial working class dominating until recently. In both countries as elsewhere, however, the class paradigm received some strong criticism during the 1990s. The possibilities for a new approach are explored in chapter 3, which then introduces the context for the local studies.

CHAPTER 2

The Rise of Labour
in Britain and Sweden

Comparative studies remain rather rare in labour history; direct comparisons of Britain and Sweden are even less common. Those studies which do exist have mainly been concerned with the development of either industrial relations or social policy during the twentieth century, rather than with the formative years of the labour movement.[1] Swedish social democracy has also attracted considerable attention from policy makers and advisers, and was sometimes held up as a shining example of what successful social democratic government should look like, against which British 'failings' were unfavourably compared.[2] Certainly, the background to the study of labour history in Britain and Sweden could hardly be more different. Few would disagree with Richard Tomasson's observation that the Swedish Social Democratic Labour Party could be described as 'the most successful – by almost any criteria – Social Democratic movement in Western Europe.'[3] The party's unbroken run of over fifty years in government meant that Swedish historians, whether or not they were sympathetic to its politics, seem almost to have taken its existence for granted. By contrast, for much of the twentieth century, British labour history has been studied against a background of Conservative hegemony and Labour weakness, and the history of working-class politics has often been subtly affected by notions of 'absence' or 'failure'.

Despite these different contexts, labour history research in Britain and Sweden has followed a remarkably similar agenda, even though its practitioners have often been ignorant of developments outside their own national tradition. In both countries, labour history has long been recognised as a distinct sub-discipline, and has generated an impressive volume of research. From the 1960s it came to be associated with two related developments: the turn to the social sciences in historical research on the one hand, and the aspiration to write 'history-from-below' (*historia underifrån*), arising from the political convictions of mainly left-wing historians, on the other. This resulted in the production of an extremely rich and varied literature, which has moved beyond the history of the labour movement's institutions to examine all aspects of working-class life. In both countries, the term 'labour history' (*arbetarhistoria*) has carried a double meaning, where developments within 'narrow' or 'institutional' labour history (*arbetarrörelsenshistoria*) have usually been understood with reference to 'broad' labour history, or the history of work and working-class life (*arbetslivshistoria*).[4] This chapter surveys the debates surrounding the 'rise of labour' in Britain and Sweden. Three areas of debate in particular are discussed: industrialisation and the formation of the working class, the response of the state, and the ideological influences on the two parties. What were the main differences between the two cases and how significant were they? Finally, since the very notion of the working class has been challenged in recent years, the chapter examines the implications of these most recent debates for the comparative study.

I

Until recently, historians largely agreed that the emergence of the Labour Party in early twentieth century Britain was primarily the result of social change, namely the twin processes of industrialisation and urbanisation, and the formation of an industrial working class. In a European perspective the British Labour Party was a relative latecomer, and a major concern therefore has been to explain why it took so long for the world's first industrial nation to develop a politically conscious working class. If the British working class was 'made' by 1832, as E P Thompson has suggested, why was there a hiatus of over fifty years between the decline of Chartism after 1848, and the emergence of the Labour Party in 1900? Mid-Victorian politics seemed to be characterised by industrial harmony rather than class conflict, and by popular support for the Gladstonian Liberal Party, a phenomenon partly explained by the presence of an influential 'labour aristocracy' of skilled working men.[5] From the 1870s, however, the economic prosperity and stability on which this social peace was based began to break down, as the British economy experienced growing international competition. Industrialists responded to declining profits by introducing new and more impersonal forms of capitalist organisation. The small family firm was superseded by larger corporations and more bureaucratic forms of labour management; the work process was restructured; new machinery and payment systems and new methods of supervision and control were adopted. These changes were to have a profound impact on the structure of the working class. Skilled workers in particular lost out as a result of the adoption of less labour-intensive production methods, and experienced a loss of autonomy over their work. The result was the erosion of fundamental differences of skill and status among groups of workers, and the emergence of a more homogeneous working class, sharing a common experience as waged labour in subordination to capital.

These economic and social changes found political expression in the upsurge in trade union membership from the 1880s, and in increased support for radical political ideas, including socialism.[6] Trade union membership grew by about 90% during 1889–90, and by about another 60% (and over 1.5 million members) during the period 1910–13.[7] Particularly dramatic was the rise in union organisation among unskilled and previously unorganised workers: the so-called 'new unionism' of 1889–90. But the escalation in labour conflict after 1900 affected all groups of workers, as skilled workers fought to defend their position against increasing incursions from their employers. The rise of trade unionism represented 'an attempt to find a formal voice for workers in a new context in which informal modes of communication and co-ordination were losing their currency... to restore by formal, institutional action the autonomy and discretion of skilled men which was under threat.'[8] This interpretation has not gone unchallenged. A reinterpretation of the 'new unionism' suggested that it owed little to changes in the labour process or to the dissemination of new socialist ideas. Instead, it was caused by the overall shortage of labour within the economy, which temporarily improved the bargaining power of unskilled workers in particular.[9] Meanwhile, studies of individual industries have revealed the limited ability of employers to transform radically the division of labour, due to the fragmented structure of firms and markets in the late Victorian economy. This inhibited the development of a unified corporate infrastructure similar to that in Germany or the USA, and allowed craft unionism to flourish.[10] The extent of regional and sectoral diversity in British industry ensured that the working class remained fragmented, economically, organisa-

tionally and culturally.[11] Above all, of course, it was divided along gender lines as male trade unionists struggled to preserve their superior
position in the labour market compared to women.[12]

Generally, however, from the late nineteenth century class consciousness replaced older loyalties, such as those derived from religious or
ethnic affiliation, or social patronage and deference, as the main deter-
minant of political alignment. The main source of contention was the
timing of the maturation of class consciousness. For some, the failure
of the Liberal Party to accommodate working-class demands led to the
establishment of the Labour Representation Committee (LRC) in 1900,
and the beginnings of a serious electoral challenge to the Liberals.[13]
Legal judgements against the trade union movement, notably the Taff
Vale case of 1901, strengthened the convictions of trade unionists that
supporting the Liberal Party was becoming increasingly inappropriate,
and contributed to the electoral breakthrough of 1906 which led to the
establishment of the Parliamentary Labour Party.[14] Other historians,
however, while accepting that social class was important in defining
political alignment during the early twentieth century, argued that the
Liberals, as the traditional working-class party, were able to contain the
challenge of Labour before 1914.[15] The 'New Liberalism', expressed in
a series of major social reforms from 1906, was able to rally working-
class support for the Liberals before the war. The negotiation of an informal 'Progressive Alliance' in 1903 between the Liberal Party and
Labour, by which Labour agreed not to contest constituencies where
there was strong working-class support for Liberalism, was also successful in containing Labour as the junior partner to the Liberals before
1914.[16] Labour did make some progress immediately before the outbreak of the war in 1914, but 'no shred of evidence existed anywhere
which might suggest that within ten years the Labour Party would be
forming the government of the country.'[17] Instead, it was the strains
of the war itself, and the resulting split in the Liberal Party, which eventually led to Labour's ascendancy over the Liberals.

Historians have also debated the impact of the First World War on
class formation and labour politics. According to some accounts, workers were radicalised by their experiences of the war, to the extent that
social relations were transformed for a generation or more.[18] In the
face of increased state control and a major restructuring of work practices, a new sense of class unity emerged which found expression in
outbreaks of political radicalism. The widespread experience of food

shortages and rent increases also contributed to this heightened tension. Inevitably, the Bolshevik Revolution of 1917 had a major impact on already radicalised workers, and the labour movement split into reformist and revolutionary camps with the foundation of the Communist Party of Great Britain (CPGB) in 1921. Even those working-class political organisations firmly within the reformist group, such as the Labour Party, were radicalised by the experience, as the adoption of the socialist objective in the 1918 constitution testifies. Thus, 'by 1919–20 large numbers of workers had an intense class awareness that encompassed an elementary critique of capitalism as a social system, a sense that reasonable alternatives existed and a confidence that Labour was solid and strong enough to bring about major change.'[19]

Against this thesis other historians, of whom Ross McKibbin is the foremost example, have denied that the war produced a major shift towards the left among the British working class, compared to France for example.[20] The war was seen as no more than a temporary interruption, which left the prevailing social structure intact, meaning that Edwardian class politics survived more or less unchanged into the 1920s. Labour remained its pre-war self, defined by a defensive class consciousness rather than a clear doctrinal commitment to socialism. If anything, it became even more solidly a trade unionists' party, and the disarray within the socialist ILP over the pacifist issue meant that the socialist influence was curtailed. More significant than social change was the 'Fourth Reform Act' of 1918. The introduction of universal male suffrage enfranchised many natural Labour voters and allowed Labour to consolidate the gains it was making before 1914, thus displacing the Liberals as the main progressive party.[21] It did so as a trade union party, united by a sense of class solidarity, but limited in its aims and outlook and demonstrating little programmatic commitment to socialism.[22]

The strength of craft unionism was considered to be partly responsible for Labour's ambivalence towards socialism, but it was not just at work that the British working class was 'remade' during the period 1880–1920. The reorganisation of the labour process occurred simultaneously with important changes in other aspects of working-class life, the result of which, it has been argued, was to strengthen class feeling among British workers. Drawing on an analysis of Anglican marriage registers, Mike Savage and Andrew Miles have suggested that while social mobility *within* the working class increased during the second half of the nineteenth century, mobility between the working class and middle class declined. While they acknowledge that increased working-class solidarity was likely to be more influential on the lives of men than women, they nonetheless identify three trends to support the thesis of a 'remaking' of the British working class during the late nineteenth and early twentieth centuries: firstly, the concentration of male manual workers in certain sectors of the economy, namely manufacturing, trade and transport; secondly, the convergence of incomes within the working class and the widening of differentials between working-class and middle-class incomes; and thirdly, patterns of social mobility which tended to reduce differences within the working class.[23] Perhaps more interestingly, they also insist that class formation was a spatial process, and that heightened working-class solidarity was associated with changes in late nineteenth century urban development. After the 1880s, the rise of the suburb enabled the middle class to withdraw from active participation in urban institutions such as schools, churches and local politics. Meanwhile working-class solidarity was fostered by the growth of stable and highly cohesive working-class neighbourhoods within the cities, and the emergence of a distinctive urban culture associated with such neighbourhoods.[24] While acknowledging that this did indeed constitute an authentic working-class culture, some historians have suggested that its presence was hardly conducive to collective political action, arguing that, on the contrary, it actually worked against it. Urban cultural institutions such as the music hall had more to do with the development of a commercial leisure industry, offering a 'fantasy escape from poverty', than with a display of working-class solidarity.[25] Although class was never absent from the music halls, it had no political definition; instead what was offered was a 'culture of connotation': '[f]atalism, political scepticism, the evasion of tragedy or anger and a stance of comic stoicism.'[26] Even where working-class people formed their own associations, their organisational energies were just as likely to be channelled into clubs and societies centred around hobbies as they were into political activities.[27]

The implication here is that Britain lacked an alternative workers' culture which was able to form the basis for a challenge to the prevailing social order, similar to that which developed around the SPD for example, or institutions such as the *maisons du peuple* in France and Belgium. Institutions such as the music hall helped to produce a highly developed consciousness of class, but one which was defensive and inward-looking. This is probably too negative a view. For many working men, especially in the north of England, social life centred around working men's or labour clubs, which also had important political functions.[28] Even more important, and probably at least as significant as the SPD's workers' taverns, was the consumer co-operative movement. Although some have regarded the success of the Rochdale system of co-operation (based on the redistribution of the trading surplus to members as a quarterly dividend) as further evidence for the 'defeat' of working-class radicalism after the demise of Chartism, more recent research provides convincing evidence to suggest that there was more to the 'co-op' than mere shopkeeping.[29] Co-operation retained at its centre a critique of capitalist systems of distribution and exchange, and a vision of an alternative society: the 'co-operative commonwealth'. More practically, by 1900 the co-operative store was a highly visible element of most working-class neighbourhoods, and even the humble 'divi' was 'part of the 'practical knowledge' used by working people to cope with and simultaneously reconstruct capitalist social relations.'[30] Co-operative societies also had an important role in providing alternative educational, recreational and social facilities, especially for working-class women through the Women's Co-operative Guild. In some districts, such as Plymouth and Woolwich, the co-operative society was instrumental in the development of independent labour politics, following conflicts over the rationing of food during the First World War.[31] The sheer size of the movement – over 1.7 million members in 1900, and over 4.5 million in 1920 – indicates the importance of co-operation in working-class life, a position which has been surprisingly neglected in studies of working-class and labour history.[32]

II

If Britain could be described as the world's first industrial nation, then Sweden, although certainly not the last, is usually thought of as a latecomer in the industrial economy. According to the traditional view, the Swedish economy underwent a 'great transformation' from the last third of the nineteenth century, largely as a result of international demand for Swedish products: iron, timber, pulp and paper.[33] This view requires some qualification, of course. The eighteenth century Swedish economy was neither especially backward nor marginal.

There was for example a well-established iron industry producing for the export market, and rural handicraft industries in textiles, wood and metal production.[34] The roots of the later industrialisation probably lay not so much in external events as in the quiet transformation of agrarian society which had been taking place since the late eighteenth century at least. Despite these caveats, however, most economic historians agree that the period 1880–1910 was one of rapid, even spectacular, growth in the Swedish economy. It was also one of profound social change. Whereas industrialisation in the mid-nineteenth century was concentrated in those sectors producing raw materials for export – timber products above all – and was therefore to a large extent located in the countryside, economic development was now driven by the advance of new, technologically sophisticated industries producing for both the home market and for export: shipbuilding and heavy engineering, chemicals, pulp and paper, and also mining. The growth of such industries brought with it rapid urbanisation, so that between 1880 and 1900 more than half of the national population growth was accounted for by the fifteen fastest growing towns.[35]

Earlier studies suggested that it was these twin processes of industrialisation and urbanisation in themselves which explained the social and political changes of the late nineteenth century.[36] From the late 1970s, however, historians began to direct more attention towards the development of industrial capitalism and the formation of a working class.[37] Above all, they suggested, it was at the workplace that the Swedish working class was 'made' during the decades either side of 1900. The introduction of mechanised and 'rational' methods of production in the new industries necessitated an increasingly specialised division of labour, which deprived the industrial worker both of opportunities to exercise his skill, and of autonomy over his work. The workforce became more homogenised, subjected to tighter supervision, and to other methods of control such as piecework. The result was 'concrete, qualitative changes in the relationship between labour and capital,' which left workers alienated and demoralised, and resulted in the formation of a politically conscious working class.[38] As in Britain, this altered relationship found expression in the very rapid growth in trade unionism: union membership increased by 182% between the years 1896–1900, and by 71% during 1906 alone.[39] Trade unions were seen as a fundamentally modern form of protest, which sought to improve wages and conditions through collective negotiations with employers, and seemed to be the only effective way to combat changes in the organisation of work. As such, they generally replaced older forms of workplace relations, whether the liberal workers' societies or *arbetarföreningar*, or informal methods of protest such as initiation and drinking rituals, spontaneous and unorganised riots and strikes.[40]

Reaction to these changes in the organisation of work was also expressed in the growth of popular support for socialist ideas, which had first been introduced to Sweden in the 1880s through German and Danish activists. (It was no accident that Malmö, with its close ties to Copenhagen, has a strong claim to be considered the original hotbed of Swedish socialism). Unlike Britain, however, where the emergence of the Labour Party in 1900 appeared to proceed from the upsurge in class conscious trade unionism during the previous two decades, the foundation of the Social Democratic Party (SAP) in 1889 largely pre-dated trade union activity in Sweden. During the first decade of its existence, the SAP concentrated its activities on building up trade union organisation rather than on exercising the traditional functions of a political party. This helped to stifle the fracturing influence of craft unionism, which became one of the defining features of the British labour movement, and encouraged instead the formation of more centralised industrial unions.[41] The foundation of a national party, and in 1898 of a national trade union federation, *Landsorganisationen* (LO), pointed towards the increased centralisation of the Swedish labour movement and the erosion of local autonomy. For some radical historians, the party's subsequent espousal of parliamentary reformism amounted to a betrayal of its roots in the radical class consciousness of the shop floor, driven by the reformist outlook of its core activists.[42] It might be added, however, that the working class itself is curiously absent from many of the SAP histories, which have focused on the party's ideology and organisation to a much greater extent than the literature on the British Labour Party.

From a comparative perspective, the implication is clear: the greater degree of organisational coherence and centralisation in the Swedish labour movement may be explained by the rapidity of late nineteenth century industrialisation. The upheaval of late industrialisation was not as severe in Sweden as it was in Norway, but it accounted for the emergence of a largely homogeneous working class, which was more willing than its British counterpart to espouse radical socialist ideas.[43] This point requires some qualification. Craft unionism was strong in Sweden during the 1880s, and it was only gradually replaced, not by industrial unions, but by a distinctive type of 'work material' union. Even so, craft sectionalism continued to cause internal problems, especially at a local level, for large federations such as the Metalworkers' Union.[44] Nor can it be assumed that the Swedish working class was religiously, ethnically or linguistically homogeneous, although it clearly lacked a schism similar to that between Catholic and SPD unions in Germany, for example.[45] It was of course divided by gender. Women workers often found themselves doubly disadvantaged by both their class and their gender, while collective solidarity among male workers could be reinforced by the assertion of a specifically masculine culture.[46] Moreover, Sweden was a large country, and the formation of an industrial working class has generally been treated as a set of regional and local variations on a national theme, producing a very rich tradition of micro and local studies in Swedish labour history. Studies of individual factories suggested that the Braverman-inspired portrayal of workers as the passive victims of processes of mechanisation and rationalisation beyond their control did not always square with the evidence, for workers were frequently able to resist new management strategies and maintain a degree of autonomy over their work.[47] By providing their own welfare benefits and other services, trade unions were also able to challenge the paternalist strategies of their employers, and help to generate a distinctively proletarian oppositional culture (*motkultur*).[48] Even so, in some instances the endurance of paternalism could explain why a class-conscious labour movement developed relatively late in certain districts.[49]

The labour process studies cited above have also been criticised for concentrating on urban factory production, which could hardly be considered typical of a country where the proportion of the population who could be classed as living in towns averaged only 27% in the years between 1911 and 1920.[50] Over half the workforce was still employed in agriculture, and many more in mining, forestry or other primary extractive industries. Here, the organisation of work was more flexible than in the factory, often characterised by seasonal patterns and workers who were more often migratory than settled.[51] The scattered agrarian workforce remained difficult to organise, while in many other industries material change and class consciousness generated support not for reformist trade unions but for more radical political currents, in particular syndicalism. In the quarrying industry of Bohuslän, as Lennart Persson has shown, it was not so much the loss of autonomy which radicalised the workforce, but instead the independence of the young workers which made syndicalism so attractive to them.[52] Critical of both their employers and also of the official trade union leadership, the quarrymen turned instead to more direct strategies. As one of their number expressed it, '[I]t was no wonder that the stonecutters (*stenhuggarna*) became both young socialists and then later syndicalists, after the treatment they received from the employers and the authorities.'[53] For this reason, Bohuslän was to become one of the strongest districts within the syndicalist organisation SAC, after it was founded in 1910.

These differences suggest that it would be difficult to identify a distinctively urban proletarian culture in Sweden, similar to that discussed above for Britain, despite the existence of some attempts in the literature to distinguish an 'all-embracing national sense of class unity and class struggle'.[54] Equally, however, there must be some question over the existence of a nationally unified culture in Britain during this period. Earlier studies in labour history tended to associate the rise of class politics with the erosion of regional and sectional particularism, as part of the formation of a modern, centralised, nation state. The rise of the ILP, for example, was symptomatic of a trend where '[r]egional political divergences slowly gave way to a more national political argument based around class differences; trade union sectionalism diminished as small local unions gave way to larger national organisations.'[55] Even where historians based their studies on a specific region, they were confident that apparently local trends could be extrapolated to form a wider national picture. The new urban working-class culture was characterised by a 'basic consistency of outlook' found across the country.[56] Local difference could not be ignored, of course, but was often explained in terms of exceptional circumstances which might have prevented the development of 'normal' patterns of working-class formation. The unusual strength of working-class support for Conservatism in Liverpool, for example, was attributed to the dominance of commercial distribution over manufacturing industry, compounded by ethnic and religious divisions.[57] The survival of Gladstonian Liberalism in Cornwall meanwhile was a symptom of the economic and political backwardness of a region where the strength of nonconformity delayed the emergence of modern class politics until well into the inter-war period.[58]

The proliferation of local and micro studies in labour history has made the thesis of local exceptionalism hard to sustain.[59] Working-class politics was never monolithic; it was always rooted in specifically local conditions.[60] The expansion of labour politics was based not on a nationally unified class consciousness, but on political ideas which could be shown to have a practical and moral relevance in a local context. There have been some attempts to construct more sophisticated typologies to explain the diverse forms labour politics might be expected to take in different localities, based on variations in skill and the structure of the labour market for example.[61] Gunnar Olofsson proposed a three-part typology for analysing the roots of different forms of working-class politics in Sweden, encompassing not only the rural-urban division, but also the distinctively Swedish 'company town' or *bruksort*. Understood both in its traditional meaning – referring especially to the small settlements dominated by individual firms in the iron-producing region of mid-Sweden – and also in the less specific sense of a small or medium sized town dominated by one industry, the *bruksort* functioned as a distinctive social enclave separated from the surrounding countryside. It thus lacked the more diverse economic and social structure of a larger industrial town. According to Olofsson, many Swedish towns, among them Landskrona, Borlänge, Kungälv and Västervik, were best analysed in this way.[62] The function of Olofsson's model though, as with Michael Savage's three-part typology for analysing the roots of working-class politics in Britain, was to explain *differences* in the forms local politics took. Over the validity of the underlying process – the formation of an industrial working class – there could be little doubt. Class formation, and class politics, were seen as the result of exogenous processes over which workers themselves had little influence, even though they sought strategies to resist them.

Despite the intricacies of the different debates considered here, then, there are nonetheless some broad similarities in the ways in which historians have approached the study of the rise of the labour movement in both Britain and Sweden. In both cases, the formation of a socialist labour movement during the late nineteenth century has been understood as a consequence of the changes in social relations resulting from the continuing development of industrial capitalism, and the formation of an industrial working class. Class consciousness was itself a product of the upheavals of industrialisation and urbanisation, whether these developments were relatively recent, as in Sweden, or more longstanding, as in Britain, where historians identified a *remaking* of the working class as a result of a further evolution in industrial capitalism from the closing decades of the nineteenth century. Historians debated the nature of class consciousness, whether radical or reformist, and the timing of the maturation of class experience into political consciousness. In particular, they have been concerned with the impact of the First World War and the revolutions in different parts of Europe during this period. Yet the phenomenon of class formation, rooted in the economic and social realities of early twentieth century capitalist transformation, remained the principal dynamic of political change. In both countries, the sub-discipline of labour history, in its broadest sense, had quickly moved away from a narrow focus on the institutions of the labour movement towards a concern with the details of work and everyday life within the working class, often within local contexts.

The emphasis on class meant that the formation of socialist labour parties as an historical phenomenon was understood in two related ways. Firstly, it was conceived as *an entirely modern process*, part of the transition from traditional, pre-industrial society to modernity. The teleology of this view is expressed within the language often used to describe the historical process by which 'mature' class consciousness – organised protest, trade unionism and centralised collective bargaining – came to replace older more 'spontaneous' forms of action, such as the tradition of St Monday.[63] In political terms, modern forms of collective class solidarity replaced older loyalties such as religion or deference to traditional authority. In Sweden, the emergence of the Social Democratic Labour Party as a modern, mass membership, political party went hand in hand with the modernisation of the entire political system: the so-called 'democratic breakthrough' (*det demokratiska genombrottet*) which began with the reform of the assembly of the estates in 1866.

It follows, therefore, that the rise of Labour was understood, secondly, as representing *a major discontinuity in the nineteenth century trajectory of popular politics*, when social class replaced older allegiances such as religion, ethnicity or deferential loyalties as the main basis for political alignment. Socialism was a modern ideology for modern age, a novel import for a new working class. Its own quasi-religious imagery suggested the idea of a clean break with the past, firstly through the possibilities for personal 'conversion', and secondly in its messianic vision of a new society to come.[64] The socialist politics of class transcended existing political divisions, leading to the emergence of a new phenomenon: political parties claiming to organise the working class. The problem for labour historians was to explain why the organisation and ideology of these working-class movements seemed to vary so greatly in different countries. As we have seen, in some accounts these variations were attributed to differences in the speed and timing of industrialisation. The problem with this approach, however, was that it often ignored the profoundly diverse experiences of industrialisation within national boundaries, meaning that it was difficult, therefore, to generalise about the implications for labour politics at a national level. Comparative labour historians have thus turned to their attention to the political context for the rise of labour in different national settings, and this work is now considered in more detail.

III

In trying to answer the question of why labour politics varied between different countries, comparative labour historians have often cited differences in the nature of the state and the political system. Most have placed Britain among the more liberal and less authoritarian regimes in Europe, where the sovereignty of Parliament was an established principle, as was individual representation on the basis of one-man-one-vote. Although the franchise remained restricted, suffrage reforms in 1867 and 1884 encouraged working men to seek political influence by giving electoral support to the established bourgeois political parties, especially the Liberal Party. The movement for independent labour representation thus emerged out of a long tradition of 'lib-labism'. Popular faith in the relative benignity of state institutions also ensured that working-class support for revolutionary movements remained negligible.[65] By contrast, the Swedish state of the early twentieth century remained fairly authoritarian, influenced by a *riksdag* that was 'one of the most reactionary of European Parliaments, surpassed only by the Prussian *Landtag*.'[66] Although the constitution of 1809 had ended absolutism, it was by no means intended to be a step towards parliamentary government, unlike the Norwegian and Danish constitutions of 1814 and 1849 respectively.[67] Rather it provided for a system of power-sharing between monarch and parliament, where the role of the monarch in choosing the council of state (*statsråd*) was intended to protect government from the struggles of parliamentary factions. The four-estate Diet was reformed in 1866, and replaced by a bicameral parliament. In-built conservative guarantees remained in the form of an indirectly elected first chamber dominated by landowners, public officials and big business, and of a monarchy with revived personal ambitions.

The contrast appears to be particularly marked if a direct comparison is made of the pre-war franchise in Britain and Sweden. In Britain,
following the Third Reform Act of 1884–5 which gave the vote to about
two thirds of adult males, contemporaries and historians alike tended to assume that the long struggle for suffrage reform was more or
less won. Keir Hardie wrote in 1895 that 'there is no need now to fight
the battle of the franchise. Our fathers did that, and today only the
details remain to be adjusted.'[68] The 'details' included female suffrage
of course, but with this exception suffrage reform never provoked the
level of political conflict seen in late nineteenth century Sweden. Here,
it was undoubtedly one of the most controversial political issues of
the 1890s and 1900s, and remained so until it was partly settled by
reforming legislation in 1909. Inevitably, therefore, the suffrage was
also important in the early campaigns of the Social Democratic Party – whether it was viewed as an end in itself or as a means towards
more fundamental change – but it also meant that bourgeois liberals
never competed to win working-class votes like their British counterparts. Liberals and Social Democrats collaborated temporarily during
the 1890s, for example in organising the first 'people's parliament' as
part of the suffrage campaign in 1892–3, but split over the Social
Democrats' support for a general strike as a further tactic.[69] As this
suggests, while the franchise remained restricted to under a quarter
of the adult male population, other strategies seemed more attractive
to many in the working class. Accordingly, the suffrage reform marked
a major turning point for the party, in that it made parliamentary influence a reality for the first time, and induced many to abandon their
earlier commitment to revolutionary ideas.[70]

The implication here is that whereas the British Labour Party took
its place within a political system which had assumed its recognisable
modern form as early as the 1870s, the development of the SAP was itself
part of the 'democratic breakthrough' of late nineteenth century Sweden. In Britain, Labour campaigned for working-class votes in competition with the established parties, and sought to displace the Liberals
as the main party of progressive politics. In Sweden, it was not until
the 1880s that informal *riksdag* groupings began to assume the form and
functions of recognisable political parties, and only after 1900 that these
groups established national extra-parliamentary organisations: the liberal *Frisinnade landsföreningen* (1902), and the conservative *Allmänna
valmansförbundet* (1904).[71] These organisations appeared more than a

decade after the foundation of the SAP, which thus could claim to be the first political party – in the modern sense – in Sweden. Although there was always the possibility for informal collaboration between liberals and Social Democrats at the local level, working-class voters never had the opportunity to attach themselves to the Swedish Liberal Party (*Liberala samlingspartiet*) in the same way that they did to the Gladstonian Liberal Party in Britain.[72] Nor did the SAP have to overcome a tradition of working-class conservatism expressed formally in electoral support for a rightist party, in contrast to the concerted, and often successful, efforts of the British Conservative Party to campaign in working-class districts after 1867.[73] On the contrary, Swedish conservatives remained extremely ambivalent about the principle of campaigning actively 'in the streets and squares' for the popular vote.[74]

How significant are these differences? It is clear that there were some important contrasts between Britain and Sweden which influenced the development of the Labour Party and the SAP respectively, but these should not be overstated. Nor does it seem particularly helpful to try to place the two cases somewhere on a scale ranging from 'more democratic' to 'more oppressive' regimes, and to make predictions about the form of working-class politics on that basis. Explanations which seem plausible in one comparative context often fail to stand up in another. The relatively early development of parliamentary democracy in Britain compared to Sweden could account for the lukewarm commitment to socialism in the British Labour Party, but in Norway it seemed to suggest exactly the opposite. Here, the major democratic 'breakthrough' came in 1884, several years before the foundation of the Norwegian Labour Party (DNA). This excluded DNA from possible collaboration with the liberals (*Venstre*) over suffrage reform, and has been cited as a major cause of the party's subsequent radical turn.[75]

Returning to the comparison in hand, the political systems thesis is unsatisfactory on several accounts. In the first place, although the suffrage was undoubtedly relatively restricted, the characterisation of the pre-war Swedish regime in its entirety as repressive is questionable. Indeed, this portrayal seems quite at odds with the traditional view of the Swedish state as relatively benign, where tyranny was abolished once and for all by the peaceful constitutional settlement of 1809. The principal beneficiaries of the 1809 constitution were the freeholding peasant farmers, who came to be regarded as the symbolic bearers of the traditions of peasant democracy, but who also exercised a degree of practical influence: through their dominance of the second chamber of the *riksdag* the farmers were able to hinder effectively the passage of repressive legislation through the upper chamber.[76] This meant that ruling class responses to the 'labour question' were more likely to be favourable than repressive. Further, even though the working class was denied the franchise, the establishment of alternative corporatist channels of representation gave it access to the state, and showed the state to be not entirely hostile to working-class demands. There was relatively little legal hindrance to unions and strikes, and no tradition of violent military or police repression.[77] Moreover, the firm central control exercised by the Crown was counter-balanced by a long tradition of local autonomy, which actually increased during the last decades of the nineteenth century as municipal governments responded pragmatically to the problems of urbanisation.[78] The state apparatus of control – including the police and the courts – was also decentralised, which made it open to local democratic influence.

Conversely, in no sense was the late Victorian British state a model of democratic accountability and openness. The reforms of 1884–5 were undoubtedly a watershed in the establishment of electoral democracy, but political participation remained restricted by wealth, class and gender. Britain still lagged behind France and Germany, where over 80% and 90% of adult males respectively had the vote.[79] The sheer complexity of the pre–1918 franchise, 'cumbersome, confused, incomplete and riddled with anomalies', and based on property ownership rather than citizenship, left it open to manipulation by party agents.[80] Party influence over the registration of voters continued to have a significant influence on the outcomes of elections before 1918. To take a local example: following a legal ruling in 1901 it was announced that the unusually high number of 'latch-key tenants' resident in Plymouth were to be placed automatically on the electoral roll, with the result that the franchise rose dramatically, from 37% to 58% of adult men in the Devonport division, and from 51% to 65% in Plymouth. As many of these 'lodger voters' were thought to be Liberals, the decision provoked political controversy, and the Unionists fought, partially successfully, to get the decision overturned in a court of appeal.[81] This sort of action required substantial financial support, and even after the passage of the Corrupt and Illegal Practices (Prevention) Act in 1883 fighting parliamentary elections remained expensive. Wealthy candidates expected to contribute their own funds towards 'nursing' their constituency, as the

TABLE 2.1. *Changes in the Electoral Roll in Karlskrona, 1887–1911.*

Election	No of voters on electoral roll	Electors as % of total population
1887	1 587	8.3
1888	1 235	6.3
1891	1 299	6.3
1894	1 310	6.1
1897	1 566	7.0
1900	1 714	7.3
1903	1 965	8.0
1905	2 619	10.0
1908	4 223	16.1

SOURCE: Sveriges officiella statistik.

TABLE 2.2. *Changes in the Electoral Roll in the Plymouth constituencies, 1892–1918.*

Election	No. of voters on electoral roll (Plymouth and Devonport combined)	Electors as % of total population
1892	20 123	13.89 (1891 population)
1895	21 371	
1900	21 917	12.31 (1901 population)
1906	33 174	
1910	30 210	15.61 (1911 population)
1918	119 117	56.71 (1921 population)

SOURCE: F W S Craig, *British Parliamentary Election Results, 1885–1918* (second edition, Aldershot, 1989); *ibid., British Parliamentary Election Results, 1918–1949* (Glasgow, 1969).

millionaire Waldorf Astor did in Plymouth by purchasing one of the town's daily newspapers, and maintaining a large Primrose League habitation. Moreover, whether democratically elected or not, the House of Commons was still constrained by the presence of an upper chamber which was not elected at all, and by a monarch who retained an active role in the selection of prime ministers. For this reason, the adoption of extra-parliamentary tactics remained an attractive option not only for the labour movement, but also for other groups, most prominently female suffrage campaigners.

A further problem with the emphasis on political systems to explain variations between labour movements is that such explanations often present rather a static picture, which ignores the profound changes taking place in the political systems of *both* countries before the First World War.[82] The legislative milestones of suffrage reform – 1866, 1909 and 1920 in Sweden, 1867, 1884 and 1918 in Britain – do not tell the whole story of the democratisation of electoral politics. In systems where competence to vote was determined by income or property ownership, the franchise was gradually and automatically extended during periods of rising real incomes.[83] Even before the great electoral reform of 1909, a growing proportion of Swedish men found that they were qualified to vote. Indeed, it has been suggested that the reform made little impact at all in the towns, where the suffrage had grown rapidly from 1900, in contrast to the situation in the countryside where the electoral role doubled between 1908 and 1911.[84] This was certainly the case in Blekinge *län*, where the number of electors in some of the rural districts increased four- or fivefold after the suffrage reform of 1909.[85] By contrast, the electorate in Karlskrona expanded rapidly before the electoral reform, as Table 2.1 shows. Not only this, but increasing numbers of those who were enfranchised were also inclined to exercise their rights, and to turn out and vote.[86] To take the example of Plymouth again, the population of Plymouth and Devonport increased by nearly 23% between the censuses of 1891 and 1901, but the electoral roll lagged behind, and there was a slight drop in the proportion of the population which was enfranchised. The large increase in the number of electors between 1900 and 1906 is partly attributable to the enfranchisement of the 'latch-key' voters. Even so, the pre-war franchise can hardly be considered to be democratic if we consider that the number of electors more than doubled between 1910 and the general election of 1918, even without taking into account the enfranchisement of some women. While it would be problematic to assume that these new voters tended naturally to support the Labour Party, this is not really the point: what matters is that *all* political parties, in both countries, were required to adapt to a changing electoral system.[87] In both cases, it was not until the 1920s that universal suffrage was finally introduced.

A more dynamic view of the 'franchise factor' in the rise of Labour in Britain and Sweden implies therefore that the two cases present more similarities than might have been expected. To be sure, in Sweden the franchise was more restricted than in Britain before 1909, but in both countries the overall picture was of an expanding electorate, which carried with it important implications for the conduct of electoral politics. By the turn of the century, all but the most die-hard reactionaries had accepted the inevitability of democratisation, and had turned from oppressing popular demands to manipulating them, through the active propagandising of political programmes. The same was true for the wider debate over constitutional reform. At first sight, the status of Parliament seems not to have aroused the level of political passion in Britain as it did in Sweden, but it was nonetheless a matter that was open for debate. The cause of constitutional reform, sloganised as 'Peers against the People', continued to form the main campaign platform for the Liberal Party in the two elections of 1910, following the Unionist Party's use of the House of Lords to reject the government's finance bill. In defending the Upper House, the Unionists argued that independence of the House of Lords was a guarantee against the tyranny of the party interests represented in the Commons.[88] These were sentiments which Swedish conservatives might have agreed with wholeheartedly in resisting the liberal proposals that governments should be formed according to parliamentary majorities. 'The Age of Liberty,' commented one such writer, in reference to the period of parliamentary dominance in the eighteenth century, 'had given us more than enough of parliamentary encroachment on government and rule by political parties.'[89]

If the comparison is made between historical *processes* in late nineteenth century Britain and Sweden, rather than between the *situation* as it was at any given point in time, the two cases appear to demonstrate more similarities than might at first be expected. The political background to the rise of Labour was in both cases a dynamic and evolving political system, where important issues such as the suffrage and the role of parliament were by no means resolved before the First World War. The rise of Labour must therefore be seen in the context of the wider political changes in both countries. This point will be discussed further below. First, however, it is necessary to examine another assumed major point of difference in the Swedish and British labour movements, namely the ideological inheritance, and in particular the role of socialism.

IV

In few ways did the British Labour Party seem to differ more substantially from its continental counterparts than in its ideology, or more accurately, in its lack of ideological commitment. The Swedish Social Democratic Party, like most continental parties, was defined by its socialist programme, which was first adopted at the party congress of 1897. Socialism quickly became established as the dominant ideology within the emergent labour movement, and both the SAP and the socialist trade union movement played a decisive role in the processes of class formation.[90] By contrast, the Labour Representation Committee of 1900 was characterised by the limitations of its ambitions: 'a loose and ill-defined alliance rather than a coherent party with specific policies.'[91] Speaking at the 1912 Labour Party conference, J Bruce Glasier complained that the Labour Party, 'had no confession of faith, no means of giving testimony to a whole-hearted support of the principles of the Party.'[92] Only with the adoption of the socialist objective in Clause IV part 4 of its 1918 constitution did the Labour Party 'enter the mainstream of European socialism'.[93] Even this hardly amounted to a bold statement of principles, nor could it be considered to be a clear expression of the ideological position of the working class. Instead, Clause IV was an 'uncharacteristic adornment'; a compromise designed to secure the support of middle-class socialists for what was still essentially a party of trade unionists.[94] Unlike most other working-class parties, the British Labour Party was not even socialist in name.

This is not to suggest that socialist ideas were unknown in Britain. As E P Thompson pointed out, British working-class politics was strongly influenced by the presence of continental Communist émigrés and refugees in Britain.[95] The appearance of some of the most important Marxist and socialist texts in translation from the 1880s instigated some intense debates, but it was usually assumed that the overall impact of these debates was limited, confined mainly to the Social Democratic Federation (SDF).[96] The peculiarly British faith in parliamentary democracy, individual liberty, justice and self-help was thought to be inimical to Marxism, with its roots in German philosophy and political economy. Egon Wertheimer attributed the 'programme-phobia' of the British labour movement to the general mistrust of theory and systematic thought prevalent in English political life as a whole; instead, he concluded, 'the empiric, the experimental, the improvisational has always been the deciding factor.'[97] The native socialist tradition expressed in organisations such as the Independent Labour Party (ILP) was derived from the romantic and moral critique of capitalism found in the writings of Robert Owen, John Ruskin, Thomas Carlyle and William Morris, and was strongly influenced by religious nonconformity. In contrast to the 'scientific' or 'materialist' socialism of the continental parties, especially the SPD, it was doubtful whether this 'utopian' tradition could even be called socialist at all.[98]

In recent years British historians have begun to demonstrate a renewed interest in analysing the ideological debates within the early Labour Party. Here, however, the emphasis has not so much been on socialism as on the non-socialist influences on the party's ideology. In a seminal collection of essays from 1991, Eugenio Biagini and Alastair Reid argued that the most important ideological influence on the Edwardian Labour Party was the indigenous Radical tradition, centred around demands for open government, the rule of law, the sovereignty of Parliament and universal suffrage.[99] Rather than marking a fundamental break with the broad trajectory of nineteenth century popular politics, based on heightened class consciousness, the Labour Party instead represented a 'dynamic recomposition of popular radicalism in adaptation to a new political environment.'[100] More important than socialist ideas of class conflict and economic exploitation were the traditional Radical concerns with democracy, constitutional reform, and individual rights and liberties.[101] Rather than being explained in terms of the immaturity of class consciousness and the de-radicalising aspirations of a labour aristocracy, the Gladstonian Liberalism of the mid-Victorian era was seen as providing the main ideological influence on the rise of Labour.[102] The demise of Liberalism was understood not a result of the party's failure to accommodate growing class consciousness after the turn of the century, but Labour's success in taking the ideological initiative as the main representative of progressive and Radical politics. The broad agreement between the reforming groups of the Liberal and Labour parties, which allowed the Progressive Alliance to function well before 1914, might have continued had it not been for the pressures of the First World War which allowed Labour to emerge as the main anti-Tory party.[103]

These revisionist accounts of the early Labour Party are linked to a broader methodological debate within social history, which has introduced new ways of understanding the relationship between social and political change. In his influential essay on Chartism, first published in 1982, the British historian Gareth Stedman Jones rejected conventional accounts of Chartism as a social phenomenon, arguing that economic and social grievances were not in themselves sufficient to produce such a politically complex phenomenon.[104] Instead, he insisted on the importance of taking seriously the political aspirations of the Chartists, and suggested that at the root of Chartist discourse lay the Radical critique of the corrupting effects of the concentration of political power, which provided a vocabulary for Chartists to express their grievances. This new emphasis challenged the relationship between social experience and political consciousness, for, rather than assuming that shared experiences generated a shared consciousness, for example of class, it seemed that, 'consciousness cannot be related to experience except through the interposition of a particular language which organises the understanding of experience.'[105] Following this lead, historians have turned their attention to examining the ways in which class was constituted by language, rooted in the knowledge and self-identity of the individuals which make up a social class, rather than in the social and economic structures in which these individuals lived. Drawing on methods more usually associated with literary criticism, labour historians have turned to analysing the language and ideas of popular politics, rather than the material structures which were supposed to lie behind them.

Particularly influential in the rethinking of class has been the work of feminist historians, both for their insights into how social relations and identities – whether of class, gender or any other category – are constructed discursively; and also for demonstrating how class relations were formed outside the traditional arenas of politics and the workplace. Above all, feminist historians have also shown that class was always expressed in gendered terms, and as such has to be considered merely as one identity among many available to individuals.[106] For some historians, therefore, the so-called 'linguistic turn' has provoked questions about the validity of social class at all as a way of understanding nineteenth century popular politics. Class competed with other ways for people to interpret the social order, and according to some accounts, was in fact more or less rejected by nineteenth century working people in favour of an inclusive and consensual 'populism', which in turn implied a perception of injustice and inequality as being rooted in the political rather than the economic sphere. Aspirations to fraternity and social reconciliation were more important than class conflict; indeed, there was an awareness or even a dread of divisions which class could engender, and a concern to avoid social conflict. In Britain, the Radical notion of 'the people' remained important beyond the mid-nineteenth century, while the alternative vision of class developed relatively late, and remained for a long time subordinate to other ways of seeing the social order.[107]

Swedish historians, in contrast to their British counterparts, have shown much more interest in ideology, demonstrating that the reform or revolution debate was a central feature of labour politics before 1917. Early accounts emphasised the strength of the reformist wing within the party, arguing that unlike the dogmatic Marxists of the SPD, the SAP was committed to pursuing a consensus-driven, evolutionary approach to the socialist transformation of society, largely driven by their moderate and pragmatic leader Hjalmar Branting.[108] According to the immensely influential study of SAP ideology by Herbert Tingsten, revolutionary socialism was alien to the traditions of continuity and stability within Swedish society, marked by its relatively peaceful accommodation of the industrial transformation:

> Social democracy's development ought... to be seen against the Swedish environment in which it occurred. The movement's early adoption of a moderate and reformist character was due to the strong traditions of freedom and justice which prevailed in Swedish society.[109]

Later studies challenged Tingsten's assertion that the party had adopted a reformist course from its foundation, arguing instead that socialist revolution remained the party's main goal before 1914. Historians debated the timing of the reformist 'breakthrough' within the party.[110] There is no need to examine the debate in detail here. The point is, that until the split in the movement and the exit of the revolutionary left to form its own party in 1917, both currents were strongly represented within the party, and competed for influence over the leadership. Liberal historians such as Tingsten denied that there was any serious threat of revolution in Sweden during the years 1917–18, although it is acknowledged that the difficult social and economic conditions of the war helped to fuel the split with the youth federation. The secession of the internal opposition helped to stabilise the party and consolidate its reformist position. Other historians, writing from a more radical perspective, have qualified the Tingstenian thesis by acknowledging the importance of the revolutionary tradition in the party *before* 1917, although most of these seem to agree that the debate was largely settled before the war. The suffrage reform of 1909 in particular was thought to be influential in confirming the SAP on a parliamentary course; as was also the bureaucratisation of the party, and the extension of control by the leadership over the grassroots.[111] As far as the split of 1917 is concerned, more attention in recent years has been focused on the role of syndicalism. The concessions made following the spring 1917 hunger demonstrations seemed to be a vindication of the syndicalist tactic of direct action. Once again, though, this was an uneven development, which questions the extent of national integrity and homogeneity within the national labour movement during this period. In some districts, notably the forestry and mining communities of northern and mid Sweden, syndicalist leaders were able to draw on an established tradition of support for syndicalism, and it was here that the Left Socialists performed best after 1917.[112]

The influence of anarcho-syndicalist ideas in the Swedish labour movement cautions against a monolithic interpretation of labour party ideology. As Rolf Karlbom has demonstrated, ideological debate within the early SAP was conducted in wider terms than the reform or revolution dichotomy suggests. Although an anarchist motion was defeated at the party's Norrköping Congress in 1891, that decision in itself did not mark a straightforward victory for parliamentary reformism. Instead, many other tactics and strategies were debated within the party throughout the 1890s. These included the People's Parliament (*folkriksdag*), with international precedents in Frankfurt, Belgium and the British Chartist movement; the general strike, also discussed with reference to precedents abroad; and municipal socialism (*kommunalsocialism*), perhaps the most genuinely native tradition, rooted in the struggle for municipal autonomy.[113] Ideological heterogeneity was perhaps most marked at the local level, and often emerged in opposition to the party leadership.

At first glance, the related debate over the centrality of class, and the so-called 'linguistic turn' appears to have had less of an impact on Swedish labour history, but on closer inspection there are similar trends discernible within the Swedish historiography.[114] Here, feminist historians have, like their British counterparts, been at the forefront of broadening the traditional understanding of class, based on an understanding of gender as 'a dynamic process which shapes power relations in society, and must necessarily form a part of the analysis of class.'[115] Moreover, Swedish labour history has been greatly enriched by the contributions of ethnologists, whose emphasis on cultural formation and identity building has helped to broaden materialist understandings of class formation. In the hands of these scholars, 'culture', conceived as an 'all-embracing concept' (*helhetsbegrepp*) which offered the individual the means to negotiate and interpret the world, does not appear to be so very different to the 'languages of class' found in recent Anglo-Saxon accounts.[116] It was acknowledged that language, memory and *mentalité* were as important in contributing to a sense of class as was the lived experience of the labour process. Ronny Ambjörnsson's influential study of Holmsund showed how workers used the traditions of diligence and respectability encountered through the local temperance lodges and study circles as resources for the construction of a collective culture.[117] They were united not only by shared memory and experience, but also by their collective vision of a better life in the future. In the same vein, rather than seeing 'respectability' as a bourgeois imposition to 'tame' an unruly working class, Olle Josephson has argued that revivalist and temperance concepts of reading, salvation and popular enlightenment (*folkupplysning*) were central to the labour movement's development of a new political language in the late nineteenth century.[118] Thus, although Swedish scholars have not been explicitly concerned with language itself and its deconstruction, at least within labour history, their work does in fact deal with competing interpretations of the social order: in Ambjörnsson's own terms with 'a popular history of ideas' (*en folkets idéhistoria*), or 'everyday ideas' (*vardagens idéer*).[119] This work has attracted some criticism, however, especially for the distinction made by Ambjörnsson and others between the culture of respectability (*skötsamhet*) and that of 'disorder' or 'wilfulness' (*bråkighet, egensinne*) which it was thought to replace. Rather than been seen as competing or mutually exclusive, both *skötsamhet* and *bråkighet* offered potential strategies for collective action.[120] The same criticism could be made of the way in which class and populism have sometimes been seen as competing, mutually exclusive discourses within the British debate. Ironically, in their attempts to destabilise the materialist understanding of popular politics as rooted in class relations, some historians have merely succeeded in replacing it with a new orthodoxy.

The importance of these new types of work for labour history – the emphasis on language to open up and broaden understandings of class and other social identities in Britain, or on culture and mentality in Sweden – is unquestionable. In both countries it has revealed new and exciting fields of enquiry for social historians, and has presented a fundamental challenge to many long-held assumptions within labour history. Naturally, these recent trends have attracted criticism, and the debate has frequently been heated and lively, which undoubtedly reflects the very real political significance of the issues discussed here.[121] In a comparative context, the emphasis on political languages has helped to highlight the cross-national exchange of ideas across national boundaries, and demonstrate how people adopted similar political analyses of their experience despite the very different social and economic environments in which they worked. Seen in this light, the British left's ambivalence to socialism before the 1880s was not evidence of the 'peculiarities of the English', but symptomatic of the general ambivalence of these ideas among the artisan and peasant classes across Europe. More important were notions of community and democracy: 'the spirit of village politics, the direct democracy of the town meetings, a sort of British *landesgemeinde* – a fact reminding us of the common heritage of European democracy, stretching from New England to the Swiss cantons, and back to the Italian republics of the Middle Ages.'[122] A generation or two later, European socialists certainly tended to view the revitalisation of Radical ideas about democracy as a major cause of the apparently limited success of British socialism. Yet this did not mean that British Labour was isolated from the continental debate. On the contrary, as Duncan Tanner has shown, the ideological discussions in the early Labour Party were in fact very similar to the contemporary debates among continental socialists. The Labour Party leaders, rather than being isolated from the continent, 'drew on parallel intellectual debates which were taking place across the political spectrum and across Europe and on direct knowledge of circumstances in other countries.'[123] Ramsay Mac-Donald followed the revisionist debate in the SPD with great interest. He befriended Bernstein during the latter's stay in Britain, and wrote in the introduction to Jaurès' *Studies in Socialism* that it was 'of the utmost moment that British socialists should study continental socialist methods.'[124] Further, Tanner suggests that the assault on Mac-Donald's revisionism contained in the Green Manifesto of 1910 mirrored Kautsky's attack on Bernstein more than a decade previously.

Nonetheless, this approach also presents some specific problems in a comparative context. In the first place, there is a danger that attempts to trace the evolution of popular mentalities or political languages can fall back into the nationally specific, ignoring the particular social circumstances in which they were produced. Ambjörnsson's attempt to extrapolate a national ideal-type from his study of the Holmsund workers must certainly be regarded as problematic in this respect.[125] The 'currents of Radicalism' argument is in some ways a restatement of the exceptionalist thesis. Attempts to trace the political thought of the Labour Party in terms of its Radical inheritance, via popular Liberalism and Chartism back to the Levellers and the Puritan revolution of the seventeenth century suggests that this was an ideology which could only be understood in terms of its Englishness. The emphasis on democracy, liberty, parliamentarianism and the rule of law makes it easy to criticise such approaches as 'neo-Whiggish'. Similarly, analysis of the political language of the SAP has revealed the prominence of populist (*folkelig*) vocabularies in Sweden too, but again this is understood in terms of its deep historical roots in the democratic institutions of traditional peasant society.[126] There is still a danger here of making determinist assumptions based on the subsequent course of the party's history once in government, and ignoring the open and contingent nature of labour politics before 1914.

Secondly, a more practical problem lies in what Marc Bloch described as the 'Babylonian confusion' in European history, where 'every national tradition of historians has elaborated its own vocabulary'.[127] Any attempt to compare political languages in different national contexts will present severe linguistic difficulties. To take one example, the Swedish term *folk* is usually translated into English as 'people', but, as Lars Trägårdh has shown, in its early twentieth century usage it did not necessarily carry the meaning of 'the people' as an association of individuals.[128] Instead, it had its roots in nineteenth century notions of 'community', partly derived from national romanticism, but also, unlike the term *Volk,* from a concept of the people as the bearers of democratic tradition. Given these difficulties, a cross-national comparison of political languages might do best to take its cue not from the 'languages of class' debate which has dominated Anglo-Saxon labour history, but from a *Begriffsgeschichte* approach which examines how key concepts acquired and changed meaning over time.[129] Indeed, seen in this light, what seemed in Britain to be a 'new' approach to popular politics and political discourse might not in fact be so very novel.[130] Nor is the charge that 'traditional' labour history was hopelessly old-fashioned in its methods and principal concerns entirely fair. Questions of experience, identity and consciousness have always been at the forefront for those concerned with the history of working-class politics, at the very least since the publication of E P Thompson's *The Making of the English Working Class.*

A further problem with the interest in political languages, however, has been the inevitable tendency to shift the focus towards the elite and relatively small groups of politicians who produced these languages: those who wrote pamphlets, and speeches and newspaper articles. This is perhaps not quite a fair criticism in all cases. Patrick Joyce, to take one example, drew heavily on popular ballads and other more 'informal' discourses in exploring the language of populism in *Visions of the People*. Yet his later work, *Democratic Subjects,* was concerned with the lives of two men only, explored through their own words expressed in diaries, letters and memoirs.[131] The enthusiasm for using autobiographies and other writings as sources inevitably shifts the focus towards those who had the means and inclination to write their own life stories. On the other hand, as those historians interested in politics have turned towards elite politics, many social historians have turned away from politics altogether, and have directed their focus towards the many other aspects of popular culture, especially concerning consumption.[132] There are indeed other things to life than politics, and as historians such as Ross McKibbin have demonstrated, other activities frequently took precedence over politics in working-class lives. It is entirely legitimate – indeed necessary – and fascinating for historians to investigate these activities. But equally, there have been occasions when very many ordinary people have demonstrated an interest in politics. Social history traditionally had a radical, highly politicised concern to investigate and reveal the ways in which ordinary people have been able to influence historical events, and it would be regrettable if this were to be abandoned altogether.

This brings us to a third and perhaps most serious criticism, that the linguistic approach is weak in that it fails to offer an adequate explanation for the *dynamics* of political change, especially when seen in a cross-national comparative context. As one reviewer has pointed out, in the rush to avoid privileging one historical explanation over another, causal explanations appear in some cases to have been almost abandoned altogether. Instead a curiously static picture seems to have emerged.[133] If Gladstonian Liberalism really did have a genuinely widespread popular appeal in the mid-Victorian period, why did it then fail to accommodate a growing body of working-class radicals after 1900? Moreover, why did the Labour Party emerge onto the British political scene at more or less the same time as social democratic labour parties were gaining ground across Europe? The linguistic approach fails to offer a satisfactory explanation for the political changes of the late nineteenth century, especially when seen in a comparative context. Indeed, as one British historian has suggested, few recent histories of nineteenth century British politics, for all their professed revisionism, offer any real challenge to the established narrative and chronology of the rise of class politics: early nineteenth century Radicalism giving way to quiescence during the mid-Victorian era, and a renewed burst of militancy associated with the rise of Labour from the late nineteenth century.[134] Even attempts to answer this criticism seriously can be read merely as attempts to push the 'rise of Labour' further forward into the twentieth century.

In the light of these criticisms, a consensus appears to be emerging about the need to contextualise political languages, and to pay close attention to the specific circumstances in which they are produced and consumed.[135] As John Breuilly has argued, '[r]ather than seeing ideas as the primary forces which shape political perceptions, one should rather treat them as a rhetoric which is used to justify prior objectives.' The use of 'respectable' Liberal languages by mid-Victorian trade unionists should not be taken at face value as representing their belief in such ideas; it was also a conscious attempt to project a particular image.[136] These difficulties become even more apparent within a cross-national comparative context. Examined across Europe as a whole, it is clear that class was not the only way of interpreting the social order, but equally it is the case, as Dick Geary has suggested, that divisions among groups of workers can be explained in terms other than cultural ones.[137] The political sphere was constructed not just by a 'repertoire of discourses', but also by different political structures and different forms of government. 'The point is not that it is always wrong to deny the centrality of class but rather that its significance as an organising construct of the lives of the workers is chronologically and spatially variable, and that the variability is often explicable in terms of differing economic and political structures or conjunctures, as well as language and culture.'[138] A meaningful explanation of the rise of labour in a cross-national comparative context requires a re-engagement with such 'political structures or conjunctures', and the way in which this might be done is discussed in chapter 3.

Local and National Politics in the Rise of Labour

Accompanying the so-called 'linguistic turn' discussed in the previous chapter has been a marked broadening of the definition of what could be considered 'political'. In recent research, the understanding of political activity has extended beyond the realms of the state or labour relations to include 'struggles over status, power and resource allocation, whether in households, neighbourhoods or governments.' This might include for example domestic quarrels between husbands and wives, or disputes between neighbours.[1] Equally, class identification and the process of class formation were not confined to the political arena, but were 'realit[ies] located in the intimate locale of the body, the home, and the locality.'[2] Studies of this type have undoubtedly contributed to enriching the field of labour history, not least in furthering the radical concern to understand working-class culture on its own terms. At the same time, however, this turn seems to be characterised by a reluctance to engage with possible explanations for large-scale historical change. This seems to be particularly problematic in a comparative context, for it means that important events such as the rise of Labour in Europe may end up being attributed to nationally specific causes, or simply to historical accident: in the case of Britain, to the split in the Liberal Party during the First World War.

A more fruitful approach to the comparative 'why' question, it seems to me, lies in the various demands in recent years for labour historians to pay renewed attention to labour *politics*, and in particular the political institutions of the labour movement.[3] Indeed, as one review article has pointed out, historians of nineteenth-century Europe seem to have 'rediscovered' formal politics, and broad processes of political change, as a legitimate field for their enquiries.[4] The major challenge arises from the need to integrate these two approaches, and to explore the relationship between 'high' or 'formal' politics on the one hand, and informal, local politics and 'political culture' on the other. Drawing on recent contributions to the literature on both British and Swedish labour, the first part of this chapter explores the possibilities for such an approach. One of the most useful points, it will be argued, is that it may help to shed some light on the dynamic relationship between local and national politics during the period in question. The second part of the chapter discusses the implications of this approach for the comparative study of two naval dockyard towns in Britain and Sweden, which forms the second part of the book.

I

One of the central concerns for labour historians has been to explain the link between economic and social changes, which are frequently felt in the local context of workplaces or neighbourhoods, and formal political alignment. The British social historian Michael Savage, in his study of the Preston labour movement, proposed a conceptual division between 'formal' and 'practical' politics in an attempt to explain this link.[5] Although *formal* political alignments could exist independently of social relations, politics remained closely tied to material interests at the more informal, practical level, because workers were engaged in a constant struggle to reduce material insecurity in their lives. The 'resources and capacities' which people drew on in organising these struggles were rooted in the social structure in which they lived. Savage identified three distinctive types of working-class 'practical politics': 'mutualist' strategies, where workers established organisations for the independent provision of jobs and services, such as co-operative and friendly societies; 'economistic' strategies, where workers attempted to force their employers to guarantee job security through trade union activity and collective wage bargaining; and 'statist' strategies, where the state was seen as the principal means to guarantee material security, through its provision of welfare. The character of the social structure, including the local skill structure, gender relations, and neighbourhood relations, was the main influence in determining which strategy was most likely to be adopted in any particular place.

The distinction between 'formal' and 'practical' politics thus allowed Savage to investigate the connections between 'practical' political struggles and everyday life in a working-class community, and also to acknowledge the diverse forms which these struggles could take. More problematic, however, is the question of the relationship between 'practical' politics, rooted in local material conditions, and the 'formal' sphere of political parties and elections. Rather than seeing 'formal' politics as existing independently of the social structure, a growing body of work insists that it is just this *relationship*, between local political struggle and formal political alignment, between politics and society in fact, which is the key to our understanding of political change. The work of the British historian Jon Lawrence deserves further discussion here. Lawrence acknowledges the difficulties in ascribing the rise of Labour in the late nineteenth century to class formation, pointing out that social tensions had existed long before that period, and that Liberal and Conservative politics were 'saturated' with languages of class long before the appearance of the Labour Party.[6] However, he insists that social explanations should not be abandoned altogether. Instead, historical investigations of the languages and belief systems of popular politics must also be concerned with the social context in which these languages were produced and consumed, and 'studies of popular politics must focus greater critical attention on the relationship between political activists, of whatever persuasion, and those they seek to represent politically.'[7] In this way, Lawrence's approach allows space for consideration of a socially rooted 'politics of resistance', outside the constraints of formal party politics (reminiscent perhaps of Savage's 'practical politics'), but he is also concerned with investigating the dynamic tension which frequently emerged between the 'politics of resistance' and organised party politics: between the politicians and the people whom they sought to represent. More important than objective processes of structural change, therefore, were the ways in which social reality was perceived by the political élites of all parties, including Labour. He concludes that the popular mistrust of 'party' was an important constraint on Liberalism from the mid-Victorian period, exploited first by the Tories and then later by Labour, although both Labour and Tories were also involved in attempts to 'tame' popular politics through the imposition of party control.[8]

One of the most important features of Lawrence's work, therefore, is his focus on the political parties, and the active role which they played in creating constituencies of support within the electorate –

'constructing unity among fragmented groups of workers' – rather than merely responding to the 'objective' interests of particular groups.[9] These political coalitions were the products of specific historical moments, and constantly evolving.[10] Rather than seeing class formation as an exogenous process, therefore, of which labour parties were the inevitable but passive beneficiaries, this suggests a need to acknowledge the role of the labour movement itself in manufacturing a sense of class among its supporters. Class formation, in other words, is seen not so much as a *process,* but as a *project.*[11] The Swedish historian Göran Salmonsson, in his study of the Swedish Metalworkers' Union (Metall) during its formative years, rejects the conventional view that Metall was founded in response to the escalation of class consciousness among Swedish metalworkers, helping to channel already existing class grievances. Instead, Salmonsson's principal concern is with the union itself, and how it was actively involved in *creating* a sense of class consciousness among its members, or rather, 'establish[ing] a description of reality which [was conceived] in terms of class.'[12] Salmonsson shows how Metall, over the first decade of its existence, was able to institutionalise a particular definition of class, which embraced skilled and unskilled workers but excluded supervisory foremen for example. Class, in this sense, was not a reality, but a potential strategy around which the union's membership could be mobilised.[13]

There are several reasons why the 'new political history', with an emphasis above all on the active role of political parties and other institutions, is a fruitful one for labour historians.[14] In the first place, it integrates 'labour history' more fully into general histories of popular politics and political change, rather than seeing it as a discrete field of enquiry. Recent attempts to explore the influence of bourgeois liberalism on the early Labour Party are important here; as are studies which take seriously working-class Toryism in Britain, a phenomenon which sometimes used to be regarded as a troubling departure from 'true' working-class consciousness.[15] Martin Pugh has, in a recent article, argued convincingly that variations in labour politics across early twentieth century Britain have to be explained partly in relation to the local political cultures, both Liberal and Tory, which Labour faced in different districts.[16] Secondly, the renewed focus on the institutions of the labour movement has helped to reconcile the divergence between 'narrow' or 'old' labour history and 'broad' labour history or working-class history. In this respect, the novelty of this new approach might be questioned. As the American labour historian Howard Kimeldorf has pointed out, so-called 'old' labour history was also concerned with the role of the party or union in developing workers' consciousness, based on ideas derived initially from activists such as Kautsky and Lenin.[17] From the 1960s, however, this approach fell out of favour with the emergence of 'new' labour history emphasising the agency of the workers themselves in developing a consciousness of class. As Kimeldorf acknowledges, this offered a rich and fruitful approach to class formation, but one which tended to marginalise the role of unions and other institutions, and in doing so, to draw labour history away from its traditional concern with the dynamics of capitalist society. Kimeldorf's call for a new synthesis which recognises the role of the union as 'a critical component of the proletarian experience' is one which has been echoed by other scholars in recent years.[18]

A third, and related, advantage to this approach is that it offers a means to integrate studies of political change at a national level with the detailed, micro-study approach to class formation and popular politics that has proved so fruitful within labour history. A closer examination of labour movement organisation may help to address the question of the relationship between national and local political change: 'the nature and importance of the interaction between the centre and the constituencies, between municipal and parliamentary politics.'[19] As Duncan Tanner's ground-breaking study of early twentieth century British politics has shown, although there were forces encouraging the 'nationalisation' of politics before 1914, 'voters in varying areas still had very different interests, expectations and attitudes.'[20] Local political cultures remained strong and vibrant to the extent that they could hinder attempts to impose national party strategies from the centre. Nonetheless, they did not exist in isolation, and local political alignments were determined by the dynamic interaction between local political traditions and national party strategy. Political parties developed increasingly sophisticated means for influencing and controlling the constituencies – such as an official party press and party literature, activist speaking tours, and procedures to control the selection of parliamentary candidates – but Tanner shows that it was much easier for them to impose a nationally agreed strategy, such as the Progressive Alliance, in constituencies where the local party organisation was relatively weak, and thus could be easily moulded. For this reason, British politics remained geographically fragmented during the period before

1914. Drawing on this work, Jon Lawrence has also qualified the orthodoxy of the 'triumph of party', which suggests that late nineteenth century political parties, including Labour, developed strategies in order
to integrate new voters into nationally established patterns. Instead,
'localism' continued to carry an appeal for all groups of voters, and
their involvement in local conflicts and identities helped local parties
to cement electoral support in the constituencies.[21] Party control and
organisation remained incomplete and at best provisional before 1914.
Indeed, the laxness of party control could be an advantage, as Lawrence
illustrates by showing how Labour was able to exploit popular dissatisfaction with the idea of 'party', and present itself as a new and non-
party organisation.[22]

There is an important comparative point to be drawn from these
analyses of party organisation. For the organisational structure of the
Labour Party – or indeed the lack of it – has sometimes been identified as one of the more important differences separating Labour from
the continental socialist parties. Some historians have even gone so
far as to question whether, at the time of its foundation, the Labour
Representation Committee could be considered to be a political party at all, describing it as 'a loose and ill-defined alliance rather than a
coherent party with specific policies.'[23] Contrasted against the epito-
me of the well-organised, bureaucratic, centralised party machine, the
SPD, the Labour Party seemed to be 'haphazard and amateurish'. Not
only this, but the SPD could also be identified as the main blueprint
for the organisation of the Scandinavian social democratic parties,
which thus seemed to differ fundamentally to Labour. The corner-
stone of the difference was the relationship between the party and the
national trade union federation in each case. While the Labour Party emerged 'out of the bowels of the TUC', more than thirty years
after that organisation was founded, the SAP was formed nearly ten
years before the establishment of the Landsorganisationen, LO, and
played a leading role in building a socialist trade union movement with
close ties to the party.[24]

Clearly, these were important differences, but they should not be
overstated. The defining characteristic of early party organisation was
its contingency and flexibility, and comparative historians need to avoid
the teleological implications of placing too much emphasis on organisational differences by acknowledging possibilities for the development of alternative models in each case. As James Fulcher has shown,

there was a 'British LO', namely the General Federation of Trades Unions, which was founded in 1899 as a central organisation for mutual assistance and support.[25] The question then arises: why did the GFTU fail to establish itself as a similar organisation to LO? Fulcher's explanation rests ultimately on the early democratisation of Britain relative to Sweden, which is problematic for the reasons stated in the previous chapter. But his insistence on the loose and provisional forms which labour institutions took during the early years is helpful. The organisational distinction between trade union and political party was ill defined, especially during the early years. Until the establishment of the LO in 1898, the SAP operated more or less as a central co-ordinating body for trade union organisation, often intervening in local wage struggles and work conflicts. Most Swedish workers with a connection to the labour movement were organised through their trade unions rather than political associations.[26] Local labour councils (*arbetarekommuner*), which after 1900 became the building blocks of local party organisation, were essentially committees of trade unionists, and as such had a role to play in resolving industrial disputes that was equally important to that of political campaigning, although they did generally perform both roles. The boundary between party and trade union movement was therefore blurred at a local level. This was also the case in Britain, where again the demarcation between the work of local Labour Representation Committees and Trades and Labour Councils was never well defined, at least before 1910.

Turning to the relationship between national and local tiers of organisation, Göran Salmonsson, in his examination of the early years of Metall, has demonstrated that the organisation of the union was always provisional. There was no blueprint for how a trade union federation should be organised, least of all in respect to how it should define the 'trade' which it sought to represent. Although the union leadership sought to hinder the development of sectional divisions based on skill, it was not always successful in doing this, or in reconciling the disparate interests of many different local branches. From its foundation in 1888, Metall's early years were therefore marked by constant change, as it developed from 'an organisation for mutual strike support' to 'a national organisation with the capacity to operate as an independent actor and pursue a trade policy.'[27] There was, moreover, nothing inevitable about this process, which was frequently marked by conflict and re-negotiation between various groups within the union. In other words, the organisational evolution of Metall was necessarily hap-hazard and contested, rather than a smooth transition from local and spontaneous protest towards a centralised national organisation. Nor was it taken for granted that a national framework was the most appropriate: indeed, the Scandinavian trade union federation was taken seriously as a viable form in some industries until well into the 1900s.[28]

The development of the SAP's organisational geography was equally provisional.[29] At its foundation in 1889, the party had no central authority, but consisted instead of three relatively autonomous districts, one each for the southern, western and central-northern regions of the country. This system was designed to assuage concerns that one regional or local organisation should not be allowed to steer the party's activities elsewhere in the country, and partly reflected the dominance of the Malmö-Copenhagen axis over the traditional centre of government and authority in Stockholm. Even after 1900, when a more centralised structure was introduced, including a national executive committee based in Stockholm, the central bureaucracy's control over the regions was never entirely complete or unchallenged. This was partly due to the deepening gulf, ideological and social, between the full-time party activists and the ordinary workers whose support they were trying to canvass.[30] The establishment of LO in 1898 institutionalised the separation of the trade and political wings of the movement, and allowed the party to concentrate on the development of its electoral machinery. In 1905, the party congress voted to establish a separate organisational tier of districts, and following the electoral reform of 1909 the boundaries of these were redrawn to match those of the new electoral districts. While the local tiers of party organisation – the *arbetarekommuner* and below them the ward and parish committees – began to assume greater responsibility for implementing election strategies on the ground, control over this strategy was increasingly concentrated in the Stockholm-based party apparatus. The executive committee (*partistyrelse*) made important decisions about the allocation of financial resources to assist with local election campaigns, and assumed greater control over the selection of candidate lists. By the eve of World War I, therefore, the SAP had some claim to be considered as a national party, with a Stockholm-based leadership exercising some considerable authority over the network of local branches. But the party leaders could not have matters all their own way. Alternative models of political action – many of them with a syndicalist tinge – continued to generate significant support among local groups, and in certain circumstances could present a real threat to party authority. The most dramatic example of this was during the war, when thousands of workers engaged in direct action in protest at the severe food shortages. Although many of the protests were short-lived, it was significant that in many districts the principal beneficiaries politically were syndicalist organisations. The permanent legacy of this agitation was of course the institutionalisation of the ideological divisions within the labour movement, with the foundation of the Left Socialist Party in May 1917.

Labour politics in the constituencies clearly owed some of its diversity to the influence of local political cultures, which could vary substantially within the same national boundaries, and could often frustrate attempts to impose party control.[31] At the same time, however, this relationship was not one-sided. Labour parties – indeed, all political parties – had an active role in defining and creating the community of which they were a part, and which they sought to represent. The idea of community (or *samhälle*) was not neutral, nor was it fixed in meaning, rooted in the local social structure. Instead, the meaning of 'community', as much as class or any other collective identity, was a product of the imagination, struggled over by different groups. As David Gilbert has shown, by the late nineteenth century there had developed a consensus, common to small towns and large cities alike, that the town or the city was the 'proper' definition of the community, and therefore the proper arena for political action.[32] This resulted in the emergence of local patriotism as a powerful force in local politics, but it was not a force that was necessarily in conflict with other demands on collective loyalty, such as imperialism or class. Indeed, the two could reinforce each other, as illustrated by Joseph Chamberlain's successful political appeal to imperialism and local civic pride in late nineteenth century Birmingham.[33] Similarly, appeals to class loyalty were also reinforced by the notion of community. In the London borough of Poplar, the local Labour Party successfully resisted the attempts of its rival, the Poplar Borough Municipal Alliance, to set 'community' against Labour's class politics, by asserting its own definition of community. Hostile local employers were portrayed as class enemies and outsiders, and Labour activists campaigned to uphold the rights of local citizens and local government against the central state.[34] Meanwhile as Jon Lawrence has shown, the Conserv-

atives' challenge to progressive politics in the West Midlands was partly built around the defence of the local community against the supposed incursion of hostile forces – such as temperance reformers – from
outside. Labour's successes in Wolverhampton after 1900 owed something to the party's ability to offer a new 'politics of place' in response
to the more centralised programmatic politics of the Liberal Party after
1900.[35]

We should however be wary of simply equating Labour with local
political issues, in contrast to the supposedly nationalist agendas of
other political parties. Indeed, the politics of place remained under-
developed by Labour, partly because it too was concerned to stamp
its authority at a *national* level and develop a national party machinery, but also because its activists frequently lacked any real empathy
with the very local struggles which they sought to take up and
respond to.[36] Moreover, local activists often looked towards the
national state, or to other national institutions, to mediate in problems which they considered to be obstructed by powerful and arbitrary local interests. For most of the nineteenth century, the dominant trend, in both Britain and Sweden, had favoured a transfer of
power from the centre to the municipalities. There had been a long
tradition of central authority in Sweden in particular, stretching back
to the establishment of the Vasa monarchy in the sixteenth century,
but the rapid urbanisation of the last quarter of the nineteenth century served to increase the towns' freedom of action, as municipal
administrations responded pragmatically to new urban problems – sanitation, water supplies, communications, planning – which could not
be solved through private means.[37] In Britain, where central control
was weaker, and the voluntary tradition stronger, nineteenth century
local authorities had even more autonomy to develop their own
arrangements.[38] By the early twentieth century, however, there were
signs that this process was in reverse. With attempts to organise services and transfers on the basis of national citizenship – the introduction of pensions and national insurance legislation is a case in point
– and above all with the necessity to mobilise all citizens for war in
1914, the pendulum seemed to be swinging in back in the opposite
direction. This straightforward picture needs to be qualified, however. The allocation of spheres of influence for local and national government was only resolved by a long and complex process of negotiation – sometimes conflict – between the central state and the munic-

ipalities (or indeed other tiers of government). These questions were moreover central to political debates during the years in question. Even where local labour parties lacked the strength to develop exemplary reformist municipal models, as they did in Poplar and Malmö for example, the labour movement could still play an influential role in the debate. After 1918, when the principal role of municipal government was more firmly established as the agent of central government policy, the boundaries between the two remained fluid, and municipal labour representatives continued to contribute to defining them.

II

In the light of the above discussion, some more detailed questions seem to be emerging in addition to the 'why' question – why did social democratic labour parties emerge in Britain and Sweden in the late nineteenth century? – which lies at the root of this study. As I have already discussed, the broad-brush approach required by much comparative history means that relatively few comparative historians have sought to integrate the micro-study approach to popular politics with a comparison stretching across two or more nations. In focusing their efforts on nation states, comparative historians are invariably forced to make rather problematic assumptions about the national integrity of the cases they consider. This is unfortunate, because it is this very question of national integrity which seems to be central to political change during the period associated with the rise of Labour. Many of the changes which took place during the late nineteenth and early twentieth centuries seemed to point towards the partial consolidation of a national political culture, dominated by national political institutions such as parliament, political parties, and the national press.[39] In many cases, the institutions of the labour movement were at the forefront of contributing to this national political culture: class consciousness was thought to have the potential to override local and even national allegiances. On the other hand, labour activists above all were aware of the significance of local loyalties, and sought to root their electoral appeals in the realities of local people's everyday experience. This meant that there was always the possibility for conflict between the local labour movement and the national organisation. Among the questions which need to be asked of the local studies which follow, therefore, perhaps the most important one is this: *to what extent is it possible to speak of a specifically local political culture, and to what extent was local politics influenced by national developments?* 'Political culture' in this sense refers not only to the 'trappings of power', the 'rituals, symbols and other expressive mechanisms', but also the more concrete struggles between political groups over the material benefits to be gained from politics.[40] In other words, politics was always rooted in the 'objective' realities of local social relations. The study is concerned with the role of political institutions, in particular the labour movement, but also other political parties, in interpreting this experience and transforming it into a political appeal. More specifically, therefore, the study is concerned with the following questions: *What form did the movement for independent labour representation take in each case? Of what significance was the idea of class to these debates? What was the role of labour organisations in creating a sense of class identity? How did the party organisation develop? What was the relationship with other political groups, and how did this change over time?*

In the context of the two towns which are to be examined in the second part of this book, this necessitates some discussion of the political issues surrounding the navy and national defence. Plymouth in south west England, and Karlskrona in southern Sweden, were naval towns which had grown up around state-owned naval dockyards founded during the late seventeenth century. In both countries the naval dockyards were administered centrally by naval authorities based in London and Stockholm respectively, which meant that national interests were always in potential conflict with those of the local community in these towns. It also meant that the local trade unions representing the state-employed dockyard workers came into direct contact with the national state from a relatively early period, and therefore sometimes adopted unusual strategies to secure improvements in their working conditions. The management and development of the dockyard at a local level, however, has also to be seen in the context of the very heated debate over national security and the role of the navy in providing national defence, during a time of heightened international tension in Europe. In a very direct sense, therefore, questions of 'high politics', to do with defence, strategy and foreign policy, could be seen to have a direct impact on local politics and the local labour movement. For this reason, the labour politics of the dockyard town makes a particularly interesting case study in the context of a cross-national comparison.

The construction of specialised ships for war was a massive undertaking, requiring a commitment of resources on a scale which, before the nineteenth century at least, could only realistically be undertaken by the state. Consequently, most European states with naval ambitions had invested in developing specialist docks from as early as the sixteenth century, together with the infrastructure necessary to construct a warship and fit it out for action with arms and ordnance, provisions and navigational equipment. In most cases the workers who performed these tasks did so as the direct employees of the state, albeit as civilians. By the late nineteenth century they formed sizeable and well-established communities, and the naval dockyards could not only be reckoned among the oldest established industrial workplaces in Europe, but also among the largest. At their peak during the First World War, the three largest dockyards in Britain, at Portsmouth, Plymouth and Chatham, employed over 15,000 workers each, and, taken together with the smaller yards, accounted for a quarter of all shipbuilding employment in Britain.[41] In Sweden, the Karlskrona dockyard workforce, which peaked at over 2000 in 1904, was significantly larger than the 500–1000 workers employed by the three largest shipyards in Göteborg before 1914.[42]

It is possible to identify a number of common characteristics shared by dockyard towns across Europe. As with all military installations, the location of naval dockyards was determined principally by strategic requirements, rather than other considerations such as the availability of raw materials and labour. Karlskrona dockyard, strategically located in the southern provinces recaptured from Denmark in the mid seventeenth century, was intended to help assert Swedish hegemony in the Baltic, as well as providing an easily defended naval base that remained ice-free throughout the year. The establishment of the new dockyard at Plymouth in 1690 was also dictated by the presence of a natural deepwater harbour, and concerns about the vulnerability of the English Channel in a potential conflict with France. This meant, however, that by the mid nineteenth century, both dockyards were extremely isolated from other centres of industry or indeed shipbuilding. Plymouth was far removed from the heavy engineering and shipbuilding industries in the north of England and southern Scotland; Karlskrona was equally distant from the heart of the Swedish shipbuilding industry on the west coast. This presented some problems for the naval authorities over the delivery of raw materials, but, more importantly, it also placed tight constraints on the local labour market, which had in turn important implications for dockyard work and industrial relations.

A further characteristic was the dependence of the dockyard town on political matters that were usually beyond its control or influence.[43] Decisions likely to have a profound effect on the dockyard town, such as those concerning the allocation of resources, were taken by naval administrators in London or Stockholm, and were determined not by local needs, but by the demands of war and peace. Although the dockyard towns were shielded from the worst fluctuations of the business cycle, they were vulnerable to sudden contractions in defence spending, which could have devastating consequences.[44] This dependence was made worse by the determination of naval administrators to ensure that, as far as possible, military and strategic requirements were not compromised by other activities, such as commercial industry. They were not averse to blocking proposals for commercial developments which might compete with the dockyard, and they also maintained a tight control over the use of land. For their part, local authorities lobbied vigorously to attempt to influence defence policy, and the politics of the dockyard town was often dominated by this tension between local and national interests.[45]

Where national defence policies were concerned there were some important differences between Britain and Sweden, which in turn had implications for the development of the two dockyard towns considered here. British naval policy was driven by the needs of a global empire, and an ambition to remain the supreme European naval power. Plymouth dockyard formed part of a massive naval infrastructure consisting of three large home dockyards – Portsmouth, Chatham and Plymouth, augmented during the First World War by a new dockyard at Rosyth – and several smaller ones, as well as an overseas network of dockyards and naval bases.[46] Extensive modernisation at Portsmouth and Plymouth, driven by fears of the German naval challenge in the late nineteenth century, meant that these dockyards had the capacity for the construction of the largest and most modern naval warships. By the turn of the century, Plymouth dockyard was entering a period of intense activity, and its workforce continued to grow until 1918. Karlskrona dockyard was, by contrast, a much more modest undertaking. By the mid nineteenth century, it had outlived Sweden's great power status, and its role had to be adapted to serve the interests of a minor, relatively poor, European nation, which based its foreign policy on non-alignment and neutrality.[47] This meant that its modernisation was delayed, and unlike Plymouth, it never developed the capacity for the construction of the largest warships. These differences clearly have to be taken into account when comparing the two towns, but they do not in themselves imply that the two cases are incomparable. In the first place, the much smaller scale of activities at Karlskrona needs to be seen in a wider Swedish context. Although it had declined in size relative to the newer industrial towns, it was still one of the larger towns in the kingdom, and its population was continuing to grow. Secondly, both towns were affected by the very prominent public debates over national defence which took place in both Britain and Sweden around the turn of the century. These are discussed in more detail below. Finally, the unusual characteristics of the dockyards as industrial workplaces gave rise to some equally distinctive practices of work and labour relations which distinguished the dockyard towns from other industrial districts.

The peculiar nature of shipbuilding, with long production runs meaning that periods of intense activity were interspersed with periods of slack, presented particular problems for the dockyard authorities in the recruitment and retention of labour. The size of the labour market in large industrial districts such as Clydeside and Tyneside meant that most commercial shipbuilding employers could draw on a large pool of labour in times of expansion. In contrast, the isolation of most dockyard towns meant that dockyard managers had to balance the need to maintain a skilled workforce, capable of responding to an acute strategic need at short notice, with the need to keep the wage bill as low as possible.[48] Most dockyards seem to have adopted the strategy of maintaining a core group of highly skilled workers by offering them relatively generous non-wage benefits such as pensions, accident and sickness benefits, and some support for dependents. In the British dockyards this arrangement was formalised through the establishment scheme, which practically guaranteed permanent employment to an élite group of workers.[49] Karlskrona did not operate a formal establishment, but similar benefits, including pensions, were available to skilled workers.[50] The rest of the workforce was employed on temporary contracts, although the promise of permanent employment was held out as a prospect to those joining the workforce as apprentices. Remarkably, though, the naval authorities were generally reluctant to extend these paternalist arrangements outside the workplace, through the provision of housing for example. For this reason, few dockyard towns ever came to resemble the 'company towns' dominated by private shipbuilding firms, such as Jarrow in north east England, or Landskrona in Sweden.[51] On the other hand, even without paternalist intervention the dockyard workforce often seemed to be a self-contained community removed from the rest of the town, cemented by ties which had been built up over many generations.[52]

Partly because of these unusual labour practices, naval dockyards have often been thought of as difficult territory for the labour movement. The presence of an élite group of workers was assumed to work against the development of class solidarity, while the attempts of management to foster a dockyard culture of patriotism and loyalty, transmitted for example through the apprentice education system, were also thought to diminish support for a labour movement committed to proletarian internationalism.[53] For these reasons the Conservative Party has been described as the 'natural party' of British dockyard towns such as Plymouth, Portsmouth and Chatham. Secure employment, the lack of any tradition of hostility to authority, and passive acceptance of Conservative 'big navy' politics meant that in these areas there was 'little reason to support Progressive parties, with their commitment to state intervention, and traditional hostility to the military and military expenditure.'[54] Similar assumptions have also been made about France, where 'dependence on the state generally assured the triumph of reformist politics in naval shipyard towns.'[55]

There are, however, several reasons why we should be wary of making assumptions about the 'natural' quiescence of dockyard workforces. Recent research has demonstrated that dockyard labour relations were far more complex than the traditional picture of a demoralised and deferential body of workers suggests. Naval dockyards were dynamic institutions, which grew and evolved in response to new technology and the varying demands of state defence policy. They were undoubtedly places of tradition, and of shared ties developed over generations, but the dockyards were also open to wider influences, especially as they expanded and drew in new workers during the late nineteenth century. Naval industrial relations policy was constantly evolving, driven by the need to satisfy military and strategic demands within the political constraints imposed on the naval budget. The response of dockyard labour was also in constant flux, combining traditional and innovative methods of protest to defend interests and secure gains. Periods of war, when the dockyards operated at full stretch, tended to encourage labour militancy. In Britain, the period of the Napoleonic Wars in particular was a time of heightened dockyard radicalism, resulting in several long-running strikes and disputes.[56] This militancy had declined by the nineteenth century, but instead, dockyard workers turned to political lobbying, institutionalised in Britain through a system of formal written petitions to Admiralty representatives. Rather than signalling a culture of deference and submissiveness, it has been suggested that the creative use of formal petitions could challenge existing structures of authority, and foreshadowed modern channels of political influence, for example through the dockyard parliamentary representative.[57] Indeed, the unusual availability of direct channels of access to the state appears to be one of the most distinctive aspects of nineteenth century dockyard labour relations.

Towards the end of the nineteenth century there were signs that existing structures for the redress of grievances, such as the petitions system, had begun to come under strain, as dockyard workers looked increasingly towards trade unions to defend their interests.[58] Trade unions were rarely formally proscribed in naval dockyards – an exception was the naval dockyards of Imperial Germany – but up until the 1880s, the threat of dismissal from what could be a job for life was an effective deterrent against forming a union. This had changed by the late nineteenth century, when the prospect of permanent employment was becoming increasingly obsolescent for many dockyard workers.[59] As most states began to introduce more comprehensive welfare provision, they also undermined the uniqueness of the dockyard benefits system, which did much to shatter the sense of the dockyard as a community apart, and to remove an important lever in management control over the workforce. This was to have implications for labour relations. By the early twentieth century, the existence of dockyard trade unions seems to have been acknowledged and tolerated in many dockyards.[60] Often such organisations had their roots in older, looser collective associations, such as committees for drafting petitions, or mutual benefit societies. The dockyard labour protest could also take more direct, even militant forms. In November 1905, nearly 8000 French dockyard workers joined a 48-hour strike to protest against the suspension of a Brest worker, charged with distributing anti-military propaganda.[61] Even in the imperial dockyards of Germany, where labour action was constrained by the more oppressive nature of the Bismarckian state, official attitudes to unionism and labour politics were tempered by pragmatism. After the SPD was banned in 1878, dockyard workers were required to sign documents pledging that they were not members of the party. Yet this seems to have been openly defied. An investigation at Kiel the following year revealed that an estimated three quarters of all the metalworkers and carpenters were members of the party, and that their mutual societies were merely a front for political activities. Shortages of skilled labour meant that the authorities could not afford to discharge any except the most open proselytisers of socialism.[62] Paradoxically, the navy's anti-socialist position hardened after the expiry of the anti-socialist laws during the 1890s, and the informal policy of tolerance ended. By this time the imperial yards had lost their central role in new naval construction to the private shipbuilding firms, and thus the need to retain skilled labour was less pressing.[63]

If dockyard labour relations were more complex and dynamic than is often portrayed, then equally we should be wary of making assumptions about the politics of the naval town. The existence of a link between the 'objective' material interests of the dockyard workers and electoral support for 'big navy' policies and parties should not be taken for granted. Above all, the simple equation of these issues with the political right is problematic. Although it has been considerably less researched than the contemporaneous developments on the political left, especially in a comparative context, historians acknowledge that the political right was also 'remade' in the period after 1870. This process was driven by the need of right wing parties to win popular electoral support, and was influenced above all by the examples of Bismarck and Napoleon III, who demonstrated that it was indeed possible to mobilise the masses in support of conservative resistance to liberal reforms.[64] There were also signs that the association of nationalism and liberalism, which had endured for much of the nineteenth century, was beginning to break down, as non-liberal policies such as protectionism were increasingly likely to be justified in terms of national interest.

With the escalation in international tension from the last decades of the nineteenth century, nationalist attention turned towards defence, and in both Britain and Sweden the question of defence generated intense political controversy from the 1890s. Although the context of these debates was clearly very different in these two countries, given their relative size and influence, the importance of defence as a political issue cannot be overestimated in either case. The main foreign policy concern for the political Right in Sweden was the defence of the Crown's union with Norway, especially after 1884, when the Swedish king was forced to capitulate to Norwegian demands for parliamentary reform.[65] The secession of Norway in 1905 thus marked a watershed for the Right, which coincided with renewed fears over the security of Swedish interests in the Baltic, following signs of increased Russian rearmament in the Baltic region, and the policy of 'russification' in the grand duchy of Finland.[66] The role of the navy in defending these interests, and the allocation of state funds to support it, now became one of the most heated political controversies of the moment.[67] The debate became polarised along party lines, with the Liberals and Social Democrats advocating a reduction in defence expenditure, and the Right in favour of expanding the navy to meet the perceived threat. A parliamentary commission of enquiry found in favour of constructing a new fleet of 'F-type' armoured warships (*pansarbåtar*) when it reported in 1910, a recommendation which carried huge implications for the defence budget.[68] The Liberal and Social Democratic opposition in the second chamber of the *riksdag* defeated the government's bill to introduce these proposals, but a majority in the more Conservative upper chamber meant that it was passed. Following the general election of 1911, the first to be contested on the new franchise, there was a change of government, however. The new Liberal government, which had campaigned on a platform of reduced defence expenditure, appointed its own parliamentary committees to examine ways of making savings in the defence budget. Significantly, this action incurred the outright opposition of the King, who declared that reducing defence expenditure would put the country in danger.[69] When the Prime Minister, Karl Staaff, announced his intention to cancel an outstanding order for a new F-type battleship there was uproar, and a national campaign for private subscriptions raised 17 million *kronor* to ensure that the vessel's construction would go ahead: it was launched in 1915. The publication in 1912 of an influential pamphlet by the ultra-right wing campaigner and defence advocate Sven Hedin, entitled 'A Word of Warning' ('Ett varningsord'), further revived fears of the old enemy Russia, and Staaff was forced to shift his position somewhat. He chose Karlskrona as the venue for an important speech in December 1913, recommending further rearmament. This failed sufficiently to placate his critics however, and following the pro-defence Peasants' March two months later, again with the support of the King, Staaff found his position untenable and resigned.

The years 1911–1914 were thus dominated by intense public debate over naval defence. It is difficult to distinguish a clear left-right divide, however, as the more ardent advocates of increased defence spending asserted the need to transcend existing party divisions, adopting the slogan 'Homeland first!' (*Fosterlandet främst*). It was certainly true that moderate conservatives, such as Harald Hjärne and the former Prime Minister Arvid Lindman, had, since the mid 1900s, gradually shifted their position on foreign policy from advocacy of strict neutrality towards support for strengthening Swedish defences.[70] It should be noted, however, that the most energetic campaigning for increased defence expenditure was associated not with the parliamentary Right, but with a more extreme group led by Sven Hedin and Rudolf Kjellén, which drew a large part of its support from the ultra-conservative military establishment. Looking principally to Imperial Germany as a model, and influenced also by the personal ambitions of King Gustav V, these men connected the need for strong defence with the role of the King in support of this position, as the representative of the true 'will of the people' (*folkvilja*).[71] They supported their arguments with reference to historical precedent. The military strength and successes of Karl XII, celebrated by the Caroline Society (Karolinska Förbundet) founded in 1910, were contrasted favourably against the distractions of a powerful parliament and party competition during the Age of Freedom in the eighteenth century. This agitation reached its apogee in the so-called palace yard coup (*borggårdskupen*) of March 1914, when the King defied parliament in his outspoken criticisms of the government's defence policy. These events had some influence on the Right's strong performance in the extraordinary *riksdag* election later that spring, but it is also worth noting that the most extreme pro-defence advocates remained disappointed by the response of the new conservative Hammarskjöld government, which adopted a cautious approach to the defence issue.[72] Nonetheless, the events of early 1914, and the intense debates preceding them, may be considered decisive in the evolution of links between the parliamentary Right and the issue of national defence.

The gradual and complex process by which this link was forged took a remarkably similar path in Britain. A number of new nationalist organisations were founded in the 1890s, but as with similar organisations in Sweden, a common theme of their agitation was the need to transcend established party rivalries and create a national consensus around important issues such as defence.[73] It was only really after the landslide electoral defeat of the Conservatives in 1906 that the issue of naval defence began to take on a more party political significance. This shift was influenced by the escalation in international tension, which heightened fears for the security of the Empire, and which coincided with the Liberal government's proposals to cut the navy estimates. The debate reached its height in 1909, when it was alleged that the British navy was no longer able to maintain the 'two power standard' against its main rival Germany, and the proposed remedy was to be the construction of more Dreadnought-class battleships. By the time of the general election campaign which began in December that year, the Conservatives had succeeded in making the defence issue their own: support for increased naval expenditure implied support for the Conservatives, and the Navy League campaigned openly for the party.[74] The Conservatives' pro-defence platform was also associated with the party's defence of the House of Lords against the dangers of 'party tyranny' in the Commons, although this position was never asserted in such an extreme way as it was in Sweden.

In both Britain and Sweden, then, it is possible to trace the evolution of a link between patriotism, defence and political conservatism during the early twentieth century. Central to these debates in each case was the strength of the navy. Warships represented the tangible evidence of a nation state's commitment to its defence, and fears about national defence in both Britain and Sweden were largely focused on the need for more of them. Quite apart from the purely strategic significance of the navy, the armoured warship has been described as 'the most important symbol of national strength and success' at this time, intimately linked with national identity even for smaller nations.[75] In the naval dockyard towns, where economic prosperity was so closely connected with the state of the navy, it might have been expected, therefore, that this politics would be particularly appealing. There were certainly attempts to exploit it, as in 1910, when the former admiral Charles Beresford successfully contested one of the Portsmouth constituencies as an independent 'naval candidate', albeit one supported openly by the Unionist Party.[76]

It would be misleading, however, to assume that the dockyard towns were hostile to the appeals of socialist labour parties. In part, this was because the relationship between socialism and nationalism was itself ambiguous. In Britain, although some historians suggested that the possibilities for radical patriotism faded towards the end of the nineteenth century, discussions of patriotism and Englishness were in fact profoundly influential in shaping the British left during these years, as Paul Ward has recently demonstrated.[77] Further, the 'vast majority' of the left accepted the necessity of national defence, even if most of them would not go so far as Robert Blatchford or H M Hyndman in calling for increased defence expenditure against the 'German menace'. Nonetheless, leading socialist newspapers such as *Clarion* and *Justice* were prepared to give some space to writers expressing these views, and Labour MPs were divided over the issue.[78] The same also applied to Sweden, where the use of patriotic discourse was by no means confined to the political right, but also influenced liberal and socialist politics.[79] For the Swedish labour movement, as for its British counterpart, the commitment to proletarian internationalism represented a hope for a peaceful brotherhood of nations, and did not necessarily imply an outright rejection of patriotism.[80] There was a strong tradition of popular aversion to military taxes and conscription, and many within the labour movement were also suspicious of the armed forces as a potential resource to settle industrial conflict.[81] Socialist and labour attitudes to defence were complex, however, and for the SAP leadership in particular, governed by pragmatism: the party's acceptance of compulsory military service for example was seen as a useful bargaining tool in the more important struggle to secure suffrage reform. Despite the presence of so-called defence nihilists in the labour movement, especially in the social democratic youth movement, the majority of party members remained loyal to the compromise resolution on defence adopted at the 1900 party congress. The party was hostile to the Right's agitation for increased defence expenditure, but did not campaign for major reductions in the defence budget.[82]

For these reasons, it is difficult to distinguish any consistency of support for 'navalist' candidates in dockyard elections.[83] The extent of popular support for navalist politics was always influenced by the ambiguities of the relationship between dockyard town and national state, and the reputations of local politicians were thus partly founded on their willingness and ability to defend local interests against the demands of the navy.[84] The situation was further complicated by the politicisation of dockyard labour relations, as a consequence of direct employment by the state. As Donald Reid notes, writing of the French dockyards, '[f]or naval shipyard workers the relationship between workplace life and politics was less problematic than for most industrial workers.'[85] The political representatives of dockyard towns were active in parliament on behalf of their constituents, and dockyard workers were urged to cast their votes on this basis. In Karlskrona, parliamentary representatives played a leading role in negotiating a collective wage settlement for the dockyard. The presence of a sympathetic *riksdagsman* was important not only for his role in directly lobbying the naval authorities, but also in bridging the distance between Stockholm, where the decisions affecting the dockyard were made, and Karlskrona, by conveying important information. The enfranchisement of a large proportion of the dockyard workforce in 1909 was significant in developing this relationship, and by 1917 the dockyard had become an electoral issue to the extent that candidates tailored their electioneering to their dockyard constituents.[86]

Two further points may be made about the politics of the dockyard towns. The first concerns the dockyard towns as sites of 'rough culture' associated with the large numbers of young servicemen present in the towns, and the services, such as pubs and brothels, which had emerged to supply their entertainment. Prostitution in the naval and garrison towns became the subject of heated public debate in Britain from the 1860s, as a result of the controversy surrounding the Contagious Diseases Acts; few doubted that the problem existed in these towns.[87] This 'rough culture' was at odds with the values of temperance and respectability that were frequently, though not always, associated with the organised labour movement, and thus could be expected to work against Labour success in the dockyard towns. As Jon Lawrence has shown for Wolverhampton, late Victorian Conservatives gained working-class support by distancing themselves from the reforming sanctimony of progressive politicians, and based their appeal on the defence of the working man's right to enjoy his beer in peace.[88] In a naval town, this type of politics could perhaps generate support among certain groups. There is evidence, for example, that the Plymouth Conservative MP Nancy Astor, despite her strong commitment to temperance reform, based her enduring success in part on her ability to generate sympathy among the lower deck of the navy, rather than among the dockyard workers.[89]

The second point is that the politics of the dockyard town must be considered within a wider regional context. Despite the unusually close connections between the dockyard town and the apparatus of the central state, dockyard towns were often important regional centres, especially when these towns were relatively isolated from other urban districts. Crook has noted that the French dockyard town of Toulon, despite being 'a prisoner of the government's maritime strategy', was nonetheless well-integrated into the region, and that the *provençal* elements of the town's identity were equally as important as its links with the national state apparatus.[90] The focus here is on the early nineteenth century, but the point applies to the later period as well. In Britain, the new dockyard opened at Rosyth in 1916, close to the 'Little Moscows' of the West Fife coalfields, was in a very different situation to the southern dockyards. Indeed, the radical Rosyth dockyardsmen sometimes complained about what they saw to be the apathy of their southern counterparts.[91] In Plymouth, on the other hand, dockyard politics were probably influenced by a vibrant tradition of Gladstonian Liberalism and nonconformity, which dominated the declining industrial districts of Cornwall from where many dockyard workers migrated. In other words, no dockyard was a closed community, and it remained constantly open to new influences from both inside and outside the local region.

The relationship between these local and regional political cultures on the one hand, and national politics on the other, is explored in the two case studies which follow. As outlined earlier in this chapter, the main focus is on the interaction between local cultures of work and politics in these two towns, and the institutions of the labour movement which attempted to make sense of them and to translate them into electoral success. Each case is considered in turn. Chapters 4 and 5 examine Plymouth, where the turning point for Labour came during the First World War, partly as a result of the intense conflicts over food prices. Chapters 6 and 7 examine Karlskrona, where the Social Democratic Party seems to have been rather more successful than its Plymouth counterpart. The two cases are considered side by side in the brief conclusion.

Part II

A Local Case Study – Labour and the Two Dockyard Towns

CHAPTER 4

The Labour Movement in Plymouth c. 1890–1914

Plymouth was difficult territory for the labour movement in the years before 1914, as Tables 4.1, 4.2 and 4.3 (pp. 319–322) show. Labour managed to contest only a handful of wards in municipal elections before 1914, and achieved success in even fewer. None of the parliamentary elections was contested by a Labour or Socialist candidate before 1918. This apparent absence of a movement for independent working-class politics has been attributed to two causes. The first points to the survival of a popular tradition of Gladstonian Liberalism in south-west England into the inter-war period, and its close links to the strength of religious nonconformity in the peninsula. The survival of the Liberal Party, it is argued, was symptomatic of an economically and socially backward region, where religious fraternity, social deference and political patronage continued to define political allegiance, in contrast to the more dynamic forms of class politics found elsewhere in the country.[1] The second explanation suggests that class consciousness was stifled by nationalist allegiance in Plymouth, and that the Conservatives, as the unequivocal advocates of a strong national defence, were the 'natural' party of the naval dockyard towns.[2]

It is true that the Liberal Party remained a vibrant political force in some parts of south west England until well after 1918, especially in Cornwall. It was, moreover, a Liberal politics which owed relatively little to the 'new Liberalism' of social reform, and much to older traditions of Radical populism and religious dissent. 'Peace, retrenchment, reform' remained the watchword of west-country Liberals until well after 1918.[3] More problematic, however, is the assumption that this success was linked to a static and decaying political culture. In the first place, the extent of Liberal hegemony across the region is questionable. In 1885 the Liberals had won two thirds of the Devon and Cornwall divisions, only to lose all but four of these seats at the general election of 1886. Rather than being static, over the following decades south west England was one of the most politically marginal regions in the country.[4] This volatility characterised the Plymouth constituencies too. With the exception of 1895, the Devonport division voted against the retiring government at every general election during the period 1885–1910, and the majorities of the winning candidates were consistently slim. Secondly, the portrayal of the south west as a backward region is unhelpful for understanding the economic, social and political development of Plymouth. The commercial significance of the port had certainly declined since the seventeenth century, although the arrival of the railway in 1844, and the designation of the port as an official emigration terminus two years later, were of some benefit.[5] The economic consequences of this decline were, however, easily offset by the presence of the navy, following the decision to found a new dockyard and naval base at Plymouth in 1690. The dockyard, and the new town which developed around it, grew rapidly during the eighteenth century, and by 1801, in the midst of the hectic activity of the Napoleonic Wars, Plymouth was the tenth largest town in Britain.[6] Over half of the population of 43,514 resided in the settlement around the naval dockyard, known as Plymouth Dock until it was incorporated as the town of Devonport in 1824. Expansion continued throughout the nineteenth century, as the prospect of dockyard labour or naval service attracted migrants from the declining extractive industries of Cornwall and west Devon. The population of Plymouth and Devonport grew by 345% during the period 1801–1901, compared to a rate of 95% for Devon as a whole.[7] (Table 4.4) The development of the Keyham Steam Yard, opened in 1853, consolidated Devonport's position as one of the British navy's most important assets, and the dockyard was extended further towards the end of the century.[8]

The presence of the navy had an immense impact on the economic, social and political development of Plymouth. The defence sector accounted for almost half of all male employment in Devonport during the census years 1891 and 1911, not including the civilian dockyard workforce.[9] Most of these were naval ratings or officers on shore leave from Devonport-based ships, or stationed more permanently in the army or navy barracks. The dockyard itself, with a workforce of over 10,000 in 1910, was by far the largest industrial workplace in Plymouth, and indeed the entire region. The largest employer in Ply-

TABLE 4.4. *Population in Plymouth and Devonport, 1851–1921.*

Year	Population		% change	
	Plymouth	Devonport	Plymouth	Devonport
1851	52 922	38 692		
1861	63 782	51 058	+20.5	+32
1871	70 524	50 157	+10.6	-1.8
1881	76 502	49 846	+8.5	-0.6
1891	88 931	55 986	+16.2	+12.3
1901	107 636	70 437	+21	+25.8
1911	112 030	81 525	+4.1	+15.7
1921	115 186	80 993	+2.8	-0.7

SOURCE: Board of Trade report into rents, wages and prices (H.C. cd.3864 (1908) cvii.319); Census 1911, 1921.)

mouth, after the navy, was the Plymouth Co-operative Society with approximately 1000 workers, and the only other comparable enterprise was the Great Western Railway, which employed between 400 and 500 dock labourers.[10] There were many other ways in which the navy had stamped its mark on the town: in the physical presence of the naval buildings, in the Admiralty's restrictive control over the use of space, and in the public monuments and spectacles, such as dockyard shiplaunches, commemorating British naval supremacy. More informally, the navy was commemorated in the pub and street names, and in the everyday use of naval imagery in the advertising of local businesses.[11] There was also the constant presence of large numbers of uniformed personnel on the streets, and the provision of entertainment and leisure for men on shore leave. Like other naval and port towns, some parts of Plymouth were associated with prostitution and heavy drinking, and the authorities' attempts to regulate these trades through the Contagious Diseases Acts of the 1860s provoked some political conflict.[12] The impact of the navy on local politics as a whole, however, is less clear. As Table 4.1 (pp. 319–320) illustrates, there was no clear pattern of support for any party in parliamentary elections before 1910, and the Plymouth constituencies seem to have displayed the same volatility as the rest of the region. The elections of 1910, however, marked the beginning of a new period of Conservative dominance, which was sustained through the inter-war period.

The rapid expansion of the town during the late nineteenth century had a marked impact on municipal politics. Until 1914, the conurbation consisted administratively of three towns, rather than one, and was often referred to as such. Under the Local Government Act of 1888, Plymouth and Devonport had the status of county boroughs, meaning that they owned the administrative responsibilities of counties in their own right, with the corporation acting as County Council and as Urban Sanitary Authority.[13] Each returned two members of parliament. East Stonehouse, the third of the Three Towns, was part of the parliamentary borough of Devonport, but was administered by an Urban District Council of fifteen members under the auspices of Devon County Council.[14] Despite their close connections, until 1914 Plymouth and Devonport formed entirely separate and discrete administrative entities, with Devonport jealously guarding its status as an incorporated town, first recognised by Royal Charter in 1824. The situation was becoming increasingly anomalous, however. Rapid population growth necessitated further re-organisation to accommodate outlying districts into the expanding conurbation, and the local labour movement, among other organisations, campaigned for amalgamation of the Three Towns during the 1900s. A public enquiry opened in January 1914, but events were overtaken by the outbreak of war in Europe that year, and the eventual amalgamation passed more or less unnoticed. The new unitary authority, first elected in November 1914, consisted of the Mayor, 20 aldermen and 60 councillors divided between 20 wards. Devonport lost out to Plymouth in terms of representation, having only 21 councillors compared to 31 for Plymouth and 6 for Stonehouse.[15]

The two borough councils differed only marginally in their political make-up over the period with which we are concerned (Tables 4.2 and 4.3). The Liberal Party led a period of reform during the 1890s, following the 1888 local government reforms which enhanced the powers of municipal authorities. This brought a sharp rise in the local rate, however, which the Conservatives were able to exploit, gaining ground in both boroughs and winning a majority in Devonport in 1900.[16] With the support of independents, including a number of councillors elected on a platform of municipal retrenchment, the Conservatives held the balance of power in Devonport on several occasions through the 1900s. In Plymouth the Liberals were more successful in retaining control, but here too they faced a strong challenge from the advocates of restricted finance, and the party dwindled from the amalgamation of the three authorities in 1914. The importance of the rates as a source of political controversy is further illustrated by the considerable fluctuations in public interest in municipal affairs, a rough indication of which is provided by the number of council seats which went uncontested each year. In Plymouth, there was a sharp rise in the number of contested seats in the late 1890s, appearing to correlate strongly with the public debate on municipal spending and reform. A similar trend is distinguishable for Devonport, where only one out of twelve wards was contested in 1891, but where nearly all the wards were contested annually from the mid 1890s.

The labour movement's first attempts to contest municipal elections in Plymouth thus coincided with a few years of heightened political interest and controversy in the municipal sphere. As the largest workplace, the naval dockyard was a natural focus for trade union activity, and dockyard workers were among those who established the Trades and Labour Council in 1892.[17] The labour movement received a tremendous boost in 1899, when the Trades Union Congress was held in Plymouth, and the momentum gained from this was carried over into the foundation of a Labour Representation Association in 1902. This organisation had some very limited success in municipal elections before 1914, contesting wards in both Plymouth and Devonport. In this it was joined by another beneficiary of the 1899 TUC, the Plymouth branch of the Social Democratic Federation, which campaigned prominently on the issue of working-class housing. But these organisations paled into insignificance besides what was easily the largest working-class organisation in the Three Towns, the Plymouth Co-operative Society. Founded by a small group of artisans in 1860, many of them former Chartists, the society had grown rapidly so that by 1906 it was the fourth largest retail society in England, with a membership of 34,581.[18] It controlled a network of twenty-four grocery branches which stretched right across the Three Towns, together with fifteen butcheries, ten dairies and other shops offering boots and shoes, drapery and millinery, and household goods such as china and glass.[19] Its dominance was such that the Board of Trade, in a 1908 report, commented that, '[t]he Co-operative Society is a powerful factor in distribution in Devonport and Plymouth... A great deal of the working-class purchasing is done in the Co-operative Stores.'[20] Adherence to the Rochdale Pioneers' principles of political and religious neutrality meant that co-operators were reluctant to become engaged in politics, but the matter provoked much debate within the society, sparked partly by the hostility of the local private traders towards co-operative trading activities. Many leading co-operators strongly advocated closer co-operation with the wider labour movement, and attempts to secure independent labour representation were followed with great interest in the pages of the society's journal, the *Plymouth Co-operative Record*. Eventually, co-operative support did indeed prove to be the key to transforming Labour's fortunes in Plymouth; this will be discussed in chapter 5.

Labour politics in early twentieth-century Plymouth must therefore be seen within the context of wider political change, and this chapter attempts to address some of the most important aspects of that change before the First World War. The first section examines the role of the dockyard, as it entered into a period of intense activity and expansion in the years before 1914. The tightening local labour market contributed in part to a renewed assertiveness on the part of the workforce, and a mounting dissatisfaction with the existing channels for the redress of workplace grievances. Dockyard disputes had a political dimension too, and the consolidation of a tradition of lobby politics might have been expected to have had a noticeable impact on voting behaviour. This went beyond dockyard industrial relations to embrace the links between naval defence and the prosperity of the local community, a link on which the Conservatives in particular attempted to build an appeal. But the requirements of national defence could also be represented as clashing with local interests, and as being less important than municipal reforms. The labour movement campaigned energetically over issues such as housing, and presented a vision for a new municipal politics free from the factionalism of the traditional party struggle.

I

Although the industrial workforces of the naval dockyards were among the largest of the late nineteenth century in Britain, there seems to have been much which worked against the development of a common workplace culture. Above all, the workforce was divided by the entrenched sectional rivalries for which British shipbuilding was notorious.[21] The roots of this stratification were highly complex, and cannot be explained simply in terms of wage differentials, or the differences between skilled and unskilled workers. The example of the

Swedish shipyards, where the labour process was no less complex, but the workers were generally organised in industrial unions, serves to reinforce the point. Moreover, the division of labour was fluid, and was constantly being reformed in the wake of important technological changes in shipbuilding. Generally, the division of labour within the naval dockyards mirrored that in the larger private sector shipyards, but with some important differences. One major source of irritation for the shipbuilding unions was that dockyard skilled labourers often performed tasks which were demarcated as separate trades in the private sector, and therefore required an apprenticeship, such as riveting. The most important difference however was in the superior status of the dockyard shipwrights. Unlike their private sector counterparts, the importance of whose role declined with the advent of iron and steel shipbuilding, the dockyard shipwrights were retrained to work in metal, and thus retained their status at the apex of the hierarchy of trades. Equivalent to the platers and boilermakers in the private shipyards, the shipwrights were principally responsible for the construction of the hull, and working in small gangs they enjoyed a high degree of autonomy over their work.[22]

As well as the effects of these established trade rivalries, dockyard historians have also cited the role of the Admiralty in creating a workplace culture which was individualist and fragmented.[23] Particularly influential was the system for selecting and educating apprentices through the dockyard schools established in the 1840s. Although some workers, usually members of the minor trades, were recruited to the dockyard after an apprenticeship served elsewhere, for the majority entry was via an annual examination for local boys aged between 14 and 16. These examinations were highly competitive, and some local schools built their reputations around their success in coaching pupils for the dockyard examination.[24] For it was not merely enough to gain entrance to the school; what mattered was the type of apprenticeship to be served. The successful candidates were allocated a trade according to their examination results, those with the highest marks being offered a shipwright's apprenticeship, and the second highest group becoming engine fitters.[25] There seems to have been no opportunity for a boy to change trades once he had entered the dockyard school. The prestigious shipwright apprenticeships were coveted not only for their own sake, but also for the opportunities for promotion which were attached.[26] All apprentices attended the dockyard school for the first year of their six-year apprenticeships, but thereafter they were divided annually by examination and the top half of the year only were allowed to continue their formal classroom-based education. The shipwright and engine fitter apprentices attending for the third and fourth year received professional instruction in naval architecture and marine engineering, followed by instruction in the drawing offices in the fourth year, and for a few who obtained exceptional results in their fourth year examinations, there was the possibility of a scholarship to the Royal Naval College at Greenwich to be trained as a technical officer. In theory, a boy entering as a shipwright apprentice could aspire to becoming a draughtsman, an inspector of trades, or even, via a Greenwich scholarship, a naval architect or designer.

Even if very few could realistically aspire to the dizzy heights of Greenwich, there were opportunities for many craftsmen to supplement their basic wages by supervising apprentices, or by promotion to the supervisory position of chargeman. For the shipwrights, and for some members of the other major trades, there were also limited opportunities for employment in the drawing office, or performing administrative tasks such as the recording of weights. Above all, for about one fifth of the workforce, there was also the prospect of the establishment, which offered benefits including superannuation, discretionary sick pay, and a widow's allowance, and most importantly, the security of permanent guaranteed employment. The establishment system, which was intended principally as a device to retain a core group of skilled workers, was viewed as a central plank of the Admiralty's industrial relations strategy. According to the Director of Dockyards, 'the permanency of the Establishment is a privilege highly prized by the workmen and is one of the greatest inducements to secure and retain good men.' Apart from its function as an incentive, '[a]bove and beyond all this is the urgent necessity to create an establishment of workmen having important interests at stake who could be depended on in time of emergency.'[27] The size of the establishment was fixed by the Admiralty, subject to the approval of the Treasury. In 1900, it was increased from 4,760 to 7,000 men, spread across all the home dockyards, but numbers admitted each year declined as the rationalisation programme began to bite, and from 1908 admission was suspended altogether until 1913–14.[28] The proportion of the workforce enjoying established status remained stable at 18–20%, and although in theory it was open to all, most workers had no more security of employment than their counterparts in any other industry. Moreover, the spread across the different trades was defined by quota, and there was a marked bias towards the major trades. The shipwrights, for example, accounted for nearly 35% of established men in 1900, even though they made up only just over 22% of the workforce as a whole, while the prospects for an ordinary labourer to join the establishment were considerably lower.[29]

In contrast to some private sector employers, Admiralty paternalism did not extend outside the workplace, to encompass the provision of housing for example. The only exception was the reservation of a small number of jobs in the dockyard colour lofts exclusively for the widows or other female dependants of deceased dockyard or navy employees. This work was poorly paid, intended to provide a modest income in lieu of the pensions the women might have received through their male relatives, and until the First World War it represented the only employment opportunity for women in an otherwise exclusively male workforce.[30] Nonetheless, despite the Admiralty's 'hands-off' attitude, there is evidence from all the dockyard towns to suggest that internal trade hierarchies were partly reproduced and reinforced in patterns of residential segregation, and in the informal networks of kin and neighbourhood.[31] In early twentieth century Plymouth, dockyard workers were scattered across the Three Towns, and used the electric tramway to travel to work; some lived on the western side of the river Tamar in Saltash or Torpoint and travelled to the dockyard by ferry.[32] Evidence from the 1891 census returns suggests that some of the better-paid dockyard workers were clustered in neighbourhoods away from the poorer and overcrowded central districts of Devonport.[33] During the 1890s, over 300 houses were built exclusively for the use of dockyard families by a mutual company, and at the time of the 1901 census nearly all of these were occupied by dockyard shipwrights, fitters or members of the other major trades as heads of household.[34] The census returns also point to the ties between certain families and the dockyard developed over several generations, with sons following fathers into specific dockyard trades.[35]

For these reasons, it might be supposed that the fragmented and hierarchical culture of the dockyard contributed to the retardation of the labour movement in Plymouth and the other dockyard towns. Some dockyard historians have qualified this view, arguing instead that the traditions of self-reliance and independence fostered by dockyard

FIGURE 4.1. *Devonport Dockyard, Output 1885–1914.*

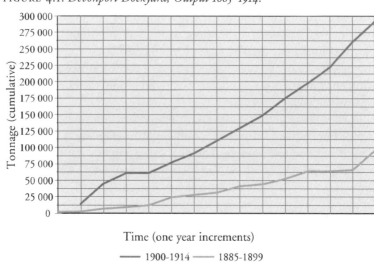

Time (one year increments)

——— 1900-1914 ——— 1885-1899

SOURCE: George Dicker, 'A Short History of Devonport Dockyard', unpublished manuscript, 1969.

work, particularly among the shipwrights, were equally important in conditioning the political outlook of the dockyard workers.[36] The problem with these interpretations, however, is that they ignore the rapid changes taking place in the dockyard during the early twentieth century. At the beginning of the twentieth century, Devonport dockyard was entering a period of intense activity. The increase in output over the two consecutive fourteen-year periods illustrated in figure 4.1 reflects not only the greater number of ships which were built at Devonport, but also the increased tonnage of the new types of battleship immediately before the war. (Figure 4.1) Before 1900, the dockyard's largest ships had a displacement of not more than 15,000 tons; after the turn of the century these were dwarfed by monsters such as the 26,350 ton *HMS Lion, HMS Marlborough* at 25,000 tons, and the massive 30,600 ton *HMS Warspite.* This new construction, and growing amounts of repair and refitting work resulted in an unprecedented expansion of the dockyard workforce, from a little over 5,000 workers in 1890 to more than 13,000 by 1914. (Table 4.5).

The cost of this expansion in output necessitated some far-reaching changes in dockyard administration. In 1905 the Naval Establishments Enquiry Committee, established by the Balfour government to

TABLE 4.5. *Devonport Dockyard Workforce, 1890–1918.*

Year	Civilian employees
1890[1]	5 206
1900[1]	8 456
1901[2]	8 116
1902[2]	8 528
1903[2]	9 475
1904[7]	9 131
1905[3]	7 187
1906[7]	7 045
1907[4]	9 799
1908[5]	8 510
1909[5]	9 323
1910[1]	9 443
1911[4]	12 493
1912[6]	11 450
1913[6]	12 226
1914[6]	13 055
1915	no data available
1916[1]	14 035
1917	no data available
1918[1]	15 803

Sources:
1 Peter Hilditch, 'The Dockyard in the Local Economy', in Michael Duffy et al., eds., *The New Maritime History of Devon*, vol. 2 (London, 1994), Table 21.1.
2 Hansard 1903, vol. 125 (15th July 1903). Number is for 1st July each year.
3 Hansard 1909, vol. 10, col. 1453.
4 Hansard 1914, vol. 61, cols. 939-40. These figures include numbers employed at the Victualling Yard, the Naval Ordnance Yard and the Naval Hospital, as well as the dockyard. The actual number employed in the dockyard was 1200-1700 less than this, based on comparison of similar figures for 1908 and 1909.
5 Hansard 1909, vol. 6, col. 1085. Figures refer to 24th October 1908, and 1st March 1909. Hansard 1909, vol. 10, col. 1902, gives 9053 for 30th November 1908.
6 PRO ADM 1/8332. Figures are for 26th December (1913), and for Easter Monday (1914).
7 WDRO Acc 2000: Henderson papers, memorandum dated 20th March 1906. Figures are for 2nd May 1904 and 1st January 1906.

investigate ways of curbing the alarming growth in the naval estimates, submitted its report on rationalisation of the dockyards. Its principal recommendation was that the dockyards should be organised more commercially, with more autonomy for the individual yards. The drive to economise took on a new urgency with the decision to embark on the construction of a new fleet of Dreadnought-class battleships, and a sweeping programme of rationalisation was imposed on the dockyards during the years 1904–6. Much of the work previously carried out in the dockyards was put out to contract, and large numbers of dockyard workers were dismissed: 8000 men in total from Devonport and Portsmouth dockyards during the winter of 1905–6.[37]

At Devonport, this period of reform from Whitehall came hard on the heels of the arrival of a vigorous new broom as the yard's Admiral Superintendent. Vice-Admiral Henderson, who oversaw Devonport from 1900 to 1905, took his role very seriously, and the period of his incumbency witnessed important changes in the organisation of the yard. One of his main concerns was to reduce bureaucracy, through simplifying the procedures by which workers obtained the materials required for their work. This, together with the move towards employing casual labour for 'services of a temporary and casual character', resulted in the discharge of 2492 workers, most of them ordinary labourers, between June 1903 and May 1905.[38] Drawing largely on his knowledge and experience of new styles of management developed in the United States, Henderson also attempted to increase efficiency by introducing internal competition between different departments. The yard officers in charge of the departments were given more autonomy over the hiring and discharge of workers, and were also asked to help root out what Henderson saw as a entrenched culture of slackness and inefficiency.[39] A controversial order in 1903, much feared and resented by the workers, required departments to submit regularly lists of employees whose work was considered to be less than adequate and should therefore be discharged.[40] Central to Henderson's attempts to improve efficiency, therefore, were the systems for the supervision and control of the workforce. Traditionally, wage rates had been negotiated individually with each worker based on the recommendations of their supervisors. For the Admiralty, so-called 'classification' was important in encouraging 'a healthy spirit of emulation and development of skill among the workmen,' by means of 'the distribution of equivalent rewards to individual efforts.'[41] It was extremely unpopular with the workers, however, who claimed that it encouraged favouritism, since promotion was left entirely to the discretion of supervisors, and 'political and other influences' could thus be brought to bear on those charged with recommending individuals for promotion.[42] When the classification system was formally abolished in 1901, dockyard managers such as Henderson were keen to find ways to maintain the culture of individual competitiveness through the authority of supervisors.

There is some evidence that these changes provoked a greater assertiveness on the part of the civilian dockyard workforce. Formal restrictions on trade union membership had been lifted in 1892, but before 1914 unions were shown at best a grudging toleration rather than official recognition.[43] The Admiralty's view was that its employees had an adequate means of expressing their grievances through the petitions system, which had become firmly established in all the home yards by the second half of the nineteenth century.[44] Workers were invited annually to submit written petitions, either individually or in groups, detailing their concerns over pay and conditions. When all the petitions had been received, Admiralty officials would tour the dockyards to hear oral evidence in support of the workers' claims, before responses were decided centrally. The formal language in which the petitions were drafted, where petitioners would 'humbly pray your Lordships', and 'respectfully solicit your most favourable considera-tion of this our petition', could be interpreted as evidence of the def-erential attitudes of the dockyard workforce, although at least one dockyard historian has insisted that dockyard workers used the peti-tions system creatively as a means of asserting their independence and self-confidence.[45]

Petitions were occasionally submitted by individual workers, but by the turn of the century the vast majority were drafted by the mem-bers of a particular trade, and were often used to protest against per-ceived loss of status against other trades. In petitioning the Admiral-ty for higher wages in 1911, for example, the shipwrights referred to their special status as the 'constructors of HM Ships from time imme-morial.' A delegation appointed to give evidence to the Admiralty made the same point: 'My Lords we are the principal trade concerned in connection with building of warships... [W]e are the principal trade in the Dockyard we are the men who are the constructors of the ship and we are responsible for the ship from the commencement to the completion.'[46] Moreover, the isolation of the dockyards, in contrast to shipbuilding districts such as the Tyne or the Clyde where employ-ers could usually draw on a wide pool of skilled men, also meant that the shipwrights as a group were less vulnerable to attempts to trim the dockyard workforce. As one shipwright put it, '[t]he Admiralty can always get a batch of labourers – a thousand if they needed them – but that, of course, does not affect our branch.'[47] For this reason alone, the shipwrights, together with other important trades such as fitters, were able to command higher wages than the minor trades such as riggers and sailmakers, and campaigned vigorously to maintain wage differentials between themselves and these other groups.[48]

From the late nineteenth century, there were signs that the petitions system was coming under strain, as dockyard workers began to turn to trade unions in their negotiations with the Admiralty. In 1903 the *South-Western Labour Journal* condemned the 'doubtful privilege of memorialising their Lordships of the Admiralty for redress', and pointed out that no answer had yet been received for the previous year's petitions, even though the current round was approaching.[49] These criticisms were echoed by one of the two MPs for Plymouth, A S Benn, who described the 'curious documents known as "humble petitions"' as 'old-fashioned' and 'cumbersome'.[50] Benn's successor, Sir Clement Kinloch-Cooke, suggested that the petitions system had fallen out of favour with the men simply because their requests were never acceded to. Moreover,

> What irritates the men is the secrecy of the whole thing, and whatever the Parliamentary Secretary [to the Admiralty] may say, he cannot deny the whole thing is done in secret... The men in the dockyard do not like the system of annual petitions, and that is the reason why there is unrest in the dockyards and why it is fostered.[51]

For its part, the Admiralty made some concessions towards the involvement of trade union representatives in the petitioning process. From 1905 deputations of workmen were invited, on full pay, to present their case to the Admiralty in London, in lieu of the annual visitation to the yards. The official line remained one of lofty disregard for trade unions.[52] In 1911, as the result of an investigation into dockyard industrial relations, the Admiralty declared that, 'membership of a Trade Union is neither a bar nor an advantage in the official Dockyard view. It is a matter of unconcern to Dockyard Officers, whose duty it is to administer the Home Dockyard Regulations with impartiality.'[53] But the situation was changing. Following the establishment of Dockyard Grievance Committees by the Trades Councils in Portsmouth and Devonport, it was conceded that these committees could present grievances at formal hearings. Concern remained, however, at the possibility of outside influence. In the words of one Admiralty official, '[t]hat method gives no assurance that such a committee actually represents the views of our employees. Indeed the probability is that they would frequently come petitioning for changes not recognised by our men, but suggested by the outside Trade and Labour Council.'[54] The conclusion remained that the petitions system offered an adequate means for the redress of grievances:

> The desire now, as it has always been, is to maintain a fair field and no favour in the Dockyards. Trade Unionists admittedly have easy access to Parliamentary influence nowadays and as a very large

number of the men in our Dockyards are believed not to be Trade Unionists, it is here that the fair field disappears.[55]

It should not be overlooked, however, that one of the main hindrances to trade union organisation in the dockyards was not the hostility of the Admiralty, or the deference of the workforce, but the entrenched rivalries between the different unions which had a claim to organise the shipbuilding trades. On occasion this rivalry could spill over into the political sphere, and it undoubtedly hindered attempts to stand a Labour candidate for parliamentary elections in Devonport in the early 1900s.[56] The growing involvement of unions in the petitioning process helped to reinforce trade rivalries, as they encouraged the different trades to submit petitions that were common to all the home dockyards. The Shipwrights' Association held a conference of its dockyard members in 1911 to draft a common petition, and the union's Labour MP for Chatham, J Jenkins, acted as spokesmen for all the dockyards at the Admiralty hearings. The union supported its case by collecting extensive data on shipwrights' wages in other shipbuilding districts, which, it claimed, indicated that the Admiralty shipwrights were hard done-by in comparison to their counterparts in the private sector, and even that this was causing a damaging exodus from the dockyard as shipwrights migrated to the north of England.[57] In fact, there is no evidence to suggest that this migration was taking place. The important point about union involvement in the petitioning process, however, is that it gave dockyard workers access to this information, and invited them to identify themselves as part of a wider trade community stretching beyond the dockyard.[58] The Admiralty's usual response was to compare the wages of its employees with those of other workers in Plymouth.[59]

The involvement of trade unions in the petitioning process was thus significant in that it enabled negotiations to be conducted on a national level. For the workers themselves, trade unions could also offer a way of circumventing the arbitrariness in the relations between workers and managers at a shopfloor level. In 1911, the Devonport branch of the Amalgamated Society of Engineers (ASE) took up the case of two of its members who had been suspended, unjustly in their view, for defective workmanship. Instead of following the usual channel of appealing to the senior officers concerned, in this case the Engineer Manager, the union wrote on the men's behalf to a sympathetic MP, who in turn took up the matter with the Admiralty. At the bottom of the case, it transpired, was dislike of a new Engineer Manager, who was alleged to have 'instituted a reign of terror' since his arrival, resulting in a complete breakdown of the accepted channels for negotiating labour relations. According to the union,

> He cannot be approached on any matter, and his treatment of deputations has been such as to prevent anyone from daring to meet him on any question affecting general or private interests. This recent happening has crowned all his previous misdeeds.... All the known laws of practical engineering were carried out during the job [by the two fitters concerned], yet we have to submit to the tyranny of the individual.[60]

Following an investigation, it was decided that the two fitters should be given the benefit of the doubt and reinstated, but the Admiral Superintendent at Devonport was inclined to view the ASE as the villain of the piece, and proposed the immediate discharge of the ASE committee, if their identity could be discovered. Significantly, the Admiralty officials in London took a much more lenient position, and were content merely to draw the attention of the men to the correct channels of protest, while also acknowledging that men were sometimes reluctant to bring minor grievances to local yard officials, 'for fear of being marked'.[61]

II

The involvement of an MP in this case illustrates a further important aspect of dockyard labour relations, namely the possibility of using political channels to bring workers' grievances to the attention of Admiralty officials. Indeed, one dockyard historian has gone so far as to suggest that the nature of dockyard work, in the direct employment of the state, 'made [the workers] politically aware and gave them the appreciation of politicised power rather than private wealth as a controller of their destinies.'[62] According to one dockyard MP, even though it was 'most distasteful' to use parliamentary pressure, 'under existing conditions there was no other method of exercising upon the Admiralty anything like the influence which the workman outside could bring to bear upon his employer.'[63] All the dockyard MPs, regardless of their party affiliation, took seriously their role as advocates of the dockyard workers' interests in Parliament, usually by putting questions to the Parliamentary Secretary to the Admiralty. The success of the Liberal MP Hudson Kearley in retaining the Devonport seat during the 1890s, despite the setbacks for his party during this period, was attributed to his conscientiousness in this role.[64] Kearley himself wrote in his memoirs that, '[o]ne of the first duties of anyone who seeks to represent a dockyard constituency is to receive, with proper courtesy, the deputations of Service electors, who came to present their "petitions"… and to indicate, so far as he can, his views upon them.'[65]

Given the involvement of the MPs in dockyard labour relations, it is not surprising that these issues made some impact on local parliamentary elections. The question of dockyard wages was reported to have dominated parliamentary elections in Devonport in 1892 and 1895.[66] Parliamentary candidates of all parties made special efforts to capture the dockyard vote. During the 1910 election campaign, candidates held daily open-air meetings outside the dockyard gates, timed to coincide with the workers' dinner hour. Not much election literature has survived, but there are some examples of leaflets and other communications aimed particularly at the dockyard workforce. It may be noted that these electoral appeals were usually addressed to the dockyard workers as a collective entity, ignoring the differences of trade and status between the workers. In 1910, for example, the Unionists criticised the Liberal government for suspending the establishment in 1908, arguing that it denied pensions to many workers who had legitimately expected them as of right.[67] As we have seen, however, established status was a realistic prospect for no more than about one fifth of the workforce during this period. By incorporating this and other similar issues into their electoral appeal, however, candidates of both Conservative and Liberal parties attempted to address the collective interests of the dockyard workforce as a distinctive bloc within the electorate. While the Labour movement was partly hindered by the rivalries of the various dockyard unions, the established parties were influential in helping to construct the identity of a distinctive dockyard community with shared interests and concerns.

No party could take the dockyard vote for granted, however. As Table 4.1 indicates, it is difficult to distinguish a clear pattern of support for either Liberals or Conservatives during this period. Government candidates in particular often found it difficult to defend their party's record on naval matters, as the Conservative candidate Sir John

Jackson found when he was severely heckled addressing a meeting before the Devonport by-election of 1904, an election which he went on to lose.[68] In 1906, with high levels of unemployment as a result of dockyard dismissals, the Liberals succeeded in winning all four seats, despite the Unionist candidates' attempts to present themselves as the defenders of the navy.[69] It was not until the elections of 1910, following the much-publicised naval scares, and the prominent campaigning of non-partisan organisations such as the Navy League, that there was any convergence between Conservative politics and the navy.[70] The Unionist newspaper *Western Morning News,* in its assessment of the Devonport contest in January 1910, suggested that the dockyard vote, 'which counts for a good deal in the borough', was affected by 'the grave state of naval matters.'[71] Although the Liberals tried to make constitutional reform the focus of their campaign, their Unionist rivals were largely successful in steering the debate towards nationalist issues such as the strength of the navy and the need for tariff reform. For the first time, nationalist organisations such as the Navy League took an explicitly partisan stance in the campaign. Particularly active in Plymouth was the Tariff Reform League, which organised daily election meetings in support of the Unionist candidates.[72] In Portsmouth there was even a naval candidate, in the person of Lord Charles Beresford, former Lord of the Admiralty, a leading figure in the Navy League and a prominent critic of the government's policy on the navy. Typically of the nationalist agitation of this time, Beresford urged voters to cast aside their traditional party loyalties ('country before party') and vote for him in the nationalist cause, even though he remained closely associated with the Unionist party.[73] No such candidate emerged in Plymouth, but the local press reported that there was general interest in Beresford's campaign, and that his election address to the Portsmouth electors was circulating widely through Devonport.[74] Such was his popularity that, when it was announced that Beresford would be visiting Devonport as part of the campaign, there was expected to be a huge demand for tickets, and potential difficulties accommodating everyone who wanted to hear his speech.[75] Beresford's visit proved to be as popular and over-subscribed as predicted, and, coming just days before polling day, was the undoubted high point of the Unionist election campaign. Much was made of his local connections, based on service as flag-lieutenant to the Devonport Commander-in-chief thirty years previously. Crowds lined the route from the station, and Beresford's carriage was pulled by sailors past the Conservative Club, decorated for the occasion in red, white and blue, while the town's brass band played *Rule Britannia*.

Beresford's speech at Devonport, reported in full in the *Western Morning News*, addressed many of the same issues taken up by the Unionist candidates during the course of the campaign. The Unionist message was that the incumbent Liberal government, with its agenda of social and political reform, could not be trusted with the maintenance of the navy and the defence of the empire. The Unionist candidate for Plymouth, Waldorf Astor, was typical in attempting to link the nationalist issues of naval defence and tariff reform, when he suggested that, 'Germany had an army strong enough to beat any other country on the Continent. There was only one other country she wanted to attack with a navy. Surely Germany was not building Dreadnoughts to send the Kaiser yachting or to bring her surplus product over here and to dump it on our markets.'[76] Meanwhile, the Tariff Reform League staged a public 'dumping exhibition' in the Conservative election committee rooms. The display, where foreign articles were placed on view marked with their country of origin, was designed "to bring home to the electors more convincingly than any speeches could do the extent to which foreign manufactured goods are dumped in this country free of duty."[77] The same theme was also reported to be prominent in the election posters around the town.

Unionist politicians did not rely on the appeal to nationalist interests alone, however. Equally important was the attempt to portray these national issues in terms of their impact on local interests. This could mean written appeals targeted at a specific group of voters, such as the Unionist leaflet directed to the Plymouth dockworkers, drawing attention to the recent closure of various manufacturing concerns in Plymouth – a tannery, a soapworks and a sugar refinery – and the implications for local employment. All three businesses, it was alleged, had been 'killed by Free-trade!'[78] Even more could be made, of course, of the link between national and local interests served by the presence of a strong navy. Here, candidates emphasised the long-standing historical links between the town and the navy: to vote against the navy, they suggested, would be to fly in the face of local history. 'Plymouth had a splendid association with the naval supremacy of England in the past,' declared Waldorf Astor in an election speech, 'and it behoved places like Plymouth and Devonport, in a time like the present, to see that their representatives took a strong line upon the question of the navy. (Hear, hear.)'[79] Beresford did not refer directly to Plymouth or Devonport in his speech, but Unionists attacked Lloyd George for his audacity in invoking the name of the sixteenth-century Plymouth naval commander Francis Drake during his speech in support of the Liberal campaign.[80] The *Western Morning News*, in its polling day leader, went further in suggesting that local electors had a duty to vote for the Unionists:

> Plymouth and Devonport at the poll have to show themselves true to the Empire. The Navy looks to them to give support to [the Unionist candidates], and thus impress upon the country the importance of a big Navy that will ensure our supremacy at sea and make invasion impossible. If our chief naval centre should at this crisis show its apathy for the Navy, what will the Empire think?[81]

The resulting Unionist election victory in Devonport was reported under the headline, 'Dockyard Borough Speaks Out on the Navy.'[82]

III

The 1910 elections marked something of a turning point for the Unionists. Having failed to gain a single dockyard seat in 1906, they were now victorious in Chatham and in the two-member Portsmouth and Devonport divisions. Plymouth remained Liberal at the first election of 1910, but the Unionists completed their victory by capturing the two Plymouth seats in December. With naval activity reaching its most intensive phase, there seemed to be a convergence between national defence interests and local interests. The dockyard towns certainly presented a wealth of possibilities to politicians attempting to forge a link between local and national interests. Apart from the unavoidable physical presence of the dockyard, with all its implications for the local economy, naval towns were also important sites for the commemoration and celebration of naval supremacy. Plymouth Hoe, the fashionable public park in the centre of the town from where most of the harbour could be seen, was noted for being 'especially famous in the naval history of this country.'[83] It was the obvious site for the erection, in 1888, of a monument to commemorate the tercentenary of the defeat of the Spanish Armada. The inscriptions on the monument evoked the continuity of the naval 'story', stretching in a direct line from the Elizabethan navy of the sixteenth century through the conflicts of the Napoleonic era to the present fleet. Next to the Armada monument, with its bronze portraits commemorating the specific role played by famous Devon men in the battle, stood a statue to Francis Drake, erected through public subscription during the 1880s. Drake was an ideal candidate as a hero of the Island Race, around which reformulations of 'Englishness' and 'Britishness' were based during the late nineteenth century.[84] Not only this, but he was also a distinctly local hero, who had made Plymouth his home port, and thus belonged to a more distinctly local narrative of the struggles of heroic west country Elizabethans against the Catholic Spanish.[85]

One of the most important opportunities for the commemoration of naval imperialism in the Three Towns was the public ceremony associated with the dockyard ship launch. Ship launches ceased to be public after 1910 because of heightened tension in the international situation, but during the decade or so before then they were important occasions in the life of the dockyard and the town.[86] The day of the ship launch was above all the opportunity for a celebration and a spectacle. The dockyard workers were allowed a day's holiday, and the dockyard, together with the streets of Devonport, was decorated with flags and bunting, in contrast to its normal 'grim and grey' workaday image. The launch was followed by a firework display during the evening, and a parade of illuminated ships. However, there was more to the ship launch than popular entertainment: the ceremony itself was a minutely choreographed event which carried a number of important symbolic meanings. In the first place, the launch represented a rare occasion on which normally forbidden spaces were made public. The strategic sensitivity of the dockyard's work meant that it was usually out of bounds to all except the workforce, even to the extent that it was represented as a void on some of the contemporary Ordnance Survey maps of the district. On ship launch days however the dockyard gates were opened to the public, who took the opportunity in their thousands to satisfy their curiosity about what went on 'behind the wall'. It was estimated that between 35,000 and 40,000 people were present at the launch of *HMS Queen* in 1902.

Secondly, the flawless execution of the meticulously planned ceremony helped to impress upon the spectators the efficiency of the Admiralty, and the orderliness with which the dockyard was run. This was important in the face of criticisms directed against the Admiralty as a prolific spender of public funds, a point to which we will return below. 'There is one charm,' stated the reporter of the *Western Daily Mercury,* 'to the spectators certainly, about Naval or Military ceremonies, and that is the wonderful punctuality which invariably characterises them.'[87] In 1902 this efficiency was demonstrated by a particularly spectacular stunt. The first ship, *HMS Queen,* was named and launched by her namesake, Queen Alexandra. Scarcely had the cord been severed to begin the ship's slide into the sea, when preparations were taking place for the next part of the ceremony. Only a few minutes later the King pressed a button, which by means of a sophisticated piece of electrical apparatus, designed especially for the occasion in the dockyard's electrical workshop, caused a thirteen-foot piece of keel plate to be lifted into place on the slip ready to begin the construction of the next battleship. The point could not be more effectively made: one ship had not been in the water fifteen minutes, yet already the construction of the next one had commenced.

Thirdly, the ship launch ceremony was carefully arranged to reflect social hierarchies, through the segregation of the spectators in the dockyard. A distinction was drawn between official ticket-holders, who arrived in their carriages at the northern gate and watched the entire ceremony from the comfort of a special enclosure, and those who were described variously as the 'dense crowd' or the 'mass of humanity', separated from their social superiors by 'stout barriers' once inside the dockyard. The non-ticket holders were obliged to arrive as early as possible and scramble for position to get a good view of events. The dockyard workers themselves were represented publicly for the occasion by the 280 of their number who were working on the slip to effect the ship's launch, their hardworking unobtrusiveness contrasted with the noisy exuberance of the holiday crowd up above. Their supervisory official who was responsible for the launch was presented to the royal party after the ship was in the water, still wearing his working clothes, in contrast to the bright dress uniforms of the navy officers attending in their official capacity. At the apex of the hierarchy were of course the King and Queen themselves, the 'Sovereign of the Seas', launching, with the aid of a bottle of colonial wine, part of the most visible manifestation of Britain's overseas domination. The sheer size of *HMS King Edward VII,* described as the largest battleship ever to be launched, was itself a clear illustration of naval supremacy. The sense of drama was heightened through hints of doubts that the ship would actually float at all once launched, so that it was slightly miraculous when, inevitably, she did not sink.

Most importantly, the ship launch was designed to represent the fusion of local and national interests, and to demonstrate Plymouth's role in the defence of the empire. Here too, there were references to the historical links between the town and the navy. The boat commandeered to convey the King and Queen across the harbour in 1902 was named for another sixteenth century Devonian sea captain, Sir Richard Grenville. The allusion was not lost on the *Western Daily Mercury's* reporter, who suggested that, '[t]he name serves to stir the memory and bring to mind the glories of the mighty past, with which the West Country is so intimately associated.' When the royal couple arrived in the town, the municipal authorities presented them with a casket containing a silver model of Drake's flagship the *Pelican,* 'as a memento of the part taken by Plymouth in the extension and defence of his Majesty's great and glorious Empire.'[88]

The relationship between national and local interests was not always so harmonious, however. The strong electoral performance of the Liberals in both Plymouth and Devonport in 1906 demonstrates that it was impossible, even at the height of the naval agitation in 1910, to take for granted that the naval connection would be translated into support for the Unionists. Nor can it be assumed that the Liberals' success was in any way related to their advocacy of 'big navy' politics, although, as has already been noted, the willingness of Kearley to lobby on dockyard matters certainly helped them. Indeed, there was always the possibility for conflict between the Admiralty and the dockyard town. Even the symbols and imagery of the Elizabethan past were open to alternative interpretations, such as the figure of Francis Drake, celebrated as an English naval hero but also as a distinctively Plymothian one. The stained glass windows of the Plymouth Guildhall, opened in 1874, portrayed Drake in two guises: in his conventional role as naval hero, playing his celebrated match of bowls before the defeat of the Spanish Armada, but also as municipal worthy, the Mayor of Plymouth who secured a safe water supply for the town. Other windows celebrated local traditions of religious and political dissent, through their portrayal of scenes such as the Pilgrim Fathers departing Plymouth for the New World in the early seventeenth century, the town as a Parliamentary stronghold during the

Civil War, and William of Orange proclaimed king in Plymouth in 1688.[89]

Such statements warn against a one-sided view of Plymouth as a town where the presence of the navy was overwhelmingly welcomed and celebrated. At times of crisis, for example during the dockyard contractions of 1905, there was frequently hostile criticism of Admiralty policy. The dockyard MPs questioned Admiralty representatives in Parliament about the prosperity of the dockyard towns, pointing to the narrowness of the economic base, and the 'great and needless hardships' caused by 'these sudden strokes of the pen' in Whitehall.[90] In Plymouth, the Admiralty's opposition to a council scheme for the commercial development of the Cattewater was cited by Kearley as an example of the extreme dependence of the town on the dockyard. The MP for Portsmouth agreed, arguing that dockyard discharges amounted to a 'public calamity' in Portsmouth, where 'there were no flourishing industries, and, rightly or wrongly, the inhabitants considered that it was partly due to the Admiralty that they were limited in their opportunities of developing their local resources.'[91] Another Plymouth MP demanded more transparency in the Admiralty's actions regarding the dockyard, stating that, '[t]he community, part of which he represented, wanted to know the meaning of what was being done, and how far it was to go… The responsibility rested upon the Admiralty, as it rested on all employers, of having consideration to the population they gathered together.'[92]

Tensions in the relationship between the Admiralty and the town surfaced again in 1907, when the Keyham Extension Works were finally completed. This marked the culmination of a scheme which had cost an estimated £4.5 million, and had consolidated Devonport dockyard's position as a vital strategic asset by extending its capacity for the construction of Dreadnought battleships. There was every sign that the ceremony to mark the opening of the extension, performed by the Prince and Princess of Wales, would be a major spectacle similar to the dockyard ship launches. In the event, the whole occasion was marred, not only by the appalling weather, but also by the Admiralty's reluctance to invite representatives of the borough to participate in the ceremony. In protest, the Mayor of Devonport returned his ticket, granted as a last minute concession, and refused to have anything to do with the ceremony. According to the Liberal *Western Daily Mercury*, popular indignation was widespread, and 'there [could] be no doubt as to the feeling of the people of Devonport in that matter.'[93] As a further attempt to smooth things over, the route of the royal party was diverted to pass through the town, but further indignation was aroused when the Corporation was asked to contribute £300 towards the cost of decorating the streets. One local politician declared that he

> could not see the utility of spending such an amount in decorating what was practically Government ground. When the Prince visited a foreign country he always recognised the municipal authorities, and did not object to an address of welcome being given him. But this was not allowed Devonport, despite the fact that its inhabitants were taxpayers and part of the nation which owned the docks.[94]

As these events illustrate, there was more to naval spectacle than merely the outpouring of unchallenged jingoist sentiment. Events which were ostensibly occasions for the celebration of naval imperialism, and the role of the dockyard town within that vision, could also bring to the surface a local critique of Admiralty actions, not least in terms of the relationship between town and state. If progressive parties were to exploit this situation for their own ends, it was clear that an articulation of local interests would be an important means of doing this. The next section of the chapter examines Labour's attempts to construct its own political appeal at both the municipal and parliamentary levels.

IV

Inevitably, given their numbers, some dockyard employees seem to have been among those involved in the development of a local labour movement. The recruitment of workers from outside the Three Towns during times of expansion could bring new ideas: one particularly influential individual was the Amalgamated Society of Engineers (ASE) activist Tom Proctor, who came to work in the dockyard from Nottingham in 1890.[95] Among other activities, Proctor was catalytic in establishing the Plymouth and District Trades Council in 1892, and, as a member of the SDF, he was also a strong supporter of the proposal that the Council should support Labour candidates in municipal elections.[96] This proved too controversial however, and failure to agree resulted in the Council's temporary demise. It was re-established in 1897, and received a major boost from hosting the 1899 Trades Union Congress in Plymouth. By December 1903 it had 31 affiliated trade union branches, representing over 6000 members, but the experience of earlier conflict left Council members wary of the question of political representation.[97] In 1905, Proctor proposed that the return of Labour representatives to government bodies be added to the Council's formal list of objectives, but by this time there was another body in existence, the Labour Representation Association (LRA), founded in 1902, and its members objected to the proposal. The secretary of the Trades Council wrote to the national LRC complaining that the LRA were attempting to ridicule the Council in Plymouth, and that only trades councils should be allowed to affiliate as local branches of the LRC.[98] The Trades Council did affiliate formally the following year, unlike the LRA which seems only ever to have been a local body.[99] Many of the unions affiliated to this organisation were trade unions which owed a large proportion if not all of their membership to the dockyard employees, and many leading activists in both the Trades Council and the LRA were also dockyard workers, as were the first two LRA candidates to be elected in Devonport.[100] The LRA concentrated its early electoral activities on the four Devonport wards – Keyham, Ford, Station and Tamar – where there was thought to be a high proportion of dockyard workers among the electorate.[101]

Despite these links, there were sometimes complaints from the labour movement about the inactivity of the dockyard workers. In particular, the latter were condemned for their failure to react more strongly to the heavy discharges from the dockyard as part of the Henderson reforms. 'Many men very probably imagine that once inside the gates of the Dockyard their future is assured, and that henceforth they will be independent of Trade Union benefits', was the comment of the *South West Labour Journal*.[102] It should also be noted that under the Civil Service Regulations, established men were prohibited from standing for Parliament, although they were allowed to become candidates for local elections.[103] The main hindrance to Labour organisation from the dockyard, however, was the entrenched intra-trade rivalry among the major dockyard unions. When one of the Devonport parliamentary seats fell vacant in 1902, the LRC contacted the local labour movement to enquire about the possibility of contesting the forthcoming by-election.[104] A candidate was available in the person of Will Lewington, an activist in the Government Labourers'

Union in Chatham dockyard who had put himself forward, but controversy surfaced when it turned out that the Devonport shipwrights had independently nominated the leader of their own union, Alexander Wilkie. Lewington, doubtless trying to defend his own position, wrote to the LRC that he would not defer to Wilkie, as this would merely provoke the ASE to 'trot out' their man, Tom Proctor, 'and as you may know there is existing between the two Societies a keen rivalry more acute in Government Dockyards which might weaken his chances.'[105] Even Proctor's credentials as the only local candidate in the field were not thought to be sufficient to overcome the hostility between his union and the Amalgamated Shipwrights' Society (ASS). The LRC made hurried efforts to conceal the damaging fact that it had two potential candidates in the field, but the candidature soon collapsed in utter confusion, once it was revealed that Lewington had initially submitted his name to the Liberals (a charge he later repudiated). The candidature was therefore abandoned, and the ensuing contest resulted in a narrow victory for the Conservatives. Some LRC members were scathing of the confusion with which the affair had been organised locally, complaining that, 'the Devonport people have hopelessly 'bungled' in the matter.'[106] The experience, followed by further controversy over another by-election in 1904, probably helps to explain the Labour Party's apparent lack of interest in the Plymouth constituencies before 1918.[107]

Instead, it was municipal politics which provided the main impetus for the development of a political labour movement, and in particular the issue of housing. The rapid expansion of the Three Towns had resulted in very high population densities and some severe overcrowding by the mid-nineteenth century, and a boom in speculative building after 1870 did little to alleviate the situation.[108] The 1901 census revealed levels of overcrowding that were well above the national average, especially in Stonehouse, where nearly a quarter of the population was officially recorded as living in overcrowded conditions.[109] This was confirmed by the 1908 Board of Trade investigation, which found that rents in Plymouth and Devonport were the highest in the country outside London.[110] Following the Housing Act of 1890, Plymouth and Devonport county councils had embarked on schemes to replace some particularly notorious slum areas with municipally owned housing estates.[111] Especially in Plymouth, these reforms were part of a wide programme of municipal expansion during the 1890s under the leadership of the Liberal Party, including improvements to the market, streets, parks, sewage works and reservoir, as well as the municipalisation of the tram company.[112] The result was a sharp rise in the local rates which began to cause political controversy from the early 1890s, and by the end of the decade had become the most important issue in local elections.[113] The Conservatives made electoral gains on a platform of municipal economy, and were supported in part by the candidates of the Ratepayers' Association from the turn of the century.

By the early 1900s, therefore, housing, and the questions it raised regarding the role of municipal government and the ratepayers who funded it, had become a major source of political controversy in Plymouth.[114] The housing issue was also important in the development of a movement for independent labour representation in the municipal sphere. The Plymouth branch of the Social Democratic Federation (SDF), revived following the 1899 TUC, took the step of convening a public conference on the housing situation early in 1900, which resulted in the foundation of the Three Towns Association for the Better Housing of the Working Classes.[115] Shortly after this, a fresh controversy arose when new land suitable for municipal housing became available, surplus to requirements for a new municipal cemetery. Given the scarcity of suitable land for building in Devonport, this seemed like an excellent opportunity for the council to address the problem. Plans to accommodate 252 families were drawn up and approved by the housing committee, an application was made to the Local Government Board to borrow the required capital, and it was resolved that repayment of this capital should be met out of the rates, not the rents of the new dwellings.[116] This last proposal proved to be the sticking point however, for when the scheme came before the full council at a special meeting in March 1901 it was rejected outright, with only two members of the council prepared to vote in favour of it.[117] The Housing Association opposed the rejection of the scheme vigorously, but, despite the presentation of a petition, it was not revived.

It was this incident, above all, which seemed to convince many of the need for a movement for independent labour representation in the Three Towns. There was little point in lobbying candidates for municipal office on a single issue if they failed to keep their promises once they were elected. More drastic action was needed, and steps would have to be taken to secure the election of independent Labour

TABLE 4.6. *Societies Affiliated to the Housing Association, 1906.*

Society	No. of delegates
Three Towns Trades and Labour Council	5
Social Democratic Federation (Plymouth)	2
Typographical Association (Plymouth)	2
Women's Co-operative Guild (Plymouth)	3
Women's Co-operative Guild (Devonport)	3
Plymouth Masons' Society	5
Operative Bakers' Society	1
Amalgamated Society of Engineers (Devonport 2nd)	2
Amalgamated Society of Brushmakers	1
Amalgamated Union of Co-operative Employees (Plymouth)	3
Amalgamated Society of Tailors (Plymouth)	1
Coachmakers' Society (Plymouth)	1
Co-operative Society Education Committee	1
Boilermakers' Society	3
Painters' Society (Plymouth)	1
Shop Assistants' Union (Devonport)	2
Rechabites' Society (Honicknowle)	2

SOURCE: Plymouth Central Library: Housing Association pamphlet, 'The Warrens of the Poor', 1906, p. 40.

councillors.[118] The Housing Association was re-organised, abandoning its original commitment to a non-partisan and broad-based individual membership to become an association of affiliated organisations, mostly trade unionists (Table 4.6). It took no direct role in municipal politics but its campaigning activities supported those organisations which did, namely the LRA and the SDF. Both these groups made the housing issue one of the main planks in their municipal programmes, and the first Labour councillor to be elected, R D Monk, promised to give his full attention to the issue.[119] There was a flurry of electoral activity, with both the SDF and the LRA contesting Council, Poor Law guardians and School Board elections in both Plymouth and Devonport, and achieving some modest success. From 1903, the movement also had its own newspaper, the *South West Labour Journal*, which was issued monthly for just over three years until its share capital ran out. Relations between the SDF and the LRA were generally amenable, described by the SDF as 'friendly neutrality'.[120] The SDF affiliated to the LRA immediately after it was set up, but left twelve months later, 'as we could not see that any good purpose would be served by being any longer affiliated with the LRA.'[121] Thereafter the two organisations remained separate from each other, but there is no evidence of any rivalry, and the relative weakness of both organisations when it came to raising candidates and funds for local elections meant that clashes of interests were unlikely. Frequently, the names of the same activists were prominent in more than one organisation. The *South West Labour Journal* gave equal coverage to the election programmes of all the labour candidates, and all interested parties were represented on the committee which ran the newspaper.

It can be assumed that many Labour activists were also members of the largest working-class organisation in the Three Towns, the Plymouth Mutual and Industrial Co-operative Society, which had a membership of over 30,000 in 1900. In keeping with the Rochdale principles of consumer co-operation, the society had been politically neutral since its foundation, but a prolonged conflict with small private shopkeepers around the turn of the century meant that some co-operators were beginning to question this position.[122] Eventually, the matter was resolved through the courts, but it also provoked some serious debate on the co-operative relationship to politics. Even if the independent traders did not engage in collective political action as traders, it was noted that they had considerable political influence in the municipal chamber, not least because of their interest, as small business owners, in the controversial issue of the rates.[123] This could also motivate a co-operative interest in politics: it was argued that the society, by virtue of its being 'a big feature of commerce in the life of the Three Towns,' was entitled to some say in local governance.[124] As one co-operator, proposing a motion on political representation to a special meeting in 1900, pointed out, 'the traders endeavoured to further their own interest by seeking seats on local bodies, and the Society had an equal right to do the same. As a Society we are large ratepayers, while a large proportion are individual ratepayers, and therefore doubly interested.'[125] A resolution was passed agreeing in principle to support candidates in municipal elections, but the meeting failed to resolve the more difficult issue of how this was to be carried out. In particular there was disagreement over whether the candidates should run on a clear electoral programme, or whether the fact that they were co-operators formed the main platform for their appeal. One speaker, an active trade unionist and SDF member, 'objected to binding the candidates to Co-operative lines alone, believing they would not do

the good they would be wanted to. He further thought those nominated should be questioned as to what they would do in case of success. For us to run without a programme would result in our becoming a laughing stock.'[126] But another speaker disagreed, arguing that,
'men of all shades would not adopt anyone with a programme. If we
ran candidates they must be Co-operators, and Co-operators only.'[127]

The formation of the LRA heightened the debate still further, over
the question of whether or not the Society should affiliate. It did so,
and sent a donation to assist with the municipal elections, following
an extensive debate. The relationship between the two organisations
was beset with controversy, however, which resurfaced at different times
over the LRA's nomination of prominent co-operators for municipal
office. Two views expressed at the original debate sum up the difference of opinion concerning the LRA. One speaker 'pointed out that
the LRA represented all shades of politics, but were one on the question of representation. He expressed an opinion that it would be best
for the Society to join with some other organisation rather than take
the matter up single-handed.' Another speaker, however, thought that
the Committee were right. 'He would not back up any other than a
Co-operative candidate pure and simple, believing that a combination would have the effect of alienating many who would otherwise
lend their aid.'[128] This view illustrates the fears within some sections
of the movement that running the candidates on a programme was a
backhanded way of introducing party political and sectarian issues to
the contest, creating internal divisions which the society was most anxious to avoid. 'It would introduce a bad element into the Society,'
seemed to sum up the consensus. 'Up to the present it had been clear
of all party questions. If we nominated Nonconformist candidates the
Church members would decline support, and *vice versa*. In the County Council politics would be stirred up.'[129] For the time being, at least,
the fear of violating the co-operative tenets of political and religious
neutrality overcame the need for representation on the Council.

Similar issues to those discussed here were also debated within the
other labour organisations, in particular the idea of party, and the precise meaning of independent labour or co-operative political representation. As the extracts quoted above demonstrate, 'politics' in this
context often meant party politics, in the sense of the conflict between
Liberal and Conservative parties. While some co-operators advocated political neutrality because of their own party allegiance, others pre-

ferred to distance themselves from party politics altogether, arguing that any attempt to nominate and support co-operative candidates would embroil the Society in the murky world of 'faction and sect.'[130] Party politics, it was argued, would merely be an unwelcome distraction from the 'proper' business of running a retail co-operative society. A similar criticism of party politics formed the LRA's main platform, although here the LRA was portrayed not as a new party, but as a challenge to the idea of party itself, which would transcend the sterility of the traditional party conflict. The *Labour Journal* pointed to the portrait of Queen Anne, hanging in the council chamber, as a metaphor for the old fashioned and meaningless division between 'the buff' and 'the blue', which was distracting and out of place in the council chamber. The traditional parties were presented as being hopelessly out of date compared to the new, young, and forward-looking Labour Party, which appealed, 'not, in the first place, to Liberals and Conservatives as such, but to all alike as men.... The ranks contain ex-Liberals and ex-Tories, men who see the folly of distinctions without differences.'[131]

Despite Labour's criticism of party, the relationship between the LRA and the Liberal Party was rather complex. As we have seen, the Labour candidature for the Devonport by-election in 1902 collapsed in utter confusion, once it emerged that Lewington had initially submitted his name to the Liberals. The chairman of the local branch of Lewington's Government Labourers Union, Mr R D Monk, wrote to the LRC that there was local hostility to a Lib-Lab candidature, but that there was also a marked reluctance to become involved in a three-cornered fight, which he felt would be 'disastrous'.[132] Richard Bell, one of the NEC members nominated to go to Devonport to assess the situation, told the LRC secretary that, '[w]ith some little knowledge of the apathy in trade unionism and everything else in the West of England, I should not be inclined to be in too great a hurry, and especially now the Liberals have a man in the field. This would be the last place in which we should have any chance of success.'[133] Further controversy arose when the Devonport seat became vacant again in 1904, even though no Labour candidate was put forward. It seemed that the local labour movement was inclined to regard the Liberal candidate as a 'Lib-lab', commenting after the event that 'the local Liberal Party have reason to be deeply grateful to Labour for assistance rendered at this election.'[134] Three prominent members of the LRC,

Arthur Henderson, Will Crooks and D J Shackleton, spoke at a meeting in Devonport, organised by the 'Free Trade and Labour Union', and held only a few days before the election.[135] Despite the insistence of the chairman, R D Monk, that no 'party significance' should be attached to the meeting, it was clear that the speakers' presence was intended to support the Liberal candidate. The event provoked a spate of correspondence from other branches protesting that the action of Henderson and the others violated the founding principles of the LRC.[136] Notwithstanding the *Western Daily Mercury's* assertion that the Liberal candidate had the official endorsement of 'Labour chiefs in London', the LRC issued a statement denying that they had authorised any such action on the part of the individuals concerned. Ultimately, however, they seemed to imply that it was local activists who were at fault in compromising the principles of independent labour representation. 'How was it that your local LRC handed over the meeting to the Free Trade League? Did the Free Trade League pay the expenses of the meeting and who arranged for the speakers?' demanded the LRC secretary of Tom Proctor.[137]

The relationship between Liberals and Labour was equally obscure at the level of municipal politics. In 1903, the Liberals withdrew their candidate from Friary ward, which they regarded as dominated by working-class voters, thus allowing a straight contest between the Conservatives and Labour. When the Labour candidate lost, this was seen in some quarters as a defeat for the progressive cause, but the *South Western Labour Journal,* in an editorial, strenuously denied that any arrangement had been made with the Liberal Party.[138] The next year, the Conservatives failed to put up a candidate in the same ward, and this time Labour won the ensuing contest with the Liberal Party. In Devonport meanwhile, Liberals and Conservatives issued a combined manifesto against the Labour candidate for Tamar ward, who nevertheless won the seat. These manoeuvrings, together with the increasing numbers of independents and Ratepayers Association candidates contesting municipal elections, 'furnishes', according to the *Labour Journal,* 'conclusive evidence that the property-owning classes are... irrespective of Liberal and Tory politics, combining "against the growing danger of Socialism." This combination is known by different names in different parts of the country. In West Ham it is "The Municipal Alliance;" in Plymouth, "The Ratepayers' Association."'[139] Opposition to this organisation was increasingly expressed in terms of class. As we have already seen, the Housing Association had sought to define itself as a working-class organisation, opposed to builders and landlords whose interests, it was argued, were inimical to the provision of better housing. The same problem applied to the council chamber, where government was in the hands of the middle classes, organised into factions who represented their own interests only: 'builders, contractors, property owners and vendors; members of the legal profession who finance jerry-builders and advise others; gentlemen who hold shares in and direct gas, water, brewery, and cemetery companies.'[140]

The concept of class was, however, ambivalent. At the SDF's first public meeting on the housing question, in March 1900, references to the class struggle were conspicuous by their absence. Instead, according to the SDF member who opened the debate, 'it was not intended to put forward any dogmatic views to the meeting, but rather to open the question to discussion. They hoped that the matter would be considered from an entirely non-political and non-sectarian point of view – (hear, hear).'[141] It was only after the disappointment over the corporation's rejection of a scheme for municipal housing at Camel's Head that the Association was reformed as a more explicitly working-class organisation. Even so, the question of how the housing problem should be addressed remained controversial. The Government Labourers' Union disaffiliated from the Housing Association over its opposition to municipal ownership of all houses, a policy which they regarded as 'downright Socialism'.[142] In the views of some, the 'better housing of the working classes' would be more readily achieved through alternative schemes, such as the new estates built by the Co-operative Society, which were ready for occupation by 1903. After a protracted debate, which generated some friction within the Society, the Co-op eventually decided that it would sell these houses to its members, rather than let them. Allowing individuals to purchase their homes, it was argued, if necessary with the help of a loan from the Co-operative Building Society, freed them 'from the caprice of the landlord', and guaranteed their security, especially during old age.[143] Others, both inside and outside the Society, opposed the decision. The Housing Association viewed the decision to sell the houses as 'regrettable', arguing that '[b]y retaining the ownership the Society could have made itself a model landlord, and could have been of great service in that respect to the less fortunate among its members.'[144] As one co-operator put it, 'to build and sell was simply carrying out the scheme of the jerry builder.'[145] It could not be denied that even the smaller houses (three rooms plus kitchen, scullery and garden) were beyond the means of many of the Society's members. Including the rates, the weekly payments on the freehold price of £310 were calculated at 8/3, nearly twice as expensive as weekly rent for the three-roomed municipal flats at Prince Rock.[146]

At the root of the debate over the disposal of the Co-op's new houses lay the central question of the relationship between the labour movement and those whom it purported to represent. The SDF and the Housing Association continued to campaign for municipal house building and ownership, and published detailed proposals in two pamphlets, which were also intended to reveal the extent of the overcrowding problem in Plymouth.[147] The Housing Association's main role, however, was understood to be educational. Housing reform would never come about until those who were in a position to benefit from it most took concerted action to demand change. The principal role of the activist, therefore, was to 'awaken' the general population, especially the inhabitants of slum quarters, to the realities of their situation. Although they were keen to distance themselves from notions that they sought to persuade slum-dwellers to improve their living habits, there was nonetheless a marked sense of moral tutelage in the attitudes of many SDF housing campaigners. The energetic secretary of the Housing Association, Arthur Grindley, who was also the most active member of the SDF, was typical of many of those involved in these campaigns. Grindley was an officer for the Inland Revenue who had worked in many other towns before he was posted to Plymouth in 1898. His journey to socialism was no less circuitous: he had been in turn 'missionary collector, Sunday-school teacher, chapel organist, Band-of-Hope secretary, Methodist local preacher, then unattached Socialist, and finally a Social-Democrat.'[148] His non-conformist background was typical of many socialists, and perhaps was most clearly articulated in his concern for education: socialism as a *personal* journey, even if undertaken collectively, towards a more refined and enlightened existence. Grindley's analysis of the housing problem was clearly similar to that of middle-class evangelical reformers, and their fears about the social and moral consequences of overcrowding.[149] More importantly than that, however, poor housing also demoralised its inhabitants, and prevented them from realising their potential as citizens and human beings. As the Housing Association's 1906 pamphlet put it:

The refinement and worthy character which a love of home develops are impracticable to large numbers of people in 'the merry homes of England'... If the people were all heroes or angels of perfection they would, of course, surmount all obstacles, and keep themselves perfectly clean; but as they are only human there are some who, discouraged by the disabilities which a grinding capitalist system has imposed upon them, fall into dirty habits.[150]

During the spring of 1906 the Housing Association launched a new campaign in Stonehouse, in protest against the council's unanimous decision not to develop Millbay barracks for housing. A series of evening outdoor meetings was organised, held in some of the district's poorest streets, and resolutions urging the council to develop the Admiralty land were passed. The reception afforded to the campaigners was not entirely friendly. The Rev J H Belcher, at this time one of the most prominent activists in both the Housing Association and the SDF, was heckled: 'Are you a ratepayer?... We don't want paid agitators here.' Similar references to 'people who had nothing to do with Stonehouse' were made when the matter was discussed by the council.[151] Revealingly, there is an inescapable sense that the activists concerned, whether paid or not (and we should probably dismiss these claims) spoke *on behalf* of those who stood to benefit from the reforms. No speaker was able to offer his own experience as testimony to overcrowding or poor housing in Plymouth. Instead they were more likely to make expeditions to the slums to gather evidence, and emerge shocked by the experience. For all the advocacy of municipal housing, and concern about the quality of such housing, there was almost complete silence from those who were re-housed in municipal housing following slum clearance schemes.

Similarly complex and ambivalent attitudes were revealed in the Co-operative Society's internal debates about its relationship with its poorer members. In 1894, the monthly business meeting debated a proposal that the Society should cease purchasing their brushes from a firm which was alleged to sweat its workers. Those in favour of cancelling the order argued that co-operative societies should be bound by principle in their purchasing policy, and use their economic muscle to discourage unfair wages and working conditions. The problem was that goods produced under fair conditions were often more expensive, and thus were not available to the poorer members. Contributing to the 1894 debate on brushes, one speaker, 'contended that the wages of the majority of members did not average more than £1 a week, and with families to bring up, they could not pay the higher prices. Trade Unionists did not support the stores as they should, and if they were allowed to govern the society it would go down (Dissent).'[152] It was hinted that the motion had been brought by representatives of the Brushmakers' Union and that this explicitly trade unionist agenda did not necessarily square with co-operative priorities. The *Record's* editorial on the subject argued that given the competitive climate, and what it referred to as the 'thirst for cheapness', price competitiveness had to be the prime consideration for the management in determining their purchasing policy.[153] Although this position was probably partly motivated by commercial considerations, it also suggests that the Society was prepared to acknowledge that many of its members did not earn sufficient wages to allow them to be discriminating consumers, and that it had a duty towards them therefore. These poorer consumers were not necessarily the same individuals as the relatively well-paid members of craft trade unions, who had their own agenda to pursue within the Society.

This issue was a difficult one for the society, and indeed for the co-operative movement as a whole. Despite the instinctive sympathy many co-operators felt towards the poor, and the earnest attempts to grasp the philosophy that poverty was a result of environmental deprivation, co-operators were unable to feel totally comfortable in their dealings with the poor. Like the SDF, which organised free children's breakfasts during the worst years of unemployment in the mid 1900s, co-operators were often deeply critical of purely charitable responses to poverty, but were forced to acknowledge that to refuse charity was to overlook some appalling instances of deprivation. The Plymouth Co-operative Society ran its own charitable relief scheme, administered by the local branches of the Women's Co-operative Guild. Revealingly, though, the women complained that they sometimes found it impossible to assess whether applicants for relief were deserving or not, and that the discussions which sometimes took place about individual cases were unedifying, in that they subjected 'our unfortunate brothers and sisters' to 'cheap talk'.[154] That the role of taking co-operation to the poor was ascribed to the women's guilds mirrors the perception that charitable work was an acceptable domain for middle-class women. In 1900, there were some discussions about proposals for a co-operative 'colony' in a poor district, modelled on a similar venture in Sunderland. The colony would combine practical help, in the form of a special low-price store, a cheap eating house and a loans department, with education in self-help carried out from a settlement. The use of terms such as 'colony' and 'settlement' may provide some indication of the depth of the gulf between co-operators and the slum dwellers whom they wished to help. Inevitably, the work of the proposed settlement took on a tutelary aspect. There was to be a coffee shop to counteract the public house, and the loans department would exist not only to offer practical help, but to undermine the habit of regular weekly pawning. If co-operation was not reaching the poor this was partly because it failed to respond to the needs of the poorest, by refusing to offer credit for example, but also because of the habits of the poor themselves, which would have to be overcome by education.

In November 1907, the society's monthly meeting considered a motion to reduce the re-entry fee from one shilling to sixpence. The fee had been introduced to discourage members from withdrawing all their share capital on a regular basis, and waiving it would recognise that some poorer members were frequently obliged to do just this in order to make ends meet. Those in favour of the reduction argued that the rule constituted a heavy tax on the poorer members of the society, some 10,000 of whom had withdrawn all their share capital and incurred what was in effect a one shilling fine during the previous four quarters. The motion was eventually carried by a narrow margin, but the arguments put by those who opposed it indicate the complexity of co-operative attitudes towards the poorer members. The preferred route out of poverty was via self-help, and the role of the society should be to encourage behaviour which was thought to enable this to happen. One speaker, for example, believed in 'elevating the poor by teaching thrift and economy.'[155] These virtues would not be encouraged by allowing them to participate in a cycle of investment and withdrawal, similar to the weekly cycle of pawning. As the correspondent to the *Record's* women's page put it in 1910:

> Catered for the very poor, I am going to say right off that we do not; no society does. Cheap food in our shops for a certain class I do not believe in. Right through Co-operation there should be no question of class. Co-operation I have always understood to be working together for the good of all, and cheap food and clothes

means adulterated food and sweated labour, and co-operators have laid themselves out not to encourage sweated goods.[156]

For the Co-operative Society, as with other labour organisations, the key to social reform was education. Co-operators made frequent complaints about the apathy of the rank and file members, and their reluctance to take part in society activities unless they were entertaining. One member complained of the Plymouth Education Committee that, 'their ideas of educational work [are] in striking contrast to the ideas that governed the men of Rochdale. These latter stood for efficiency and improvement. Whether or not they organised Cinderella dances I will leave to the person who cares to study the original programme.'[157] These were echoed by the other labour organisations, in their struggle to understand the political apathy which was a serious obstacle to the success of their campaigns. Arthur Grindley recognised the problem within the SDF: 'People come to our Sunday evening meeting because it is a pleasure to them to do so; but the smaller number who come to the Tuesday meetings do so because it is a duty. Well, the SDF is not likely to neglect to cater for the latter; and it will be well worth our while to cater to a large extent for the former.'[158] The blame for the severe overcrowding in Stonehouse was laid firmly on the existing councillors, but also with the working men of the ward who re-elected them.[159] 'The worst feature of all is that the disinherited have lost hope,' commented an SDF activist in 1906. 'They don't care a straw for the politician, be he Liberal, Tory, or Socialist. Having been humbugged for years by the two orthodox political parties, it takes a lot to convince them that the Socialists or Labour Party can be any good.'[160] Education was seen to be the key to overcoming this problem, and in this light, election campaigning was understood as being valuable not only as a means to an end, but also as a way of educating the electorate. Arthur Grindley made this point to an SDF branch meeting (note the clear religious overtones):

Then there is the opportunity which is afforded us of discussing Socialism with the people on their doorstep in a quiet way, which I regard as a very valuable means of spreading the light, and for that reason I do not believe in the abolition of canvassing. For those parties which have no gospel to preach it would be right to prohibit canvassing, but in our case canvassing gives the opportunity to enlighten the people on Socialism, without any cost to ourselves except the labour we put in. And finally there is the moral advantage gained by demonstrating to the public the ever-increasing strength of our party.[161]

Given the limited resources at the disposal of the movement, campaigning tended to be concentrated on certain wards only. No attempts were made to contest the poorer wards in the town centre. Nor was there a conscious effort to appeal to the large number of servicemen in Devonport, in particular the large numbers of naval seamen present in the town. Meanwhile, the SDF concentrated its efforts on a handful of Plymouth wards, especially Sutton ward in central Plymouth, characterised by the *Western Morning News* as a 'purely working-class ward', which they contested consistently between 1905 and 1912, with some limited success.[162] The North Quay at Sutton Harbour was consistently the site for outdoor meetings organised by SDF and other labour movement organisations, so the branch had a visible presence in the ward even without working it further.

In 1906, an unexpected opportunity presented itself for the SDF to raise its profile in a different part of the Three Towns. In July, the branch had organised a series of Sunday morning open-air meetings in Manor Street, which attracted little attention until a police superintendent attempted to break up the gathering. Undaunted, the branch resumed the following Sunday, and this time the main speaker, John Tamlyn, was warned that he was breaking the law. With the extra publicity, the meetings had begun to attract a larger crowd, indicated by the steep rise in the amount of money collected: one shilling on the first Sunday, 6s 1d the following week, and 16s 8d the week after. The matter had by now got completely out of hand as far as the police were concerned. Tamlyn found himself arrested and charged with obstruction, and spent a few days in prison for non-payment of his fine. On his release he was welcomed by a crowd of 300 people. The weekly stand-off with the police had become a major event for the local population, and the branch prospered from the publicity and funds which it generated. Despite their outraged protests, activists were keenly aware how positive the whole affair was. Those SDF speakers who received custodial sentences emerged from prison as heroes, and exploited their experiences to the full through their accounts of their treatment inside.[163] The affair dragged on into September, and culminated in a mass demonstration, supported by the Trades Council and the LRA, with a speaker from London. The following week the police relented and announced that meetings could continue as long as the speakers undertook to maintain a clear passage through the street on one side of the crowd.[164] The 'Free Speech Fight', as it came to be known, generated a tremendous amount of positive publicity for the SDF, and turned a modest series of meetings into a major milestone for the entire labour movement in Plymouth. The relative (if still limited) success of that autumn's municipal elections owed something at least to the whole affair. John Tamlyn, the hero of the Free Speech Fight, stood for election in Millbay ward, and gained a credible second place, even though the ward was not thought to be promising – it had a high concentration of shopkeepers and was a stronghold of the Ratepayers' Association.[165] Yet the branch lacked either the will or the resources to capitalise on this relative success and contest the ward again, and Tamlyn's moral victory was an isolated triumph. With such tiny numbers of candidates, the SDF could never really hope to generate much of an impact.[166]

V

Common to the different organisations of the pre-war labour movement in Plymouth, therefore, was the emphasis on education as a means of social change. A sense of class solidarity was part of this, but class was often understood in a negative sense. As one activist wrote, 'The essence of the Labour Movement... is not class struggle, but a sense of the dignity and sanctity of life.'[167] As the *Labour Journal* commented, 'the sneer implied in "class legislation" is an old one,' class, in this sense, drawing on older constructions of the term denoting the assertion of sectional interests in the constitutional balance of power.[168] An example of such class legislation was felt to be the decision of Devonport council to increase the salaries of its officials, but to refuse claims for higher wages for the corporation electricity workers on the grounds that this was class legislation. All council members, both Liberal and Tory, were, in characteristically antagonistic terms, described as 'self-interested jobbers representing private interest and privilege.'[169] The labour movement, by contrast, sought to transcend class, and to act in the interests of the whole community. Local government should not be based on the pursuit of sectional interests. The strength of independent labour representation was that the interests of the workers were also, by definition, the interests of the whole community. 'Is not all social legislation class legislation?' asked the *Labour Journal*. '[I]t's just this great working class that wants legislating for so badly. The builders and lawyers and doctors and successful businessmen, these have no housing question, no living wage question, no bread and butter question, they don't feel the pinch so they don't know the pain.'[170] Moreover,

> Municipalities throughout this country and throughout all civilised countries are coming to the conclusion that in the welfare of the unit lies the welfare of the community. If a section of the people are half-fed, badly-clothed, inadequately housed, untaught, not only is it bad for them but for the whole. The whole suffers with the part. The whole must protect, sympathise with, and if necessary maintain that part until it be restored to the state of well-being desired.[171]

Despite references to co-operators' 'duties as workers', and 'the power of organised labour' to remedy 'the wrongs of a downtrodden class', co-operators often displayed a similarly ambivalent attitude towards the idea of class.[172] The Plymouth co-operator W H Watkins, addressing the 1910 Co-operative Congress in Plymouth, suggested that, 'Co-operation knows no class. And in this connection it will perhaps be of service to again proclaim that the Co-operative movement countenances no policy of exclusion or class division.'[173] Against this assertion, the co-operative movement was undeniably an overwhelmingly working-class association. There seem to be few grounds to doubt that the majority of those who did their shopping in the co-operative store, and drew their dividends every quarter, considered themselves to be working class, and that the co-operative store formed an important focal point for working-class neighbourhoods. It also played an important role in the development of a strong associational culture, which was independent from and at times explicitly opposed to alternative or competing cultures.

Even though labour activists were forced to respond charitably to some of the worst instances of deprivation, they continued to campaign for the administration of municipal services on the basis of justice rather than charity. SDF and LRA candidates for the Boards of Guardians included in their election programmes proposals to institute a new system of outdoor relief, which would avoid the degradation of applying to charity for those who applied. This recognition

126

of the rights of the poor to relief further emphasises the notion of a community of which all were equal members, as citizens. These rights were, moreover, defined in terms of historical continuity: 'The Poor Rates… are the revenues of the Poor, all that is left to them of the monastic endowments, mediæval charities, and common lands, and as such they are justly entitled to them.'[174] Independence remained the central tenet of the organised labour movement and the impetus to independent labour representation, but this went beyond independence from party to embrace a notion of collective dignity and self-reliance. Although this was embodied in the continuing appeal of self-help movements, especially the friendly and co-operative societies, Labour discourse does reveal an acceptance of the state provision of certain welfare benefits. Importantly, Labour arguments for state intervention in welfare were concerned with the provision of welfare benefits as a right. Unstated yet implied was also the assumption that the only way in which such benefits could be justly administered was universally. The LRA programme for the Guardians' election of May 1906 is indicative of the piecemeal, rather ad hoc approach to different areas of welfare provision. In part the proposals stem from a distrust of the ability of locally elected Guardians to administer the rates fairly uninfluenced by their conflicting interests as local ratepayers: it was proposed therefore that the poor rates should be a national, rather than a local charge. Old Age pensions were likewise to be funded, and also administered, at a national level. The other major concern was that outdoor maintenance was always to be preferred over workhouse relief, in order to avoid breaking up the home, but also to reduce the most publicly visible manifestations of pauperism. The main reason for suspicion of the Guardians arose not from their inadequate distribution of relief, but in their ability to confer upon individuals or families the status of pauperism. Another proposal was to remove the responsibility for providing for needy children to another body, for example the Education Authority, with once again the explicit aim of avoiding the status of pauperism which became official upon an individual's contact with the Guardians.

This concern with the geography of municipal politics and the boundaries between local and national state was also expressed in the aspiration for the administrative amalgamation of the Three Towns. Proposals to construct a new asylum for Devonport in 1904, at a cost to the borough of £100,000, were protested by the two Devonport

Labour councillors, who argued that it made much better sense to seek co-operation with Plymouth.[175] Sharp rises in the rates in both boroughs strengthened the case further. An LRA meeting in 1904 voted unanimously in favour of amalgamation, and the Labour candidates noted their support for the scheme in their election addresses.[176] Opposition to the proposals came mainly from Devonport, whose councillors expressed fears that the economies of the two towns were too dissimilar, and that their smaller borough would simply be swallowed up.[177] W H Welsford, a former dockyard civil servant and councillor for Molesworth ward gave evidence to the Local Government Board against amalgamation, and claimed that the agitation in favour had been brought about solely by the local Labour Party. If this is the case, then amalgamation must be reckoned as the outstanding success of the pre-war labour movement in Plymouth, for it was achieved in 1914 (although over-shadowed by the outbreak of the war).

The amalgamation of the Three Towns was a victory for Labour over the interests of the Devonport councillors, but the conflicts of interest which beset local government remained. Labour itself was prepared to capitalise on public dissatisfaction with the rates, and the party's municipal programme emphasised the need for 'efficiency and economy' in carrying out the undertakings of the town.[178] Yet Labour found itself in an anomalous position as far as the rates were concerned, advocating financial prudence on the one hand and the pursuance of an extension in municipal activity on the other. In 1904 Plymouth Corporation was forced to undergo an exhaustive investigation into its finances, as a result of its growing indebtedness, and as a result of this was allowed to undertake further borrowing only under the stringent conditions set down by the Local Government Board. The curtailment of municipal expenditure which this implied was strongly criticised, and taken as evidence of similar attacks on municipal autonomy throughout the country.[179] On the whole, though, the national state was seen as a progressive force against the arbitrariness of local administrations. The cost of poor relief should be met from general taxation rather than the local rate, it was argued, otherwise Guardians might be swayed by their interests as ratepayers, and tempted to keep the rates down rather than provide relief where it was needed most.[180]

The prominence of these two ideas in Labour discourse – the emphasis on education and self-improvement as the key to social reform, and the concern to remove social welfare from the arbitrariness of local interests, looking instead to the national state as a guar-antor of justice – might be explained with reference to the occupa-tional culture of the dockyard. Dockyard workers in several commu-nities including Plymouth seemed to have had a vibrant tradition of co-operative and mutual societies stretching back to the era of the Napoleonic wars or even earlier. We know for example of a retail co-operative society formed by dockyard shipwrights at Deptford, Wool-wich and Chatham in the 1750s; a co-operative flour mill at Portsmouth in 1814, and a Union Dock Mill Society at Plymouth in 1817.[181] These organisations had disappeared by the late nineteenth century, but there remained an equally strong dockyard tradition of informal mutual benefit and friendly societies. Admiral Henderson's order prohibiting the transaction of dockyard business during work-ing hours was thought to affect 'hundreds' of unregistered clubs for sickness, injury, infectious diseases, money-lending and the like. Some of these clubs attracted a very large proportion of dockyard workers: the Western District Government Employees Infectious Diseases Club had approximately 5000 members in 1914.[182] It is harder to trace a direct link between the dockyard and the prominence of the con-sumer Co-operative Society in Plymouth, but there are parallels here with other dockyard communities in southern England that also had strong and locally influential co-operative societies, including the Roy-al Arsenal Co-operative Society in Woolwich, and the New Bromp-ton Co-operative Society in Chatham.

It proved more difficult, however, to transform these ideas into polit-ical success. Overall, the example of Plymouth supports the case for the fragility of Labour's advance before 1914. The party had managed to contest only a handful of municipal wards before 1914, and had been temporarily successful in even fewer. Moreover, activity in municipal elections dwindled steadily from its peak in 1906. This lack of suc-cess, compared to elsewhere in the country, has sometimes been attributed to the economic backwardness of south west England, which meant that an old-fashioned combination of religious allegiance and social deference continued to determine political alignments before 1914. As this chapter has demonstrated, however, this explanation is not entirely accurate. Plymouth was in fact undergoing a period of rapid expansion during the late nineteenth and early twentieth cen-turies, which had important consequences for political activity in the Three Towns. The expansion of municipal intervention in response to problems of housing in particular necessitated a sharp rise in the rates, which provoked in turn a political challenge to the ruling Liberal Party. Conservatives achieved some success in municipal politics on a platform of municipal retrenchment. Labour organisations, even if not conspicuously successful in electoral terms, played an important role in shaping the debates over the appropriate boundaries of municipal activity, by campaigning vigorously for more action to tackle the housing shortage, and for the amalgamation of the Three Towns.

Nor can Labour's lack of success in Plymouth be attributed simply to working-class support for the Conservatives, as a pro-navy party, at least in the early part of the period. The Conservative association with the naval interest probably worked to their advantage in 1910, when the dockyard was working at full stretch and it was easy to point to the benefits of the navy for local prosperity, but these links could never be taken for granted. The naval dockyard and its workforce was clearly influential on local politics, though it cannot be assumed that the dockyard workers showed a 'natural' tendency to vote for the Conservatives as the 'big navy' party (or indeed for any other political party). Instead, dockyard workers relied on local MPs to lobby for their interests in Parliament, and some dockyard MPs, whether Liberal or Conservative, could command a high level of personal loyalty. These ties were not easily overcome by Labour, despite the changes in dockyard work and organisation. Further, the isolation of the Three Towns from other industrial centres where Labour was expected to advance was probably significant. Following the collapse of the Labour candidature in the Devonport by-elections of 1902 and 1904 little interest was shown in Plymouth by the national organisation, and all initiatives came instead from the local level. Here, the bitterness of the sectional rivalries within the dockyard helped to prevent united action, and other trade unions outside the dockyard were not strong enough to make an impact. The one organisation which might have contributed to a successful Labour campaign was the Co-operative Society, which also had the advantage of being able to offer generous funds, but although the question of political representation was discussed before 1914 the Co-op remained committed to the Rochdale principle of political neutrality. The events of the war were to be decisive in changing the attitude of the Co-op towards political representation, as will be discussed in chapter five.

CHAPTER 5

Plymouth during World War I and after

The war was a major turning point for the labour movement in Plymouth. In the space of just a few years Labour advanced from a position where it was able at best to contest a handful of municipal seats, to one, in 1918, where it could claim to have displaced the Liberals as as the main challenger to the Conservative Party, in both municipal and parliamentary elections. What were the causes of this transformation? Many historians have emphasised the economic and social changes which occurred as a result of the war, specifically the radicalisation and militancy of the workforce in certain parts of the country.[1] Revisionist accounts have played down the escalation of class consciousness, and suggested instead that political changes were more important, namely the split in the Liberal Party which threw its supporters into disarray.[2] One of the main questions, therefore, is whether wartime politics in Plymouth was primarily influenced by economic and social conditions, or whether political events in London were equally or more influential. As the present chapter will show, local conditions were certainly important, but it was the role of the Co-operative Society and campaigns within the sphere of the politics of consumption, rather than production, which were most influential. The chapter begins, however, with a discussion of the dockyard during the war. Intense levels of activity during the war helped to strengthen the position of the workforce, though this did not spill over into political activity as it did in the shipyards of Clydeside for example; indeed the dockyard dispute had become much less politicised by 1918. Instead, it was the growing problem with the food supply which had the most significant impact on wartime politics. From 1916 the Co-operative Society found itself increasingly embroiled in conflicts which were to shift it from its historic position of political neutrality by 1917. Conflicts over the distribution of a scarce food supply also contributed to a growing sense that the war had brought about – or at least had hastened – a profound change in the nature of politics.

I

The outbreak of war in August 1914 resulted in a further intensification of the level of activity in the dockyard, already working at a high rate. The yard's fifth and final Dreadnought was launched in 1914, and work then shifted from new construction towards the refits and conversions necessary to prepare ships for active service. This work was sometimes carried out under such pressure that dockyard workers were forced to sail with the ships. The civilian workforce continued to expand, and within a tight local labour market, many dockyard workers made some gains in pay and conditions. In December 1914, all permanent male employees, regardless of trade, were issued with war service exemption badges as members of reserved occupations. They were also allowed pay increases, a supplementary war bonus and new overtime rates in an attempt to offset the rising costs of living.[3] The developing manpower crisis meant however that by 1916 it was necessary to consider alternative strategies to maintain the dockyard workforce at the required level. Some dockyard pensioners were re-engaged at their previous trade rates.[4] In February 1916 the Director of Dockyards wrote to the different yards to ask them to consider 'dilution', that is, the employment of labourers, and more radically, women, in trades where there were shortages. In keeping with dockyard tradition, according to which a small number of naval widows had earned their living through employment in the colour lofts, preference was to be given to women who were the widows or dependent relatives of deceased sailors and marines.[5] Even so, by August 1916, the number of women employed in all the home dockyards was still only 1630: hardly a revolution in the workplace, although it did represent a significant increase on the tiny numbers employed before the war.[6] But in March 1917 the skilled and unskilled labourers were debadged, thus allowing them to be called up (most of the trades remained reserved occupations), and by July 1917 the number of women employed in the home yards had risen to 4,200.[7] Women remained very much in a minority in the dockyards therefore, but they were present in much greater numbers than they had ever been before.

The dilution of dockyard labour, especially the employment of women, was challenged by the dockyard trade unions. In response to similar pressures in the private sector, the five largest engineering unions, spearheaded by the ASE, had reached an agreement with the Engineering Employers' Federation that restrictions on the dilution of skilled labour were to be relaxed only for the duration of the war. When workers were informed of equivalent changes in the dockyards early in 1916, the ASE sought meetings with dockyard management in Devonport and Portsmouth yards. The main issue at stake was not so much the question of dilution itself, however, but the official recognition of dockyard trade unionism, and the maintenance of union control over important aspects of the labour process. The petitions system had been suspended for the duration of the war, but the Admiralty stated that it would continue to recognise the established, informal traditions of consultation, and that officials would be willing to receive delegations from the men to discuss the dilution issue. The recognition of trade unions as formal partners in the bargaining process remained out of the question, however. The relationship between Admiralty and unions had been fundamentally altered in any case, following the introduction of the Munitions of War Act of 1915, by which the government attempted to centralise its control over the industrial workforce vital to the war effort.[8] Under the provisions of the Act, the functions of the Admiralty in relation to its employees were formally transferred to the Ministry of Munitions in July 1915. The unions contended that this meant the Admiralty was obliged to recognise and consult trade unions over the waiving of demarcation agreements, but the Admiralty responded that the dockyards were not considered as controlled establishments, and thus fell outside the provision of the Act.[9] In an internal memo to dockyard superintendents, the Director of Dockyards expressed his concerns that admitting trade union officials as a party to discussions of this kind would imply that they held the power of veto over any arrangements, and the Admiralty was unwilling to create potential 'hostages to fortune' in the postwar period.[10] Heightened industrial unrest elsewhere in the country seemed only to deepen support for this position. The Sheerness ASE, in one of their communications with management, threatened that the present situation, 'might cause a similar upheaval in the Dockyards, as is already in progress on the Clyde.'[11] There is no evidence that there was ever any likelihood of this, but it was a risk the Admiralty was not prepared to take. The dockyards remained different to other industrial establishments, and they would continue therefore to be run differently. The Admiralty put it thus:

> It is considered that, whatever may be the practice in respect of the recognition of shop stewards in private establishments, any official recognition of them would be quite unsuitable to the conditions obtaining in the Royal Dockyards; and it would be particularly objectionable for the Dockyard officers to be required to recognise Shop Stewards, in compliance with an Admiralty Order issued in accordance with an undertaking conceded to a trade union.[12]

There is no evidence that the dockyards were ever seriously threatened by wartime industrial unrest, however. Although some dockyard workers clearly had grievances, whether over the dilution of the workforce or the lack of control they had over the labour process, this was not translated into militancy and political radicalism. Nonetheless, the Admiralty was bound to acknowledge the greater involvement of trade unions in the informal bargaining process, and the 'professionalisation' of the dockyard dispute as matters were more and more likely to be handed over to paid union officials. The Devonport ASE's deputation in February 1916 was organised not by Devonport men, but by the Organising District Delegate from Swindon. For their part, TUC-affiliated unions such as the ASE were also hostile to the continuing existence of more informal, local workers' organisations, as in 1916 when the Portsmouth ASE wrote to the Admiralty stating that they refused to recognise or have dealings with a Mr Bates of the Portsmouth Steam Engine Makers' Society.[13] During the latter part of the war there were indeed moves to establish a formalised bargaining process. In 1916 the government established a committee under the chairmanship of J H Whitley, MP for Halifax, to enquire into industrial relations in the context of heightened wartime industrial unrest. The committee's first report recommended the establishment of a joint council of employers' associations and trade unions in private industrial establishments. A new report in October 1917 suggested that this should also apply to the public sector, and that state and municipal authorities should form joint councils with state sector trade unions. Pressure on the government to act as a model employer meant that state departments such as the Admiralty were obliged to adopt the scheme. In May 1918 it was reported that the Admiralty had set in motion a scheme for the establishment of different trade and shop committees, and presented draft proposals on these to the dockyard workers, a move which met a largely positive response from the workforce.[14] Most dockyard employees seemed to consider the Admiralty Joint Industrial Councils to be a huge improvement on the old petitions system, and that the management of labour was generally approached more sympathetically.[15] For its part, the Admiralty appeared to be willing to accept the Whitley councils as the best system for guaranteeing industrial peace.

The introduction of Whitley councils was not considered entirely satisfactory, however, and it may have contributed to undermining the influence of TUC unions within the dockyards. Dockyard MPs expressed their concerns to the Admiralty officials that the draft proposals fell short of the recommendations of the Whitley report, in that they by-passed the recognition of existing trade unions.[16] Even in operation, the new system for consultation indicated that old habits died hard, and that 'the formality of the proceedings in many ways continued to reflect the old patterns of authority.'[17] Worker representatives presented grievances, and the employers often rejected them, in a process that showed its clear inheritance of the traditions of the old petitions system. The establishment system was retained as an important part of the Admiralty's industrial relations strategy. Civilian state employees were not banned from taking part in strike action, but the pension payable to an established worker was dependent on 'faithful and satisfactory service', which could be jeopardised by participation in a strike, and thus acted as an effective deterrent.[18] In 1927, in response to the Trade Disputes Act and the General Strike preceding it, the Admiralty decided to make non-membership of a TUC-affiliated trade union a condition of establishment. This provoked an upsurge in membership of non-official associations, which again helped to limit the impact of TUC labour organisations in the dockyards. Moreover, dockyard workers sometimes avoided TUC unions in order to circumvent trade union restrictions on certain types of payments.

For these reasons, dockyard workers continued to remain relatively isolated from the national labour movement. In the case of Devonport in particular this isolation was exacerbated by their geographical position far removed from the main centres of industry and trade union and labour movement activity. There is no evidence to suggest that workplace conflicts ever threatened to generate the radical political movements experienced in other parts of the country, among the shipbuilding workers of the Clyde for example. On the other hand, the experience of the war was clearly decisive in the formation of a political labour movement in Plymouth. It was, however, conflicts within the sphere of consumption, not production, which proved to be most influential in these developments, and specifically in changing the relationship between Plymouth Co-operative Society and the wider labour movement in Plymouth.

II

As was discussed in the previous chapter, the influence of Plymouth Co-operative Society cannot be overstated. Compared to the very rapid expansion of the early 1900s, the society's growth had slowed following the jubilee year of 1910, but even so, by the outbreak of war it was the second largest retail co-operative society in England and Wales, with over 40,000 members and annual trade worth just over a quarter of a million pounds. In 1914 there was a change in the management of the society, following the victory of the so-called 'White Party' in the internal elections of that year. W H Watkins, who became the new president, was a product of the dockyard apprentice school, who had served as a clerical assistant in the naval stores at Chatham and Portsmouth, before returning to his native Devonport in 1912. His education was continued via a Co-operative Union scholarship and the university extension scheme, which allowed him to teach co-operative classes in Plymouth.[19] His rival for the presidency, who eventually succeeded him in 1919, was J Hayne Pillar, who was a committed member of the Liberal Party and served as a local councillor of that persuasion for many years. In contrast to Pillar, who remained staunchly opposed to political alliance between the Co-operative Society and the labour movement, Watkins represented the 'labourist' strand within the movement. His was to become one of the principal voices calling for the co-operative movement to engage with politics, and he became the first chairman of the Co-operative Party in 1918, while simultaneously serving as a Labour councillor in Plymouth. Watkins' vision for Plymouth Co-operative Society on his election is not clear, but he immediately signalled his commitment to the educational and propagandist work of the society by establishing a full-time paid position of secretary to the education department. The choice of incumbent for the new post was also significant. T W Mercer may be described as a professional co-operator who had made his career entirely within the movement, beginning in the grocery department of Reigate Co-operative Society. He was relatively young, only 30 years old in 1914, and his five-year tenure at Plymouth seems to have been the making of his career, for he went on to become a highly prolific pamphleteer and propagandist for the Co-operative Union. Personally, Mercer shared Watkins' commitment to co-operative political representation in partnership with the wider labour movement.[20]

The outbreak of the war caused no major upset in the day-to-day running of Plymouth Co-operative Society. The new president stated emphatically that 'business as usual' was the management's position in an address delivered to the Devon District Co-operative Association conference in September 1914.[21] The *Plymouth Co-operative Record* for August 1914 carried a front page notice appealing to members for their patience, and offered the management committee's pledge to do their best to maintain normal supplies and keep prices low. The outbreak of the war was passed off as nothing more dramatic than a new business challenge, and the committee was subsequently congratulated for its handling of the situation.[22] The prevailing mood within the society, and indeed the co-operative movement as a whole, seemed to be what one co-operative historian described as a 'volunteer spirit' of acquiescence to the privations of war, and a determination to make a patriotic contribution to the war effort.[23]

From 1915, the society faced some major challenges, however. The first of these resulted from the Asquith government's introduction of Excess Profits Tax in 1915, in a rather clumsy attempt to assuage public concern over wartime 'profiteering'.[24] In the confusion over what exactly constituted profiteering it was decided to include the trading surpluses of co-operative societies as profits which were liable for the tax, and the Joint Parliamentary Committee of the Co-operative Union agreed to accept the tax on the grounds of patriotic expediency.[25] The Plymouth Co-operative Society decided from the outset that it would oppose the tax, and in doing so it thus confronted not only the government, but also the Co-operative Union. In January 1916, the quarterly meeting of members passed a resolution authorising the management committee to take whatever action they felt appropriate in campaigning against the tax.[26] A legal appeal drawn up by the society's own lawyers was launched, to be backed up by a propaganda campaign among the membership and the public at large. The appeal was heard in London before the Special Commissioners of the Inland Revenue, early in January 1917. The society's case was based on two grounds, firstly that co-operative societies made surpluses, not profits, and that there were therefore no profits per member within the meaning of the act, and secondly that the amount assessed was in fact excessive.[27] When the court found in favour of the Crown, the management committee made a formal request to take their case to the High Court.

The experience of the Excess Profits Tax led many co-operators to call for political representation in defence of co-operative interests. 'It is time the [Co-operative] Movement had its own Members of Parliament to strongly protest against the position,' was the view of one member at the quarterly meeting in January 1916.[28] There were also references to the 'co-operators' Taff Vale', and the three million voters who could potentially be mobilised in defence of the movement. 'A new attack upon our funds will work a miracle within the Co-operative Movement like that which the Osborne Judgement worked in Trade Unionism,' wrote the editor of the *Record*.[29] Of the 136 local retail societies which declared their support for the Plymouth campaign, 110 promised to communicate with their MPs, and a deputation from Plymouth waited on a Labour MP and the Chancellor of the Exchequer to put their case.[30] Calls for political representation were echoed throughout the entire movement, which eventually resolved, at its extraordinary Congress in Swansea, in the summer of 1917, to take steps towards seeking independent co-operative political representation. The eventual vindication of the Excess Profits Tax campaign, following a parliamentary amendment to the Finance Act in July 1917, came hard on the heels of this decision and thus could be attributed in part at least to the increasing clamour of co-operative demands for parliamentary representation.

On the surface, the decision of the Swansea Congress to seek co-operative political representation seemed a surprising volte-face for a movement with a long tradition of political neutrality and hostility to the state.[31] Beneath the pragmatism, however, lay a deeper sense of inequality and injustice arising from the war, and an attempt to differentiate consumer co-operation from wartime 'profiteering' and the capitalist system of which it was a part. As Mercer explained to the quarterly meeting, co-operative dividends were not profits, but savings, restored to the members at the end of each quarter. 'Everyone who has studied our case knows that no such thing as profit exists within the co-operative movement. Profit can only be made by one man, or one set of men, out of other men. We trade with ourselves, and it is impossible for us to make profit out of ourselves. That which our opponents desire to tax us is non-existent.'[32] The Co-operative Union's argument, that the war situation made the tax expedient, cut little ice with Plymouth co-operators, and disillusion with the movement's leadership was frequently expressed within the society. The president W H Watkins, as a member of the Co-operative Union's Central Board, formally disassociated himself from the Parliamentary Committee when the matter was debated at the 1916 Co-operative Congress.[33] The tax was merely one example of the broader wartime trend to undermine fundamental rights and principles in the name of expediency. It was necessary to oppose the tax, according to Watkins, 'because to me it is astonishing what the working classes of the country are submitting to in the name of the war. Rights which our forefathers fought for and secured have been swept away by those people who are always doing their best to keep the workers of this country under.'[34]

The society found itself embroiled in further conflict over the growing problems with the wartime food supply. Food prices had risen sharply from the outbreak of war, attributable mainly to the sudden peak in demand as consumers stockpiled essential goods.[35] The society responded with determined efforts to keep its prices for basic foodstuffs low. This strategy continued during the winter of 1916–17, when prices rose again due to restrictions in supply. Although the evidence for stability in the food supply and calorie consumption may be convincing in historical perspective, it nonetheless belies the sense of crisis which was experienced at the time, and is clearly distinguishable from the co-operative sources. During the winter months in particular, there was a strong perception that the food supply problem was dangerously close to undermining the entire war effort. An editorial from the *Record* early in 1917 stated dramatically that the war 'has brought us within measurable distance of starvation,' and continued the apocalyptic tone by describing the new register of members for rationing purposes as 'our Domesday book'.[36] The society attempted to respond to these problems in two ways. In the first place, it sought to keep its prices low, and undercut those in privately owned stores. The strength of the society in Plymouth meant that it was able to have

TABLE 5.4. *The composition of Plymouth Food Control Committee, August 1917.*

Name	Trade/organisation
Councillor J O Brown	Wholesale grocer and provision merchant
Alderman W Littleton	builder
Alderman S H Phillips	wholesale grocer
Councillor Modbury	ice merchant
Councillor Ross	butcher
Councillor S Stephens	baker and confectioner
Councillor F Viggers	dairyman
Mr Law	grocer
Mr J Smale	Trades and Labour Council
Mr C White	Plymouth Co-operative Society
Mr A E Wonnacott	Plymouth Co-operative Society
Mrs Daymond	women's organisations

SOURCE: *The Co-operator,* 1st September 1917.

some influence over general prices locally, as in April 1917, when the master bakers agreed that the price of the standard two-pound loaf would rise to sixpence, but were eventually forced to match the Co-op's 5d.[37] The general committee's report for the trading quarter ending 2nd June 1917 presented some comparative prices, suggesting for example that confectionery products were at least 20% lower in co-operative stores than they were elsewhere, and that coal was being sold for at least two shillings a ton less.[38] From 1917, the society ran a new publication, *The Co-operator,* which was intended as a weekly newsletter about the society's activities, and published comprehensive lists of prices in comparison with those of other traders.[39]

As the war progressed, it became increasingly apparent that the price mechanism was inadequate as a device for regulating the food supply. The Plymouth Co-operative Society introduced a scheme to ration potatoes in the spring of 1917, and this was followed by similar arrangements for bread and sugar as these commodities became scarcer. By August 1917 it was reported that 183,000 people, out of a total population of just under a quarter of a million, were registered with the society for the consumption of potatoes. These schemes were set up within the context of growing dissatisfaction with government efforts to organise food control.[40] In December 1916, the new coalition government had appointed Lord Devonport – formerly, as H E Kearley, Liberal MP for Devonport until 1910 – as Food Controller with extensive authority under the Defence of the Realm Act. Devonport was not conspicuously successful in his new role, however, and was succeeded in May 1917 by Lord Rhondda, generally regarded as being the more competent in the post. One of Rhondda's first actions was to set in place the machinery for the establishment of local Food Control Committees, which would be appointed by local authorities in order to regulate the food supply in particular districts. In anticipation of this development the co-operative management committee wrote to the Plymouth Town Clerk, to present their case for a level of co-operative representation on the committee which they felt would take into account their status as major distributors of food in the locality. The composition of the committee when it was announced was therefore felt to be bitterly disappointing (Table 5.4).

The perceived under-representation of consumers on the new committee brought the society into conflict with the local authorities. A protest campaign was launched with a demonstration and a petition to the Mayor, who refused however to meet the co-operative delegation in order to discuss the committee.[41] Sixteen hundred people attended a public demonstration in October, and were told by the main speaker that the affair went beyond the question of representation on the Food Control Committee to embrace the wider issue of how business was conducted in the council chamber.[42] Unrest grew as the autumn progressed, to the extent that public demonstrations and disturbances prompted the municipal authorities to close the public gallery of the council chamber to the public.[43] By December the matter had come to the attention of the Food Controller himself, and although he was powerless to impose a solution to the conflict, Rhondda was prepared to suggest that the committee be reformed to take greater account of working-class interests. The borough council did indeed agree the following month to appoint three new members to the committee, but the eventual outcome was disappointing in that it secured only one other co-operative representative. Three thousand people attended the demonstration on the North Quay in protest, and a deputation was sent to the Ministry of Food.[44]

Just as with the Excess Profits Tax, the difficulties over the Food Control Committee raised the question of the need for independent co-operative representation, this time in the council chamber. 'The British House of Commons has become the frontier of the Co-operative Commonwealth,' wrote Mercer in the *Record*. 'The Municipal

Council Chamber is now our first line of defence… Those who resist Co-operation in the workshop and the distributive store must be compelled to accept it in the legislative assembly and the Council Chamber.'[45] The council's decision to ban public demonstrations in the Guildhall Square, and to close the public gallery of the council chamber, was seen as further evidence of the erosion of fundamental rights and liberties in the name of the war effort.[46] There was growing dissatisfaction with the wartime electoral truce, which had prevented the municipal elections being held in the usual way. 'Was there ever such a self-satisfied body of men as the Plymouth Borough Council?' asked a 'member of the fourth estate', writing in *The Co-operator.*

> They are a law unto themselves – an Assembly of Unrepresentatives, who recognise no authority higher than their own…. It is so long since they have faced the electors at the polls that they have quite forgotten the existence of an outside public.[47]

The co-operative society reminded its members that it, by contrast, had not jeopardised its own democratic principles, even where the conditions of wartime might have made it convenient to remove these particular constraints on the actions of its management. Further evidence of the management's commitment to principle over pragmatism even in wartime was indicated, they argued, in their determination to maintain the educational grant at its pre-war level, and indeed to increase it.[48]

The food situation worsened during the winter of 1917–18, so that queues for basic supplies became a common sight during the first months of 1918. In response to the inactivity of the borough council, the Co-operative Society continued to make its own arrangements to try to secure the equitable distribution of a growing list of scarce commodities. Arrangements for the rationing of margarine and meat were introduced early in 1918, and efforts continued to maintain low prices.[49] But the presence of the queues was also giving rise to a growing sense of injustice, frequently expressed in terms of class. 'Labour is on the doormat again!… represented by the persons of thousands of working-class womenfolk and kiddies waiting in the rain for Margarine and Meat. No! not always for margarine and meat, but merely for the chance of getting some… Few happenings have gripped the public imagination as firmly as this spectacle of long files of people standing in the wind and rain for food.'[50] It was, moreover, an increasingly political sense of class. '[W]orking-men ought not to permit their womenfolk to stand in queues in the streets,' one co-operative activist told the February monthly meeting.[51] Action on the part of these 'working-men' would in fact be inevitable, it was suggested, driven by the inherent justice of their cause.

> For who could deny that Councillor Moses was right when he said that working-class political opinion had reached a high pitch of indignation? Who could tell what Trade Unionists would not do if something was not done to pacify them? Suppose the dockers did cease to work and the railwaymen take a holiday?[52]

In contrast to the Excess Profits Tax campaign, the struggle over food control was confined to the local arena. Co-operators re-encountered their old enemies of the pre-war struggles against the private traders, and some of the criticism levelled at individual councillors in the *Co-operator* noted the familiarity of these names. The national state was regarded as an ally, against the arbitrary operation of local vested interests, rather than an enemy. The deputation of labour and co-operative representatives who visited Rhondda declared themselves highly satisfied that he was attempting to do his very best for the interests of working-class consumers, and his correspondence with the municipal authorities was presented as further evidence that he could be counted on to be fair.[53] This view of the state as the just arbiter of local disputes, accessible through petitions and deputations, was perhaps reminiscent of the dockyard tradition of petitioning the Admiralty. There was no attempt to enlist the support of any of the four local MPs, however, and the deference which seemed to characterise attitudes to Lord Rhondda was in stark contrast to the criticism of 'millionaires' found in the co-operative newspapers, a probable reference to the Plymouth MP Waldorf Astor. Class conflict, then, seems to have been confined to, or at least expressed most strongly in, the local arena.

This increased local emphasis was to find further expression in the development of other aspects of co-operation in Plymouth during this period. Apart from the conflict with the Co-operative Union over the Excess Profits Tax, the Plymouth Society also became embroiled in a dispute with the Co-operative Wholesale Society (CWS) over an accounting practice known as 'invoicing through'. These difficulties can only have been exacerbated by the physical distance between Plymouth and the centre of the co-operative movement in Manchester, made worse by wartime disruptions to transport. Moreover, the continued expansion of the society's activities helped to reduce the dependency on the Manchester institutions. By the end of the war, in addition to its seven new grocery stores, Plymouth Co-operative Society had also extended its productive capabilities, acquiring its own farm, milk depot, and coal ship, and expanding its bakery and sausage and jam factories. Other activities developed by 1918 included life assurance, a legal aid scheme to assist members campaigning against high rents, a Junior Comrades organisation for children, holiday homes and a summer school, and co-operative kitchens and dining rooms for the use of members. By the end of the war, co-operative leaders were portraying their society and its activities as a co-operative island in a sea of competition, and even extending this analogy to Plymouth as a whole, noting that the society was the second largest employer in Plymouth after the state-owned dockyard. This sense of isolation, and independence from connections with the wider movement, is also distinguishable in the steps to formalise the 'fusion of forces', from 1917.

III

Although they followed the national debate with interest, Plymouth co-operators took their own steps towards political action independently of the Co-operative Congress at Swansea in July 1917. In April that year a joint committee, consisting of trade unionists and the management committee of Plymouth Co-operative Society, met in order to agree a provisional constitution for a new local body devoted to seeking independent labour representation. Following this initial meeting a conference of delegates representing local trade unions and the co-operative society voted all but unanimously to form the Plymouth and District Labour and Co-operative Representation Association (LCRA). The various organisations involved spent the summer consulting their members via branch meetings, before the new organisation was launched with a major demonstration in August. The association organised itself quickly: by September 1917, 30 trade union branches and independent labour organisations had affiliated, and local ward organisations had been formed, spurred on by the conflict which had arisen over the Food Control Committee, and the joint demonstrations organised as part of this campaign. Prospective candidates for the next municipal elections were selected and it was also agreed to contest all three parliamentary seats.

According to its provisional constitution the aim of the LCRA was the election of working-class representatives to public bodies. Some co-operators continued to insist that the LCRA was born of necessity, a pragmatic response to the wartime trials inflicted on the movement by the government. Perhaps seeking to reassure the more cautious members of the society, T W Mercer wrote that,

> In other circumstances, the arguments [against political representation] would be unanswerable... It is because the politicians have become the catspaws of private trading interests that we now demand direct representation in the House of Commons. Co-operation is independent of State help, and Co-operators scorn State patronage, but is it expected that we should look on whilst our enemies shape a weapon to destroy us?... We still believe that voluntary Co-operation transcends State collectivism, but 'New occasions teach new duties.'[54]

For others, however, the formation of the LCRA was driven by a more ambitious aim, to found a united working-class party, which would work for the 'complete emancipation of the people'.[55] At its first quarterly meeting in December 1917, the LCRA was described as a 'People's Party', a step towards overcoming the 'demon of division' which had hitherto prevented workers from gaining political representation.[56] Division in this sense meant not only the traditional party divisions, but also splits within the labour movement, between trade unionist and co-operator. For co-operators and trade unionists alike, the 'fusion of forces' was probably in part a conscious attempt to overcome the lingering bitterness resulting from a drawn out conflict between the Co-operative Society and its employees. In April 1915 the Dockers' Union, which organised many co-operative employees, made a claim for a three-shilling increase in their weekly pay. The demand was referred to an Advisory Board set up by the Plymouth Trades Council to liaise with the Co-operative Society, but during negotiations the other union involved in the dispute, the Amalgamated Union of Co-operative Employees (AUCE), raised the demand to five shillings a week. The negotiations broke down and in September both unions began an eleven week strike, with the AUCE complaining that, 'craftsmen on the Co-operative Management Committee, earning good money themselves in the Dockyard, were prepared to "sweat" the Co-operative employees in order to maintain a good "divi".[57] The conflict was resolved when the society agreed to pay nationally agreed trade union rates in all its departments.

The formation of the LCRA was thus seen as a means to overcome the bitterness engendered by this conflict, not only between the Co-operative Society and its employees, but also between different trade unions. The Plymouth Trades Council had voted by twenty-one votes to fourteen to support the Co-op's position in the conflict, and had thus distanced itself both from the Dockers' Union and the AUCE. The latter had in any case seceded from the Trades Council in 1915, without discharging its financial obligations.[58] It is not clear, from the sources which are available, from where the initiative for the 'fusion of forces' plan came, but the names of many of those who took part are familiar as pre-war activists in the Trades Council, the different trade union branches and the LRA, as well as the Co-operative Society. The association was to be composed of delegates from local trade unions, the Co-operative Society and the Co-operative Guilds, and other local labour and socialist organisations, together with associate members who agreed to abide by the association's rules. Although political representation was to be the main goal, there were also proposals to take the fusion of forces beyond the LCRA, through for example trade union branches investing their surpluses in the Co-op in preference to other funds.[59] The support for the LCRA was taken as evidence for the extent to which conditions of war had broken down the sectional rivalries within the wider labour movement. According to one co-operative speaker, 'it was hardly fair to assume that the Co-operative Movement had come into politics simply because of the taxation of its dividends. For years men of ideas, who stood for democratic culture and the education of the masses, had worked for the day when Co-operators and Trade Unionists would act together.'[60]

There remained, however, some disagreements over the precise nature of the LCRA's relationship with the national Labour Party. For some co-operators, the pre-war uncertainty over the exact meaning of independent labour representation had still not been satisfactorily resolved. Was the new organisation in fact a distinct political party with its own programme, or did it draw its main rationale from its independence from party? At the district meetings held in the summer of 1917 to approve the new LCRA several co-operators expressed their reservations about the ideological direction of the new organisation. One member condemned a scheme which, he claimed, 'excluded everybody except the Socialist and the Labour man who adopted the Socialist programme.' Another member, 'enquired if the Association would embrace all Labour bodies, including the section represented by men of the Philip Snowden and Ramsay MacDonald type. If so, he would have nothing whatever to do with it in any shape or form.'[61] Even though the Parliamentary Labour Party had been instrumental in securing the co-operative exemption from the EPT through its amendment to the Finance Act, there was still some dissatisfaction with the record of the Labour Party in the co-operative ranks. Mercer, in a lecture to the society, gave his view that, '[a]ffiliation with the national Labour Party, so ardently desired by enthusiasts who hoped to bring about a fusion of forces, was not yet desirable, for the record of that Party was not encouraging, nor did the spectacle of Mr John Hodge as the first Minister for Labour inspire confidence.'[62] At the district meetings organised by the Co-operative Society, the proposed LCRA constitution was thus amended to exclude the obligation of members to conform with the national Labour Party rules. The trade union representatives objected to this, and a compromise was agreed whereby delegates had to be eligible for Labour Party membership (i.e. not members of any other party), but no steps to formal affiliation were taken.[63] Five months later, however, this position had changed, and an LCRA meeting 'heavily endorsed' the proposal to affiliate formally to the Labour Party.[64]

The ambivalence within the Co-op was reflected by similar attitudes among those on the Labour side. The Trades and Labour Council had affiliated to the Labour Party in 1906, and from 1913, both Plymouth and Devonport were listed as having local Labour Parties affiliated to the national Labour Party. In September 1917, the LCRA applied for affiliation, its application endorsed by a letter from the Plymouth Trades and Labour Council waiving their right to affiliate in favour of the new body.[65] The Labour Party committee which dealt with the matter, however, declared that it was unable to accept the affiliation since the title of the association, and its rules for candidature and the organisation of individuals, were not in harmony with the national rules. It resolved that, if necessary, a deputation should be sent to Plymouth to secure a satisfactory arrangement. This decision was endorsed by the National Executive Committee (NEC).[66] There is no evidence to suggest whether or not the proposed visit ever actually took place, but only a month later the NEC resolved to accept the application for affiliation from the LCRA, without, apparently, requiring it to change either its name or its rules.[67] The Labour Party's Annual Conference Report for January 1918 suggested that there were two affiliated Labour organisations in Plymouth: the LCRA, and the Labour Party, which, incidentally, paid only half the subscription rate of the LCRA. The following year, this second organisation had disappeared, and the LCRA stood alone as the sole affiliated organisation.

The precise nature of the relationship between the national Labour Party and the local representatives of the movement in Plymouth is therefore not clear. The LCRA was formed in response to a local situation, independently of either the Co-operative Union or the Labour Party. The main initiative seems to have come from the Plymouth Co-operative Society, although there were also those in the society who staunchly opposed the development. One of these argued that for most members political allegiance to the traditional political parties would over-ride their support for co-operation, and that it was therefore pointless to campaign for political representation. Exclude these members from the equation, not to mention the 45,000 women members who had no vote, and,

> You are confronted with this situation, that not the slightest argument, nor the strongest argument, will have any weight in diverting the Chancellor from the path he is pursuing. It is useless you going forward unless you are backed up by a considerable number of votes, and after you have taken from your ranks those I have mentioned [Liberals, Conservatives and women], what have you left?... [W]here are you going to get the force which is to alter the law? I say the whole thing is futile and tin-pot and you are beating your heads against a stone wall, and, in addition, wasting money.[68]

In August 1918 opponents of the LCRA attempted to suspend publication of the society's weekly publication, *The Co-operator*, which they argued was, 'the most untruthful publication which had disgraced the printing presses of Plymouth within the last quarter of a century.'[69] The motive was ostensibly the wartime shortage of paper, but there seems little question that the real reason stemmed from political objections. At a meeting to discuss the Educational Committee's half yearly report the following month, the question of political affiliation was raised again, in the form of challenges firstly to the committee's affiliation to the Fabian Research Department, and secondly to the involvement with the LCRA. The chairman of the committee defended their actions, stating that '[t]he Education Committee were not afraid of the word "Socialism". What they were concerned about was that the Society, through them, should be in touch with all progressive elements in the town. They thought affiliation with other organisations was helpful to the Society, and proposed to continue the policy which they had adopted.'[70] Opponents to political action objected that the decision to form the LCRA was unconstitutional; its supporters, including the President himself, responded that the matter had been conducted entirely properly.[71] As so often in co-operative debates, both sides sought to justify their position in relation to that most sacred of co-operative icons, the Rochdale pioneers. In the words of one member, '[they] had decided in a constitutional way to adopt a certain course, and until that decision had been altered, they, as loyal Co-operators, should support it. They had passed through four years of war, in which the Co-operative Movement had been very severely tried, with the result that they decided upon political action. They were out to realise the ideals of the Rochdale Pioneers, who built far better than they knew.'[72]

Despite this dissent, the views of the leadership, as presented through the society's organs, were united in their view of the significance of the new movement. The formation of the LCRA was seen as symptomatic of the emergence of a new type of politics, resulting from the conditions of war, and the general breakdown in established party alignments. Those who dissented were frequently portrayed, or indeed caricatured, by their opponents as an older generation out of touch with the spirit of an extraordinary age. These political changes were partly the result of the extension of the franchise and the redistribution of seats, but were also attributed to the politicisation of new issues: the prices of basic goods, wages, rents and taxes.[73] Moreover, it was not merely working *men* who were part of the new politics; there was also growing recognition of the changing role for women as political actors. Within the co-operative movement the Women's Co-operative Guild had broken new ground in establishing the principle that married women, who made up the bulk of their membership, had interests which were quite distinct from those of their husbands and indeed of single women.[74] What was new in the context of war, was that, instead of being confined to the Guild, women's half of the partnership was extended to embrace the whole movement. T W Mercer summed up this view when he wrote that, 'a new generation of Co-operators find that they cannot separate the wage-earner from the wage-spender, for he is one and the same person. In both the Co-operative and the Trade Union camps opinion is ripening as men realise that those whom industry has joined should not be put asunder.'[75] The direct reference to the marital partnership was underpinned by a sense of the correctness of women's role as wage-spenders, which would lead them automatically to defend their interests as consumers. Thus, women were expected to take a particular interest in the Excess Profits Tax, and much of the society's campaigning against the tax was directed specifically at them.

The increasing likelihood that women would be partly enfranchised after the end of the war added further impetus to this view. Some co-operators pointed to the emergence of a new, separate 'feminine' politics, a politicising of certain issues, such as the household and the family, which were identified as being situated particularly and inevitably within the sphere of women's interests.[76] Moreover, women's distinctiveness as voters rested not only on their supposed interest in certain issues, but also on their disassociation from any supposedly negative ties with political parties. This 'freedom from party' led some co-operators to suggest that women consumers were more likely to respond to political solutions for co-operative grievances. Some of the more forthright women within the Plymouth Society were even prepared to suggest that men had delayed the inevitable fusion of forces by their refusal to abandon traditional political allegiances.[77] As one co-operator put it:

> [W]e shall be surprised if women pay much heed to the sophistries of Tweedledum and Tweedledee. Working-women will be too wise to accept political shadows as a substitute for economic substance. When women vote they will vote for the things they want as housewives and wage-spenders, for high wages and low prices, and the things that vitally concern them as women.[78]

The prominence allocated to the role of women in co-operation emerged largely during the course of the war. Before the war, the Plymouth Co-operative Society took no especial notice of women's concerns. The attached branches of the Women's Co-operative Guild were mainly concerned with the familiar women's work of administering charitable relief on behalf of the society, while the various committees involved with the day-to-day management of the business affairs of the society were for the most part run by men, albeit with a few notable exceptions. Similarly, only a handful of women took a prominent role in events outside Plymouth, attending regional and national conferences as delegates of the society. What differed in comparison with the later period is the lack of any attempt to represent women in particular as the main consumers, and therefore as the main participants in co-operation. The experience of the war had changed that, firstly by politicising matters commonly regarding as belonging to the women's sphere, such as the distribution of basic foodstuffs, and secondly through enfranchising some women. It is now necessary to turn to the first election in which women were allowed to vote, in 1918.

IV

Despite the controversy over Plymouth Co-operative Society's engagement in political action, the immediate outcome was the full involvement of the society in the 1918 general election. The Plymouth constituencies had been re-organised since the previous parliamentary elections in 1910, and the two double member borough constituencies replaced by three single member divisions: Sutton, Drake and Devonport. It was originally hoped that Labour would be able to contest all three seats, but it proved possible to put up candidates in only two, Sutton and Devonport. Nonetheless, this was the first time Labour had contested any parliamentary elections in Plymouth, and as such it marked a major breakthrough. The decision not to contest Drake was partly due to the extreme haste with which the election was called, barely a month after the armistice was signed. Commentators of all political persuasions acknowledged the difficulties that this posed: the shortage of election agents and helpers, the reduced election expenditure available to most candidates, and the scarcity of petrol and paper.[79] An additional uncertainty was created by the Representation of the People Act, which had become law in February 1918, and had effectively introduced universal male suffrage by relaxing the residential qualifications for male voters, and removing the poor law disqualification. Further, it enfranchised men aged 19 or 20 who were on active service, and, perhaps most significantly, nearly 8.5 million women voters over the age of 30, who were either married to local government electors, or qualified as local government electors in their own right. Although this left five million women still without the vote, the legislation had a profound impact on the composition of the electorate, and more than doubled the overall number of voters, from 8 million to 21 million. As well as the uncertainty for the parties of how these new voters were likely to behave at the polls, there was the additional difficulty that the haste with which the election was called meant that many new electors, both male and female, remained effectively disenfranchised because they were unable to register to vote in time.

These constraints presented a considerable burden for the new and untested electoral machinery of the LCRA. Reflecting on his experiences a week after the poll (but before the votes had been counted), the LCRA agent for Sutton, T W Mercer, wrote that even 24 hours before the adoption meeting he had had 'no idea' that he would be called upon to become election agent.[80] The 'scandalous haste' with which the election was 'rushed upon us' had left no time to construct an organisation. The campaign was forced to rely almost exclusively on voluntary help, with only one full-time helper and no paid clerks or messengers. More importantly, there were only rudimentary ward organisations, and thus no possibility of conducting a full canvass. Indeed, it seems that the question of whether to contest Sutton at all hung in the balance, once the Liberals had confirmed that they were fielding a candidate in the division. Might it not be better for the LCRA to contest Drake instead, or even to concentrate resources on what was thought to be the most likely of the three, Devonport?[81] Speaking at the post-election LCRA rally, Mercer accepted principal responsibility for opting to contest Sutton, and claimed that his insistence was justified.

> Devonport did well, and he, of course, rejoiced in it. But the point was that against an exceptionally strong candidate – not an old man whose name was a byword and whose public speech a thing of scorn – against wealth and great influence, Labour with a local man, 'Old Bill Gay' – (applause) – received over 20 per cent. of the poll. Whereas in Devonport, Labour secured less than 20 per cent. That, then, was his justification for fighting Sutton.[82]

The satisfaction expressed by Mercer in outperforming the Labour candidate in Devonport (the margin of difference was in fact very small:

Labour got 19.3% of the vote in Devonport, and 20.6% in Sutton) perhaps reflected the different backgrounds of the Labour candidates and Labour campaigns in question. Labour's candidate in Sutton was a local man, W T Gay, who was an employee of the Co-operative Society, and could doubtless draw on some degree of personal loyalty, at least among the most active members of the society. The Devonport candidate, meanwhile was Fred Bramley, who was a professional Labour activist and trade unionist who appears not to have had any connection with the constituency at all. He was a member of the Parliamentary Committee of the TUC, and gave his address as Camden on his nomination papers. Co-operative speakers presented the dual candidature of Bramley and Gay as an example of the fusion of forces – Bramley the trade unionist and Gay the co-operator – but Labour's political opponents alleged that Gay's candidature had provoked serious divisions within the local labour movement.[83] The Liberal candidate for Sutton, Captain Ransom, claimed that it was 'an open secret that one powerful Labour organisation with considerable voting strength in Sutton has up to the present declined to accord him their support,' probably a reference to the 1915 conflict between the Co-operative Society on one side and the Dockers' Union and AUCE on the other.[84] This allegation was strenuously denied by George Neilson of the Dockers' Union, who appeared on Gay's election platform to be greeted with cheers and declare that, '[i]t has been stated that Labour is not anxious for the return of either Mr Bramley or Mr Gay. This platform gives the lie to that statement. The Labour Movement of Plymouth recognises its responsibilities, and is prepared to fulfil them. Mr Dan Hillman and myself are here to show where we stand in this fight, and we are prepared to use all our efforts to see that our members vote Labour.'[85] Gay stated publicly that he was the 'authorised candidate' of the Labour Party, and his agent referred to the strength of this 'new Labour Movement that has been created here in Plymouth'.[86] Gay and Bramley shared a platform throughout the campaign, and both were supported by Arthur Henderson on his visit to Plymouth just before the poll.

Of the four retiring Unionist members who had represented the Plymouth constituencies since 1910, three re-contested the new divisions. In Devonport, the candidate was the veteran Sir Clement Kinloch-Cooke, whose name had appeared regularly in the parliamentary reports as an advocate of dockyard interests. Introducing his candidature, the

Tory newspaper the *Western Morning News* described his efforts on behalf of the constituency as 'indefatigable', and reported that, as founder of the Dockyards Members' Committee, he had 'never neglected to press with all his force matters affecting the services and Dockyards.'[87] Although there is no surviving evidence of written election addresses aimed specifically at the dockyard workers, Kinloch-Cooke did use his platform speeches to emphasise his record on dockyard matters. The Unionist candidate for Sutton, Major Waldorf Astor, had, like Kinloch-Cooke, held his seat since 1910, and was a prominent figure in the constituency. The Astors' success in Sutton, that of both Waldorf and his wife Nancy who succeeded him, was undoubtedly due in part to their willingness to devote part of their considerable personal wealth towards 'nursing' the constituency.[88]

All the Unionist candidates contested the election as the 'couponed' candidates of the Coalition. By declaring their support for Lloyd George, they could claim the patriotic 'country before party' slogan of the pre-war period. Indeed, all three candidates emphasised this very point at both their adoption meetings and their eve of poll rallies. They had been sent to Parliament as Conservatives and Unionists, they argued, but had selflessly laid aside their party loyalties for the wider good of the country in its hour of need.[89] When Auckland Geddes visited Plymouth to support the Coalition campaign, he too was presented to the meeting as a non-party man, who had been brought in from outside by Lloyd George to carry out a particular role.[90] In response to this, the Liberal and Labour candidates argued for the necessity of restoring parliamentary government, the principles of which had been sacrificed for the sake of wartime expediency, and were being perpetuated through the Coalition. The Gladstonian slogan of 'Peace, Retrenchment, Reform' remained the rallying cry of west country Liberalism even after 1918.[91] The Liberal candidate for Devonport, Samuel Lithgow, stated that although he would not oppose Coalition policy on principle, electing him as a Coalition candidate would be the equivalent of sending him to Parliament gagged and bound.[92] His counterpart in Sutton, Captain Sidney Ransom, insisted that he had refused to 'barter his freedom' for 'a scrap of paper'.[93] The Marquis of Crewe, addressing the Liberal faithful on the eve of poll, decried the 'no party' slogan as false.[94] The point was also taken up by the Labour candidates. The Coalition rally with Auckland Geddes was described by one LCRA speaker as 'nothing more or less than a good old Tory affair', despite the Coalition's claims to place country before party.[95] Since the Labour Party had withdrawn from the Coalition immediately the election was called, it could no longer claim to be a Coalition worthy of the name, consisting merely of the Unionists and a certain faction of the Liberal Party. Writing in the *Co-operator,* Mercer declared that Labour was determined to have no part in Lloyd George's 'attempt to destroy our Parliamentary system of government… no National Coalition exists; and… none who hate "the old party politics" can possible support candidates pledged to establish the political dictatorship of a political adventurer of the worst type.'[96]

As the campaign progressed, however, these political points became increasingly submerged in an intensely personal focus on the different candidates, and their experiences of the war. The Sutton Liberals responded to attacks on the inadequacies of their leader Asquith by extolling the personality of their candidate. Captain Ransom had served as an electrical engineer in the armed forces for three and a half years during the war, and suggested that his experience of war and empathy with servicemen was one of the main reasons for seeking election.[97] At the start of the campaign, Ransom was commended by the Liberal press for his modest refusal to refer to his experience of the front, but as the campaign progressed it was to become the central plank of his campaign. Comparing the experience of himself and Major Astor, Ransom drew on his war experience as his trump card. He told his audience that, '[m]y records of the last four years are not to be found, I agree, in the archives of Downing-street, [a reference to Astor's work as MP and minister] but they are to be found in the aerodromes of France… It might have been more pleasant for me to spend the last four years in a Downing-street office: I preferred to spend them in France. – (applause).'[98] The implication was that whatever Major Astor's credentials in terms of patriotism and service to his country, his experience of the war lacked authenticity because he had not actually participated in active combat. By contrast, Ransom could claim empathy with the servicemen whose votes he sought because, as a combatant, he could claim to understand their views and needs. This empathy could serve as a counter to many political charges, and he was prepared to exploit it to the full, to the apparent approval of his audience:

> According to the speech made by Major Astor last night, I am not an honourable man. – ('Shame') He says my methods are the meth-

ods of the Hun. I pass such a despicable insult. – (applause) For-
tunately or unfortunately, I have had much more knowledge of
what the Huns are than Major Astor has. – ('True')[99]

The candidates' reliance on the public meeting as the main method
of campaigning during this election was perhaps suited to the highly emotional language used, particularly with reference to the post-
war fate of the Kaiser. The Coalition rally with Auckland Geddes was
a spectacle of patriotic music and flag-waving, where, 'Sir Auckland…
stated amid prolonged cheering that the Kaiser and his satellites must
stand upon their trial before a tribunal which if the verdict be guilty
would pass sentence of death.'[100] The Coalition campaign was given
a further boost only days before the poll: the entry into Plymouth
Sound of two captured German submarines, escorted by a procession
of about thirty vessels engaged in the anti-U-boat campaign.

The two Labour candidates found themselves at a severe disadvan-
tage, accused by the Coalition of sharing the antithesis to the 'authentic' wartime experience of active service: the stigma of pacifism.
Major Astor, addressing a Primrose League meeting, made an explicit connection between bolshevism, pacifism and the Labour Party:

> The other day Mr Gay expressed doubt whether England was right
> or wrong in standing by France and Belgium. If that was Mr Gay's
> view he had come to the wrong place when he offered himself as
> candidate at Plymouth. He fancied the electors would remind Mr
> Gay that had Mr Snowden and Mr MacDonald had their way the
> German navy would not now be safely and quietly tucked away
> in English harbours, that the Kaiser would still be on his throne,
> and that the women of Lille would still be slaves in Germany. We
> did not want men of that type to reconstruct the country. They
> used to be in favour of peace by negotiation. Trotsky and the Bol-
> sheviks tried that, with the result that the Germans did the Rus-
> sians in. Thank heaven we had a Government which prevented
> the Trotskys of this country letting us be done in – (applause).[101]

The taunt of pacifism rested not on personal experience, but on association with the ILP. Gay, it was suggested by the *Western Morning
News,* 'chiefly represents an extreme and somewhat discredited section
of the great Labour party – the ILP, which never at any time command-
ed any considerable measure of support from the more sober-minded
workers in Plymouth, and certainly not during the war, when the paci-

fist edge of its character has become so discreditably prominent.'[102] Gay responded that he was 'not ashamed' to be a member of the ILP.[103] He denied strenuously that he had been a conscientious objector, but responded to the charge of patriotism by attempting to rise above it. The labour movement, he suggested, 'was the only movement that recognised the sacredness of human life. No wonder it was said that the Labour movement was a pacifist movement. They did not believe in the destruction of human life, nor in the man who hurrahed for his own country and for the destruction of another. He believed in all that was just in the world.'[104] His colleague Bramley, however, responded to the allegations of 'shirking', betrayal and cowardice in a way that suggested he was stung by the taunts. He announced his readiness to, 'box, wrestle, or run either of his opponents' in an attempt to defend his *personal* integrity against the charge against him, and more importantly against his masculinity.[105] The only truly authentic experience of war was blood and gore: those who had avoided it had failed to reach an ideal of masculinity, and were by definition lesser men. In contrast to the dashing Captain Ransom, 'a splendid type of British manhood, perfectly frank and open-hearted, a man of arresting speech and magnetic personality', Bramley was portrayed as a 'Pacifist and a Bolshevik, and generally a spineless and sentimental creature.'[106] In the extremely militarised environment of December 1918, the gap in consciousness between those who had experienced active service and those who had not came to dominate the public discourse. For Captain Ransom, soldiers, sailors and airmen were his colleagues, and 'he could use no claptrap electioneering phrases about them.'[107] Taunted that he had no connections at all with Plymouth, he responded, 'at any rate I may at least say that I have done my bit for my country... I have wounds which I shall carry to my grave.'[108] Even a woman like Nancy Astor, although obviously a non-combatant, could legitimately claim some first-hand knowledge through her involvement with nursing the wounded at a makeshift hospital set up in her home at Cliveden. William Gay, meanwhile, was engaged in the distinctly unglamorous work of managing a co-operative boot factory.

Co-operators did not forget that the main reason for their involvement in the campaign was the wartime experience of conflicts over consumer issues. In Sutton at least, Labour was quick to issue election placards casting the 'profiteer' as an alternative villain to the Kaiser and the Hun, and the President of Plymouth Co-operative Society,

W H Watkins, appeared on Gay's election campaign to remind voters about the local campaign against the Excess Profits Tax.[109] Nationally, the National Co-operative Representation Committee (NCRC) endorsed ten official co-operative candidates, and prepared test questions for other constituencies. The 'new politics' of food and consumer affairs was thought to be one area at least where Labour could appeal to newly enfranchised women voters. 'Woman is the Chancellor of the Exchequer of the home', declared the Labour Party's manifesto.[110] Domestic economy could easily be translated into political economy, and the intimate knowledge women were thought to have of this sphere reflected the way in which only the men truly understood the trenches. As the *Co-operative News* put it, '[w]hile their brothers, husbands, and sons, have been away fighting, [women] have had to fend for themselves, and they know even better than the men how prices have soared, and how hard it has been to make ends meet.'[111]

For Fred Bramley, however, who did not share Gay's close ties with the co-operative movement, the profiteering issue could not be separated from the war rhetoric discussed above. In condemning monopolists and profiteers he made reference not to the women who had queued, but to 'Tommy's babe [which] had been dying in slums in order to swell the abnormal profits of the agricultural interests.'[112] He pledged, somewhat melodramatically, that, '[w]hen he had secured the same comforts for the worker's baby as were enjoyed by Lady Gwendoline's pampered poodle, he would retire. While society ladies were extravagantly indulging expensive Pekingnese poodles, starving children in the East End were picking rotten fruit fallen from costers' barrows.'[113] Inequality was represented as a gendered issue. Upper- and middle-class women were condemned in two respects: for their class and unequal share of wealth, and also for their idleness, which took on a new aspect in the context of war. Men of the same class were irreproachable in one respect at least, they had taken part in active service, they had endured privations, many of them had fallen. For Bramley, women of the same class represented as heinous a war crime as the conscientious objectors did for his opponents: they were frivolous, extravagant, distracting from the war effort in their pursuit of luxury. The main victims of the inequalities engendered by their profligacy were not working-class women themselves, but their children and their soldier husbands.

Thus, even if there was a political sphere which was recognisably women's domain, even if women's active participation in politics could be construed as a chance for women to apply their particular expertise to national political economy, then this was still a sphere in which women's experiences were mediated through their relationships to men. The editor of the *Western Morning News* noted that the Coalition candidates needed to concentrate on winning women's votes by drawing attention to the policies in the election programme thought to be of especial interest to women: housing, public health, education. Major Astor's record of service on issues such as TB, milk, housing and infant mortality, concluded the paper, should make him popular with the 'wives and mothers' of Sutton.[114] Sir Clement Kinloch-Cooke announced at his adoption meeting that the first priority of social reform was the compensation of the wounded and dependants.[115] Women's concern with social reform stemmed not from their own interests, but from their interests as wives and mothers. Just as they were asked to vote on the peace settlement in terms of their positions as dependants of those who had fought, they were invited to vote for social reform with this in mind too. Women's role as the defender and propagator of the race (as opposed to the nation) was vital to the regeneration of the country in the aftermath of the war, and although it was not mentioned in so many words, to the replenishment of the thousands of men killed or maimed. Even Margaret Llewellyn Davies, national secretary of the Women's Co-operative Guild, urged women to take an interest in politics on account of those for whom they were responsible.

> Let no wife, or mother, or any woman say that voting is no concern of hers. What! Do not her husband's wages and hours of work, unemployment, and pension affect her? Are not comfortable homes her concern? Should she have no say as regards the education of her children? Has she no interest in prices, in taxes, in profiteering? Does she not want to help the sweated workers, the poor in workhouses and all the sufferers from poverty, not with charity, but with justice? Does she not want to abolish War off the face of the earth altogether?[116]

Despite the attempt to promote an alternative politics based on the wartime experiences of food shortages and hardship, what seemed to matter ultimately was the candidates' personal experiences of the war, and neither Gay nor Bramley was able to escape the taunt of pacifism. In a highly personalised campaign, Gay in particular seemed to be hindered by his unwillingness, or indeed inability, to respond to the allegations and engage in the campaign in the same emotional, deeply personal level of the other candidates. His addresses on the 'sacredness of human life' and the value of education reflected his background as a self-educated co-operator, typical of many within the movement. Equally typical, perhaps, was the frustration expressed by these earnest autodidacts when it appeared that despite their efforts many poorer voters found the glamour of the Astors the more attractive proposition. Speaking at the LCRA rally immediately after the election, Gay summed up these views:

> He had seen the deplorable spectacle at Palace Court of men and women being brought to vote and told how to vote. These people were victims of the present social system, the victims of ignorance, the victims of oppression. They had to be helped and developed. Into dark places they must throw the searchlight of education, and enable men to realise the dignity of manhood, women to realise the dignity of womanhood, each walking to the poll with head erect to exercise a sacred trust (applause). From now onward they must organise and educate these people to revolt by constitutional methods against the oppression under which they suffered, carrying to them the gospel of truth and of light.[117]

Even before the result was announced, Mercer had cast doubt on the ability of the Labour campaign to penetrate into the poorer districts:

> In Sutton, self-respecting working-men and women voted for the Labour man last Saturday. It was the middle-class residents of Mannamead and Compton and the submerged tenth who dwell in Vintry Ward who voted for Major Astor and Lloyd George… On the morning of the poll, the polling station at Palace Street Schools resembled the Pool of Siloam. At the very moment when the star performer of the Coalition was denouncing me as a villain who preached hate and stirred up strife, the aged poor – halt, maimed and crippled – were being brought up in carriages and motor cars from the slums of Vintry Ward to vote against the interests of the working-class. The unorganised and uninstructed workers, the rack-rented and sweated women of Vintry Ward were conveyed to the polls to vote for the millionaire! In the light of that fact, all other memories of the fight are insignificant… Organised Labour must organise those who cannot organise themselves. The Ply-

mouth Co-operative Society must take help to those who cannot achieve self-help. Sutton will be won for Labour when the workers of Plymouth fight the rack-renters and slum-owners of Vintry Ward.[118]

V

The scale of Labour's defeat in 1918 was heavy, but even so, the post-election meeting of the LCRA was an upbeat affair. It was, after all, the first time Labour had contested any parliamentary constituency in Plymouth, and in gaining 20% of the poll their reaction was, in public at least, that they had performed better than expected.[119] 'Rome was not built in a day,' was Mercer's conclusion. 'The lesson of this election is that a change has taken place in the character of British politics.'[120] It was thought that the decision of the Co-operative Society to throw the full weight of its support behind the campaign, by voting in its December meeting to pledge whatever support was appropriate to the LCRA candidates, had undoubtedly been the crucial influence in securing this breakthrough.[121] By the beginning of 1919, however, there were some signs of a shift within the society. At the end of 1918 T W Mercer left Plymouth to take up a new position with the Co-operative Union, a natural move for a young and gifted co-operative activist. The loss of his energy and commitment must have been a blow for the supporters of political action. It is not clear whether Mercer acted as agent in a his own capacity, or as part of his duties as an employee of Plymouth Co-operative Society, but there was however some feeling that debate on the matter had been stifled. When the report of the delegates to the LCRA was debated in February 1919, one member made the point that, '[t]his was the first opportunity any of the Co-operators, who were not Socialists, had had to protest against the action of the Co-operative Society at the General Election.' In a reference to the forthcoming internal elections within the society, the same speaker declared that, '[t]hey were walking a perilous path, and there must be a surprise packet for them in April. If that were so, short work would be made of this Socialist intrigue to use the money of Co-operators for what was really not Labour at all... And yet those behind this political movement called themselves democrats! It was coercion, and he warned them that they were endangering the future of the Society.'[122]

The internal elections, in the spring of 1919, did indeed result in some change in the management of the society. Perhaps most significantly, there was a new president, J Hayne Pillar, who represented a different strand within the movement since, in addition to his co-operative activities, he had also served as a Liberal member of Plymouth Borough Council since 1905. He was still a councillor during the war, although there is no mention of his activities within the Co-operative Society at the time of the conflict over the Food Control Committee. Pillar's voice was absent from the various debates on political representation before 1919, but another Liberal, and one of the strongest and most consistent critics of the LCRA, Mr Carling, was elected as chairman of the Education Committee at the same poll. One of Carling's first actions in his new role was his refusal to let the Committee's rooms to the LCRA for a meeting, acting, he claimed, in accordance with the mandate given him by the members who had supported him.[123] The quarterly meeting decided, by a majority of 356, to instruct the Education Committee to let the rooms, but there was now every sign that a damaging rift was deepening within the society. One prominent co-operator seems to have spoken for many when he stated that, '[h]e was sick to death of the nagging and bickering going on, and was anxious that the Society should drop its petty quarrelling and step out upon a higher plane and get on with the business.'[124]

The debate simmered on throughout the summer. A members' meeting on 10th April confirmed Watkins' nomination as the LCRA's prospective parliamentary candidate for Devonport, and the management committee agreed unanimously to support him. Meanwhile, the LCRA's opponents sought to overturn affiliation on the grounds that it was unconstitutional under the society's rules.[125] Supporters argued that since affiliation had been agreed through voting at constitutional district meetings of members, and confirmed at a special meeting, it could therefore only be rescinded by members at a special meeting. Opponents then questioned the legitimacy of paying affiliation fees, but on this point the legal advice from both the Society's own solicitors and the Registrar of Friendly Societies seemed to be on the side of the supporters of political action. They were also encouraged by the ruling on the case brought by five members of the Barrhead Co-operative Society, trying to prevent that society from spending money in promoting co-operative candidates in local elections. The presiding judge, Lord Ormidale, 'expressed the opinion that all Societies registered under the Industrial and Provident Societies Acts could apply sums of money taken from the profits for any purposes whatever, provided that a properly formed rule gave them the necessary power to do so. This being the case, all that any Society desiring to take political action need to do is to see that its rules are properly drafted.'[126]

The matter was bound to come to a head, however, and did so at a special meeting of members in October 1919, called to consider a General Committee proposal to alter the rules, that is to disaffiliate the society from the LCRA. The meeting was reported to be very well attended. LCRA supporters wore red buttonholes to declare their allegiance, and draped the balcony with banners bearing the legends, 'Labour saved you £47,000' and, 'Fight the Profiteers, not one another.'[127] The mover of the resolution made the point yet again that affiliation had been decided on by a very small number of members, at a time when many others were away fighting in the war. Even so, the district meetings had originally voted to reject affiliation with the Labour Party, so it was surprising that six months later this had been agreed. The proposed amendment was defeated by 668 votes to 332, and two prominent pro-Labour co-operators, J J H Moses and Mr Prince, spoke afterwards of their hopes that the meeting had finally decided the matter. Yet this was not to be the case. The following month the question of political affiliation was back on the agenda again, following a further refusal by the Education Committee to let its lecture hall to the Plymouth Trade Union, Socialist and and Co-operative Educational Alliance, ostensibly on the grounds that the meetings were to take place on a Sunday evening which was the caretaker's day off.[128] Once again the anti-political faction was defeated, and the minute sent back, this time by 260 votes to 53.

On the surface, the debate centred on the question of the management of the society during the war, and whether the formation the LCRA was constitutional. The real source of controversy concerned not merely the question of whether the Co-operative Society should be involved with politics, but the wider question of its relationship with the Labour Party. The incoming president, J Hayne Pillar, summed up the position of those who felt that the movement for political representation had gone too far. 'We have to admit that there are times when democratic associations have to take a stand to safeguard their own interests,' he said. 'There was such an occasion when the question of excess profits was being dealt with by the Government.

A stand had to be made to prevent an imposition on the movement. That stand was made, but somehow or other the Plymouth Society was led perhaps a little farther than was really anticipated at the out-set.'[129] Political action in itself to defend the interests of the society was all very well, as long as it was confined within the movement. As another speaker put it, 'they were not averse to seeing a Co-operative member of Parliament, or a Co-operative member of any other organisation, but they held that the policy of the Co-operative Movement must be confined within its own ranks. If the members had to find the funds to do this work they must be able to call the tune and return the men they wanted. They did not want to be the milch cow for others to drain dry. They appealed to members in the cause of Co-operation to stand by the cause and the Committee would stand by them.' Others argued that the difficulty lay with Labour itself, and its ideological position, claiming that, '[i]t was not Labour with which they were affiliated, but with the Socialist group who had been carrying their shoes through while the Service-men were away.'[130] Meanwhile, for supporters of the LCRA, the dissenting voices were portrayed as those of old men, who had failed to move with the times and were out of touch with the contemporary political situation. Mr J T Davis, 'asked Mr Carling and Mr Wedlake not to think uncharitably of the younger school of Co-operators, who found themselves in the same position as both those gentlemen would have been in had they been confronted with similar conditions in their earlier life.'[131]

Supporters of the society's involvement with the LCRA could also point to the success of that organisation in political terms. The first post-war municipal elections, held in November 1919, also represented a significant advance for Labour. For the first time the party was able to contest every ward, and it won nine seats on the new amalgamated authority, a huge improvement on the very modest victories of the pre-war period. Particularly satisfying was the defeat of some of the LCRA's most prominent opponents in the conflict over the Food Control Committee. Labour performed more strongly in the Devonport wards than in Sutton, but nonetheless the results were thought to be encouraging for the Sutton parliamentary by-election, held less than twelve months after the general election in November 1919. The by-election was caused by Waldorf Astor's elevation to the peerage on the death of his father, and it excited considerable national interest once it was announced that the Coalition candidate would be Astor's wife

Nancy. It was widely assumed that Nancy's candidature would merely be a stop-gap, allowing her to keep the seat 'warm' for Waldorf until he was able to divest himself of the title and return to the Commons.[132] Even so, the prospect of her candidature caused some disquiet because of her commitment to temperance, and shortly after the announcement of the by-election, the possibility of an alternative candidate, Alderman Jacobs, was floated. Jacobs denied that he had allowed his name to go forward at the instigation of the licensing trade, but he nonetheless declared that, 'if the licensees support me I shall go for their support, because I believe in the working man having his glass of beer as well as the millionaire having his champagne.'[133] By 4th November, however, eleven days before the poll, Jacobs had confirmed that he did not intend to allow his name to go forward for nomination.

For the LCRA, the by-election offered an opportunity to consolidate the gains made in 1918 and at the recent municipal elections. The Labour candidate was once again William Gay, nominated by the LCRA, and supported by the main labour organisations in the town, including the Trades and Labour Council and most of the prominent trade unionists. The National Executive Committee of the Labour Party had made some tentative enquiries about introducing a candidate, and it was reported that Gay was willing to stand aside in this case, but they eventually decided that the seat would be better fought by a local candidate who had contested the constituency previously.[134] Despite this, and the show of unity at Gay's adoption meeting, it was thought likely that the internal rifts within Plymouth Co-operative Society would have some impact on Labour's campaign. The newspaper most hostile to the Labour cause, the Conservative *Western Morning News,* suggested that these differences had helped to delay the announcement of Gay's candidature, because of the question mark it placed over the funding of his campaign.[135] Labour activists were, however, quick to deny any suggestion that Co-operative Society funds were being used to support their campaign, maintaining instead that they were relying on voluntary donations. In this at least, they seemed to have been very successful, for the NEC's report on the by-election remarked on the 'splendid example' set by Plymouth in raising the full election costs of £634 through subscriptions and collections during the campaign.[136]

The Liberal Party candidate, Isaac Foot, was a young lawyer from a prominent west country Liberal family. Although a native of Plymouth – a point which he did his best to emphasise during his campaign – Foot had unsuccessfully contested the Bodmin division in 1918. His politics amounted to a textbook statement of traditional Liberalism: 'a strengthened Opposition in the House, the defence of Parliamentary liberties, the restoration of the authority of the House of Commons, the stoppage of all waste, the return to solid finance and honest government, and fair play for all classes'.[137] Throughout his campaign, Foot and his supporters attempted to link these principles to a specifically west country and even Plymothian Radical tradition, with frequent references to the town's role in the civil war, and 'the great days when famous Westcountrymen like Pym and Eliot, Strode and Valentine fought for the liberties of Parliament against the King.'[138] In doing this, he implicitly compared his local origins with his American-born rival Nancy Astor, though there is no evidence that he attempted to use this against her directly. Yet Astor found her own way to draw a link between her own origins and the constituency, by drawing an analogy between herself and the Pilgrim Fathers, and challenged Foot on his own ground with her references to the political and religious liberties of the New World. As she put it, in a speech to a women's meeting, '[i]t is, after all, a very natural thing you should have a Virginian-born woman who lives in Devonshire. Virginia is the first offshoot from England, and I think it is only proper and right, if I do come back here, I ought to fight about the same things for which the Pilgrim Fathers went out. That is what it really amounts to.'[139] Foot's adherence to a 'classical' Liberal position also made it easy to portray him as a reactionary, who would seek to introduce out-dated party conflicts into a new political era. According to the Conservative *Western Morning News,* 'he stood as a reactionary, whose only idea was to turn the clock back to where it stood at the end of July, 1914, and ignore totally the great lesson of the war, namely, that we must sink minor differences and stand shoulder to shoulder together against the enemy, who is no longer the enemy without our gates, as in the war, but the enemy within, whose champion was Mr Gay, the spirit, that is, of class hatred, class selfishness, and class domination.'[140] Astor, like her husband in 1918, used her position as a Coalition candidate as proof of her freedom from party loyalties, a point which was emphasised by careful attempts to ensure that those who supported her on her platform represented as wide a variety of political position as possible.[141] She also exploited her position as a woman in this way, arguing that, '[a] woman in many cases has a more courageous and unfettered mind. She is not bound down by traditions; and as women have no political past they will have a clearer political future.'[142] Throughout the campaign she was to stress her independence of mind, illustrated partly by her unorthodox methods of electioneering, effectively negating the point made by the Liberals that there was a need for an effective opposition in Parliament.

The prospect of a woman contesting an eminently winnable seat meant that the Sutton by-election attracted an extraordinary amount of interest in the national press. Much of the coverage could only be described as trivial. Many hundreds of column inches were for example devoted to discussions of whether Astor would need to remove her hat once she entered the House of Commons. Astor did nothing to discourage this style of reporting. On the contrary, from early on in the campaign there was every sign that she intended to make the issue of 'personality' a central feature of her campaign, and the immense press interest in her dress and person suited this tactic perfectly. Undoubtedly she was also helped by the resources the Astors had been able to pour into the constituency since Waldorf had first contested the seat in 1910. The local habitation of the Primrose League, which they had revived to a point where it had 3,000 members, provided a solid grounding for the Unionists' organisation, and it was reported that large numbers of Primrose League members had helped to prepare the postal addresses and the polling card envelopes.[143] But in a relatively short campaign, it was Astor's extensive tours of the constituency, often in her motor car, and her impromptu exchanges with groups of voters which seemed to make the most impact. The press seized in particular on her visits to the poorer parts of the constituency around Sutton harbour, where she would pose for photographs on a trawler, or stop briefly to speak to small groups of voters, especially women.[144] She was reported to revel in engagements with hecklers, and the following report of an encounter with some fishermen would appear to be typical. Heckled about the slum conditions of the capitalist system, the exchange continued as follows (the heckles of the crowd in brackets):

> If you had no greed you would have no capitalism. ('You can't be greedy when you are poor.') If you took out of the hearts of all men and women all greed and selfishness, you need not have any laws. Greed is rampant among the capitalists and the poor. ('There

is a difference between the producer and the non-producer.') You have to have brains as well as hands. ('And a little of your greediness.') If you had what I had, you would not be standing here. ('Yes, I would, if I was as interested in your own class as you are.') I am not interested in my own class. I am interested in all classes. If you don't think I am honest and sincere, if you really think I am out to better myself, I implore you not to vote for me. (Applause.)[145]

Astor was also able to exploit her position as a woman candidate, by organising meetings for women only, where she addressed them in 'a homely fashion', which was reported to be extremely popular.[146] Many also suggested that the absence of men at these meetings allowed women to speak up, and engage with the candidate in a way that they might not normally have done. Astor's charity work in the constituency had also helped to raise her profile, especially among the poorer women. One reporter found, 'a quiet but sincere admiration of her ladyship's activities at the crèches and maternity centres,' of the constituency.[147] Although she denied that she was 'a woman's candidate', Astor nonetheless played on her sex, arguing that she had a natural empathy with the concerns of ordinary women. She made much of the fact that she was a mother herself, and suggested that '[s]ound practical national house-keeping is what we need,' for the national finances. Political economy 'was not a woman's province, and that would not be her job in the House of Commons. She was going there to put a different aspect on things. But she did pretend to have her own views on questions affecting women and children…'[148]

The evidence suggests that those involved in the Labour and Liberal campaigns felt a sense of frustration at Astor's style of campaigning, and the overwhelming focus on 'personality'. At her adoption meeting Astor announced openly that she did not intend to lay her detailed programme before the electorate, because 'they knew what she stood for'.[149] It was suggested that some in her own party had private reservations about her style. The *Morning Post,* which, like many of the national newspapers, interviewed Astor, reported that Waldorf 'switched his wife off' when any difficult or dangerous topic was broached.[150] This apparent determination to avoid serious debate was frustrating to the other candidates, who felt that their earnest attempts to engage with political principles and issues were therefore doomed to failure. For Labour supporters, the biggest source of frustration was

Astor's apparent success among the poorer inhabitants of the division, whom they might have regarded as their own constituency. In particular, just as in 1918, they were concerned to condemn what they saw as attempts to seduce working-class voters through charity and glamour. J J Moses, speaking at Gay's adoption meeting, suggested that Astor was a camouflage, a distraction:

> Attention was already being focused on the personality of Mrs Astor, and the photographers of the capitalistic Press were busy gathering together the children of the Barbican as a background for Mrs Astor's winning smile. (Laughter.) Sutton did not want blankets or coals, nor to have their children photographed at a tanner a time. Sutton did not intend to be sold for foreign gold, and they did not intend that Sutton should be libelled in that way. They meant to see behind the glamour of American millions.[151]

The act of kissing babies came to express Labour's distaste for Astor's campaigning style, as different speakers argued that socialism, not charity, was the only sound means of abolishing poverty.[152] Labour's biggest problem, however, seems to have been their candidate's lack of charisma, and his failure therefore to achieve anything like the personal popularity of his rival. Gay was summed up as 'a good debater, but not an inspiring platform man, because after the preliminary pleasantries he is inclined to get back to his textbooks, of which he is a diligent student, and talk over the heads of his audience. He makes no pretence to be content with trade unionism; Socialism is his creed, and he preaches it without hedging.'[153] The *Western Daily Mercury* described the Labour campaign as 'a dark and gloomy one, unrelieved by any sunshine or laughter', and characterised by Gay's 'earnest, closely-reasoned' speeches.[154] Astor herself was quite prepared to poke fun at the seriousness of the Labour candidate, caricaturing the 'young intellectuals' of the ILP as 'long-haired and wild-eyed men who were not working-men.'[155] The self-educated trade unionists and co-operators of the Labour Party were at a clear loss to know how to deal with this, and comforted themselves with the reflection that even if Labour failed to win then at least the educational work of the election would have been useful.[156]

Against this Labour made some attempt to win political support from concerns over the future of the dockyard and its workforce. It was clear that the dockyard's output would be forced to contract following the end of the war, and by May 1919, rumours had begun to circulate in Devonport of an imminent discharge of 5000 men from the dockyard. These were denied by the Admiralty, but few doubted that heavy discharges were unavoidable, and 1700 had been reported by the end of October 1919, with a projection of a further 2,200 by Christmas. Devonport escaped the fate of Pembroke and Rosyth dockyards, both of which were placed on a care and maintenance basis in 1926, but nonetheless the scale of the contraction had a considerable impact on local employment, and there remained many uncertainties surrounding the yard's long-term future. By late 1919, 6,000 men were without work in Plymouth, and dockyard discharges were expected to average 200 every week in the weeks leading up to Christmas. The discharges had caused major dissatisfaction, which might be expressed in a vote against the Coalition government.

Gay declared at his adoption meeting that the main plank of his platform was the maintenance of the dockyards 'in their full efficiency of staff'.[157] 'Sack the Coalition or be sacked' advised the Labour posters.[158] The problem for Labour was that they, and indeed any other politicians, were powerless to offer a solution to the problem. Both Labour and Liberals advocated the use of the dockyards to construct merchant ships, but with little apparent conviction. The predicament of the dockyard towns was recognised sympathetically by the Colwyn Committee, which reported in 1920 on the possibility of alternative uses for the dockyard infrastructure. In the words of the report:

> [W]e feel that this is a national emergency during the continuance of which it is the duty of the Admiralty to provide work in the Dockyard Towns for the men whom they retained and collected into their service during the war. It must be borne in mind that the Dockyard Towns depend almost entirely upon the Navy for their existence, and have incurred considerable expenditure in public utilities which cause a recurring charge on income, and that the Admiralty policy in the past has tended to discourage any extension of the Ports on commercial lines which might otherwise have taken place. It follows therefore, that these Towns have no immediate means of filling the gap caused by the decline of Admiralty expenditure.[159]

Even so, the committee was cautious about concluding that the dock-yards should take on the construction of merchant vessels, suggesting that the 'rapidity of delivery and economy of construction were not invariably the guiding factors' in the pre-war dockyards. It made the rather cautious recommendation that the dockyards could be used temporarily to construct mercantile ships, though more commercial influence on the production process would be necessary if this policy were to work. There was little willingness on the part of the Admiralty or the government to address the question of dockyard unemployment, and the situation did not really improve until the rearmament of the 1930s. Dockyard workers continued to look to their parliamentary representatives to lobby on the issue, but it seems that the most likely reaction was probably one of fatalism, and a sense that little could be done to improve the situation. The entire workforce was balloted in November 1919 on the question of short time over the winter, but the results were thought to be inconclusive as over 7500 workers failed to take part.[160] The position of trade unions was severely weakened, as these had little to offer against the situation either; and the labour movement's analysis of the causes of unemployment probably lacked the relevance that they had elsewhere.

VI

Labour activists declared themselves pleased with Labour's further advance, and increase in its share of the vote in the 1919 by-election. The failure to win the seat outright was attributed to a curious alliance between 'the poverty of Vintry on the one hand and the vested interests in Mannamead', a reference to the poorest and wealthiest districts of the constituency respectively.[161] Although it had yet to make the parliamentary breakthrough, Labour could now claim to have displaced the Liberals as the main opposition to the Conservatives. The party had also made considerable advances in the municipal elections. The fact that it could now call upon the wealth and influence of the Co-operative Society had undoubtedly been important in this respect. The divisions in the co-operative movement over political activity were not laid to rest in 1919, however, but simmered on into the 1920s. The outcome of the 1920 municipal elections was disappointing, with some suggestions, admittedly from hostile sources, that Labour was hopelessly split, and that certain trade unionists had even supported opposing candidates. The Labour Party's NEC approved the appointment of J C Turner, Mercer's successor as the Co-op's Education Secretary in September 1920, but the Labour and Co-operative Representation Association seems to have fallen apart.[162] No Plymouth organisation was affiliated to the Labour Party between 1920 and 1922, and by then the Co-operative Society seems to have withdrawn its involvement altogether, although it was to remain a prominent feature of Plymouth life more generally throughout the interwar period and beyond.[163]

There has been a recent tendency to play down the radicalising effects of war in twentieth century Britain, so that the First World War is no longer seen as the watershed it once was. Historians have played down the extent to which popular opinion became radicalised by the war and brought about changes in political alignment; continuity is emphasised over upheaval. There is some evidence to support this view in Plymouth. There were those who opposed the Co-operative Society's political adventure, which they saw as an aberrant response to the extraordinary circumstances of war, to be swiftly replaced by a return to business as usual after the armistice. After 1918, the prominence of the food supply as a political issue was replaced by the grave concerns over the long-term future of the dockyard, and perhaps for this reason did not have the impact on immediate post-war electoral discourse that might have been expected. Although this view may be persuasive from a longer term historical perspective than is possible here, it nonetheless ignores the contemporary sense of crisis and profound social change which was experienced by ordinary people during the war. The war's impact on local society in Plymouth was decisive, although it was conflicts in the sphere of consumption, rather than labour militancy in the workplace, which proved to have most impact. Undoubtedly the war was a watershed for the development of Plymouth Co-operative Society, and, whatever the longer term repercussions of the internal co-operative disputes, also for the wider labour movement in Plymouth. The First World War was a period of unprecedented expansion, activity and innovation for the society, but the most profound consequence was the intervention of the state in and the politicisation of the food supply.

The co-operative decision to seek direct political representation in 1917 should thus be seen as more than a pragmatic response to the erosion of rights and freedoms during the war, equivalent to the trade unions' Taff Vale. Instead, it was a response to, and an attempt to forge a new type of politics. This was based in part on the acceptance that consumer issues such as the regulation of the food supply were a legitimate area for state intervention. It was also linked to the enfranchisement of some women, although the definition of women's role as independent voters was far from resolved in 1918. Further, the war had, in the eyes of many, hastened the pre-war trend towards the erosion of the existing party system. Adoption of the coalition coupon allowed the Conservative candidates to distance themselves from what was perceived as an old-fashioned notion of party difference. This perhaps helped to draw the sting of Labour's own claims to have transcended the sterility of the pre-war party divisions.

Although the First World War may thus be seen as an important turning point in local politics, the period also demonstrates some elements of continuity. The prominence of consumer politics in the period 1914–18 had some precedence in the years before the war. The Co-operative Society's struggles over the control and distribution of food during the war had its roots in the conflict with the private traders in the early 1900s, although the wartime conditions clearly exacerbated the difficulties and crucially, the tendency to interpret them in terms of class. What also seemed to have changed after 1918 was the way in which these conflicts were expressed politically. Where the Co-op had been content to resolve its pre-war difficulties with the private traders through the courts, this changed after 1914 with the involvement of the state in the regulation of the food supply. Another recurring theme was the appeal to the national state as the neutral arbiter of interests and dispenser of justice against the arbitrariness of local interests. Yet the traditions of independence, education and mutual support, expressed through the Co-operative Society as well as the strong tradition of mutualism in the dockyard, continued to dominate Labour discourse.

CHAPTER 6

The Labour Movement
in Karlskrona c. 1890–1911

Karlskrona was a town dominated by the navy, perhaps to an even greater extent than Plymouth. It owed its very existence to the Crown's decision, in 1690, to re-locate the Swedish navy to an ice-free port in the southern part of the country. Unlike Plymouth Dock, however, which developed next to an existing town, the site chosen for the new naval dockyard at Karlskrona was more or less uninhabited, occupied only by a single farm. The removal of the entire Swedish navy, and the thousands of personnel connected with it, was an immense project, which illustrates the extent of the power and resources the Swedish state had at its disposal at this time. The new town grew rapidly from its foundation, so that by the second half of the eighteenth century it had become the third largest town in Sweden and second only to Stockholm in strategic importance. Unlike Plymouth, which formed part of an extensive naval infrastructure including several other dockyards and a network of colonial naval bases scattered across the globe, Karlskrona had a unique status as the main base of the Swedish navy.

As in Plymouth, the presence of the navy had profound consequences for the long-term economic development of the town, not all of them favourable. By the 1860s the dockyard had outlived Sweden's great power status, and its role had to be adapted to serve the defence interests of a minor, relatively poor, European state which based its foreign policy on non-alignment and neutrality. With the advent of iron and steel shipbuilding at about the same time, it was fast becoming apparent that extensive modernisation was necessary if the dockyard were to continue to serve a useful role. Following several decades of stagnation, the construction of new workshops, a new railway system and new docks in the 1880s created the necessary infrastructure for the production of modern steel battleships, although, unlike Devonport, Karlskrona dockyard never developed the capacity to take on the very large vessels of the immediate pre-war era. Such construction went to the developing private shipyards of Malmö and Göteborg, and Karlskrona consolidated its role as a base for the maintenance and repair of the existing fleet. Until the end of the First World War it was able to hold its own, and even to expand its workforce, but this could not be sustained after the war. Following the defeat of Germany in 1918, and the retreat of the Russian threat, economy in military spending became a political priority, and this was duly reflected in the sharp contraction in the dockyard workforce between 1918–1920.[1]

Like many other dockyard towns, including Plymouth, Karlskrona's vulnerability to the vicissitudes of government defence policy was exacerbated by its lack of a commercial industrial sector.[2] Some commercial manufacturing developed around the port during the 1870s and 1880s, including various clothing factories, but this had stagnated by the late 1890s, beset by problems of poor communication. The commercial port trade was also in decline, despite the modernisation of the quay in the early 1900s. The archipelago, which made Karlskrona such an attractive port from a strategic point of view, was a severe hindrance to the development of a commercial traffic, and Karlskrona lost out to its rivals. By 1912 the port of Kalmar, with an easier approach from the sea and better connections inland, was earning three times as much in customs duties compared to Karlskrona. After the war, with the need to attract much larger ocean-going ships, the problem became even worse. The town council made numerous attempts to address the situation, but with only limited success, bearing out the comment of one of their number that 'the town is a military and civil service town and can never be an… industrial town.'[3]

Nevertheless, late-nineteenth century Karlskrona was a relatively large town by Swedish standards, and was continuing to expand. The population grew from 15,666 in 1862 to a peak of 28,414 in 1923, although it thereafter declined somewhat.[4] The rapid expansion of the town during the late nineteenth century, mainly on the back of the modernisation of the dockyard, put considerable pressure on land-use and caused concerns about housing in particular. The dockyard was not the only naval establishment competing for space on the increasingly crowded islands which formed the town, but shared them with a number of naval companies.[5] These and the other regiments stationed in Karlskrona had their own schools, training facilities and other accommodation, but they were also a constant uniformed presence throughout the town. At times of crisis the naval presence became even more visible, as other companies crowded into the town, and the archipelago became the site for extensive naval exercises. The highest military authority in Karlskrona, the admiral-in-chief for the port (*befälhavande amiral*) could exert considerable influence on the daily life of the town, as in August 1914 when he recommended the total evacuation of the civilian population.[6]

Karlskrona's hinterland, the county (*län*) of Blekinge, was dominated by agriculture, with the exception of a quarrying and stonemasonry industry based around the neighbouring port of Karlshamn. Although this region did not experience the absolute depopulation seen in some parts of nineteenth century rural Sweden, it nonetheless declined in comparison to the more dynamic, industrialising regions, especially after 1890. In 1913, Karlskrona, with 27,446 inhabitants, accounted for just over 18% of the total population of Blekinge *län*. (Table 6.1) Outside Karlskrona, the majority of the population was classed as living in the countryside (*landsbygden*), with the remainder divided between the three small towns of Karlshamn, Ronneby and Sölvesborg.[7] (Table 6.2) The relative stagnation of the region is also indicated by the fact that the proportion of the population emigrating during the decades either side of 1900 was higher than average, in common with other largely agricultural regions. Karlskrona itself continued to expand throughout the nineteenth century, but it did so relatively slowly, so that by 1913 it had dropped from third to tenth largest town in Sweden, behind expanding industrial centres such as Malmö, Norrköping, and Eskilstuna.

Like Plymouth, therefore, late nineteenth century Karlskrona was relatively isolated from the expanding industrial districts and centres of population elsewhere in Sweden. There was not even a direct train to Stockholm. The politician Erik Palmstierna, who lived in Karlskrona for some years after 1900, recalled in his memoirs the 'long way... up to Stockholm on a creaking railway with a change in Alvesta.'[8] It was no better by sea, for the difficulties of navigating the Blekinge archipelago meant that most commercial maritime traffic went instead to Kalmar on the east coast, which was also better connected inland. For all its status as a metropolitan outpost, Karlskrona has generally been seen, by historians and contemporaries alike, as largely peripheral to the

TABLE 6.1. *Population in Karlskrona, 1850–1940.*

Year	Population	% change
1850	14,097	
1860	15,330	+8.5
1870	16,558	+8.2
1880	18,300	+10.5
1890	20,613	+12.6
1900	23,955	+16.2
1910	27,434	+14.5
1920	27,056	-1.4
1925	27,716	+2.4
1930	25,491	-8.0

SOURCE: Sveriges officiella statistik.

TABLE 6.2. *Population of Blekinge län, 1st January 1913.*

District	Population
Karlskrona	27 446
Karlshamn	7 266
Ronneby	3 437
Sölvesborg	3 167
Rest of county (*landsbygden*)	108 739
Total for Blekinge *län*	150 055

SOURCE: Sveriges officiella statistik.

upheavals of the late nineteenth and early twentieth centuries, and, like Plymouth, it has largely been ignored by historians of popular politics. In particular, it was often supposed that the dominance of the defence issue precluded widespread popular support for the social democratic party, as the advocates of disarmament.[9] As the following two chapters will show, however, just as in Plymouth, the relationship between local interests and national defence was actually rather more complex than it first appears. It certainly did not prevent the social democrats from challenging the political status quo in Karlskrona, initially as part of a broad coalition with the liberals campaigning for democracy, and then later adopting a more independent, class-based position.

After a discussion of the significance of the dockyard in the local economy and the labour market, the chapter begins by examining the organisation of the workforce and the nature of dockyard work.

Although the workforce was nominally civilian, it was however, like its counterparts in Britain, subject to military structures of organisation and supervision that might have been assumed to work against trade unionism or other forms of labour protest. Indeed, it was sometimes assumed by contemporaries that this was the case. There were attempts to organise the dockyard workers, however, and the forms which these attempts took are examined. These developments seem to have had relatively little impact on the parallel development of the wider labour movement in Karlskrona, however. This is discussed in the next section, beginning with the foundation and early development of the main labour organisation, the Labour Council (arbetarekommun). From the turn of the century, the council took on an increasingly political role as the local branch of the social democratic party, although it frequently acted in co-operation with the liberals. As in Plymouth, the early years of the labour movement in Karlskrona were characterised by a constant debate over the meanings of independent labour representation, and the understanding of the role of class in that politics. How did these debates evolve, especially in response to changes in the electoral system after 1909? Finally, the chapter examines the extent to which developments in Karlskrona were influenced by attempts to impose national structures and tactics from the centre, and the extent to which they were derived from local experiences, rooted in activists' understanding of local issues and local social relations As in Plymouth, the question of naval defence was always going to play a very significant role in these debates in Karlskrona, but this is discussed in chapter 7.

I

Karlskrona dockyard was not only one of the oldest industrial workplaces in Sweden, it was also one of the largest. The civilian dockyard workforce, which peaked at over 1500 in 1904, can be compared with the 500–1,000 workers employed in each of the three largest shipyards at Göteborg, and the 1000 or so at factories in Motala and Huskvarna at the turn of the century. (Table 6.3)[10] The status of these workers was ambiguous: nominally civilian, but part of a centralised, bureaucratic system which relied primarily on military chains of command. The head of the dockyard (*varvschefen*) was of military rank equivalent to a commodore (*kommendör*), responsible to the Royal

TABLE 6.3. *Karlskrona dockyard workforce, 1898–1930.*

Year (1st working day in March)	Naval Officers	Naval ratings	Monthly workers	Day workers (civilian)	Total civilian workforce
1898	76	294	43	966	1009
1899	73	211	43	1 079	1 122
1900	80	266	43	1 105	1 148
1901	89	199	42	1 299	1 341
1902	111	209	46	1 333	1 379
1903	104	389	46	1 444	1 490
1904	98	545	48	1 505	1 553
1905	1 19	205	44	1 434	1 478
1906	139	352	49	1 320	1 369
1907	129	328	49	1 326	1 375
1908	163	302	50	1 234	1 284
1909	99	274	52	1241	1 293
1910	1 42	203	60	1 290	1 350
1911	153	261	67	1 255	1 322
1912	126	269	68	1 211	1 279
1913	138	159	78	1 357	1 435
1914	118	299	89	1 397	1 486
1915	49	220	90	1 358	1 448
1916	59	219	88	1 503	1 591
1917	54	415	102	1 688	1 790
1918	122	345	127	1 903	2 030
1919	209	153	145	1 846	1 991
1920	272	198	143	1 519	1 662
1921	272	297	137	1 639	1 776
1922	296	240	140	1 601	1 741
1923	277	194	126	1 659	1 785
1924	286	257	130	1 693	1 823
1925	292	391	127	1 743	1 870
1926	242	297	131	1 671	1 802
1927	180	248	114	1 520	1 634
1928	202	337	106	1 549	1 655
1929	192	315	116	1 607	1 723
1930	180	293	242	1 375	1 617

SOURCE: Krigsarkivet: KÖV Varvschefens militärexp, serie D I, volym 8–9, "Journal över Uppgifter beträffande Varfsdriften" (1898–1910); KÖV, Varvschefens militärexp. Journaler 1911–1939, Serie D I, vol 9–11 (1911–1930).

Naval Administration in Stockholm (*Kungliga Marinförvaltningen* or KMF), and in military matters to the port's commander-in-chief (*Stationsbefälhavaren för Karlskrona station*).[11] Where Karlskrona dif-

FIGURE 6.1. *Karlskrona dockyard civilian and naval workforce 1898–1934.*

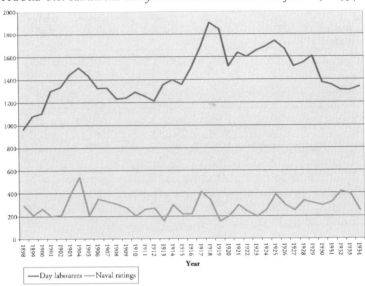

SOURCE: Krigsarkivet, Karlskrona Örlogsvarvet, Varvschefens militärexpedition, Serie DI: vols 8–9 Journal över Uppgifter beträffande Varfsdriften, 1898–1910; vols 9–11, Journaler 1911–1939.

fered from the British dockyards was in the involvement of military personnel in the day-to-day activity of the yard. Naval officers of various ranks were employed in supervisory roles, while men from the lower deck provided general unskilled labour, performing tasks such as transporting materials, loading and unloading ships, and acting as guards and porters on the dockyard gates. From the 1860s, the proportion of civilian to naval workers had risen, following a number of official enquiries which criticised the employment of naval personnel in dockyard work as an inefficient use of resources.[12] In 1868, naval ratings made up over 58% of the total workforce, excluding supervisory officials and officers, and prisoners.[13] By the turn of the century, however, they were reduced to just over 16% of the total. (Figure 6.1) Their presence or absence could still have a profound impact on the yard, most notably in 1905 when they were temporarily ordered to sea as a result of the Norwegian secession crisis.

By the turn of the century, therefore, the majority of the yard's work was performed by the civilian day labourers (*dagslönare*) and their salaried supervisors (*månadslönare*). Under the naval regulations, these

180

men were allotted a special non-combatant military status, with ranks equivalent to that of ordinary seaman for day labourers, and non-commissioned officer for *månadslönare*.[14] This meant that the day labourers were bound, under the terms of their contracts, to accept the naval regulations, and could, in theory, face military punishment if these regulations were infringed.[15] Although this did not amount to an outright ban on trade union activity, the regulations proscribed the employment of anyone likely to, 'disrupt the harmony between supervisors and workers,' and forbade the circulation of any kind of printed matter among the dockyard workforce, a measure which seems expressly designed to hinder collective organisation. Nor was it officially allowed to collect money during working hours, or even to engage in 'unnecessary' conversation, although it is not clear to what extent these formal provisions were enforced in practice.[16] It is not certain that these restrictions were necessarily more severe than those experienced by workers in comparable private industries during the same period, but the conventional view suggests that military organisation and discipline worked against the establishment of trade unionism in the dockyard, and that the dockyard workers 'quite simply, did not dare to form a trade union.'[17]

We should, however, be wary of making assumptions about the quiescence of the dockyard workforce. Collective action and protest was always a possibility for the dockyard workers. In 1855, for example, 700 workers had demonstrated against a rise in the prices of rye and potatoes brought about by the Crimean War.[18] Although there was no equivalent of the formal petitions process found in the British dockyards, Karlskrona workers were entitled to seek redress for a specific grievance through a written petition to the Crown. The civilianisation of the workforce and the re-organisation of work itself in the wake of technological changes was undoubtedly influential in challenging established practices in the yard, even if the rate of change was never as intensive as that experienced at Devonport. During the spring of 1900, day labourers founded the first known workers' organisation, the Karlskrona Dockyard Workers' Association (*Karlskrona Varvsarbetareföreningen* or KVAF), with the aim 'to work for the interests, economic or otherwise, of the workers, by all legal and humane means.'[19] The KVAF attempted to co-ordinate petitions on matters such as wages and pensions, and in 1907 it was reported that 747 dockyard workers, most of them not actually members of the association, had signed a petition to the head of the dockyard asking him to change pay-day arrangements.[20] It also took steps to establish a mutual sickness benefit fund for its members. Some members argued that the fund was unnecessary because of the official benefits available to workers: half their wages if they were absent from work through sickness, full pay if they were hospitalised or suffered serious injury at work, free medical treatment and drugs, and a naval pension on retirement.[21] In contrast to the British dockyards, these benefits were available to all employees, not confined to an elite group of established men. To claim official sickness benefit, however, workers had to have written confirmation of their incapacitation from a naval doctor, and the mutual fund was possibly a means of avoiding this constraint. It was reported that 50 men had received help during the first year or so of its existence.[22]

In most matters the KVAF displayed extreme caution, perhaps understandable in view of its rather precarious existence. In the first flush of enthusiasm following its launch, the KVAF signed up nearly 300 members, but like many labour organisations it struggled for survival. It was beset by the permanent problems of dwindling interest and poorly attended meetings, together with the difficulties of finding a suitable venue to hold meetings, and of persuading members to keep up their monthly contributions. Its existence was also threatened by internal controversy over a decision, in May 1904, to use 1,500 *kronor* of the association's funds to subsidise a members' outing to Stockholm, to the tune of 50 *kronor* per person (a sum which was roughly equivalent to a month's wages).[23] The association's chairman distanced himself from the matter by resigning, but nothing further happened until August, when the matter was debated again at the association's meeting. It was alleged that the executive committee had orchestrated support for the proposal through a special meeting which they had no authority to call, and that non-members had been permitted to take advantage of the offer.[24] Coming on the heels of other allegations that money had disappeared out of the association's funds without the knowledge of the executive committee, the scandal was a major blow for the association: membership fell drastically, and activities were scaled down. A new 'compromise committee' had to be elected to oversee the association's activities in place of the old executive. This attempted to tighten procedures by insisting on a roll call at the start of each meeting, but often found that there were simply not enough members present to take any decisions.[25]

Apart from the controversy surrounding it, the incident suggests that the KVAF was seen above all as a social club, and, according to the minutes of its first years of existence, much of the association's energy and resources was put into organising outings, treats and teas for members and their families, as well as a sports club and a music group. Some of these events seem to have been lively affairs, far removed from the earnest respectability often associated with the organised labour movement during this period. A meeting in December 1900 was forced to compensate one member for injury and others for stolen property, and following one particularly rowdy event in 1901, which necessitated an extra payment to the caretaker to clear up the resulting mess, and threats that the rental contract would be terminated, the association agreed that spirits were no longer to be purchased in the name of the KVAF.[26] Two years later, however, the KVAF co-ordinated a campaign against two local distilleries, protesting at the rise in the price of *brännvin*.[27] Actions such as these may not have amounted to trade campaigning as many understood it, but they undoubtedly helped to reinforce a sense of camaraderie and shared culture among the dockyard workforce. They may also have contributed to external perceptions of the dockyard workforce as a largely homogeneous group, but one which was set apart from other communities in Karlskrona. Erik Palmstierna described the dockyard workforce as 'that hermetically sealed world, where [membership of a] trade was inherited from father to son.'[28] The same attitudes prevailed in the labour movement. J A Henricsson, who came to Karlskrona from Sundsvall in 1906 to take over the editorship of *Blekinge Folkblad*, noted the distinctiveness of the island of Björkholmen, where dockyard workers had lived for many generations, and even the existence of a separate, virtually incomprehensible, dialect: 'björkholmskan'. Henricsson's overriding impression of Karlskrona was that it was a closed and tight-knit community, where 'all are related to each other, more or less.'[29] This sense of distinctiveness was perhaps also strengthened by the historic legacy of entitlement to certain privileges as Crown employees. Among the achievements of the KVAF reported for its first year was the special members' price negotiated with local tailors and shoemakers, and a similar deal with a local farmer for the purchase of grain. A request to the *varvschef* for the right to buy cloth, leather and similar direct from Crown stores was rejected however.[30]

In this respect, it should be noted that the KVAF was open, nominally at least, to all the different trades working in the dockyard. This point should not be over-stated. Even at its peak, the KVAF never succeeded in organising more than a quarter of the civilian workforce, and for most of its existence the proportion was considerably less than that. Without membership rolls, there is no means of knowing whether the association was dominated by one particular trade or trades. Nonetheless, the founding meeting agreed that the executive committee should be elected regardless of their trade, and it seems that this applied to the general membership as well.[31] This was despite the existence of a division of labour which was no less complicated than that obtaining at Devonport, or indeed in any other shipyards, private or state-owned. Administratively, the dockyard was divided into five departments: artillery, torpedo, equipment, mines and engineering. The largest of these, the Engineer's Department, employed 773 civilian day labourers in 1896. Of these the major shipbuilding trades were the most numerous, including the carpenters (*timmermän*), platers, fitters, and other metalworkers, together with their helpers (*hantlangare*).[32] (Table 6.4) After 1900 there were some attempts by established trade unions to organise groups of dockyard workers. The Labourers' Union (*Grovarbetarefackföreningen*) succeeded in signing up 55 dockyard workers at a special meeting held for their benefit in 1907, but there is no evidence of any subsequent activity, suggesting that the branch was short-lived.[33] During the same year, Branch 96 of the Swedish Metal Industry Workers' Union (*Svenska Metallindustriarbetare-förbundet* or Metall) succeeded in establishing a more permanent foothold in the dockyard. The Karlskrona branch of the union had been founded in 1901 by workers employed elsewhere in the town, and gained a substantial boost in membership when it managed to attract several hundred dockyard workers, though interest waned rapidly once the dockyard management rejected the union's wage proposals outright.[34] That none of these attempts was particularly successful indicates, and perhaps partly explains, the ambiguity of the relationship between the dockyard workers and the wider labour movement in Karlskrona. It will be necessary to return to this point below, but first some discussion of the Karlskrona labour movement is necessary.

II

The Karlskrona labour movement traced its roots not to material changes in the dockyard, but to August Palm's campaign tour of Blekinge during the spring of 1883, two years after he is normally cred-

TABLE 6.4. *Day labourers by trade in the Engineering Department of Karlskrona dockyard, 1896 (excluding pensioners).*

Trade			number
Carpenters (timmermän)			205
Fitters			82
Platers			73
	Plater helpers		37
Woodworkers (snickare)			34
Lathe turners and other machine workers			28
Smiths			24
	Smithy helpers and apprentices		21
Painters			21
Bricklayers			11
Foundrymen			10
	Helpers in foundry		5
Helpers (hantlangare)			114
Other trades			(34)
	Tinsmiths		7
	Tinsmith helper		1
	Blockmakers		4
	Electricians		4
	Planers		4
	Coppersmiths		3
	Coppersmiths helpers		8
	Patternmakers		2
	Sawyer		1
Offices and stores			(20)
	Draughtsmen		7
	Assistant writers		9
	Office assistants		3
	Storerooms		4
Supervisors and foremen			(12)
	Foremen		9
	Supervisors		3
Divers			4
Runners			4
Stonemasons			4
Plumbers			3
Others			9
Unknown			15
TOTAL			**773**

SOURCE: Krigsarkivet: Karlskrona Örlogsvarv, Varvschefens militärexpedition, Series D II h; Vol 2 Ingenjör Departementets daglönare den 1 Aug 1896.

ited with officially 'introducing' socialism to Sweden.[35] Arriving in Karl-shamn on 'a beautiful April day', Palm campaigned here before con-tinuing to Karlskrona, where his attempt to hold a public meeting encountered some disruption from local youths, and thereafter to Lycke-by and Sölvesborg. His Blekinge tour did not lead directly to the estab-lishment of a permanent labour organisation in any of these towns, but his socialist ideas were received with some sympathy among small groups of craftsmen, and persuaded them to found the region's first trade unions in the late 1880s.[36] Of some influence regionally were also the Karlshamn stonemasons, who migrated between Blekinge and the Danish island of Bornholm in search of work, and through this were exposed to Danish attempts to establish a Scandinavian Stonemasons' Union. This organisation was relatively short-lived, but held its con-gress in Karlshamn in May 1897.[37] Trades that had some organisation in Karlskrona by 1890 included the painters, shoemakers, tobacco work-ers, stove-builders, tailors, pattern makers and bricklayers.[38] The same year also saw the establishment of a short-lived socialist club, although it is not known whether this was involved in the campaigning which led to the success, against all expectations, of a social democratic can-didate in the People's Parliament (*folkriksdag*) elections of 1892–3.[39] Palm returned to Karlskrona in 1896 to address a May Day demonstration, organised, like that of the previous year, by a campaigns committee (*agitationskommitté*) made up of trade unionists. This committee also took steps to establish Karlskrona *arbetarekommun*, which held its inau-gural meeting on 15th September 1896. The meeting minuted its par-ticular thanks to one Oskar Kloo for his work in the campaigns com-mittee.[40] Kloo was a native of Karlskrona who had encountered social-ist ideas through contact with Palm and Branting while serving with his regiment in Stockholm. He returned to Karlskrona in 1893 deter-mined to put these into action, and shortly afterwards abandoned his military career to take employment in a hat factory. Despite his mid-dle-class background, he was undoubtedly one of the most prominent and energetic social democratic activists in Karlskrona, and was later to be distinguished as the town's first social democratic municipal rep-resentative and *riksdagsman*.[41]

Although the efforts of Palm, Kloo and others were certainly influ-ential in introducing new ideas to Karlskrona, the development of the local labour movement has also to be seen against the background of a broader movement for reform. The municipal reforms of 1862 laid

TABLE 6.5. *Occupations of local councillors in Karlskrona, 1904.*

Councillor	Occupation
E Albrecht	Vice-consul
O Beckman	Colonel
Fr Bäckström	Regimental physician
H Berggren	Company director
J A Bergström	Pharmacist
G Enblom	Lieutenant
C Haase	Naval lieutenant
N Hussénius	Naval pastor
J W Lannerstjerna	Commodore (kommendörkapten)
H Liljevall	Vice-consul
J F Mårtensson	Customs officer
L Nilsson	Shopkeeper
Gustaf Olsson	Wholesaler
Ad Palander	Vice-consul
C Puke	Commodore (kommendörkapten)
G Ringhelm	Factory owner
Ad Rudberg	Naval physician (first class)
G R Schlyter	Lecturer
S Carlsson Sparre	Stationmaster
E Swanlund	Pharmacist
W L Thörn	Vice-consul

SOURCE: *Blekinge Folkblad,* 2nd December 1904.

the foundations of elected municipal administration in Sweden and ushered in a period of conservative hegemony in Karlskrona.[42] Military officers were prominent within this ruling elite, and two of the council's most influential chairmen, Colonel C V v Heidenstam (1863–75) and Admiral F W v Otter (1889–1900), were drawn from the armed forces, though representatives of commercial business interests were equally influential.[43] (Table 6.5) From the turn of the century, however, the expansion of the town – the boundaries were extended in 1881 to take account of the growing population – and the increased opportunities for municipal autonomy and action which had developed since the 1862 reforms, were provoking the beginnings of a challenge to the political *status quo* in Karlskrona.[44] One of the leaders of this challenge was Erik Kule Palmstierna, who was later to become a prominent social democratic politician. Like Kloo, Palmstierna had embarked on a military career, and he first came to Karlskrona with his regiment in 1897.

He soon became disillusioned with subaltern social life, however, and turned instead to the local temperance movement, campaigning for improved education in the navy. His growing interest in social reform was also channelled into the Karlskrona Lecture Society (*Karlskrona föreläsningsforening*), founded in 1898 by the Good Templars, and a debating society (*diskussionsforening*), which made the local housing situation one of the main areas of its concern.[45] The presence of these organisations, and the public debates on social reform topics which they organised, were thought to be influential in challenging established local attitudes. 'We have noted with satisfaction,' wrote the editors of the liberal newspaper *Blekinge Läns Tidning,* 'a growing interest among the inhabitants of the town for everything concerning public affairs.... A feeling has been generally spreading that Karlskrona has been left behind, that we have not paid enough attention to new and beneficial ideas in social policy.'[46]

As this comment suggests, by the early 1900s, supporters of progressive politics believed that they were witnessing the beginnings of a major shift in local politics. Palmstierna himself took some personal credit for this change, and especially for his actions in persuading the dockyard workers en masse to support the liberal candidate at the 1902 *riksdag* election. According to him, 'it was...taken for granted that [the conservative Admiral] Dyrssen would be elected. The dockyard workers did not dare to vote against the admiral.' Palmstierna claimed that he was able to persuade the dockyard workers to vote for the opposing candidate by suggesting that they could hide the liberal ballot paper in their pockets while outwardly appearing to vote for Dyrssen. He was convinced that the dockyard vote had been decisive in securing the election of a liberal candidate in this case.[47] Although it would be unwise to take this at face value, what is interesting is the assumption that the dockyard workers would tend to vote as a group, and that winning the 'dockyard vote', therefore, was a vital part of electioneering which could help to turn an election result. The perception of the dockyard workers as a community apart, with separately identifiable interests, was thus carried over into the political sphere, especially as ever more dockyard workers gained the vote in the years before 1909. As they did so, there was a shift away from assumptions that the dockyard workers could be relied upon to cast their votes for certain candidates out of tradition or deference, towards active campaigning aimed at winning their votes.

The KVAF was also involved in municipal politics. In June 1902, the *arbetarekommun*'s executive committee (*styrelse*) had approached the local temperance societies and the KVAF to discuss the possibilities for joint action in that year's municipal elections, and agreed to form an electoral association (*valmansförening*) with these groups.[48] The council had already agreed to support the candidature of K V Dahlström, a dockyard employee who had been nominated by the same groups for a municipal by-election. Neither campaign was successful, but there was sufficient support for the electoral association to be revived again the following year. In 1904 the first social democratic councillor for Karlskrona, Oskar Kloo, was elected as part of a slate of three candidates, along with the liberals Ulrik Leander and Leonard Key. This election was felt to mark a turning point in local politics. The last uniformed chairman of the council had already left office in 1901, although the military presence persisted. The success of the 'progressive' candidates was partly attributed to the raised levels of interest in municipal politics, fostered in part by organisations such as Palmstierna's debating society. The recently founded labour newspaper, *Blekinge Folkblad,* hailed the election result enthusiastically as a 'victory for the Left', and expressed its satisfaction that it was not only 'we socialists, we stirrers and instigators of rebellion (*vi upprorsmakare och fristörare*)', but others as well, who had 'opened their eyes, and come up against the stark and naked fact, that the town council, composed as it currently is, is incompetent.'[49]

Encouraged by Kloo's success, the labour council now turned its attention to the *riksdag* election scheduled for the autumn of 1905. When the council met to discuss the issue, several months ahead of the election date, a few members were in favour of running an independent labour candidate, but the meeting resolved to call a meeting with its electoral partners from the previous year.[50] At its meeting later in the year, the electoral association duly nominated four candidates: the sitting *riksdagsman* G W Roos, the liberals Ulrik Leander and J Jansson, and the social democrat Oskar Kloo. Yet when the candidates presented themselves to the alliance's hustings meeting, serious doubts were raised over Roos' commitment to the liberal cause, in particular his commitment to the most important liberal cause, suffrage reform. 'It is fashionable at election time to declare oneself a liberal,' as one speaker put it, 'and that is why most of the candidates appear to be liberal, but there is a difference between liberal and liberal. The hypocritical liberal disappears on the way to Stockholm.'[51] Although he now professed to support the liberal position, Roos was known to have voted against suffrage reform in the *riksdag*, and was therefore prone to changing his views. This position proved intolerable for the labour council, which eventually decided to withdraw from the alliance and run its own candidate, Oskar Kloo, independently. The election was not an easy one for them though. However much Kloo's supporters tried to portray Roos as a conservative, particularly over suffrage reform, they were forced to admit that his liberal associations were a burden to them, and that they would have preferred to campaign against an out and out reactionary.[52] The outcome was indeed rather disappointing for the *kommun*, with Kloo securing just 299 votes against 1,198 for Roos.

The *kommun's* suspicions of Roos threatened to expose divisions within the electoral alliance. There was also unease about the motivation of Palmstierna as one of Roos' key supporters, since he was known to be sympathetic towards trade unionism, but was thought to be strongly opposed to the secular socialism of the organised labour movement.[53] When Palmstierna's name surfaced as a potential candidate for the municipal elections later in 1905, many social democrats were of the view that the *kommun* should not entertain his candidature, because of his anti-socialist views. Indeed, some felt that his priorities lay with preventing the election of a socialist candidate rather than supporting a progressive one, especially after he condoned the decision of the Right not to put forward a candidate of their own, arguing that this would play into the hands of the social democrats.[54] Despite these misgivings, the electoral alliance was revived for the municipal campaigns of 1906 and 1907, but it came under strain again when thoughts turned towards the next *riksdag* election in 1908.[55] Although some members were reluctant to act unilaterally until the actions of other groups had been confirmed, the *kommun* nonetheless went ahead and adopted Oskar Kloo as its candidate at the beginning of August. The editor of *Blekinge Folkblad* made it quite clear that the *kommun* had been forced into this action by the experience of the previous election.[56] Controversy surfaced again, however, when the temperance societies refused to support Kloo on the grounds that he was not a pledged teetotaller, and declared that they would be supporting Leander instead.[57] At its election meeting a week or so later, the liberal group confirmed Leander's nomination.[58] But by this time there was also another candidate in the field in the person of O Holmdahl, sponsored by the conservative General Election Association (*allmänna valmansförbundet*), which generated concerns that the progressive vote would be destructively split between the social democrats and the liberals.[59] All three candidates addressed an election meeting in early September, but barely a week later came the news that the *arbetarekommun* had decided to withdraw their candidate, and would lend their support instead to Leander. The decision was apparently uncontroversial, and even hints at some relief on the part of *kommun* members.[60] Moreover, it was supported unequivocally by the candidate himself, who announced that he had resigned 'in order to avoid splitting the left wing vote'.[61] *Blekinge Folkblad* gave its full support to Leander, and exhorted its readers to vote for him on election day. His eventual victory was hailed as ample justification for the *kommun*'s action.[62]

III

As this analysis of the 1905 and 1908 elections suggests, the early years of the labour movement in Karlskrona were dominated by a series of debates over the meaning of labour representation, and the best tactics by which this could be achieved. At each election, whether municipal or parliamentary, the *arbetarekommun* faced the dilemma of whether to run its own candidates independently, or to nominate candidates together with other organisations as part of a broad slate. Pragmatically, this strategy was probably more reliable in achieving limited success, but it meant publicly endorsing the political views of individuals and organisations who were very likely opposed to social democracy. By 1906, the electoral alliance had expanded to include the Subaltern Officers' Association, the Constables of the Watch (*vaktkonstaplar*), and the Policemen's Association, as well as associations of postmen and railwaymen. On at least two occasions the *kommun* found itself unable to endorse proposed candidates for municipal office because the individual in question was a military officer.[63] Moreover, the fluid, *ad hoc* nature of the electoral alliance meant that it was not always clear what it actually stood for ideologically. Nominally, it was associated with the embryonic liberal party, especially from the middle of the decade with the hardening of divisions between left and right. The 1908 *riksdag* election, when the liberal Ulrik Leander opposed the former mayor O Holmdahl, was certainly understood in these terms.[64] But the precise meaning of the term 'liberal', or more commonly *frisinnad*, was extremely difficult to pin down. The liber-

al faction within the Swedish *riksdag* espoused the two most important concerns of nineteenth century European liberalism – free trade
and suffrage reform – and the Liberal Party itself had emerged from
the public debates generated by these controversies in the last two
decades of the nineteenth century. It was also associated with the emergence of the modern press from the mid nineteenth century.[65] 'Liberalism' was linked to, though not synonymous with, the term *frisinnad* (literally, free-thinking).[66] It certainly implied freedom in the traditional liberal sense, but the broader term *frisinnad* perhaps
encompassed a political sense of freedom from ties to existing factions
and élites, and it seemed to carry this meaning in Karlskrona. *Frisinnad* also implied free thought in a religious sense; indeed, many prominent *frisinnade* in Karlskrona were also associated with the Free
Church movement (*frikyrksrörelse*). Politically, however, an appropriate translation might also be 'progressive' (*framstegsvänlig*): *frisinnad*
was the antithesis to reaction. One of the candidates adopted by the
electoral alliance in 1904, J Jaensson, was described as 'a very progressive (*frisinnad*) schoolteacher'. *Frisinnad*, in other words, implied a
broad grouping, rather than a tightly organised political *party*; an informal association of liberal and progressive-minded individuals; a movement which was 'merely a political conglomerate of all possible political opinions and shadings', in contrast to the ideological distinctiveness of the labour movement.[67] Alternatively, this electoral grouping
was often referred to simply as 'the left' (*vänstern*), a term which was
no more specific in meaning than 'liberal' or '*frisinnad*'.

If the *ad hoc* electoral arrangements discussed above could best be
described as a 'progressive alliance', then the basis for this alliance was
probably no more than opposition to the established élites in the council chamber at the local level, and a commitment to suffrage reform
at the national level. The town council had been elected from within its own ranks for too long: 'its inhabitants should not be represented solely by Messrs. Businessmen and Officers, [but], in the name of
all reason, the People ought also to have a voice in decisions.'[68] The
roots of the alliance lay in the campaigns for suffrage reform during
the 1890s, and labour activists had acknowledged then that the suffrage issue was a cause to which all people's parties (*folkpartier*) ought
to affiliate, and for which social democrats and temperance reformers would make common cause.[69] Where the *arbetarekommun* differed
from its liberal allies, however, was in its analysis of municipal poli-

tics in terms of class. The town council was not merely out of date; it was an enclosed and self-perpetuating oligarchy, bound by its class loyalties. 'Class' here could carry a negative meaning, in the sense of the people versus the classes. 'A vote for Roos is a class vote,' was the social democratic message in the 1905 *riksdag* election, implying that although elected as the people's representative, Roos was more likely to support the interests of a much narrower group. The alternative was for the workers to recognise their own class interests, and support the social democratic candidate:

> If you want a straightforward solution to the suffrage issue, do you not think then that it is better to elect as *riksdagsman* a candidate from the class which still lacks the vote, or from the class which will have to concede it?... [The voter] who fully understands that the upper class and the under class have opposing interests will not vote for any other than one of his own. This is what the upper class do, and this is what the workers also ought to understand that they should do.[70]

Despite his protestations of liberalism, Roos was constrained by his social class from acting in a way which was truly liberal or progressive. Similarly in 1908, *Blekinge Folkblad* warned its readers not to be lured by the attempts of the Right to broaden their appeal by presenting themselves as a popular front against socialism. The Right were described as 'cunning as snakes' in their attempts to win over 'moderates and liberals, small farmers, smallholders (*torpare*), tenant farmers, agricultural labourers and the less clear-sighted workers.' The result of voting for them however would be to send to the *riksdag* 'large landowners, chimney barons (*skorstensbaronerna*) and the ubiquitous militarists'.[71]

The *riksdag* election of 1908 was the last to be contested by the social democrats in alliance with the liberals, as part of a broader, left wing alliance. Already there had been some signs of strain in the arrangements for the municipal elections. The *arbetarekommun* expressed its reservations about the selection of one candidate in 1906, because he was a naval officer, and could only offer a half-hearted endorsement of the alliance's list for 1907. Indeed, the *kommun* had discussed the possibility of asking its supporters to return blank ballot papers, as a more effective protest against the restricted franchise.[72] During the spring of 1910 the *arbetarekommun* decided, after some discussion, that its candidates would contest the elections for Blekinge county council (*landsting*) independently, under the designation 'labour party'.[73] Some members remained in favour of continued co-operation with the liberals, mainly because it was assumed the dockyard workers would continue to vote, as a block, for a liberal candidate. But these views were outweighed by the general acceptance of the principle of independence in the *kommun*'s electoral campaigning, and the need, as part of this, to create a clear distinction in electoral discourse between the liberals and the workers' party.[74] Reporting on a liberal election meeting in Karlskrona in March 1910, the *Blekinge Folkblad* reporter observed how the liberal speaker spoke disparagingly of the social democrats, 'in the well-known style of [Karl] Staaff.'[75] The following year, when the next *riksdag* election was due, there seemed to be little doubt that the election would be fought as a three-way contest. This election was of course the first to be held under the new reformed franchise, which was undoubtedly very significant in imparting an increased confidence and seriousness to the *kommun*'s electoral campaign. A central electoral office was set up, workplace committees founded, and non-affiliated workers canvassed to cast their votes for the *kommun*'s list.

Although the *kommun* had now abandoned all thoughts of a broad electoral alliance, it is noticeable, however, that this did not lead to the adoption of a more explicitly class-based analysis of social wrongs and remedies in their electoral rhetoric. Instead, political campaigning continued to draw on the populist language of the electoral alliance, with the party seeking to appeal to the 'ordinary people' or *småfolket*. It is clear that this strategy was partly dictated by the introduction of a proportional electoral system to replace the majority-elected one member constituencies of the limited franchise, and the realisation that every vote counted. The 'natural' constituency of social democracy, the 'working class', were just one group making up the broader category of the 'people', and much energy was diverted into campaigning amongst the rural population in particular. Indeed, so much more confident were labour organisers about the votes of the Karlskrona workers, that activists were advised not to waste time and resources distributing election literature in urban working-class districts. Instead, '[t]he leaflets should be taken out into the countryside, and distributed among small farmers, smallholders, tenant farmer and agricultural labourers, those who need to come in with us for they are of our flesh and blood and in the same oppressed position as us.'[76] The call to arms was heeded, and *Blekinge Folkblad* carried reports of Sunday excursions by Karls-

TABLE 6.6. *Distribution of votes in Second Chamber Election 1911, Blekinge län.*

District	Social Democrats		Liberals		Right	
	No of votes	%	No of votes	%	No of votes	%
Eastern district rural division	174	12.92	755	56.05	418	31.03
Medelstad rural division	851	30.13	888	31.44	1 085	38.42
Bräkne rural division	603	34.52	387	22.15	757	43.33
Lister rural division	544	20.38	1 026	38.44	1 099	41.18
Ronneby	148	38.14	95	24.48	145	37.37
Sölvesborg	124	37.8	132	40.24	72	21.95
Karlshamn	251	35.35	234	32.96	225	31.69
Karlskrona	636	28.28	747	33.21	866	38.51
Whole of Blekinge	3 331	27.17	4 264	34.77	4 667	38.06

SOURCE: *Blekinge Folkblad,* 23rd September 1911.

krona *arbetarekommun* members and young socialists, out into the surrounding countryside to canvass the electors in the villages.[77]

The use of this type of language could be read as an appeal to a democratic populist tradition, but it was overlaid with an economic critique of the existing social order, which appears to owe more to conventional socialist analyses of class. The bonds between the 'people' were created not by their exclusion from the political process, but by their experience of capitalist exploitation. The small farmers 'have come to see the means by which the land is governed from the same point of view as the entire working class… The workers and the tillers of the earth are obliged for the most part to struggle against the same capitalist power as the industrial workers. The many tentacles of capitalism reach everywhere, and the poor man, whether he lives in the town or the countryside, is hemmed in on all sides by those who wish to harvest the fruits of others' work.'[78] Perhaps to make this distinction clear, the term 'working people' (*arbetande folk*) was preferred over 'workers' (*arbetare*), with its connotations of urban, industrial work. The 1911 election results vindicated this approach, for although the social democrats were unable to obtain a clear majority in any of the Blekinge electoral districts, their achievement of just over 27 % of the vote overall was enough to secure two out of the six Blekinge mandates, and the election of the first social democratic *riksdagsman* for Blekinge. (Table 6.6)

The need to campaign for votes across a much larger electoral district required close co-operation between Karlskrona *arbetarekommun* and the other labour organisations in Blekinge. In 1905, the first steps were taken by the Social Democratic Party at the national level to establish a more formal structure to party organisation at the grassroots, by setting up regional party districts.[79] Karlskrona differed in many respects from the other, smaller Blekinge settlements; but there had been contact and co-operation with the other Blekinge towns from the 1890s, for example over securing external speakers for May Day demonstrations. By 1907, there were eight *arbetarekommuner* in Blekinge, and these met in Ronneby in January 1907 to discuss the formation of a regional party district.[80] There was some debate over the geographical scope of the proposed district: should it include parts of Småland (the southern part of Kalmars *län* and the island of Öland), or should it be confined to Blekinge?[81] That the latter option won the day perhaps owed something to the precedent set by the establishment of *Blekinge Folkblad,* founded in 1902 as the 'organ for the popular movements in Blekinge *län.*' The newspaper's main editorial offices were to be based in Karlshamn, although there was also an editor in Karlskrona, and the costs were to be borne by a levy on all labour movement organisations in Blekinge. *Blekinge Folkblad* was thus from the outset a truly regional organ rather than a specifically Karlskrona one, carrying reports on events in specific towns and villages across the county and across Sweden. The editorial committee brought together activists from across the region. In 1904 it was decided to register the *Folkblad* as an official party organ, and this led to the establishment of a Blekinge newspaper district, formally recognised by the party following the party congress initiative of 1905.[82] The main objective of the Blekinge district of the Social Democratic Party was to undertake 'collective [and] methodical campaigning for the labour press, political and trade union organisation, and parliamentary and municipal elections.'[83] There was some discussion over the most preferable location for meetings. Karlshamn and Ronneby were the most central points geographically, but it was eventually agreed that meetings should be held in Karlskrona, as the largest town in the region. The new district had a catalytic effect on the development of the labour movement across Blekinge. Financial support from the SAP's national executive committee (*partistyrelse*) and the LO helped to fund a campaign tour by August Palm, which resulted in the foundation of six new *arbetarekommuner*. This initial success were also measured by the large increase in membership during its early years: from 2200 at the founding district congress in January 1907 to 3600 by 1908.[84]

IV

The evolution of labour politics in Karlskrona during the first decade of the twentieth century was therefore partly related to the growing evolution of the party bureaucracy, and the *arbetarekommun's* developing status as a local branch within a national party structure. Following the 1900 party congress, the national executive committee (partistyrelse) had emerged as the most important instrument of central control within the SAP, communicating regularly with local *arbetarekommuner*, and attempting to co-ordinate their activities.[85] Karlskrona *arbetarekommun* communicated increasingly regularly with the national executive in Stockholm, and many of its campaigns and public events were organised in response to circulars from Stockholm, although the final decision over whether to respond to a national call to demonstrate was more likely to be dictated by pragmatic considerations. For example, serious doubts were expressed in Karlskrona over the likely success of the demonstration called by the party in the spring of 1901.[86] Some *kommun* members suggested that the practical difficulties could be overcome by combining the party demonstration with the annual 1st May event, a course of action which the national executive was anxious to avoid. Others felt however that the credibility of the local labour movement depended on taking the initiative, and that 'if nothing were done the old perception that Karlskrona was dormant would be further underlined.'[87] Another party initiative for a general strike during the suffrage debate the following year was rejected outright.[88] In the spring of 1905 a further call for action from the national executive was received, relating to a proposal to change the laws on striking (the so-called *Åkarpslagen*) then before the *riksdag*. This time there seemed to be more of a will to participate in a nationally co-ordinated campaign, and although nothing actually came of the discussions, most who took part in the relevant meeting declared their willingness to take whatever action was necessary in the campaign. The *kommun* resolved to call a meeting with the local trade unions, and to make arrangements for an immediate strike if necessary. The meeting went ahead and assembled in time to receive a telegram containing the news that the proposed law had been defeated by a narrow margin.[89] The *kommun* could also expect a limited amount of assistance from the national executive, sometimes in the form of much-needed financial support. In 1901 it was announced that an official party campaigner was to be allocated to Karlskrona for one month every year, and by 1904 there were regular visits from speakers from Stockholm and elsewhere, some of whom had quite high profiles within the movement.[90]

The relationship between the different tiers of organisation was not always harmonious, however. As elsewhere in Sweden, the presence of a social democratic youth club was a source of some friction, described as 'brutal…and not an example of educated youth,' when it submitted a motion in protest against a speech by a visiting party activist.[91] The club was also involved in the controversy over the labour newspaper, *Blekinge Folkblad*, in its early years. It was not founded as an official party organ, although when it officially became one it was described as 'a really dreadful rag' (*en riktig gristidning*) by one *arbetarekommun* member, an expression for which he was chided by his comrades.[92] Controversy arrived in the shape of Carl Schröder, a left-wing youth activist who was later suspended from the SAP for his anarchist leanings and advocacy of the general strike tactic. He took over the editorship of *Blekinge Folkblad* and caused uproar by inserting an article from the radical social democratic youth paper *Gula Faran*. The debate was heated, and Schröder was berated by several members of the *arbetarekommun* executive committee. Several members went so far as to accuse Schröder of causing a major setback to the progress of the labour movement in Karlskrona. 'Schröder had contributed to halting the success of the labour movement here [in Karlskrona]… [It is] certain that if Herr Schröder had represented the workers' views factually and with dignity in the newspaper then the labour movement here would have been stronger both internally and externally.' There was also concern that Schröder's editorship had damaged relations with the party leadership, and would prevent recognition of *Blekinge Folkblad* as an official party organ. The meeting agreed a resolution protesting against the editor's use of material from *Gula Faran*, 'because its tone is absolutely in conflict with the social democratic programme', although opposition was not unanimous, and one member suggested that the paper had been singled out merely because its associations with the radical youth movement.[93] Schröder attended an *arbetarekommun* meeting to answer his critics, and stood by his criticism of the party leadership, arguing that their experience as members of the *riksdag*, 'where they come into contact with the upper class', meant that they were becoming 'intolerable' (*ohållbara*). The strongest argument against his editorship seemed to be the need to follow the party line, and thereby to avoid losing the party's financial support for the newspaper. Yet this was by no means a majority view, for when the matter was put to the vote, 36 members voted against the resolution to censure Schröder's editorship, while 79 voted for. The minority group adopted their own resolution, which is worth quoting in full:

> Since there are different opinions over how the newspaper should be edited in relation to the Swedish Social Democratic Party programme, but its contents have never shown themselves to be in conflict with the interests of the working class against the upper class;
>
> and since our party programme itself demands freedom of speech, thought and the press;
>
> and since possible deviations from the party programme cannot in all cases be thought to be of any significance, and the task [of the newspaper] was to promote the development of our views;
>
> and since those from outside are not prevented from expressing their views in the newspaper;
>
> the meeting does not feel called upon to do anything other than express its continued belief that the newspaper with its current editor is in the best sense a free and independent organ, and in this way is the best weapon against our opponents and a means for our own development.[94]

This resolution suggests not so much support for the radical or anarchist currents represented by the youth wing, but an assertion of independence against the growing mechanisms of control from the party leadership. There was possibly further vindication for Schröder's position when the meeting moved on to debate its response to the Russian revolution and Schröder, advocating a demonstration on the grounds that the SAP was 'a revolutionary class struggle party', received the support of a clear majority of the members present. Similar views were expressed a year later, when the party executive voted to suspend Schröder, who had now left Karlskrona, and another youth wing activist, Hinke Berggren. The Karlskrona *arbetarekommun* passed a resolution supporting the leadership's decision, but again there was a substantial majority opposed to this decision, on the grounds that the party was the healthier for being able to accommodate a breadth of views, and should avoid a potentially damaging split.[95] Such was the importance of the matter that the affiliated trade unions were asked to ballot their members on the question, and the result of this showed a clear majority in favour of the party's action.[96]

There was also the possibility for conflict between the different tiers of regional organisation. In 1908 the Blekinge district executive stated that Karlskrona *arbetarekommun* should support a liberal bourgeois candidate (*en frisinnad borglig*) in that year's *riksdag* election.[97] In allowing himself to be nominated as an independent labour candidate Oskar Kloo was thus defying these wishes. He expressed his distaste over the use of party district money in support of a liberal candidate, though it is not clear whether these differences were influential in persuading him to stand down.[98] The suffrage reform of 1909 heightened the need for party discipline, and following the announcement of the new electoral districts some slight adjustments were made to the district party organisation to ensure that the electoral boundaries coincided with those of the party. The campaigns for both the *riksdag* and *landsting* elections were now to be co-ordinated by the district's election committee, which circularised local labour councils with information about planned actions. Blekinge was divided into four separate areas, and Karlskrona *arbetarekommun* was required to take responsibility for that covering the town of Karlskrona and its environs. Meanwhile, an extensive web of committees was established to cover every village and hamlet, and ensure that no potential social democratic vote went uncanvassed. Election activity was also more closely tied into to the national strategy, with speakers and printed pamphlets available from Stockholm.[99]

The evolution of a national party structure also implied a shift in the relationship between *arbetarekommun* and trade unions. The British equivalent to the Swedish *arbetarekommuner,* the Trades and Labour Councils, had a dual role as co-ordinating committees for the trade unions in a locality, and also as the local representative of the Labour Party, at least until 1918. As we have seen in the case of Plymouth, this relationship between political and trade functions was not to be taken for granted, and could lead to conflict. During its early years, at least, Karlskrona *arbetarekommun* was acting more as a trade body than a political one, in its role as the central co-ordinating committee for the town's trade unions. Special *ad hoc* committees were set up to try to induce different groups of workers to organise trade unions, and practical support was offered where possible, by arranging a rent-free meeting place, for example.[100] The *kommun* was also a central source of information on labour matters in the town, and provided moral and practical support to workers involved in conflicts with their employers, for example by holding collections and passing resolutions in support, although it avoided becoming involved as a mediator in any particular conflict. In its early years, the majority of the *kommun's* campaigning was therefore internal, directed towards building up the local labour movement rather than seeking to campaign for political change. This is not however to suggest that the desirability of political action was overlooked, for, as we have seen, the *kommun's* roots lay not only in the local trade union movement, but also in the suffrage campaigns and the *folkriksdag* of the 1890s.

The question of the relationship between trade union and political work came to a head with the foundation of the national trade union federation, *Landsorganisationen* or LO, in 1898. The existence of the LO alongside the Social Democratic Party implied a more formal demarcation of the activities of the two wings of the movement, and the SAP congress in 1900 responded by establishing a more formal party machinery, as we have seen. These moves created some controversy in Karlskrona. When the proposed constitution for LO was discussed at a *kommun* meeting in July 1898, one member supported the official position, arguing that LO's principal role should be as a statistical bureau to collate information on the movement, and also that it should avoid undermining the autonomy of branches or federations, by intervening only in larger conflicts. The member elected to attend the conference as the branch's delegate disagreed, arguing that the new organisation should support the party through its political engagement.[101] The consensus within the branch seems to have been that trade and political work did indeed go hand in hand, but there was some opposition to this view. In 1899, the tilemakers' union proposed that the eight-hour day should be the sole cause of the May Day demonstration, untrammelled by the distractions of the suffrage campaign. The motion was rejected, those against it arguing that workplace reforms would be the natural consequence of suffrage reform, and that political and trade work did indeed go hand in hand therefore.[102] The dualism of this situation was unsustainable in the longer term, however. When the matter came before the party congress in 1900, the LO delegate admitted that he had changed his view since 1898, and was now in favour of the LO being run exclusively as a trade organisation, even though he had originally voted in favour of compulsory affiliation in 1898. Most members agreed that it was desirable

FIGURE 6.2. *Members of Karlskrona Arbetarekommun, 1897–1914.*

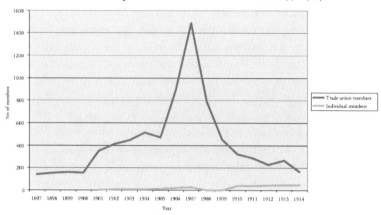

SOURCE: Karlskrona arbetarekommun protokoll, *passim.*

to keep party membership voluntary, on the grounds that it was better to maintain a smaller group of committed activists than a nominal membership ten times the size.[103]

Pragmatically it was difficult for the *arbetarekommun* to avoid
becoming engaged in trade union affairs. It made some key interventions in local labour conflicts; acting for example to establish a strike
fund for the chimney sweeps involved in a pay dispute in the spring
of 1902, and even acting as mediator on one occasion in 1906 when
the chairman and secretary met the master sweep to try to resolve
another dispute.[104] At the annual meeting for 1907 it was reported that
eight trades had been organised with the help of the *kommun*, but that
a significant proportion of the town's workers remained unorganised,
and that efforts should be concentrated on reaching these groups. This
strategy bore fruit with the formation of a new fireman's union with
26 members two months later.[105] Despite the abolition of compulsory affiliation, the *kommun* continued to draw the bulk of its membership from affiliated trade unions, and the number of individual
members remained extremely small before 1910. (Figure 6.2)

1909 was a major turning point not only in terms of the suffrage
reform, but also because of the general strike of that year, which
involved over 1300 workers in Karlskrona. The effect on the local trade
union movement was disastrous. All branches recorded significant

losses in membership, and several ceased to exist altogether. Overall, membership of the SAP in Blekinge fell by over 2000, and nine out of nineteen *arbetarekommuner* in Blekinge folded altogether.[106] Karlskrona *arbetarekommun* also suffered a severe drop in membership, which meant that it took no part in electoral campaigning that year, and was even forced to cancel its New Year's Eve party for lack of funds.[107] The Metalworkers' Union was typical in seeing its membership more than halved after 1909, and noted the subsequent years as being very quiet in contrast to the pre–1909 flush of enthusiasm.[108] The Labourers' Union began 1909 with a healthy roll of over 100 members, of which only twenty-six remained at the year's end, and it was not until 1918 that membership reached its pre–1909 levels.[109] The blow to morale was equally severe, and the branch sought disaffiliation from the *arbetarekommun* in 1910. The strike was thus a severe blow to the stability and strength to the labour movement in Karlskrona, but it was not entirely isolated as figure 6.2 indicates. The decline in membership in many trade union branches during 1908 must be attributed partly at least to the rise in unemployment of that year.[110]

A further result of this setback in the trade union movement, and the failure of the general strike tactic, was also that the distinction between political and trade activities was more marked than it had been previously. For the *arbetarekommun,* trade union work now took second place to election campaigning. The establishment of national trade union federations meant that most local branches were by this stage tied into a rather different institutional relationship in any case. The Karlskrona chimney sweeps approached the *arbetarekommun* in 1911 to ask for assistance in a conflict, but were informed that the *kommun* was not able to help them if they were not affiliated to their national federation.[111] In 1910 the *arbetarekommun* voted to establish a committee with special responsibility for trade union issues, formed from delegates elected by each trade union branch. With this committee in place, trade matters could be referred back to it, thus leaving the *kommun* to focus on its political work.[112] Nonetheless, activists were anxious to avoid a complete separation of functions. The Painters' Union was publicly chided at a *kommun* meeting in 1913 for their request to secede, with J A Ingvarsson, one of the two social democratic *riksdagsmän* for Blekinge *län,* reminding them that it 'would not be right to overestimate the trade union movement and underestimate the political one, since the reality [was] that both movements complement each other.'[113]

The sense of collective belonging to a unified movement could also be strengthened by the *arbetarekommun*'s role in organising social activities. In 1898, the *kommun*'s executive committee organised the first of what was to become an annual summer outing to Kalmar. Four years later, as many as 300 people took part.[114] Such events were mainly motivated by practical considerations, as they were an important means of raising ever-scarce funds, and not even the most earnest activists attempted to impart any political significance to the trips. Bazaars, or stalls and games organised at events staged by other organisations were also regarded as essential to support the *kommun*'s fragile finances. More controversial was the question of how to spend the funds raised. Since its foundation in 1896 the *kommun* had discussed its need for a band, and in 1903 it was agreed to allocate the funds raised from that summer's outing towards buying a set of musical instruments. Progress stalled over the question of where the instruments were to be bought, since German instruments were reported to be cheaper, but Swedish ones were of course preferable.[115] Regardless of origin the instruments undoubtedly represented a substantial investment, and the Karlskrona Labour Council Music Association was established as a separate organisation with its own rules.

The *arbetarekommun* band was partly seen as a fundraising tool, required to return 10% of any income raised from public performance to the *kommun*'s central finances, but its most important duty was to provide the music for the annual May Day demonstration, and for any other demonstrations and public events organised by the *arbetarekommun*. Indeed, the decision to establish a music association and to purchase instruments stemmed originally from the difficulties which arose in finding suitable bands for May Day. In 1902 the *kommun* had still been prepared to consider hiring the Naval Music Corps to provide the music, although this was not considered to be ideal. Some members objected to involving military institutions on ideological grounds, while others suggested that the band in question could simply not be trusted to turn up, as there was always the risk that their officers might prohibit them from taking part.[116] May Day parades were partly associated with the navy in Karlskrona in any case, through the traditional 1st May reveille.[117] The first workers' May Day demonstration in Karlskrona was held in 1896 with August Palm as speaker, and led directly to the establishment of the *arbetarekommun* later the same year. Banners demanding universal suffrage were prominent within the procession, but the central demand of the demonstration, in recognition of the international significance of the event, was the trade union goal of the eight-hour day.[118] The demonstration was also a means of asserting the presence of the labour movement within the town. When the *arbetarekommun* moved to new premises in 1903, it was decided that members should march there through the streets, accompanied by banners and music.[119] While the demonstration remained political, in that it usually culminated in the agreement of a joint resolution following an address by an invited speaker, after the turn of the century there were signs that the demonstrations had lost some of their political urgency, and were instead taking on the characteristics of a popular festival.[120] In preparing for the annual demonstration, the organisers' energies were as likely to be taken up with organising refreshments and evening entertainment as they were with the political content. Moreover, in so doing they were also concerned to maintain control over the event and prevent it from becoming too rowdy. In planning for the 1903 demonstration, for example, it was decided to request that the local authorities took action to close the public bars, and strictly soft drinks only were to be sold at the demonstration.[121]

At other times of the year social activities centred on the 'People's House' (*Folkets hus*). The need to find suitable rooms for meetings was a constant problem for the *arbetarekommun*, and indeed for trade unions and other labour organisations. In 1899 these groups established a People's House Association, the main function of which was to raise funds for the acquisition of a suitable property. In the meantime the association negotiated an agreement with the Labour Society (*arbetarförening*), which allowed labour organisations in Karlskrona to hire its rooms for their meetings. In 1902, the People's House Association was able to buy a plot, and earned some valuable funds by organising outdoor entertainment during the summer months. This, combined with the money raised through other means, such as bazaars and the modest donations of trade unions, meant that the association acquired their own property in 1906. By 1904, advertisements for summer theatre, music and variety performances were appearing regularly. Although the organisation of these events was largely driven by pragmatism, the political significance was not entirely forgotten. In a circular to trade unions, the association complained that workers' loyalties did not always lie where they should. 'The workers should,' it pointed out, 'much more than is the case now, regard the People's House as their own company, and as such, support it and take care of it, and not be so willing to patronise the entertainment organised by Messrs Capitalists while the People's House stands empty.' The People's House served another, more important, political function, providing a location where labour organisations could hold their meetings without fear of 'disruptive interventions from any quarter.'[122]

A similar concern to avoid 'disruptive intervention' also lay behind the attempts to found a party newspaper. In one of its very first actions, the *arbetarekommun* set up a committee to investigate this possibility, though this group later reported that it would not yet be financially viable to establish a labour newspaper. Instead, the *kommun* would concentrate on distributing the social democrat organ *Arbetet* among its members, and it was decided that every affiliated society would be obliged to appoint its own newspaper campaigner.[123] Many activists remained dissatisfied with what they saw as anti-socialist bias in the existing local newspapers, especially *Blekinge Läns Tidning,* and the *kommun* attempted to undermine the influence of the bourgeois press by organising a boycott. The only satisfactory solution to the problem however was felt to be the establishment of a social democratic newspaper.[124]

There was one group of workers in Karlskrona with whom the *arbetarekommun* seemed to have less contact, namely the employees of the naval dockyard. Although the *kommun* co-operated with the VAF in its electoral campaigning, some members were rather wary of the latter organisation, and suspicious that it could be regarded as a 'proper' trade union. One *kommun* member even went so far as to describe the VAF as a 'sewing circle' (*syförening*) and suggested that its programme contradicted the aims of trade unions.[125] The editors of *Blekinge Folkblad* were exasperated by the Stockholm trips affair, but concluded that the association's other members had only themselves to blame for their apathy and failure to hold the leadership to account.[126] For its part, although the question of closer links with the social democratic labour movement was discussed on several occasions, the KVAF was reluctant to commit itself to an openly political position by affiliating formally to the *arbetarekommun*. Requests that the association should become a member of the People's House Association or help to publicise the social democratic newspaper *Arbetet* were also turned down, as was an invitation from the *arbetarekommun* to take part in the 1901 1st May demonstration, although in this last case a donation was sent in lieu.[127] As far as it is possible to tell, it seems that the reason for this reluctance was not due to fear of disapproval on the part of the dockyard authorities, but to the disparate political views of the members, which made it impossible to reach agreement. It was noted, for example, that workers in the sister dockyard at Stockholm had been allowed the day off to attend the 1st May demonstrations, and some members were in favour of petitioning for a similar concession in Karlskrona the following year, but the association was not able to agree on this and the matter was dropped. As this implies, some members were certainly seeking to move the association much closer towards the labour movement, but opinion within the association was by no means unanimous on this point. When the *arbetarekommun* called a demonstration on the suffrage question in 1902, the VAF chairman agreed unilaterally that the union's banner could be taken on the march, since there was not time to call a members' meeting to debate the issue. But when the matter was discussed, at the next meeting, there were several objections, and those opposed complained that the chairman had allowed the banner to be damaged by being exposed to bad weather.[128] Later the same year, the union also declined to be formally involved with the organisation set up to run *Blekinge Folkblad*, because of the newspaper's 'red tone'.[129]

V

The conventional view suggests that in Karlskrona, as in Plymouth, the dominance of the naval dockyard contributed to retarding the development of the local labour movement during the late nineteenth and early twentieth centuries. In fact, as we have seen, this is not quite a fair assessment, for there was indeed an active labour movement in Karlskrona from the 1890s and even before. The *arbetarekommun* could not afford to ignore the dockyard workers. By the mid 1900s *riksdag* candidates were appealing directly to the dockyard workers for their votes, on the basis of their willingness and ability to tackle dockyard issues such as pensions, wages and working conditions. G W Roos, seeking re-election in 1905, made much of his efforts to improve dockyard pensions, although supporters of his labour opponent did their best to play down the significance of these actions.[130] Clearly, though, the dockyard workers were seen as one of the most important groups among the electorate, possessing the ability to affect the outcome of the election. The liberal candidate's victory in 1908, by 1049 votes to 890, following what was described as an unusually lively election, was attributed by his supporters to the dockyard workers' steadfastness in resisting the appeals from the Right and voting instead for Leander. 'To the working-class voters and not least the naval dockyard workers, who have been most exposed to the campaigning of *Karlskrona Weckoblad,* today we say **thank you!**'[131]

Conflicts over industrial relations and working conditions in the dockyard played a relatively small role in the formation of a labour movement, however. More significant was the common cause between social democrats and liberals in forming a progressive opposition to the élites who had dominated local politics during the part of the nineteenth century. The relationship between the social democratic *arbetarekommun* and the liberal groups was ambiguous, driven above all by pragmatism. Even before the suffrage reform of 1909 there were signs that the alliance was coming under strain, as the labour movement began to articulate a separate politics, influenced by ideas of class. The suffrage reform seems to have been decisive in producing a final break between liberals and social democrats, although the movement for independent labour representation was also influenced by organisational developments within the Social Democratic Party at a national level. The period should not be seen as one of linear development towards a national party structure concerned mainly with parliamentary elections, however. Instead, the boundaries between national and local organisations remained fluid, at times leading to conflict between the pressures for local autonomy on the one hand and national control on the other. The dockyard workers co-operated to some extent with the *arbetarekommun,* but they remained at arm's length, and were often seen as a community apart, a separate group with disparate interests. Although sectional rivalries were not as significant in Karlskrona – and indeed in the Swedish shipbuilding industry – as they were at Devonport, nonetheless, internal divisions among the dockyard workers perhaps also helped to hinder full co-operation with other labour organisations.

CHAPTER 7

Naval Politics
in Karlskrona c. 1911–1921

The year 1909 was an important turning point for the Swedish labour movement, in Karlskrona as elsewhere. The general strike of that year resulted in a substantial decline in trade union membership, and helped to confirm the commitment, at least within the mainstream of the SAP, to parliamentary reformism as the principal strategy for achieving the party's socialist goals. This process was helped by the suffrage reform of 1909, which meant that parliamentary representation and thus influence was now a real possibility for the SAP. Consequently, further steps were taken towards the development of a comprehensive electoral machinery, which had its first important test during the second chamber *riksdag* elections of 1911. These represented an important advance for the SAP, not only nationally but also in Blekinge, where the social democrats succeeded in winning two of the six mandates.

The three years after 1911 were challenging ones for the SAP, however, particularly in Karlskrona. The dominant issue in political debate was now defence, brought to a head by the mounting international tension, and the controversy surrounding the new Liberal government's attempts to control the defence budget. These questions carried, of course, particular resonance in a town like Karlskrona which was so intimately connected with the navy. The loss of the second social democratic mandate to the Right in Blekinge during the spring election of 1914 must be partly attributed to the defence issue, although the loss was made good later the same year, and March 1914 seemed to mark the high tide of the naval agitation. In fact, the second *riksdag* election of 1914, conducted against the background of the outbreak of war, generated remarkably little attention when compared to the bitter campaign fought during the spring. Given Sweden's neutral status, the impact of the war itself was likely to be less dramatic in Karlskrona than it was in Plymouth, but its effects were felt nonetheless, politically, economically and socially. As in Plymouth, activity in the naval dockyard reached an unprecedented level of intensity during the war, and this provided a boost to the ongoing attempts to develop dockyard unionism. This expansion took place, however, against the background of the permanent question mark over the yard's future, which developed into an acute crisis after 1918. The importance of the dockyard for the long-term economic interests of the town was a permanent subject of political debate during this period. Meanwhile, the consolidation of a dockyard trade union movement implied a growing separation between trade and politics as legitimate spheres for labour movement activity, amounting to a partial withdrawal of trade unions from political life. Against this, it was instead consumer issues, namely the severe food shortages from 1916–7, which provided the greatest impetus for working-class political activity during the war years.

This chapter begins by examining the defence debates of 1911–14 in Karlskrona, in the context of the elections of 1914 and the events leading up to them. Of particular interest are the ways in which politicians, especially those of the Right, connected national defence with local interests in their attempt to appeal to Karlskrona voters. The presence of the navy also attracted criticism, however, and it is necessary therefore to consider Labour and Liberal responses to the defence agitation. As in Plymouth, it cannot be assumed that political attitudes in Karlskrona were driven simply by support for 'big navy' politics. Questions of national defence and material interest were most closely linked in the case of the dockyard workforce, of course. From 1914 there was a new assertiveness on the part of these workers, marked by attempts to establish a national trade union federation, and to secure formal arrangements for collective bargaining. The chapter considers the extent to which these developments stemmed from changing local conditions within Karlskrona dockyard, or whether they were driven instead by responses to changes outside the yard. The relationship between the dockyard workers and the rest of the local labour movement is also examined. As in Plymouth, it seemed that conflicts over the control and distribution of a scarce food supply were important in shaping wartime politics in Karlskrona.

I

There could be no doubt about the importance of the navy to Karlskrona, or indeed, the importance of Karlskrona in the naval defence of the nation. The very name of the town, from its founder Karl XI, marked its historic associations with Sweden's era of great power status, which had begun to possess something of a nostalgic attraction for conservatives during the early twentieth century.[1] The links with that period were commemorated physically throughout the town, in its parks, streets, public buildings and monuments. Further, the presence of the navy was also acknowledged through the performance of public rituals and spectacles. The dockyard ship launch never took on quite the significance that it did in Plymouth and Portsmouth during this period, perhaps because Karlskrona dockyard was not, after all, constructing Dreadnoughts. But ship launches were nonetheless public events, performed in the presence of the naval authorities from Stockholm as well as all the luminaries of the local military establishment.[2] More informally, the 1st May reveille was, by the early twentieth century, a well-established tradition, which took the form of an early morning musical parade to the most important naval sites in the town. The tradition was thought to have its roots in the early morning tour of Björkholmen by the town watch to rouse the dockyard workers, or the use of a band of drummers to summon off-duty naval servicemen in the event of a potentially disastrous fire in the dockyard.[3] The music was usually provided by the fleet band, and the itinerary of the parade included the houses of the most important personages in Karlskrona, including the head of the dockyard and the Admiral-in-Chief. Between two and three thousand citizens took part in May 1914, and a general holiday atmosphere was reported in the town, with the various restaurants and other meeting places extremely busy.[4]

In September 1911 Karlskrona residents witnessed a spectacle of a very different kind when a large-scale naval exercise was held in the archipelago. This was in effect a mock sea-battle which took place over five days, with the 'Red' side off Karlshamn preparing to attack Karlskrona, which was itself defended by the 'Blue' side. Each day's events was reported by the newspapers in great detail, almost as if it was a real war, with special correspondents filing reports from different locations in the archipelago. '[W]e can expect an attack on Karlskrona at any time,' it was reported in *Karlskrona-Tidning*, and the town 'must thereafter be considered as being in a state of siege for some days. War and imaginary bloodshed will be in the air for at least four days, and the inhabitants of the town are doubtless waiting anxiously for the first shot [to be fired].'[5] This was an uncomfortable reminder, perhaps, of what the town might face in the event of a real war. The exercises were timed to coincide with the visit to Karlskrona of the King and Queen, the first such visit since their accession. Most of the royal itinerary was taken up with military duties, including a trip out into the archipelago to watch the naval manoeuvres, and a tour of the dockyard to inspect the various workshops and facilities. The right-wing newspaper *Karlskrona-Tidningen* noted the significance of the visit in terms of the developing political links between the monarchy and the defence and also, it was claimed, the loyalty of the population of Karlskrona to what the monarchy represented.

> It should be a matter of particular satisfaction to us, that [this visit] is occurring at a time when Karlskrona presents herself at her best as she does just at the moment. Despite the anti-social forces (*samhällsupplösande makter*) which are now appearing, the Swedish people are, to their credit, for the most part a royally-minded people, and it is with the most upright feelings of loyal veneration and appreciation that the population of Karlskrona now welcomes Their Majesties.[6]

The town was decorated for the occasion with blue and yellow flags across all the streets that the royal entourage would pass through, and many also turned out to line the route, only to be disappointed when the route was changed at the last minute.[7]

Such public commemorations of Karlskrona's role in Swedish naval defence were not universally welcomed, however. The labour newspaper *Blekinge Folkblad* criticised the expensive arrangements for the royal visit, which would have to be borne by the town's taxpayers.[8] Before 1911, Karlskrona had seemed to be anything but the 'natural' territory of political conservatism. On the eve of the 1905 *riksdag* election, the editors of *Karlskrona-Weckoblad* were pessimistic about the chances of a Rightist candidate winning much support in Karlskrona, where most of the electors were thought to be either liberal or moderate in their political views.[9] In 1896, one of the most recent occasions when there had been a straight fight between liberals and conservatives, the liberal candidate had won convincingly. The tables were turned in 1899, but the victory of Admiral von Otter was attributed to the candidate's personal following. Indeed, the existence of a clear delineation between left and right cannot be taken for granted, at least before 1914. The contests of the 1900s were represented as the struggle between two strands of liberalism, more or less reformist although clearly anti-socialist. Typically of the time, the winning candidate in 1905, G Roos, was not aligned with any political party, although, as we have seen, his views were beginning to awaken suspicions among the social democrats.[10] By 1908, there was a tendency in some circles at least, notably among the social democrats, to view the election as a straight contest between left and right, even though the candidate associated with the Right, Holmdahl, did not describe himself as such. Instead, speaking to 2000 people at a hustings meeting organised by the progressive electoral alliance, he announced that he preferred to take specific issues as they arose, rather than align himself to a particular party.[11]

Even before 1911, however, the question of defence had gained some prominence in electoral discourse. All candidates appealed directly to the dockyard workers for their votes, citing their willingness and ability to tackle dockyard issues such as pensions, wages and working conditions. G W Roos, seeking re-election in 1905, emphasised his efforts to improve dockyard pensions during the previous *riksdag*, although supporters of his labour opponent did their best to play down the significance of these actions.[12] Three years later, with Roos no longer in the race, the pledges of the rival candidates over dockyard and naval matters were even more hotly debated. The 1908 campaign seemed to be a particularly bitter one, with the first result being declared null and void after the losing party alleged that election irregularities had taken place, and a new ballot had to be organised several months later.[13] Both candidates declared that they thought it desirable to reduce military expenditure, but neither was prepared to make a firm commitment. The nominal candidate of the Right, O Holmdahl, argued that he could not support reductions in the military budget where local interests were concerned.

> If, for example, the question of dredging the eastern channel to Karlskrona arose, and it seemed that current expenditure would be exceeded, should he then say no, if he were convinced of the

necessity of such a scheme for maintaining the naval base in Karl-skrona? Or, if it were necessary for Karlskrona's defences that one of the islands should be fortified, should he then say no for economic reasons, even though he knew that it was necessary in order to save the millions which had already been put into fortifying Karlskrona?[14]

It was thought to be in Holmdahl's advantage that he was a local man, a former mayor of Karlskrona, who had therefore 'a living knowledge and experience [of the fact] that Karlskrona has and will depend on the fleet for its existence.'[15] His supporters pointed approvingly to the dockyard employee reported to have urged his colleagues to 'vote for a native of the town, who knows our and the town's real needs.'[16] Later, the opposing candidate Leander was to reflect that Holmdahl had achieved some success in playing up his local connections.[17] The latter was adopted as the official candidate of various military societies, although the absence of two local ships and their crews was thought to undermine his support.[18] For his part, Leander also pledged his support for the dredging scheme, and for maintaining the naval base in Karlskrona; as he put it, 'local patriotism urged everyone in the community to try to keep the fleet in Karlskrona.'[19] Leander also drew attention to his efforts to secure improvements in dockyard wages, pensions and holiday entitlement, although in doing so, he was accused by his opponents of political opportunism. After all, it was argued, what Karlskrona *riksdagsman* would not state his intention to improve conditions for the dockyard workers?[20] Clearly, though, the dockyard workers were seen as one of the most important groups among the electorate, possessing the ability to affect the outcome of the election.

The public debates over the defence issue during the years 1911–14 were followed with close interest within the Karlskrona labour movement. Despite the importance of the navy in Karlskrona, there is little evidence to suggest that social democrats were inhibited in their criticism of pro-defence nationalism. A *Blekinge Folkblad* editorial in 1907 condemned the 'dark fatalism' which insisted that there was no future for Karlskrona outside the naval base, looking forward instead to 'a future Karlskrona [sustained by] peaceful means'.[21] Karl Staaff's famous speech on defence, delivered in Karlskrona in December 1913, was also criticised in *Blekinge Folkblad,* for overturning the Liberal promise to prevent further increases in the defence budget put forward at the 1911 election, although the writer acknowledged that Staaff 'showed that he understood the people's (*småfolkets*) resentment of defence.'[22] No specific comment was made about the implications of what Staaff said on this occasion for Karlskrona, however. The *arbetarekommun* passed a resolution in January 1914 expressing its 'determined protest against the armaments frenzy and scare campaign (*rustningshets- och skrämselagitation*) which is presently happening in our country.' The military system was simply another tool of capitalist oppression, and the working class were thus urged to campaign with all their strength and energy 'not only against increased military expenditure, but also against militarism as an institution.'[23] The social democrats were steadfastly opposed to the Peasants' March (*bondetåget*) of 1914, arguing that it represented a cynical attempt by the Right to manipulate the peasant population in order to claim that the voice of the people was behind their demands.[24] It was suggested that most of the participants in the demonstration had little idea of why they were really taking part, and had simply been lured by the promise of a cheap outing to Stockholm. In Karlskrona, the *arbetarekommun* organised a protest demonstration and rally, attracting over 3000 people, it was claimed, to pass resolutions against increased defence spending and the monarchy. It was reported that about ten young officers in the crowd attempted to raise a shout for the king, but were heckled down.[25]

Following the resignation of the Staaff government in the wake of the Peasants' March, there was a new election in the spring of 1914. It was obvious that defence was going to be the main issue of debate, though this was now coupled to constitutional reform following the intervention of the King in the so-called palace yard coup (*borggårdskupen*). The divisions between the parties were clearly drawn with the Right adopting the slogan 'For King and country' and attempting to portray their Liberal and Social Democratic opponents as dangerous republicans.[26] The election campaign was an unusually bitter one. Karl Staaff was closely linked with the Liberals' campaign and attracted much vitriol from his right-wing opponents, even to the extent of being threatened and spat upon. The turnout, at 70% of those entitled to vote, reached record levels, and the polling stations attracted long queues.[27] All the parties organised election meetings, often headed by high-profile invited speakers. There were also a number of interest groups actively campaigning in the election, especially on behalf of the Right.[28] The campaign for the second election of 1914, which fell during the autumn as part of the normal electoral cycle, was much quieter by contrast, overshadowed by the outbreak of war in Europe.

At both elections defence was the foremost campaign issue for the Right party. Campaigning under the patriotic slogan 'For King and Country', the Right linked its advocacy of defence with its strong support of the monarchy, asserting the need for a strong individual to take responsibility for the defence of the country, free from the distraction of party ties or parliamentary majorities. The example of Germany under the strong hand of the Kaiser was contrasted approvingly with the French Republic.[29] Both the Liberals and the Social Democratic Party attempted to turn this patriotic language to their own advantage. For the Social Democrats, this meant campaigning for the 'people's country' (*folkets fosterland*): a democratic nation in which all could take pride.[30] The Liberals argued for the need to consider the defence question in 'its broadest sense', taking up the temperance slogan of campaigning against 'enemy forces… within the nation'; in other words, drunkenness.[31] This was in the context of the mobilisation of troops in response to the outbreak of war, and the demands of local temperance campaigners for tight restrictions to be placed on the sale of alcohol, a move which was condemned by the Right as a slur on the exemplary behaviour of the servicemen stationed in the town.[32]

A simple assumption that big navy policies would benefit Karlskrona, and would thus work automatically in the interests of the pro-defence Right, was misleading. The problem lay in the obsolescence of the dockyard infrastructure, which had been allowed to decay for a period during the mid nineteenth century, and had since been overtaken by technological changes in shipbuilding. An attempt to modernise the dockyard was made at the time of the first defence scare in the 1880s, with the construction of new workshops, a new railway system and new docks. During the last quarter of the nineteenth century the balance of work carried out by Karlskrona dockyard was shifting however, as the construction of new vessels was contracted out to larger private yards, and the dockyard concentrated on the repair, maintenance and fitting out of the existing fleet. There was indeed a fair amount of this work available during the 1880s and 1890s, as the fleet did not spend much time at sea, and there were many older ships requiring refits. Some new construction of smaller torpedo boats did take place, but it is noteworthy that during the period 1882–91 not a single vessel was launched at Karlskrona.[33] The trend towards the deployment of larger battleships from the turn of the century raised further questions about the dockyard's long-term future. The largest ship constructed at Karlskrona during the period 1885–1910 was only 210 tons displacement, and even after 1910 the dockyard did not have the capacity to build anything larger than 1600 tons.[34] The period from 1910 was one of prolonged enquiry into the dockyard's future, which produced little in the way of concrete results. The *F-båt* furore raised some concerns over the quotations for construction tendered by the private shipyards, and an investigation to establish whether the hull of the 7000-ton *Sverige* could be constructed at Karlskrona. The scheme was rejected, as the necessary expansion would require the costly purchase of private land outside the existing dockyard site. The naval adminstration and the minister concerned supported the first two stages of the modernisation proposal, but balked at the third, citing the uncertainty surrounding the future of this class of vessel.[35]

These uncertainties over the future of the dockyard complicated the defence debate in Karlskrona. Defence campaigners justified their advocacy of increased military spending with reference to the alleged threat from Russia and the need to protect Swedish neutrality. But their demands had to be tailored to perceptions of local circumstances and interests. The preference for very large battleships would be unlikely to benefit Karlskrona directly, since these ships would almost certainly have to be constructed in larger, private shipyards. Moreover, any move to concentrate the fleet in the Stockholm area, in the face of a potential Russian threat, would undermine Karlskrona's status as the main base of the Swedish navy. The Right party issued a leaflet to all citizens suggesting that this was indeed the aim of Liberal naval policy, which would therefore have disastrous consequences for Karlskrona.[36] By advocating a more modern, high-speed fleet, the Right party's policy provided for a navy which would not be bound to Stockholm, but would continue to be based in Karlskrona. The implications of this were straightforward. 'How should a Karlskrona resident vote? For the pro-defence [party], for in their programme the interests of the country are one with the interests of Karlskrona.'[37] The Right's defence plans 'would be greeted with satisfaction not least in Karlskrona,' stated one of the candidates, O Holmdahl.[38] He emphasised the need for a strong fleet of smaller torpedo boats alongside the largest battleships such as *Sverige*. The question over the preferred form for the navy was also taken up by the naval minister Broström, who visited Karlskrona during the election campaign for an opportune tour of the dockyard. He responded to the comment of a local social democrat that the government was deciding to concentrate on large ships only, to the detriment of Karlskrona's dockyard, by citing the failure of the outgoing government to set in motion the promised enquiry on the future of the dockyard, and promised that steps should be taken forthwith in this direction.[39] In an interview with *Karlskrona-Tidningen* following his tour of the dockyard he agreed that it would not be in national economic interests not to use the existing resources at Karlskrona, before also hinting at the possibility to develop the dockyard further for the construction of larger ships.

As in Plymouth, there is evidence to suggest that the dockyard workforce, which numbered almost 1500 in 1914, was seen as an important target of this campaigning. Certainly the Right party was prepared to campaign aggressively for the dockyard workers' vote. Special election meetings were organised for the dockyard workers, sometimes held together with meetings for new military conscripts, at which different speakers warned of the dire threat from Russia, and described the 'work opportunities' for the dockyard which the Right's defence programme would offer.[40] Opponents were highly critical of what they saw as political opportunism, accusing the pro-defence campaigners of hiding their propandising behind evenings of light entertainment – music, singing, recitations and even cinema – laid on for the dockyard workers and other groups, a tactic which they condemned, interestingly, as American (*amerikanska agitationsmetoder*): 'scare tactics and...election promises for lower ranked officers and dockyard workers.'[41] The Liberal newspaper *Blekinge Läns Tidning* also condemned the dockyard authorities' willingness to grant permission, against normal regulations, for the display of posters on the dockyard gates advertising these meetings, while simultaneously refusing to display liberal political posters.[42] Both papers addressed columns specifically to the dockyard workers, advising them to vote one way or the other in the yard's and their own interests. The Liberals drew attention to the record of their candidate Leander in the *riksdag* during the Staaff government, when, they suggested, he had been active in drawing attention to dockyard affairs, and in particular bringing a motion on dockyard expansion and modernisation.[43] The introduction of paid holidays for dockyardsmen was cited as another achievement of the

Staaff government. *Karlskrona-Tidningen* countered with its own address to the dockyard workers, suggesting that the Right had been equally influential in securing dockyard holidays.[44] But the main issue was not changes in conditions of employment so much as the future of dockyard employment altogether. Social democrats and liberals linked the debate over the future of naval construction with their critique of the big business interests behind the Right party. Karl Hildebrand, who addressed a meeting of dockyard workers on the need for improved defence, was condemned by the Liberals as a prominent supporter of private ownership, who would therefore do all that he could to ensure that new construction went to private shipyards. 'Do Hrr Dockyard Workers know who Hr Hildebrand really is?' they asked.

> [He is] the most ardent supporter of private capital in Sweden.... Now, Hrr Dockyard Workers know very well that the previous government wished to enlarge the dockyard and for that reason induced the *riksdag* to buy land next to the dockyard wall. The idea, of course, was that armoured warships (*pansarbåtar*) should also be built here. But how do Hrr Dockyard Workers think it will turn out if Hr Hildebrand and the Right win the election? It is certain then that only smaller ships will be built here, as has been the case up until now. Everyone knows, after all, where the *Sverige* is being built! The Right will *always* favour private shipyards and hold back the state dockyards. It is in the nature of the thing.[45]

It is difficult to gauge how the dockyard workers themselves responded to these attempts to win their votes. The 300 or so dockyard employees reported to have attended one of the Right's political meetings in 1914 accounted for only a minority of the dockyard workforce. There is evidence that some members of the dockyard union were uncomfortable with the Right's attempts to woo them, and the matter was debated at a branch meeting in March 1914. The prevailing view seemed to be that the union should avoid political controversy at all costs, and no action was taken.[46]

II

The prominence of the defence debate within political discourse, and the Right's attempts to take advantage politically by campaigning aggressively on defence issues among the dockyard workforce, coin-

TABLE 7.1. *MVAF minimum wage proposal for all dockyard workers, November 1914.*

Workers	Minimum age	Years in service	Basic pay rate (per day)
Craftsmen (*yrkesarbetare*)	18	-	2 kr 50 öre
	21	4	3 kr 30 öre
	24	7	3 kr 70 öre
	-	10	4 kr 20 öre
Labourers	-	-	3 kr 30 öre

SOURCE: Folkrörelsearkiv i Blekinge län, 1984/67, FCPF avd 36, ankomna skrivelser 1913–1925: Varvschefen to KMF, 24th November 1914 (copy).

cided with a new assertiveness on the part of the dockyard workers. A meeting in February 1913 resulted in the foundation of a new organisation, the Naval Dockyard Workers' Union (*Marinens Varvsarbetareförbundet* or MVAF), which from the beginning co-operated with workers at the sister dockyard in Stockholm, and soon became a branch of an embryonic national federation with common rules. The KVAF continued to exist as a separate organisation for a number of years, but in practice the two organisations were the same, at least in terms of the leading activists, and the formal merger, on 1st January 1916, passed almost unnoticed. At the MVAF's first official meeting, K V Dahlström, who had also been one of the most active members of the KVAF, clarified the status of the new organisation, and outlined the most important issues facing it: working hours, free health care, pensions and wages. The pensions issue occupied the union for most of 1913, but in April the following year they put forward a proposal for a new wage system, which was to dominate activities for the next few years. Workers' incomes were formed partly by a basic day rate, set according to the individual contract agreed between the workman and the Crown when the former was first hired, and adjusted on the recommendation of a foreman or other supervisor. The basic rate was supplemented by a complicated piecerate system, and after 1914, workers could expect to negotiate a war supplement (*krigstidstillägg*) to offset inflation, and also to earn overtime.[47] Indeed, the union argued that the amount of overtime expected of the workforce, as the Swedish fleet was made ready for active service to defend the country's neutrality if necessary, undermined the management's argument that there were not sufficient funds for a general pay rise.[48]

In November 1914 the union proposed the replacement of individual tariffs by a collective system which guaranteed a minimum basic rate for all workers in a particular category. The first such proposal, in 1914, set the pattern for later proposals (Table 7.1). Because of Swedish neutrality, the outbreak of war in August 1914 was not felt in Karlskrona dockyard with the same intensity as in Plymouth, but it did nonetheless generate a sharp rise in the cost of living, and this certainly helped to drive the MVAF's campaign. But there was more at stake here than merely wage rates. Fundamentally, the union's proposal was concerned with the issue of management control of the workforce, and the formal contractual relationship between worker and management. The union argued that the existing system was arbitrary and encouraged favouritism. Like the 'classification' system in operation at Devonport before 1901, it left decisions about pay, 'in the hands of one or other foreman or supervisor, who, with the best will in the world, on many occasions cannot entirely free himself from personal sympathies and antipathies.'[49] For their part, the officers in charge of the dockyard departments at Karlskrona were deeply sceptical about the new wage system proposals, arguing that it was vital to the smooth running of the dockyard to retain a system for rewarding merit and sanctioning workers who underperformed. The Dockyard Director reported to the Royal Naval Administration (*Kungliga Marinförvaltningen* or KMF) in 1914 that, 'the [proposed] system is fundamentally wrong in that wages are not linked to labour productivity, but to other considerations, namely age and length of service, by which the feebly talented and least productive individuals will be favoured.'[50] Minimum wages would be acceptable only if management retained the right to withhold them from workers who did not do their jobs properly.[51] Particularly striking is the view, expressed by the Head of the Buildings Department, that the increased job security by dockyard employees, compared to workers in private industry, meant that a discretionary wage system was an important means of maintaining motivation and productivity.[52] For what this implies is the acknowledgement of problems which were specific to the management of dockyards as a state-owned industry, problems which, as we have seen, were also encountered by dockyard managers at Devonport.

Included in the MVAF's minimum wage proposal was the further demand that the union should be involved in the negotiation of the basic rates; in other words that wages should be set through a centralised, formal, collective bargaining system, the so-called 'right to negotiation' (*förhandlingsrätt*). Pre-empting such an agreement, the union attempted to remove the influence of local management by directing its campaigning towards the KMF, through locally elected delegates who travelled to Stockholm and joined their metropolitan colleagues to lobby in person. In the absence of established channels of communication similar to the British petitions system, this strategy relied on the co-operation of the KMF to establish a dialogue. The admiral who received the delegates in the summer of 1915 made it quite clear that his tolerance of a delegation was an exception, which could not be expected to establish a precedent, and he refused to allow the representatives to attend the discussions of their proposal in person. Labour sources suggest that the workers felt themselves to be fobbed off with promises to put the wage matter to an inquiry, a process which could take many months or even years.[53] The union began tentatively to discuss the possibility of more militant action, and threatened to make inquiries along these lines in a resolution to the authorities in 1916, but the general feeling remained that this was still not a viable option.[54] The 1914 parliamentary decision to exempt the dockyard workers from the operation of the 'war laws' (*krigslagar*), which placed them under military discipline, might have been thought to have give a boost to the campaign, but the situation remained far from clear. When the MVAF sought clarification from the authorities in 1916, the response was that although the *krigslagar* no longer applied to dockyard workers in times of peace, this was not the case during wartime mobilisation, and thus the situation was in effect unchanged. The grounds for caution were confirmed by the *varvschef*, who pointed out that, even in peacetime, the relaxation in the law did not allow the possibility of a strike, as workers remained prevented from carrying out such action by their individual contracts, which placed them under the naval regulations. If dockyard workers wished to pursue strike action, their only lawful possibility was to resign and work out their contractual notice before withholding their labour, otherwise they would be subject to a disciplinary hearing in a military court.[55] Nevertheless, despite these restrictions on the available tactics, the MVAF gained confidence from the wider developments within Swedish industry at this time. A resolution from 1917 stated boldly that, 'the right of workers to be consulted is of course a generally acknowledged fact in private industry, and is therefore an essential condition for peaceful labour relations in the royal dockyards.'[56] Dockyard management resisted comparisons with private industry, however, and argued that while they had nothing against hearing workers' views, they were under no formal obligation to take these into account when deciding wages or any other matters of work conditions.

By 1917, it seemed that the management position could no longer be sustained, and the first collective minimum wage agreement, covering all dockyard workers in Stockholm and Karlskrona, came into force on 1st September 1917. It is not clear what brought about the change of heart on the part of the authorities, although it is possible that they were motivated by the tightening labour market and the fear of losing skilled workers at a time of increased intensity in dockyard work. Some concessions were also made regarding the union's other campaign goal, the right to negotiation. Under a new system, dockyard workers were entitled to elect delegates, one for every 200 workers, to represent them in negotiations with the authorities on wages and other aspects of working conditions.[57] The system ignored the existence of the MVAF, but in practice the union was able to exercise control over the election process, by running its own internal elections before those officially organised in working hours by the dockyard authorities.[58] The union's main goal was now to secure its recognition as a partner in the wage bargaining process, so-called *förhandlingsrätt*. By the early 1920s, the dockyard workers had succeeded in discrediting the delegation system by voting with their feet and simply not participating, and *förhandlingsrätt* was eventually conceded in 1922.[59]

Apart from the distinction made between apprenticed craftsmen (*yrkesmän*) and ordinary labourers, the MVAF campaigned for a wage agreement that would apply to all workers across the dockyard, regardless of their trade. Whereas Devonport dockyard workers petitioned according to trade, and campaigned to maintain existing wage differentials between trades, this type of sectional rivalry seems to have been absent from Karlskrona dockyard. Like its predecessor the KVAF, the MVAF was an organisation for all dockyard employees. Just under half (48.5%) the membership was drawn from what may be described as the major shipbuilding trades; the rest included helpers (*hantlangare*) and members of the minor trades, together with many workers who were not involved in shipbuilding at all. This last group included workers employed to maintain the yard's buildings and infrastructure, storemen and transport workers, dockyard guards, general labourers, and a small group of women workers employed in the sail and colour lofts. The largest trade group within the union was the platers, which formed just over 17% of the total membership.[60] At its first meeting in 1913, the union elected representatives (*uppbördsmän*) charged with collecting membership dues in each individual workshop, right across the dockyard.[61]

Not only did the MVAF organise all dockyard workers, it is also important to note that, from 1914 at least, the union was nominally a branch of a national federation. At a national level, attention was being increasingly drawn towards the possibility of merging the MVAF with unions representing other civilian defence workers. Three delegates from the MVAF attended the founding conference of the Civilian Army Employees' Union (*Arméns civila personals förbund* or ACPF) in Stockholm in December 1917, and the two organisations co-operated fairly closely during the following years. Among early campaigning successes may be noted the achievement of the statutory eight-hour day for all civilian defence industry workers, the first group in the country to achieve this milestone. The ACPF's 1920 congress took up the issue of the unification of the ACPF with the MVAF, and from 1 January 1921 naval workers from Stockholm and Vaxholm joined their colleagues in the renamed Civilian Defence Employees' Union (*Försvarsverkens civila personals förbund* or FCPF). The Karlskrona workers were more reticent, however, and it took a visit from the new federation's rather belligerent chairman, Edoff Andersson, to persuade them to affiliate six months later.[62] The Karlskrona branch had in fact moved to align itself with state employees in general, and a branch meeting in 1916 had voted unanimously for full co-operation with the Civil Servants' Co-operation Organisation (*Statstjänarnas samorganisation*) in Karlskrona, to lobby for wartime wage supplements.[63] During the years immediately following the war, this co-operation was extended to national campaigns for pensions and holidays. At its meeting in October 1918, the Karlskrona branch voted to affiliate formally to the organisation, and in doing so aligned itself with the interests of the state railwaymen, postmen, customs workers, prison warders, and telecommunications workers, both male and female.[64] The loose co-operative federation which developed during and immediately after the war was the forerunner of the Civil Servants' Union (*Statstjänarnas Centralorganisationen* or SCO) founded in 1923.

The FCPF, of which Karlskrona dockyard workers made up Branch 36, appears to conform to the conventional model of a Swedish trade union federation: national in scope, highly centralised, and tightly controlled by its Stockholm-based executive committee. The autonomy of the branch was restricted, and local activity was to be confined to negotiating everyday working conditions: the ventilation of a particular workshop, or the provision of overalls and tools for a specific group of workers. Other activities were discouraged, and in 1917 the MVAF's Stockholm-based chairman, C A Nyström, wrote to his Karlskrona colleagues to warn them that wage negotiation with the local dockyard authorities at a branch level was not likely to gain a result.[65] Attempts to organise outside the auspices of the MVAF were barely tolerated, as indicated by the rejection of affiliate status for the torpedo workshop club in 1915.[66] As the FCPF grew in size during the 1920s, attempts were made to form workshop-based sections, primarily intended to make the collection of membership fees easier, and thus reduce the burden of work on committee members.[67] Even so, the FCPF's supremacy in the dockyard did not go entirely unchallenged. Branch 96 of the Swedish Metal Industry Workers' Union (Metall), founded in 1901, had managed to retain its foothold in the dockyard even after the formation of the MVAF. As late as 1929, the branch retained 41 members in Karlskrona, most of them working in the engine workshop.[68] This number was insignificant compared to the 1000 or so in the MVAF, but it was enough to fuel a long-running dispute between the two unions over representation of the dockyard workers in the bargaining process. With members in other branches of the defence industry, Metall was able to block FCPF affiliation to LO for a number of years.[69]

The success of the MVAF, and its successor the FCPF, relied on the union's ability to create a common identity among its members which stretched across the dockyard trades, and following the foundation of the FCPF, across the entire defence industry. The members' newsletter, which was produced on two occasions in 1919, and monthly from 1920, was intended to cement this collective identity, as was the official tenth anniversary history of the union written by its first chairman Edoff Andersson. This later generation of activists such as Andersson regarded earlier attempts to establish a dockyard organisation with a degree of suspicion, and were generally inclined to dismiss the KVAF as a social club which encompassed only a minority of dockyard workers, and lacked the functions of a genuine trade union. It should be noted, however, that these comments were often made in the context of attempts to justify rather different forms of labour organisation in the dockyard. Where earlier organisations did not fit into the preferred model, they tended to be regarded as doomed to failure. The MVAF was itself described as a 'very primitive' organisation in comparison to the one which succeeded it, but unlike the misguided KVAF it could at least be portrayed as part of the transition towards the emergence of a modern, industrial trade union for the dockyard.[70] According to the official history, the foundation of the Karlskrona branch of the MVAF stemmed from the initiative of Stockholm workers, and thus had no connection with the KVAF. In fact, from the local minutes it appears that the KVAF was indeed more or less moribund by this time, but that it was more or less the same activists who called a meeting of dockyard workers in the spring of 1913 and established the MVAF.[71]

III

The efforts of the Stockholm-based union officials were undoubtedly influential in contributing to the development of dockyard unionism in Karlskrona. The increased publicity for the union's activities generated by the wage negotiations played its part in recruiting members to the MVAF, as did also the tightening labour market in the context of the war. The order to mobilise the dockyard in response to the outbreak of war prevented workers from resigning, but paradoxically, tighter restrictions may have helped to strengthen the assertiveness of the workforce. Dockyard workers who did leave their employment in the yard stood more chance of gaining shipbuilding employment elsewhere, and a number of Karlskrona workers joined the workforce at the new Öresund shipyard at Landskrona.[72] Equally important in developing the links between the dockyard workers and the wider labour movement in Karlskrona, however, were the events outside the workplace. As in Plymouth, it was not so much conflicts surrounding work and employment, as those over consumer issues and the distribution of increasingly scarce food supplies, that had the greatest political impact during the years after 1914. In Karlskrona problems related to the food supply were felt as early as the outbreak of war in August 1914.[73] Even though Sweden was not a belligerent state, there were nonetheless fears for the country's security, and Karlskrona was witness to a massive mobilisation of troops during the early days of August. The town was suddenly transformed by the presence of large numbers of uniformed men on the streets, and the bars and restaurants in the town centre were reported to be extremely lively.[74] Two days later the Admiral-in-Chief issued an official notice requesting all citizens who were able to leave the town, 'so that food shortages should not arise.'[75] It was stated that the request should not be interpreted as suggesting that Karlskrona was in any immediate danger, but it can only have contributed to raising the level of tension in the town. By the following day it was reported that 6000 inhabitants had already left, and the neighbouring town of Ronneby had taken out a substantial loan in order to provide for Karlskrona citizens who had left their homes.[76] Within 48 hours, however, the admiral, perhaps in an effort to calm panic, made a further announcement to the effect that Karlskrona was not directly threatened, and thus his initial request 'was not to be taken as a command but merely as guidance for those who could leave the town without inconvenience.'[77]

The admiral's statement was prompted not by any threat to the security of Karlskrona, but rather a concern over the strains placed on the local food supply.[78] *Blekinge Folkblad* criticised the irresponsibility of the authorities in allowing a state of public hysteria to develop. 'There was a catch here, people thought, Karlskrona would be bombed and it was a matter of life or death. And thus there was panic – a rush to the railway and another rush to the food shops.'[79] Throughout Europe, this was a common concern, and prices rose considerably during the first month of the war as people rushed to stock up for fear that supplies would shortly be disrupted. As early as 6th August the Swedish state had taken action to establish local food committees in each *län*, in an attempt to regulate the food supply, and the machinery for these committees was quickly in place in most of the towns.[80] Once the initial spate of panic-buying had subsided the price level stabilised, and civilian life returned to something near normal, although the autumn *riksdag* election was severely subdued, especially in comparison to the heated agitation of the spring.

The problem of food shortages and rising prices remained a threat throughout 1915, resulting in some limited action on the part of the committee (*livsmedelsnämnden*). The situation worsened across Europe as the war progressed, even for non-belligerent countries like Sweden. By the winter of 1916 the submarine war was causing severe disruption to merchant shipping, and the resulting shortages were compounded by a poor harvest during the autumn of 1916. In Karlskrona matters became more acute when the coastal fleet (*kustflottan*) was moved from Stockholm to Karlskrona during the winter of 1916–7. Local schools and other public buildings were pressed into service to quarter the personnel, who announced their presence in the town with a daily musical procession.[81] Early in 1917 it was thought necessary to take the first steps towards the rationing of basic foodstuffs, in the first instance of bread and flour, but other scarce commodities such as bacon, potatoes and firewood followed shortly afterwards. The *arbetarekommun* expressed further concerns at these measures, with some members suggesting that rationing was unnecessary, brought about by failures in government policy, particularly in allowing exports to continue. It was pointed out that the situation in Karlskrona was relatively good compared to the privations in the north of Sweden, and there was also some resentment that there seemed to be adequate military supplies in the town, despite the shortages in the civilian shops. The resolution eventually agreed by the *arbetarekommun* at its meeting in February 1915 recognised the need for rationing, but protested that the allotted ration was inadequate. Working-class families were now relying more heavily on bread to make up the bulk of their diet as other commodities such as potatoes were so expensive as to be beyond the means of many consumers. Given the 'intensity of work which present-day working methods require, [workers] use at least as much physical effort as farmers, and for this reason it should be a priority for the state authorities to provide at least as great a quantity of bread or flour for these groups of workers as for the maintenance of the farmers.'[82] If prisoners were deemed by 'experts' to require a ration of 500–680g bread per day, and 680g flour per week, then workers were also 'worth a ration large enough to keep him from starvation.' There was also a marked concern that grain should be reserved for bread only, and not used for brewing or distilling.

The spring of 1917 was marked by heightened levels of tension and excitement. News of events in Russia was followed with great interest throughout all sections of Swedish society.[83] Within the labour movement the February revolution was hailed as the first signs of the beginnings of a wider movement for democratic reform. With the 'sun risen in the east' (a common metaphor), Sweden now held the dubious distinction of being one of the most reactionary regimes in

Europe.[84] Karlskrona *arbetarekommun*'s call to demonstrate on 1st May 1917 referred to 'society shaking to the foundations as never before'.[85] The call from Blekinge district SAP was no less apocalyptic, citing the developments across Europe, and condemning the actions of the 'profiteers harvesting gold' while the Swedish people neared starvation. 'Never before have the workers of the separate countries of the world sought to win such far-reaching demands as just now…'[86] The district party organisers insisted that parliamentary reformism represented the best tactics to achieve the 'peace, bread and justice' demanded by the demonstrations, but also thought it necessary to absolve themselves from responsibility in case the demonstration got out of hand. 'It will be our opponents' affair if they meet us with any other means, and in that case they bear responsibility for what might happen,' they stated, hinting that they were not entirely confident that they were in full control of the situation. A *Blekinge Folkblad* editorial hinted at the potential trouble in the situation:

> The Swedish people are world renowned for the calm and loyal means by which they have constantly presented their demands, for example the general strike of 1909, but there is still a boundary here, and it is important not to play too carelessly with fire, for it could be dangerous and have consequences more disastrous than many have imagined. That one drop can tip the balance ought to be borne in mind in these times.[87]

As it happened, the labour movement was overtaken by events in Karlskrona. At the end of April, a group of military conscripts assembled in the centre of the town to protest against the declining quality of their rations. Joined by members of the civilian population, they formed a substantial crowd of 5000 which marched up to the main square and met the Admiral-in-Chief with a cry of 'More food, more bread!' The Admiral responded that he would meet a delegation of five individuals, and asked the rest of the crowd to disperse peacefully. When this was ignored, the chairman of the *arbetarekommun*, Vilhelm Carlsson, appealed to the demonstrators in the name of the Swedish people's reputation for 'calm and self-control' (*lugn och besinning*), and asked them to disperse. His message was repeated by the leader of the social democratic youth club, O W Andersson. The majority of the demonstrators did indeed depart, but tensions remained high, and in the immediate aftermath a small group of youths took out their frustration by breaking the shop windows of some prominent traders and merchants.[88] The authorities reacted swiftly to stamp out expressions of discontent within the military population. All military personnel were confined to barracks and required to wear uniform at all time, and soldiers were forbidden from gathering in large groups.

The reaction of the labour movement to the hunger demonstrations of April 1917 is interesting. Labour leaders found themselves torn between their understanding of the 'resentment of profiteering' (*förbittring mot jobberiet*) which lay behind the demonstration, and the need to assert their control over the more unruly elements of popular protest, which they felt undermined their longstanding demands for full political responsibility. 'Merely to demonstrate, without having appointed a speaker in advance, will naturally not bring the result that collective action can otherwise deliver,' the demonstrators were reminded in a *Blekinge Folkblad* editorial.[89] The 'excesses' which followed the peaceful demonstration were attributed partly to the actions of the police in raising tension by drawing their weapons at a crucial moment, but were for the most part associated with a few boys, 'who do not belong either to [labour] organisations or to other collective groups.' In an attempt to take back control over the situation, the *arbetarekommun* co-ordinated the drafting of a series of petitions to various local bodies, agreed at a meeting held on the same Thursday evening between the *kommun*, the SAP group on the town council, the workers' representatives on the food committee, and the editors of *Blekinge Folkblad*.[90] (It is unclear whether this meeting took place independently of the demonstration or as a result of it.) A further demonstration was organised for the following Saturday, at which 5000 people gathered to hear an address from the social democratic *riksdagsman* Oskar Kloo.[91] Kloo told the crowd that the food shortages were the result of the failings of the Hammarskjöld government, and contrasted the situation in Sweden with that of the neighbouring Scandinavian countries where the governments were rooted in the will of the people through parliament, and the food question had consequently been handled much more competently. The petition which was handed to the magistrates in the town hall was directed against the local authorities, however, urging them to take a series of practical measures which should be taken by the local authorities to improve the distribution of the food supply. The proposals included: tighter controls to prevent black market trading; a ban on whole-sale purchasing before 11 am; an increased bread ration for workers on low incomes – offset by a corresponding reduction for all those with higher incomes; the sale of potatoes and firewood to be organised through the food committee; and a reorganisation of this committee to include the appointment of one or more paid employees, and the 'election... of more people who have the support and trust of the ordinary people (*småfolket*)'.[92] The response was felt to be positive. The magistrate promised to forward the demands to the relevant authorities, and as early as 3rd May it was reported that action had been taken. The town's employers were required to act to ameliorate their employees' situation, and the police had issued an order regarding the regulation of the sale of foodstuffs.[93] These announcements were taken as an illustration of what could be achieved through organised action. The demonstrations culminated in the 1st May demonstration, which was reported to be the largest seen in Karlskrona, with at least 8000 people taking part. The food issue remained prominent, with banners bearing the slogans, 'Bread for the people', 'Down with profit-making on basic provisions', and 'We demand a ban on the export of all basic provisions.' But it passed off peacefully, to the relief both of the authorities and also of the labour movement. The main speaker, Oskar Kloo, 'hoped that Karlskrona workers at that demonstration as at future demonstrations would show that they had political maturity.' He concluded his speech by exhorting 'all to maintain the same dignified self-control as hitherto and not to squander their strength on minor riots and other stupidities, addressing himself here especially to the younger unorganised element. May 1st would today end with people's consciousness of the majesty of the people.'[94]

Conflicts over the supply of food were thus important in the development of labour politics in Karlskrona, just as they also were in Plymouth. The major difference between the two towns was the role played by the consumer co-operative movement in Plymouth. There was a small consumer co-operative society in Karlskrona, which ran two shops in 1900 and had a modest membership fluctuating between about 200 and 400 in the years before the war. During the war the society attempted to keep its prices as low as possible, but was hampered in its efforts by the sheer difficulty of getting hold of sufficient supplies.[95] This meant that most of the initiatives for political action over the food supply were taken by the *arbetarekommun*. Nonetheless, closer examination of the way in which this consumer politics was articulated reveals some important similarities between the two cases, despite the much less significant role played by the co-operative society in Karlskrona. In the first place, the problems with the food supply were attributed not merely to the war, but to the failures of the capitalist system of distribution. The drastic price rises of August 1914 were caused by 'the most hateful profit hunger, profiteering (*ocker*) on misery'. The *arbetarekommun*, together with other labour organisations, observed the situation carefully, attributing the problems not only to the wartime situation however, but to 'monopolies and trusts' and the failure of the government to introduce regulations to curb financial speculation. A well-attended public meeting on the 'inflation question' (*dyrtidsfrågan*) early in 1915 agreed a resolution pressing for the temporary suspension of customs duties on corn imports, and the agreement of a fixed price for corn.[96] The banners at the 1915 May Day demonstration carried a new word which was rapidly becoming commonplace in the labour vocabulary: 'Down with the food profiteers' (*Ned med livsmedelsjobbarna*).[97] *Jobberi*, which was to become a familiar term during the war years, seems to correspond to the English term 'profiteering'. Nor was profiteering merely attributable to the large trusts. Despite the pre-war efforts of the Social Democratic Party to base its appeal on a broad alliance of the 'little people' or *småfolket,* it seemed unavoidable that the situation would drive a wedge between urban consumers and rural producers. Local fishermen were rumoured to be taking their catch as far away as Denmark where they could get a better price, while farmers sent their milk to Stockholm for the same reason, or even slaughtered their animals in preference to milking them. When the authorities set a national price for firewood they were condemned for setting a price 'which the farmers and forest owners of Blekinge never dreamed that they could get, even if profiteering in wood had continued unchecked.'[98]

Although the high prices were consistently attributed to the actions of capitalist profiteers throughout the course of the war, there was however a subtle shift in emphasis, which replaced the 'period of inflation' or *dyrtiden* of the period up to 1916 with the 'period of crisis' or *kristiden.* With basic commodities not merely soaring in price, but vanishing altogether from local shops, the focus of the labour movement campaigns turned towards local control of the food supply. The Karlskrona municipal food committee had begun to take some limited action from the beginning of 1915, exploring the possibilities for making bulk purchases of commodities such as wheat and rye grain which could then be sold to the public at the lowest possible price from the committee's rooms near the town's main square.[99] As the situation worsened, though, its efforts seemed to be increasingly inadequate. There were complaints that the provision made for the sale of goods below the free market price – bacon for example was sold for less than 1.85 *kronor* per kilogram compared to anything up to 3 *kronor* – was exercised indiscriminately, with the result that supplies had frequently sold out altogether before working-class consumers could purchase them.[100] 'The bread question is forgotten, the need for firewood is handed over to the goodwill of the Welfare Committee, the town council's decision on the purchase of pork is ignored, and the provisions for cheap potatoes are restricted to a modest consignment which the town owns itself. And finally an appeal to conserve eggs – to people who scarcely have the means to buy bread.'[101]

The demand for fairness, accountability and the adequate representation of working-class consumers thus dominated the debates over food control in Karlskrona, just as they did in Plymouth. The obvious difference between the two cases was the role of the Co-operative Society in Plymouth. In Karlskrona, before the war, the *arbetarekommun* and its affiliated trade unions had showed themselves willing to support the struggling co-operative society, by helping to publicise the society among their own members, and lending its support in specific campaigns, such as the Co-operative Federation's margarine boycott in 1909. As food prices rose after the start of the war, there is evidence that some within the labour movement now saw co-operation in a new light, as a genuine alternative to existing systems of distribution. A labour meeting to debate the high price of milk was told that more commitment to co-operation would have prevented the profiteering of the trusts.[102] The MVAF had campaigned hard to secure 'crisis supplements' (*kristidstillägg*) for its members, but warned that in itself this presented no solution to the problem; instead, 'a lively interest in co-operation is just as necessary as improved wages.' Certainly, membership of the co-operative society more than doubled from 247 in 1913 to 671 the following year, and the society took out a front page advertisement in *Blekinge Folkblad* to explain the workings of the dividend system to potential members. It was also agreed, partly for financial reasons, that the society's chairman should be the Karlskrona delegate to the Social Democrats' first 'inflation congress' (*dyrtidskongress*) in December 1916.

With the introduction of bread rationing in early 1917, the situation became even more acute. Criticism was directed towards the government for allowing food exports to continue, and for setting the ration so low as to 'gamble with the people's health'. But the greatest concerns arose over evidence that the rationing system was still failing to ensure that scarce goods were distributed fairly to all citizens.[103] The petition handed in to the local authorities in the wake of the hunger demonstration demanded that 'substantial measures be taken to ease the burden of this crisis on those members of society with less means (*de mindre bemedlade i samhället*).' Despite the concessions made in response to the petition, the allegations that essential provisions were not distributed fairly to the '*mindre bemedlade*' continued. Speakers at a labour meeting, called to debate the issue, expressed their concerns that those with the luxury of a telephone could often secure their supply at the expense of those for whom the only option was to wait in a queue.[104] There were also demands that the food committee should conduct more of its business in public, and that it remained largely unaccountable despite the inclusion of more labour representatives. Indeed, the *arbetarekommun* discussed whether it might not be more effective for them to resign altogether, and, following a public meeting, its representatives were withdrawn and the committee was reconstituted.[105]

IV

The years 1917–18 marked a crucial period for the labour movement in Sweden and elsewhere, resulting in a permanent split between reformist social democracy and the revolutionary communist left. Although the Bolshevik revolution had an enormous influence on this development of course, the separation of the left wing from the SAP marked the institutionalisation of an internal dispute which had been developing since the early years of the century, or even before. Most historians of the SAP have tended to focus on the reform versus revolution debate as it was played out at the centre of the party, and Branting's struggle to keep control of his party during the revolutionary tensions of the years 1917–18. The ideological split within the party turned on the issue of defence in particular, and views were also divided within the Karlskrona *arbetarekommun* on this point, between those in favour of a 'struggle against militarism in all its forms' and those advocating a more moderate stand to protect the party's support.[106] But there was more to the 1917 schism than ideological difference. In part, it was the result of a developing current of opposition towards the bureaucratisation of the party, and the ever more heavy-handed attempts of the leadership to impose discipline and authority on the party. Young socialists and other opponents became increasingly vociferous in their argument for greater independence and freedom of expression within the party, and a chance to express their radical views on defence, religion and temperance. The radical protests which erupted throughout Sweden during the spring and summer of 1917 should be seen above all therefore as a challenge to central organisation, rooted in local conditions and experiences. On that basis, it was hardly surprising that anarcho-syndicalist ideas were as important to these protests as doctrinaire Marxism: the main influences Kautsky and Krapotkin rather than Lenin.[107]

These currents were also present within the Blekinge labour movement, though, not surprisingly, the social democratic histories of the movement in Blekinge tended to play down the extent of the split in 1917, suggesting that few bothered to join the new party.[108] Nevertheless, the region was by no means isolated from the events of 1917–18. By the beginning of 1917, before events in Russia or the hunger demonstrations of the spring, it was clear that the relationship between the party and its youth wing was becoming strained, and Karlskrona *arbetarekommun* met to debate this. After a long discussion, the *kommun* eventually passed a resolution against the national executive committee's proposals for a settlement between party and youth federation. This was by no means a unanimous decision: it was agreed by 21 votes to 15, and at least one member insisted on having his dissent from the resolution minuted.[109] Interestingly, most of the contributors to the debate played down the significance of the growing split, arguing that it was the prerogative of youth to be more radical than their elders – as indeed their elders had been themselves in their own youth – and that the youth federation played an important role in recruiting new members to the movement. Others insisted that there was nothing particularly novel or indeed unusual about the youth federation's politics; merely that divisions had been inflamed over the defence issue. Above all, the minutes convey a strong sense that this was a quarrel for the Stockholm-based party leadership, which had little relevance for the day to day activities of the movement in the rest of the country, except inasmuch as a formal split would benefit the bourgeois parties.[110]

When the *arbetarekommun* received an invitation to send a delegate to Stockholm to the founding congress of the new Left Socialist Party, it was agreed to reject it out of hand, though in any case it was thought unlikely that the financial costs could be met out of *kommun* funds.[111] The prevailing mood seems to have been expressed by the member who hoped that the two sides could 'separate but separate as friends', and the formal divorce did indeed seem to be treated amicably and pragmatically. When one member of the *arbetarekommun* executive, O V Andersson, announced that he was resigning from the *kommun* and the party in order to join the Left Socialists, other members expressed their regrets, 'but hoped that when the war was over and the world was quiet again their paths would cross again.'[112] Following the establishment of a Left Council (*vänsterkommun*) the *arbetarekommun* announced that it was willing to co-operate with the new organisation where appropriate, although in practice it did not always prove possible to resolve differences of opinion satisfactorily. In 1918 efforts were made to co-ordinate an alliance in support of Finnish workers, but it proved frustratingly difficult to find a speaker who would satisfy all parties, and the *arbetarekommun* was forced to conclude that if they could not agree a compromise candidate then they were prepared to go ahead unilaterally. The meeting eventually took place without the *vänsterkommun*.[113] The 1918 1st May demonstration, in which 8000 people were reported to have taken part, was more successful as an example of co-operation. Banners bearing the standard social democratic demands for parliamentary reform appeared alongside those calling for the release of anarchist prisoners, and for revolutionary socialism. The rally following the demonstration passed official resolutions drafted by the SAP and the Left Socialists.[114] There was also more success in co-operation over local elections, which the *arbetarekommun* considered worthwhile both for financial reasons and 'for the sake of quiet'.[115] Negotiations between the two parties focused on the composition of the list of candidates which would be offered to the electorate under the rubric of the 'Labour Party', and it seemed that the *arbetarekommun* were prepared to make concessions from their original proposal for the sake of keeping the *vänsterkom-*

mun with them, and thus avoiding splitting the left wing vote. Under the terms of the arrangement which was eventually worked out, the *vänsterkommun* agreed to fill the second and sixth places on the list for the first district, and the fourth and the eighth places for the third district. This agreement was to stand for four years; meanwhile for two years only it was agreed that the *vänsterkommun* would take the fourth and eighth places in the list for the first district, and the fifth place for the third district.[116] It seems unlikely that these arrangements endured for as long as they were intended, given that there is no trace of the *vänsterkommun* after 1919. Even looking beyond the social democratic sources, however, there is little evidence to suggest that the revolutionary left made a significant impact in the longer term. There are no records for what eventually became (in 1926) the Blekinge district of the Communist Party pre-dating 1925, when it was reported that a campaign tour had resulted in the founding of left socialist *arbetarekommuner* in both Karlskrona and Karlshamn.[117] The Karlskrona organisation did not appear to be greatly successful, as only a couple of months later it was reported that nothing had been heard of the branch since it was set up.[118] A Karlskrona member reported that the dockyard workforce was proving to be a particularly hard nut to crack in terms of support for communism. Even at the district level there had been little campaigning undertaken as a result of poor finances and low membership.[119]

V

In fact, the 1918 May Day demonstration was noted not for the presence of the Left Socialists, but for the prominence of the dockyard workers, and the evidence which this provided of the 'spectacular' growth of the MVAF during the latter part of the war.[120] As was discussed above, the official 'story' of the development of trade unionism within the defence industry attributed the foundation and growth of the MVAF to a growing consciousness among defence industry workers of their status and common interest as state employees. There was also a growing insistence that the union was concerned strictly with trade issues, and that political activities were to be considered inappropriate. Writing in one of the first editions of its members' newsletter in 1920, the union leadership reminded its members that, until now all politics has been scrupulously avoided in 'Medlems-bladet' and we intend to avoid political controversy in the future as well. There is a difference between a radical political and a radical trade union movement: it is however understandable that a few members mistake the two. A self-interested egoist can be a radical trade unionist, but not really a radical politician. The Union combats its opponents because they combat us, not for their political views… With this we present an appeal to the members: try to distinguish between the political and the trade union movements. Do not set an equals sign between them. Do not discuss politics in your articles.[121]

The insistence that the union was concerned strictly with trade issues meant that no mention was made from official quarters about the links between the union and other groups within the organised labour movement, including political organisations.[122]

There were, however, the signs of a growing affinity between the dockyard union and the *arbetarekommun* during the years after 1914. As we have seen, relations between the MVAF's predecessor, the KVAF, and the wider labour movement were rather ambivalent, and the union never formally affiliated to the *arbetarekommun*, even though the two organisations co-operated over local elections and other campaigns from the early days of the KVAF's foundation. But the election of two social democratic *riksdagsmän* for Blekinge in 1911, under the new extended franchise, helped to change this relationship, and dockyard workers were urged to consider the possibility of using the *riksdag* as a source of redress for their workplace grievances.[123] One *riksdagsman* in particular, J A Ingvarsson, became active not only in the wage campaign, but also in lobbying for dockyardsmen's pensions and cost of living wage supplements, using his position to table motions, ask parliamentary questions, and set up meetings between the union and the KMF. Through his work, other Blekinge *riksdagsmän* also came to be involved: it was reported for example that three Blekinge colleagues had seen the naval minister to forward the dockyard wage proposals in 1914.[124] At its meeting in July 1915, the Karlskrona MVAF formally recorded its thanks to the *riksdagsmän* for their help.[125] This action was not confined to the social democratic representatives, although the involvement of Ingvarsson clearly helped to develop the links between the union branch and the party, and the majority of the union members seemed instinctively inclined to support the social democrats. A branch meeting in 1916 condemned comments printed in *Karlskrona Tidning* which insinuated that Ingvarsson's interest in dockyard wages was merely an electioneering strategy, and that the only true guardians of dockyard interests were the Right.[126] A year later, the branch agreed to stop using *Karlskrona Tidning* to advertise its meetings, on account of its political views, and instead extended its contacts with the social democrats, donating funds towards the *arbetarekommun*'s election funds and urging members to vote for the labour candidates.[127] In 1918, the MVAF agreed to share half of the total costs of the *landsting* election campaign with the *arbetarekommun,* and also nominated its own candidates.[128] Dockyard workers were urged to support the Labour candidates for pragmatic reasons, since a strong social democratic presence in the *landsting* had a direct bearing on the composition of the First Chamber of the *riksdag,* and could therefore have an impact on dockyard questions when these were dealt with by the *riksdag.*[129] The result was seen as a great victory, with the social democrats doubling the number of votes received compared to 1914.[130]

Over the space of just a few years, therefore, the role of local *riksdagsmän* in dockyard affairs had become more clearly defined. By the time of the second chamber election in 1917, the pay and conditions of the dockyard workforce had become an electoral issue. The social democratic candidate W Karlsson promised that he would use his influence as best he could for dockyard affairs, and published an electoral address aimed directly at MVAF members. 'If your wish is that the particular dockyard issues, which may be dealt with by the parliament, should be settled favourably, then it is absolutely necessary that you use your vote in order to secure strong representation for the labour party.'[131] The extension of the franchise meant that the dockyard workers now accounted for a significant proportion of the Karlskrona electorate, which no candidate could afford to ignore. This identification of the dockyard workers as a constituency with distinct political interests was a process which was confined to Karlskrona, however. It was the Blekinge *riksdagsmän* who took up the dockyard issues on behalf of all dockyard workers in Stockholm as well as Karlskrona, with no evidence to suggest that their Stockholm colleagues were also involved. Although the social democrat, Ingvarsson, seemed to be particularly active, the dockyard workers also received support from other local representatives from different parties. Apart from political lobbying, it seems that the most important role of the *riks-dagsman* was to act as a local contact in Stockhholm. Karlskrona was remote from the metropolis, and some of the correspondence between Ingvarsson and the MVAF suggests that the former had an important role to play in forwarding information, for example concerning the passage of dockyard related legislation through the *riksdag*.

The lobbying role was confined not only to the work and conditions of the dockyard, but also concerned the wider interests of the town as a whole. The county governor (*landshövdingen*) for Blekinge, *greve* Axel Wachtmeister, brought a motion to the *riksdag* to set up a formal parliamentary enquiry into the possibilities for expansion, the *riksdag* itself having acknowledged the need to make best and most economical use of the existing capacity in Karlskrona. The commission began its work in April 1914, chaired by the *varvschef*. Its conclusion, presented the following year, was that new construction work could be a means to take up the slack in the workforce at certain times of the year, thus helping to maintain a larger, permanent and economically viable workforce for the yard's principal role, the mobilisation of the fleet for sea at short notice.[132] With this end in view, the commission proposed a modernisation programme costing 2.3 million *kronor*, which would increase the capacity for new construction, and eventually enable the dockyard to produce the largest armoured battleships. The programme was to have three stages: firstly, essential modernisation in order to maintain the capacity for the work already carried out, i.e. repairs and maintenance; secondly, expansion so that four submarines (or one destroyer and two submarines) could be under construction simultaneously; thirdly, a final phase to create the capacity to build first class armoured warships. The naval administration and the minister concerned supported the first two stages of the modernisation proposal, but balked at the third, citing the uncertainty surrounding the future of this class of vessel. The outcome of this investigation set a pattern for the enquiries of this period: the parliamentary commission, chaired by the *varvschef*, was positive in each case, but the naval authorities in Stockholm blocked any development.[133] The debate may thus be seen to some extent as a conflict between local actors, desperately trying to secure the future of the town, and the very different considerations of the Stockholm-based naval administration. The social democratic *riksdagsmän*, Oskar Kloo and J Ingvarsson, put a motion to the *riksdag* in 1915 concerning the modernisation of the dockyard, and attempting to revive the stalled proposals of the 1913 enquiry.[134] The town council was also involved in lobbying the naval administration, especially when there were very grave concerns about the future of employment in the yard in 1919. In the words of the motion to establish the committee, 'It is generally known that the interests of Karlskrona are intimately connected to the state of the royal dockyard. It has already been shown in the town council to what extent the town's economy is dependent on retaining the dockyard in its entirety.'[135]

Because of the considerable difficulties attached to creating a role for Karlskrona in the construction of new vessels, the various enquiries of the 1910s and 1920s also contemplated civilian uses for the yard. The use of the dockyard to establish a state-owned merchant fleet was considered in response to a motion from the left wing socialists Fabian Månsson and Fredrik Ström, both well-known defence nihilists. Once again, this proposition met with some welcome, if a cautious one, in Karlskrona, but was rejected out of hand by the naval administration. In July 1916 a new commission of enquiry began, with the participation of social democratic *riksdagsman* J A Ingvarsson, to 'investigate the desirability of organising the operation of the dockyard in Karlskrona so that it is placed on a footing to undertake repairs and new construction of ships other than warships for state purposes.'[136] The commission noted the disadvantages faced by Karlskrona, especially in terms of labour and raw materials, but its eventual proposal was to establish a civilian dockyard alongside the existing naval installations, and to run the two enterprises in tandem. This was a very ambitious proposal, which would have meant fundamental change for the whole of Karlskrona, and was estimated to cost three times as much as the 1915 proposal for modernisation. Perhaps unsurprisingly, the naval administration reacted firmly against it, suggesting that it was inappropriate for a naval dockyard to compete in the civilian sphere, and that the dockyard's future developments should involve military purpose only.[137] There was moreover, it was suggested, a fundamental difference in the nature of the dockyard's work and that carried out for civilian purposes in the private sector, in that private shipyards sought to compete economically, while the state dockyard had to be concerned with quality. No progress had been made, although it is interesting that there was a marked willingness to consider other uses for the dockyard apart from naval defence. In 1919, there were further proposals, this time originating from the dockyard workers themselves, and backed up by a motion from the Social Democratic group on the town council, to turn some of the spare capacity over to work for the state railway board, and thus avoid the expected contraction in the dockyard workforce.[138] A small amount of this work was indeed carried out, but it was always problematic, and no transition in the main areas of the dockyard's work ever took place.[139] The upshot was that the dockyard's position within the wider naval establishment shifted very little during this period: its main role continued to be the repair and maintenance of the fleet, and new construction was confined to the private shipyards.

VI

The dominance of the naval dockyard in Karlskrona posed some difficulties for the local labour movement, just as it did in Plymouth. This was especially the case during the years 1911–1914 when the naval agitation in Sweden was at its height, and the Right's gain of a third Blekinge mandate in the extraordinary *riksdag* election of March 1914 must partly be attributed to the resonance of pro-defence arguments in the region. It might also help to explain why the more unequivocally anti-defence left socialists failed to make more of an impact in Karlskrona and Blekinge after 1917. The Karlskrona social democrats compromised: nominally in favour of reducing defence spending but at the same time willing to recognise the significance of the navy for Karlskrona. The social democratic group on the town council acknowledgement the need for pragmatism during the difficult years of the early 1920s. A resolution from 1923 stated that,

> The town has grown up with naval defence and the naval institutions continue to play a crucial role in the town's economy. As long as the international situation persuades the state authorities to maintain a naval defence system to a greater or lesser extent, it is obviously in Karlskrona's interests that the naval institutions remain here.[140]

For many years the relationship between the dockyard workers and the organised labour movement had been relatively cool, with the dockyard workers frequently regarded as a community apart, with separate interests from the rest of the town's workers. With the development of a dockyard trade union after 1913, and its eventual incorporation into the FCPF, came more control through the union federation and in particular the insistence that the union was to be concerned with trade matters only, not politics. Despite the efforts of union officials to distinguish between trade and politics, however, the development of the union was clearly affected by political events in the town. The links between the dockyard workers and the social democratic *arbetarekommun* were strengthened through the willingness of the social democratic *riksdagsmän* to take up dockyard workers' concerns about pay and working conditions. Also influential were consumer politics and the political struggles over the food supply during the war. The importance of consumer politics may help to explain the very rapid growth in membership of the MVAF during May and June 1917, when over 300 new members were enrolled.[141] Karlskrona did not have a large and influential consumer co-operative movement like the one in Plymouth, but despite this difference, reactions to the food situation and analysis of its causes were similar. There were two main issues here. Firstly, labour campaigners expressed their moral outrage at a capitalist system which allowed individuals to benefit materially from the scarcity of essential goods. The term profiteering – in Swedish *ocker* or more commonly *jobberi* – seems to have emerged as a new concept during the course of the war; there are no references to it in the local sources before 1914. Secondly, as the supply of essential foodstuffs became scarcer, and some form of rationing became inevitable, the role of the state in regulating the food supply emerged as ever more important. The *arbetarekommun* argued for working-class consumers to have a voice in organising the practical matters of food distribution, and concerns were constantly expressed that the existing arrangements were abused against the interests of the least powerful or 'those of limited means' (*mindre bemedlade*). Just as in Plymouth the main goals of the food demonstrations of 1917 were accountability, fairness and adequate representation of working-class consumers in the distribution of the food supply.

CHAPTER 8

Conclusion

Despite frequently reiterated calls for more cross-national comparison, much labour history remains insular, even microscopic, in its focus. The movement which was conceived as internationalist continues to be studied within the confines of the national framework. This insularity is not confined to labour historians of course. Quite apart from the practical and institutional difficulties which it presents its practitioners, cross-national comparative history sometimes seems to generate more problems than it can claim to resolve. As Peter Baldwin has commented, comparisons imply a level of generalisation that seems to go against the historicist emphasis on the particularity of specific historical cases.[1] As I discussed in the first part of this study, in some cases the implied comparison may even be with an abstract model or ideal type, which does not stand up to detailed empirical scrutiny. Moreover, there seems to be a lack of agreement over what comparative history should actually be *for*. Marc Bloch's attempt to define comparative history as a method found some resonance among the historical sociologists in particular, but more generally it has been treated with scepticism.[2] Instead, it has been suggested that comparative history should be treated not as a method but more as a 'mode of analysis', a 'way of considering a problem', or even merely as an intellectual tool to stimulate thought.[3]

It is this broader understanding of comparative history which has largely informed this study. One of the great advantages of any form of cross-national or transnational history is above all is that it exposes the assumptions of fairly discrete national historiographical traditions to the questions and problems arising from a different national context. The first part of this study focused on the 'rise of labour' debates in British and Swedish labour history. As I showed in chapter 1, British labour history has been characterised by a tradition of exceptionalism which understood the British working-class movement as different from those on the continent in several ways, notably in its lack of programmatic commitment to socialism, and its diffuse and decentred organisation. The exceptionalism of British labour was consistent, moreover, with a more general understanding of British 'difference' from continental Europe. Nonetheless, as the discussion of the historiography in Britain and Sweden revealed, in both countries the 'rise of labour' itself was understood in similar ways, as part of universal processes of industrialisation and modernisation. As Europe's first industrial nation, the situation in Britain undoubtedly differed in important ways from that in Sweden, where industrial development happened very rapidly during the last decade or so of the nineteenth century, but the outcome of the economic and social changes of that period were the same in both cases: the formation of an industrial working class and the articulation of its demands in the context of both the workplace and in politics. In Britain, the emergent labour movement took its place within a party political system that was already well developed, leaving working-class men to throw their lot in with the Liberals or Conservatives instead. In Sweden, by contrast, the rise of the social democratic labour movement should be seen within the context of the 'democratic breakthrough' of the late nineteenth century, and in its early years the labour movement made common cause with other liberal and popular movements in campaigning for suffrage reform. It is possible to overstate these differences however. Britain with its restricted franchise was hardly a model of a reformed democratic state in the early twentieth century, while conversely the Swedish state should not be seen as an autocratic monolith. In both cases, the rise of labour should be seen as part of the wider historical processes of suffrage reform and the development of party politics which took place over many years.

In recent years historians in both Britain and Sweden have turned away from structural explanations of the rise of labour. Indeed, it might also be added that in many cases they have lost interest in the history of labour altogether. Particularly in Britain, social historians turned their attention to the languages of popular politics, and in some cases this has led to the suggestion that the idea of 'class' was less influential than a broader and consensual populism in informing popular politics.[4] As a historical phenomenon, the labour movement was understood not so much as a fundamentally new and modern form of politics, influenced primarily by ideas about class, but as the reformulation and continuation of an older political current of Radicalism, expressed in demands for parliamentary sovereignty and the rule of law. These ideas could be traced back to the Chartists of the mid nineteenth century and even beyond to eighteenth century radicalism, the Civil War and the religious revolutions of the seventeenth century.[5]

This work has been important not least in that it has allowed a reassessment of the working-class politics of the Gladstonian Liberal Party, and the case for the importance of democratic ideas in the early Labour Party has been well made.[6] But there are two main problems with the continuities of radicalism thesis. The first is that it is in many ways a 'whig' history: it locates the British Labour Party as part of a peculiarly native tradition of British radical politics and thus is a restatement of the exceptionalist thesis.[7] There are striking parallels with Sweden here. At first glance, Swedish working-class politics seemed to conform more closely to the continental 'model' of a socialist movement, albeit one which became unusually successful, but in fact Swedish history writing has its own tradition of exceptionalism. This view, which seems to have gained in prominence in recent years, emphasises the unusual degree of consensus and lack of social conflict with which the Swedish transition to modernity was accomplished, drawing on political traditions which had their roots in the early modern period.[8] The second problem is one of explanation. The so-called 'linguistic turn' has without a doubt been extremely valuable in enriching our understanding of how social categories such as class are formed discursively, and broadening our interest to include all aspects of working-class life. But the increasingly narrow, sometimes even myopic, concern with language and experience has also led to a neglect of the broader processes of historical change, especially in the sphere of politics. Eric Hobsbawm has commented on this change of emphasis in his recent autobiography, suggesting that, '[t]here was a shift away from historical models or "the large *why* questions," a shift from "the analytical to the descriptive mode", from economic and social structure to culture, from recovering fact to recovering feeling, from telescope to microscope.'[9] Why, if there was strong popular support for liberal radicalism among the working class, did the Liberal Party lose its working-class supporters to Labour over the first decades of the twentieth century? The only reasonable explanation seems to rest on the historical accident of the Liberal split during the First World War, which takes us back to exceptionalism again.

This aim of this study was to examine the exceptionalist thesis at two levels, however: not only through the national historiographies but also through the local case study of the two towns. Comparative history may not be able to provide a cast-iron method for investigating these questions, but comparative historians cannot afford to ignore the big 'why' questions; indeed, there would seem to be little point to a comparative history which did not attempt to explain historical phenomena at some level. This study has no ambition to attempt to construct an explanatory model, which could be applied to other cases. The historical specificity of the particular cases – and the particular comparison – considered here must always be borne in mind. Nonetheless, it is possible to identify some themes, which appear to be common to Plymouth and Karlskrona, and taken as a whole might suggest some more general explanations. One interpretation of the cases presented here could be that the local similarities, related to the very peculiar social and economic structure of the dockyard town, outweighed the differences between Britain and Sweden. It might be suggested, even, that Plymouth and Karlskrona fit not with general patterns of historical development in Britain and Sweden respectively, but belong instead to a small and select group of dockyard towns, which might include Portsmouth, Brest, Cherbourg and others. Ultimately, however, as Aristide Zolberg has suggested, the answer to the question 'How many exceptionalisms?' is simply, 'as many as there are cases under comparison'.[10] To paraphrase Thompson, it happened in one way in Plymouth, and in another way in Karlskrona, and neither case can be understood except in relation to a historically unique combination of local, regional and national circumstances.

The aim of the study was not to deny the existence of important differences between Britain and Sweden, Plymouth and Karlskrona, therefore. However, in seeking to compare these two cases, this study has attempted to identify and explain some of the universal historical processes which contributed to the political changes of the early twentieth century. Put in a different way, the study was concerned with a universal question: how to explain political change and the rise of labour at the beginning of the twentieth century. The most important similarity between Plymouth and Karlskrona was the dominance of the government-owned naval dockyard. With civilian workforces that peaked at over 2000 in Karlskrona and over 15,000 in Plymouth, the naval dockyard were by far the largest and most important workplaces in the respective localities. Indeed, considered in relation to national industrial development, both could be considered to be unusually large organisations in any case. The dockyards were also unusual workplaces because of their longevity as institutions founded in the late seventeenth century. This meant that in each case the dockyard had developed a very distinctive and deep-rooted workplace culture. In both towns there was a sense of the dockyard workforce as a community apart, distinguished both from the service personnel and the rest of the civilian population. Some dockyard workers also enjoyed special privileges which set them apart from their counterparts in the private sector, including guarantees of permanent employment, pensions, accident insurance and other benefits. These were available to all civilian workers in Karlskrona, but in the British naval dockyards they were confined to a small group of established workers (comprising about one fifth of the total workforce). This sense of difference was reinforced by patterns of residential segregation and to some extent by social relations outside the workplace. It was also a very male culture, since until the First World War both dockyards provided extremely limited opportunities for female employment.

Although many of the older dockyard traditions had survived intact into the early twentieth century, the period should be seen as one of unprecedented change for both yards. This change was partly a result of technological changes in shipbuilding with the transition from wood to iron and steel, and from sail to steam. But it was also a function of the changing role of the dockyard in relation to the naval infrastructure in both countries. Here, the future of Devonport dockyard seemed to be more secure than that of Karlskrona, especially after an extensive modernisation programme left it with the capacity to construct the largest and most up to date battleships. Karlskrona dockyard, by contrast, had to be scaled down to reflect the reduced naval ambitions of a small neutral state, and it was allowed to stagnate for much of the second half of the nineteenth century. Nonetheless, there were some similarities between the two cases. First, the early twentieth century was a period of expansion for both yards, which contributed to a growth in the population of both towns, and a very tight local labour market in the years immediately before the war. Second, although the dockyards were not subject to the fluctuations of the business cycle, which notoriously afflicted the private shipbuilding industry, they were however governed by a political constraint: the constant pressure on governments to keep the naval budget within an acceptable limit. By the early twentieth century, naval administrators in both countries were increasingly seeking to contract out new construction to the private shipyards, and turn the dockyards over to maintenance and repairs.

Some historians have suggested that the peculiar conditions of naval dockyard work contributed to retarding the development of trade unionism, and helped to foster a workplace culture which was inward-looking and deferential. Others have qualified this view by suggesting that the nature of the work itself contributed to a culture of independence and autonomy among an elite group of workers. In any case, by the early twentieth century there were signs that this culture was beginning to break down. The changes of the early twentieth century eroded the notion that the dockyard held out the possibility of a job for life, and the introduction of general state benefits such as pensions, for example, also contributed to undermining the value of the special privileges attached to dockyard work. Dockyard managers in both Plymouth and Karlskrona continued to argue that the nature of dockyard work was different to that in the private sector, and that this justified their resistance of various demands for change from the workers. The retention of individual wage settlements, for example, was seen in both Plymouth and Karlskrona as an important means to maintain discipline and motivation in a state-owned enterprise. The workers themselves, however, played down the peculiarity of their unusual status, and sought to make comparisons with employees in other organisations to justify their claims, helped by the presence of dockyard trade unions. Here, of course, there was an important difference between Britain and Sweden. In Devonport dockyard, workers were organised by trade, and campaigned to maintain wage differentials between trades. In Karlskrona, most of the workforce was organised by one single union, and through this developed ties with other civilian defence workers, and ultimately with other state employees. The existence of the general union in Karlskrona, despite the operation of a division of labour which was no less complicated than that obtaining at Devonport, illustrates the need to recognise the central role of the union itself in creating a shared identity among its members.

It is possible to see the development of Swedish labour movement in terms of a transition from a popular culture that was characterised by disorderliness (*bråkighet*) and wilfulness (*egensinne*) to one of respectability (*skötsamhet*).[11] Pre-industrial traditions such as heavy drinking, fighting, rowdiness and St Monday provided workers with an important means to cope with the difficulties of their everyday conditions, and cement a shared sense of camaraderie.[12] With the advent of the formal labour movement, however, workers abandoned their 'rough culture' for more disciplined forms of resistance such as collective organisation and collective bargaining.[13] In his influential study of labour movement culture in the Norrland community of Holmsund, Ronny Ambjörnsson suggested that the early labour movement was engaged in a struggle on two fronts: against capitalism on the one hand, and against the *egensinne* and *bråkighet* of its own members on the other.[14] But the culture of *egensinne* did not disappear completely. There was no national, monolithic workers' culture in Sweden, or indeed in any other country, and the triumph of *skötsamhet* was never complete. Instead, rough culture and disorderly forms of resistance continued to exist alongside the respectability of the labour movement until well into the twentieth century.[15]

This question of 'rough' and 'respectable' cultures has some relevance to the dockyard town. Naval and military towns, with their large transient male populations, were notorious as centres of heavy drinking and prostitution, as illustrated by the debates over the Contagious Diseases Acts in Plymouth and other military towns during the 1860s. Further, as unusually long-established workplaces, the naval dockyards undoubtedly had their own specific cultures of informal resistance to control among the workforce. The problem for the historian is that whereas the naval bureaucracies and labour movements left orderly records of their activities, it is much more difficult to uncover evidence concerning informal resistance, and it is only possible to guess at this from the labour sources. Nonetheless, these do provide some evidence to support Ambjörnsson's point that the labour movement was at times engaged in a struggle on two fronts: against employers and political opponents on the one hand, and against its own members and those whom it thought should be members on the other. The example of the campaigns for better housing in Plymouth makes it quite clear that many of the well-meaning, self-educated, respectable working-class activists in the local labour organisations were deeply frustrated that those whom they were trying to help failed to respond as they had hoped, indeed on some occasions they were even met with resistance. A detailed investigation, using census returns, of the neighbourhoods where labour activists were most likely to live would help to illuminate this point further, though regrettably this was beyond the scope of this study.[16] Co-operators such as William Gay and T W Mercer were clearly in no doubt that the glamour and film-star exoticism of Nancy Astor, as an American millionaire trading on her personality and looks, appealed strongly to the poorest voters of the Sutton division in 1919.

The existence of a 'rough culture' in Karlskrona is less well documented, although there are hints that the town had a reputation as the site of some heavy drinking.[17] Some of the early meetings of the KVAF seem to have been quite rowdy affairs involving heavy drinking, episodes which were brushed aside as pioneering but misguided preludes to the formation of a 'proper' trade union after 1914. But as Göran Salmonsson has pointed out, the organisational forms of the early labour movement were always contingent: there was no blueprint for the development of the centralised national federation that later came to dominate the movement, and other forms of organisation were indeed tried at different times.[18] In Plymouth and Karlskrona dockyard unions campaigned for similar ends: the removal of local control over workplace relations, with the possibilities it created for favouritism and arbitrariness, and a collective wage settlement, agreed through national negotiations between management and recognised trade unions. This was eventually achieved, though it did not remove the possiblities for other forms of organisation. But unionists were convinced that their best strategy was to seek to depersonalise the relationship between employer and employee, and they sometimes appealed to the state authorities as a neutral arbiter in a conflict of local interests. In doing so, they also turned to the parliamentary representatives of the dockyard towns as advocates of the dockyard workers' interests, and a channel of communication between the town and the naval administrators in the capital. At a time when politics remained a highly metropolitan activity, and many members of parliament had little contact with the constituency they represented, the dockyard towns were thus perhaps unusual in the closeness of the ties between constituency and representative. The importance of this relationship means that it is difficult to distinguish a consistent pattern of support for one political party or another in the dockyard towns.

Although the industrial relations and workplace traditions of the dockyard were clearly important in shaping labour politics in Plymouth and Karlskrona, events outside the workplace were equally important. In both towns, the movement for independent labour representation emerged around the turn of the twentieth century as part of a broader challenge to established elites and interests in municipal politics. Before the war, this challenge stemmed partly from the expansion of the towns, and the need for a municipal response to pressing urban problems such as housing shortages. Although their success was limited in terms of council seats, the labour movements in Plymouth and Karlskrona participated in debates about the form and extent of municipal government. A common theme of labour agitation in both towns was the need to transcend the sterility of existing party rivalries, a point echoed in the 'country before party' agitation of the nationalist campaigners of the political right. Class could be seen as a means to unite voters against party loyalty, although the understanding of class was influenced in both cases by more inclusive notions of 'the people' or *småfolket*. Equally ambiguous were attitudes to the state. In a way that was reminiscent of the dockyard workers' campaigns for collective bargaining, the state was sometimes viewed as a neutral and disinterested guarantor of justice, against entrenched local interests. On the other hand, there was also hostility towards state intervention, and support instead for mutualist provision of economic benefits.

These matters came to a head during the First World War, in the context of conflicts over the distribution of a scarce food supply. A major difference here was the unusual strength of consumer co-operation in Plymouth, but the labour organisations in Karlskrona campaigned for similar ends: fairness and justice in the distribution of scarce resources, democratic accountability of the local decision-makers, and the need for adequate representation of working-class consumers on food control committees. The Labour newspaper in Karlskrona, and the co-operative newspaper in Plymouth published monthly lists of what were considered to be the maximum acceptable prices of basic provisions so that working-class consumers could keep themselves informed about instances of 'profiteering' or *jobberi*. Once again, the national state was appealed to against the vested local interests of municipal politicians, many of them shopkeepers and traders. To some extent, this implied a shift in the role of the state, from the guarantor of free trade in consumers' interests to the protector of consumer rights and fair prices. On the other hand, this shift was not complete, as co-operators and social democrats continued to press for free trade and the suspension of customs duties, while simultaneously calling for the government to set maximum prices. It is certainly clear that these new ideas about the relationship between consumption and citizenship were undoubtedly important in the reformulation of Liberal and Labour politics, and it is an area which would repay further research.[19] Most importantly, of course, the politicisation of consumer issues had important implications for the political role of women, shortly to be enfranchised.[20] Despite this though, and despite the strength of consumer co-operation in Plymouth, Labour seemed unable to make this consumer politics central to its political appeal in 1918 and 1919.

Perhaps the most important feature of late nineteenth and early twentieth century politics in both Plymouth and Karlskrona, therefore, was the dynamic relationship between local and national politics, between the national state and local interests. The period saw the partial consolidation of a national political culture, dominated by national institutions such as parliament, political parties and the national press. For all organisations, including trade unions, the challenge was to respond and adapt to local experience, which was rooted in part in local material conditions, and transform it into political support. In some cases this meant imposing new identities onto old ones – aligning the interests of dockyard workers with other civilian defence workers in Sweden, and with other shipbuilding workers in Britain. But this was not a one way process, nor was it necessarily a complete one. Local activists responded pragmatically to attempts to impose central control, or sometimes they challenged them. The national state could be appealed to as a neutral dispenser of justice freed from local vested interests, or it could be criticised as inflexible and unresponsive to local needs and interests. Further, although it has not been possible to do more than touch on this point, the very nature of the nation state itself was one of the key issues for political debate during this period. This was a debate which perhaps had particular resonance in naval dockyard towns, but it was by no means unique to them. Often regarded as a prerogative of the political Right in this period, it is only recently that historians have begun to investigate the extent to which nationalism also informed Labour and Liberal political discourse, but it is still an area that would repay further research.[21] It is also worth noting that, despite the very different nature of the state in Britain and Sweden, nationalist debate was polarised along similar lines in both countries. This is especially the case for the political Right, which reformed during the early twentieth century around the issues of the monarchy, economic protectionism, and the demand for increased defence expenditure.

This study took its departure from a wide and ambitious *why* question: why did social democratic labour parties emerge in Britain and Sweden at more or less the same time? It has not been my ambition to provide a general explanation to this question which could also be applied to other cases. As I discussed at the beginning of this chapter, that should not necessarily be the ambition of comparative history in any case. The major advantage of the comparative approach is instead that it can help to open up the national historiographies to new ideas and suggest new ways of approaching a particular problem, perhaps even helping to challenge some of the nationalist assumptions which continue to inform national history writing. This particular study has attempted to combine this approach with a detailed comparison of two local case studies, which in themselves had some claim to be considered in terms of exceptionalism. It has not been my aim to suggest that Plymouth or Karlskrona should be considered as representing necessarily typical elements of working-class politics in Britain or Sweden respectively. But by comparing the developments in these towns over the period c.1890–1920, and identifying some similarities in the broad processes of change that were taking place in this period, my intention has been above all to demonstrate the contingency and open-ended nature of political change in the early twentieth century.

Summary

Political Change and the Rise of Labour
in Comparative Perspective.
Britain and Sweden c. 1890–1920

The main aim of this study was to compare political change and the rise of labour in Sweden and Britain, c.1890-1920. Comparative studies of the rise of labour are still relatively rare: as one historian has remarked, it remains a 'theory without much practice'. Moreover, the majority of comparative studies are variation finding; that is, they are concerned with identifying and explaining differences between two or more cases. While acknowledging that there were important differences between Britain and Sweden, the aim of this book was to investigate a more universal question: namely, *why did social democratic labour parties emerge at more or less the same time in these two countries, and indeed across Europe?* By reconsidering national cases in the light of a different historiographical tradition, cross-national comparisons can help to question sometimes problematic assumptions about national exceptionalism.

Methodologically, the book draws on the so-called 'new political history' developed in recent years by historians in both Sweden and Britain (e.g. Salmonsson, Lawrence). Rather than seeing labour parties as resulting from exogenous processes of social change such as class formation, this approach points to the role of political parties and other organisations, such as trade unions, in interpreting and representing material experience, and in constructing coalitions of support among the electorate. Class formation is thus understood not so much as a process than as a project. The relationship between political parties and those they seek to represent is thus seen as central.

For the purposes of this study I chose to investigate this relationship in a local context, through a comparison of the naval dockyard towns of Karlskrona and Plymouth, both of which had been previously ignored by labour historians. In each case, the aim was to explore the relationship between local social relations and political culture on the one hand, and national politics on the other. In both countries, national politics during the period was strongly influenced by debates over naval defence, which carried a particular resonance in the dockyard towns. It was difficult, however, to distinguish any consistency of support for 'navalist' candidates in local elections in either Plymouth or Karlskrona. Instead, the extent of popular support for navalist politics was influenced by the ambiguous relationship between the dockyard town and the national state, and the reputations of local politicians were partly founded on their willingness and ability to defend local interests against the demands of the navy.

Although there were some important differences between the Swedish and the British cases, not least the more modest naval ambitions of the Swedish state, these should not obscure the similarities. Most importantly, the development of the local labour movement was influenced above all by the dynamic relationship between the local and national spheres. This was found, for example, in the changing nature of dockyard work, as dockyard workers increasingly turned to external groups of workers to develop new models of labour organisation and campaign for collective bargaining. It could also be seen in the development of the political labour movement as part of a broader challenge to the dominance of traditional local elites in the council chamber, and dissatisfaction with their response to municipal problems associated with the rapid growth of the towns. Here, the national state was seen as a source of justice against the arbitrariness of local interests, especially in the context of struggles over rationing of scarce food supplies during the First World War.

Notes

1. Introduction

1 Peter Baldwin, 'Comparing and Generalizing: Why All History is Comparative, Yet No History is Sociology', in Deborah Cohen and Maura O'Connor, eds, *Comparison and History: Europe in Cross-National Perspective* (New York and Abingdon, 2004), pp. 1–22: 1–2. See also Patricia R Turner, 'Hostile Participants? Working-Class Militancy, Associational Life, and the "Distinctiveness" of the Prewar French Labor Movement', *The Journal of Modern History*, 71 (1999), pp. 28–55.

2 Peter N Stearns, 'The European Labour Movement and the Working Classes 1890–1914', in Harvey Mitchell and Peter N Stearns, *Workers and Protest: The European Labor Movement, the Working Classes and the Origins of Social Democracy, 1890–1914* (Itasca, 1971), p. 128; James E Cronin, 'Neither Exceptional Nor Peculiar: Towards the Comparative Study of Labor in Advanced Society', *International Review of Social History*, 38 (1993), pp. 59–75: 59.

3 Kocka, 'Problemer einer europäischen Geschichte', p. 25; Gary Marks, *Unions in Politics: Britain, Germany and the United States in the Nineteenth and Early Twentieth Centuries* (Princeton, 1989), p. 19; Friedrich Lenger, 'Beyond Exceptionalism: Notes on the Artisanal Phase of the Labour Movement in France, England, German and the United States', *International Review of Social History*, 36 (1991), pp. 1–23: 22; John Breuilly, *Labour and Liberalism in Nineteenth Century Europe: Essays in Comparative History* (Manchester, 1992), p. 20.

4 Donald Sassoon, *One Hundred Years of Socialism: The West European Left in the Twentieth Century* (London, 1996), p.15. Stefan Berger, 'Labour in Comparative Perspective', in Duncan Tanner, Pat Thane and Nick Tiratsoo, eds, *Labour's First Century* (Cambridge, 2000), pp. 309–344, gives many more examples of British exceptionalism.

5 Egon Wertheimer, *Portrait of the British Labour Party* (London, 1929), pp. xii–xiii.

6 See Theodore Rothstein, *From Chartism to Labourism: Historical Sketches of the English Working Class Movement* (London, 1983; first published 1929), p. 202; cited in Martin Crick, *The History of the Social Democratic Federation* (Keele, 1994), p. 13.

7 Ross McKibbin, 'Why Was There No Marxism in Great Britain?' in *idem., The Ideologies of Class: Social Relations in Britain, 1880–1950* (Oxford, 1990; first published 1984), pp. 1–41. See also Harvey Mitchell, 'Labor and the Origins of Social Democracy in Britain, France and Germany, 1890–1914', in Harvey Mitchell and Peter N Stearns, *Workers and Protest: The European Labor Movement, the Working Classes and the Origins of Social*

Democracy, 1890–1914 (Itasca, 1971), pp. 35–6, 41ff; Christiane Eisenberg, 'The Comparative View in Labour History: Old and New Interpretations of the English and German Labour Movements before 1914', *International Review of Social History,* 34 (1989), pp. 403–432: 403–4; Gregory M Luebbert, *Liberalism, Fascism or Social Democracy: Social Classes and the Political Origins of Regimes in Interwar Europe* (Oxford, 1991), pp. 15–25.

8 Ross McKibbin, *The Evolution of the Labour Party, 1910–1924* (Oxford, 1974), p. 247.

9 See J G A Pocock, 'History and Sovereignty: The Historiographical Response to Europeanization in Two British Cultures', *Journal of British Studies,* 31 (1992), pp. 358–389: 362–8; David Armitage, 'Greater Britain: A Useful Category of Historical Analysis', *American History Review,* 104 (1999), pp. 427–445: 428; Benedikt Stuchtey, 'Literature, liberty and life of the nation: British historiography from Macaulay to Trevelyan', in Stefan Berger, Mark Donovan and Kevin Passmore, eds, *Writing National Histories: Western Europe since 1800* (London, 1999), pp. 30–48. Antonio Varsoni, 'Is Britain Part of Europe? The Myth of British "Difference"', in Cyril Buffet and Beatrice Heuser, eds, *Haunted by History: Myths in International Relations* (Providence, 1998), pp. 135–156 discusses the myth of British difference and how this has exerted influence over decision-making process and public attitudes towards relations with other countries in the post-war period.

10 Perry Anderson, 'Origins of the Present Crisis', *New Left Review,* 23 (1964), pp. 26–53: 28; also Tom Nairn, 'The British Political Elite', *New Left Review,* 23 (1964), pp. 19–25.

11 Anderson, 'Origins of the Present Crisis', p. 36.

12 Seymour Martin Lipset, 'Radicalism or Reformism: The Sources of Working-Class Politics', *American Political Science Review,* 77 (1983), pp. 1–18: 2. For a review of American exceptionalism in labour history see Eric Foner, 'Why Is There No Socialism in the United States?', *History Workshop Journal* 17 (1984), pp. 55–80; Rick Halpern and Jonathan Morris, 'The Persistence of Exceptionalism: Class Formation and the Comparative Method', in *idem.,* eds, *American Exceptionalism? US Working-Class Formation in an International Context* (Basingstoke, 1997), pp. 1–13; for a critique see Sean Wilentz, 'Against Exceptionalism: Class Consciousness and the American Labor Movement', *International Labor and Working-Class History,* 26 (1984), pp. 1–24.

13 This debate is summarised in Lenard R Berlanstein, 'The Distinctiveness of the Nineteenth-Century French Labor Movement', *Journal of Modern History,* 64 (1992), pp. 660–685. Berlanstein suggests, however, that historians of French labour have rarely dealt directly with the question of French distinctiveness.

14 For a review of the *Sonderweg* literature see Eisenberg, 'The Comparative View in Labour History'. Also Richard Bessel, 'Workers, Politics and Pow-

er in Modern German History: Some Recent Writing on the German Labour Movement and the German Working Class in the Nineteenth and Twentieth Centuries', *The Historical Journal,* 33 (1990), pp. 211–226.

15 Charles Tilly, *Big Structures, Large Processes, Huge Comparisons* (New York, 1984); Cronin, 'Neither Exceptional Nor Peculiar', p. 59.

16 Karl Marx and Friedrich Engels, *The Communist Manifesto* (Penguin edition, Harmondsworth, 1967), pp. 92, 102.

17 Kautsky, Das erfurter Programm in seinem grundsätzlichen Theil (Stuttgart 1892, p. 250); cited in Marcel van der Linden and Jürgen Rojahn, 'Introduction', in *idem.,* eds, *The Formation of Labour Movements, 1870–1914: An International Perspective,* vol. 1 (Leiden, 1990), pp. ix–xvii: x.

18 Hjalmar Branting, afterword to Robert Blatchford, *Den glada England, eller Samhället sådant det är och sådant det borde vara,* translated A F Åkerberg, (Stockholm, 1896).

19 Branting, afterword to *Den glada England,* p. 244.

20 Selig Perlman, *A Theory of the Labor Movement* (New York 1928), cited in van der Linden and Rojahn, *The Formation of Labour Movements,* pp. x–xi.

21 Marcel van der Linden and Lex Heerma van Voss, 'Introduction', in *idem.,* eds, *Class and Other Identities: Gender, Religion and Ethnicity in the Writing of European Labour History* (New York, 2002), pp. 1–39: 13.

22 Jürgen Kocka, 'Probleme einer europäischen Geschichte in komparativer Absicht', in *idem., Geschichte und Aufklärung* (Göttingen, 1989), pp. 21–28: 27.

23 Edvard Bull, 'Arbeiderbevægelsens stilling i de tre nordiske lande 1914–1920', *Arkiv för studier i arbetarrörelsens historia,* 15/16 (1979), pp. 62–80 (first published 1922).

24 Walter Galenson, 'Scandinavia', in *idem.,* ed., *Comparative Labor Movements* (New York, 1952), pp. 104–172; also *idem., Labor in Norway* (Cambridge, Massachusetts, 1948). The debate is reviewed in Flemming Mikkelsen, 'Fra proletarisering til klassesamfund. Industrialisering, urbanisering og fremvæksten af en arbejderklasse og arbejderbevægelse i Skandinavia ca 1750–1900', *Arbejderhistorie,* 30 (1988), pp. 2–20.

25 Seymour Martin Lipset and Stein Rokkan, 'Cleavage Structures, Party Systems and Voter Alignments: An Introduction', in *idem.,* eds, *Party Systems and Voter Alignments: Cross-National Perspectives* (New York, 1967), pp. 1–64; Hugh Heclo, *Modern Social Politics in Britain and Sweden: From Relief to Income Maintenance* (New Haven, 1974), p. 37; Ira Katznelson, 'Working-Class Formation and the State: Nineteenth Century England in American Perspective', in Peter B Evans, Dietrich Rueschemeyer and Theda Skocpol, eds, *Bringing the State Back In* (Cambridge, 1985), pp. 257–284; *idem.,* 'Working-Class Formation: Constructing Cases and Comparisons', in Ira Katznelson and Aristide R Zolberg, eds, *Working-Class Formation: Nineteenth-Century Patterns in Western Europe and the United States* (Princeton, New Jersey, 1986), pp. 3–41.

26 Theda Skocpol, 'Bringing the State Back In: Strategies of Analysis in Current Research', in Evans et al., eds, *Bringing the State Back In*, p. 7.

27 Lipset, 'Radicalism or Reformism'.

28 Pierre Birnbaum, *States and Collective Action: The European Experience* (Cambridge, 1988), p. 86; Bo Rothstein, 'State Structure and Variations in Corporatism: The Swedish Case', *Scandinavian Political Studies*, 14 (1991), pp. 149–171.

29 Marina Cattaruzza, '"Organisieter Konflikt" und "direkte Aktion". Zwei Formen des Arbeiterkampfes am Beispiel der Werftarbeiterstreiks in Hamburg und Triest (1880–1914)', *Archiv für Sozialgeschichter*, 20 (1980), pp. 325–355; Edward H Lorenz, 'Two Patterns of Development: The Labour Process in the British and French Shipbuilding Industries 1880 to 1930', *Journal of European Economic History*, 13 (1984), pp. 599–634; James Fulcher, *Labour Movements, Employers and the State: Conflict and Co-operation in Britain and Sweden* (Oxford, 1991); Gerald Friedman, *State-Making and Labor Movements: France and the United States, 1876–1914* (Ithaca, 1998).

30 Luebbert, *Liberalism, Fascism or Social Democracy*.

31 Aristide R Zolberg, 'How Many Exceptionalisms?', in Katznelson and Zolberg, eds, *Working-Class Formation*, pp. 397–455. Zollberg's answer to his own question is: 'as many as there are cases under comparison'.

32 E P Thompson, 'The Peculiarities of the English', in *idem., The Poverty of Theory and Other Essays* (London, 1978; first published 1965), pp. 245–301.

33 Thompson, 'The Peculiarities of the English', pp. 255, 258.

34 See also Cronin, 'Neither Exceptional Nor Peculiar', pp. 62–63 on this point. Cronin suggests that the fondness for overarching theories such as Marxism may explain why exceptionalism was so attractive for labour historians.

35 Wilentz, 'Against Exceptionalism', p. 2; Margaret Ramsay Somers, 'Workers of the World, Compare!', *Contemporary Sociology*, 18 (1989), pp. 325–329: 325; Halpern and Morris, 'The Persistence of Exceptionalism'.

36 Foner, 'Why Is There No Socialism?', pp. 58–9.

37 Breuilly, *Labour and Liberalism*, p. 116.

38 David Blackbourn and Geoff Eley, *The Peculiarities of German History: Bourgeois Society and Politics in Nineteenth Century Germany* (Oxford, 1984), p. 10; also Eisenberg, 'The Comparative View in Labour History'.

39 Neville Kirk, *Comrades and Cousins: Globalization, Workers and Labour Movements in Britain, the USA and Australia from the 1880s to 1914* (London, 2003) uses a three-way comparison to criticise accounts which see working-class development as either 'normal' or 'exceptional'.

40 Madeleine Hurd, *Public Spheres, Public Mores and Democracy: Hamburg and Stockholm 1870–1914* (Ann Arbor, 2000), pp. 1–3, 15–21. See also Sheri Berman, *The Social Democratic Moment: Ideas and Politics in the Making of Interwar Europe* (Cambridge, Massachusetts, 1998), who points out that

Germany has suffered from an idealised comparison with Britain, even though Sweden was perhaps more appropriate as a comparative case because like Germany it only made the transition to democracy after World War I. Berman's account suggests that there was no inevitability about German inter-war history: nothing in 1918 indicated the very divergent paths which Sweden and Germany were to take during the inter-war period.

41 Blackbourn and Eley, *The Peculiarities of German History*, p. 33, suggest that the dominance of the *Sonderweg* theory of German development had imposed a 'teleological blandness', where all German history since the mid nineteenth century was written "as if the known outcome in 1933 was inscribed in every event." See also Kirk, *Comrades and Cousins*, p. 6.

42 Øystein Sørensen and Bo Stråth, eds, *The Cultural Construction of Norden* (Oslo, 1997); Eva Österberg, 'Bönder och centralmakt i det tidigmoderna Sverige. Konflikter – kompromiss – politisk kultur', *Scandia,* 55 (1989), pp. 73–95: 86–89; for a critical view see Börje Harnesk, 'Den svenska modellens tidigmoderna rötter?', *Historisk Tidskrift* (S) (2002), pp. 78–90.

43 Mary Fulbrook, 'Introduction: States, Nations and the Development of Europe', in *idem.*, ed., *National Histories and European History* (London, 1993), pp. 1–17: 8; also Stefan Berger with Mark Donovan and Kevin Passmore, 'Apologies for the Nation-State in Western Europe since 1800', in Berger, Donovan and Passmore, eds, *Writing National Histories,* pp. 3–14: 9.

44 Marc Bloch, 'Toward a Comparative History of European Societies', in Frederic C Lane and Jelle C Riermersma, eds, *Enterprise and Secular Change: Readings in Economic History* (Homewood, Illinois, 1953; first published 1928), pp. 494–521: 515; Breuilly, *Labour and Liberalism,* p. 19. See also Ilaria Favretto, *The Long Search for the Third Way: The British Labour Party and the Italian Left Since 1945* (Basingstoke, 2002), which demonstrates how the comparative method can relativise the rhetoric of exceptionalism.

45 The full implications of the so-called 'linguistic turn' for labour history are discussed in more detail in chapter two.

46 Michel Espagne and Michael Werner, *Transferts. Les relations interculturelles dans l'espace franco-allemand* (Paris, 1988); cited in Stefan Berger, 'Comparative History', in Stefan Berger, Heiko Feldner and Kevin Passmore, eds, *Writing History: Theory and Practice* (London, 2003), pp. 161–179: 169. In Britain, it is probably fair to say that investigations of cultural transfer between Britain and its colonies have been of more interest than its European connections, though there are signs that this is changing. For a study which deals with cross-national contacts – in this case in the field of early nineteenth century evangelicalism – between Britain and Sweden, see Hanna Hodacs, *Converging World Views: The European Expansion and Early Nineteenth Century Anglo-Swedish Contacts* (Uppsala, 2003).

47 Armitage, 'Greater Britain', p. 443.

48 Armitage, 'Greater Britain', p. 431.
49 Bloch, 'Toward a Comparative History of European Societies'.
50 Stefan Berger, *The British Labour Party and the German Social Democrats, 1900–1931* (Oxford, 1994), p. 1; Cronin, 'Neither Exceptional Nor Peculiar'; Richard Price, 'The Future of British Labour History', *International Review of Social History*, 36 (1991), pp. 249–260: 259.
51 John N Horne, *Labour at War: France and Britain, 1914–1918* (Oxford, 1991), p. ix.
52 Horne, *Labour at War*, pp. 15, 20–21.
53 Berger, *The British Labour Party and the German Social Democrats*, p. 85
54 Berger, *The British Labour Party and the German Social Democrats*, p. 254.
55 See chapter 2.
56 Jürgen Kocka, 'Comparative Historical Research: German Examples', *International Review of Social History*, 38 (1993), pp. 369–379: 373; Breuilly, *Labour and Liberalism*, pp. 4–5.
57 See Turner, 'Hostile Participants', for an account which challenges the notion of national distinctiveness from the perspective of a local study.
58 On coalminers see: Roger Fagge, *Power, Culture and Conflict in the Coalfields: West Virginia and South Wales, 1900–1922* (Manchester, 1996); John H M Laslett, *Colliers Across the Sea: A Comparative Study of Class Formation in Scotland and the American Midwest, 1830–1924* (Urbana and Chicago, 2000); on dockworkers: Frank Broeze, 'Militancy and Pragmatism: An International Perspective on Maritime Labour 1870–1914', *International Review of Social History*, 36 (1991), pp. 165–200; and Sam Davies, et al., eds, *Dock Workers: International Explorations in Comparative Labour History, 1790–1970* (Aldershot, 2000), both of which are extremely ambitious in their scope, extending beyond Europe and America; also Yngve Tidman, *Spräng Amalthea! Arbete, facklig kamp och strejkbryteri i nordvästeuropeiska hamnar 1870–1914* (Lund, 1998); on shipyard workers: Marina Cattaruzza, '"Organisieter Konflikt" und "direkte Aktion"'; Bo Stråth, 'Workers' Radicalism in Theory and Practice: A Study of the Shipyard Workers and Industrial Development in Gothenburg, Malmö and Bremen', *Scandinavian Journal of History*, 8 (1983), pp. 261–291.
59 See Stefan Berger, 'Working-class Culture and the Labour Movement in the South Wales and the Ruhr Coalfields 1850–2000: A Comparison', *Llafur*, 8 (2001), pp. 5–40.
60 Broeze, 'Militancy and Pragmatism', p. 166. This criticism could for example apply to Fagge's book.
61 Hurd, *Public Spheres;* Natasha Vall, 'Explorations in Comparative History: Economy and Society in Malmö and Newcastle since 1945', (unpublished PhD thesis, Northumbria University, 2000); Katarina Friberg, *The Workings of Co-operation: A Comparative Study of Consumer Co-operation Organisation in Britain and Sweden 1860 to 1970* (Växjö, 2005).

2. The Rise of Labour in Britain and Sweden

1 For example, on industrial relations: James Fulcher, *Labour Movements, Employers and the State: Conflict and Co-operation in Britain and Sweden* (Oxford, 1991); Alf O Johansson and Joseph Melling, 'The Roots of Consensus: Bargaining Attitudes and Political Commitment among Swedish and British Workers c.1920–1950', *Economic and Industrial Democracy*, 16 (1995), pp. 353–397; on social policy: Hugh Heclo, *Modern Social Politics in Britain and Sweden: From Relief to Income Maintenance* (New Haven, Connecticut, 1974); Margaret Weir and Theda Skocpol, 'State Structures and the Possibilities for "Keynesian" Responses to the Great Depression in Sweden, Britain and the United States', in Peter B Evans, Dietrich Rueschemeyer and Theda Skocpol, ed,. *Bringing the State Back In* (Cambridge, 1985), pp. 3–37; Malcolm B Hamilton, *Democratic Socialism in Britain and Sweden* (Basingstoke, 1989).

2 The fascination with the 'Swedish model' for journalists and politicians in both Britain and America dates from the publication of Marquis Childs' *Sweden: The Middle Way* (New Haven, Connecticut) in 1936, which seemed to give rise to a genre of its own. Other examples include Margaret Cole and Charles Smith, eds, *Democratic Sweden* (London, 1938); Perry Anderson, 'Sweden: Mr Crosland's Dreamland', *New Left Review*, 7 (1961), pp. 4–12, and 9 (1961), pp. 34–45. Not all foreign commentators have been so positive.

3 Richard Tomasson, introduction to Herbert Tingsten, *The Swedish Social Democrats: Their Ideological Development*, translated Greta Frankel and Patricia Howard-Rosen (Totowa, New Jersey, 1973), p. vii.

4 The terms 'broad' and 'narrow' labour history are those used by Marcel van der Linden and Lex Heerma van Voss to convey in English the difference between *Arbeitergeschichte* and *Arbeiterbewegungsgeschichte*, or *histoire du mouvement ouvrier* and *histoire ouvrière*, or indeed between *arbetarrörelsenshistoria* and *arbetslivshistoria*. Marcel van der Linden and Lex Heerma van Voss, "Introduction", in *idem.*, eds, *Class and Other Identities: Gender, Religion and Ethnicity in the Writing of European Labour History* (New York, 2002), pp. 1–39: 1. See also Sten Karlsson, *När industriarbetaren blev historia. Studier i svensk arbetarhistoria 1965–1995* (Lund, 1998), p. 22.

5 Eric Hobsbawm, 'The Labour Aristocracy in Nineteenth Century Britain', in *idem.*, *Labouring Men* (London, 1964), pp. 272–315. More recently, historians have challenged the theory of the labour aristocracy, and has emphasised instead the vibrancy of mid-Victorian popular politics. See for example, Eugenio Biagini, *Liberty, Retrenchment and Reform: Popular Liberalism in the Age of Gladstone, 1860–1880* (Cambridge, 1992).

6 Keith Burgess, *The Challenge of Labour: Shaping British Society 1850–1930* (London, 1980); Neville Kirk, *Change, Continuity and Class: Labour in British Society, 1850–1920* (Manchester, 1998); Henry Pelling, *A History of*

British Trade Unionism, (Harmondsworth, 1987; first published 1963), ch. 6.

7 Eric J Hobsbawm, 'The "New Unionism" Reconsidered', in Wolfgang J Mommsen and Hans-Gerhard Husung, eds, *The Development of Trade Unionism in Great Britain and Germany, 1880–1914* (London, 1985), pp. 13–31: 15; Henry Pelling, *A History of British Trade Unionism* (Harmondsworth, 1987; first published 1963), p. 297.

8 Mike Savage and Andrew Miles, *The Remaking of the British Working Class, 1840–1940* (London, 1994), pp. 54, 56.

9 Derek Matthews, '1889 and All That: New Views on the New Unionism', *International Review of Social History,* 36 (1991), pp. 24–58.

10 Edward H Lorenz, 'Two Patterns of Development: The Labour Process in the British and French Shipbuilding Industries 1880 to 1930', *Journal of European Economic History,* 13 (1984), pp. 599–634; Jonathan Zeitlin, 'Industrial Structure, Employer Strategy and the Diffusion of Job Control in Britain, 1880–1920', in Mommsen and Husung, eds, *The Development of Trade Unionism,* pp. 325–337, which also reviews the relevant literature.

11 Alastair Reid, 'The Division of Labour and Politics in Britain, 1880–1920', in Mommsen and Husung, *The Development of Trade Unionism,* pp. 150–165.

12 Sonya O Rose, 'Gender Antagonism and Class Conflict: Exclusionary Strategies of Male Trade Unionists in Nineteenth Century Britain', *Social History,* 13 (1988), pp. 191–208.

13 Henry Pelling, *The Origins of the Labour Party, 1880–1906* (London, 1954); Paul Thompson, *Socialists, Liberals and Labour: The Struggle for London, 1885–1914* (London, 1967); Alun Howkins, 'Edwardian Liberalism and Industrial Unrest: a Class View of the Decline of Liberalism', *History Workshop Journal,* 4 (1977) 143–161; David Howell, *British Workers and the Independent Labour Party, 1888–1906* (Manchester, 1983).

14 John Saville, 'Trade Unions and Free Labour: The Background to the Taff Vale Decision', in Asa Briggs and John Saville, eds, *Essays in Labour History in Memory of G D H Cole* (London, 1967), pp. 317–350.

15 P F Clarke, *Lancashire and the New Liberalism* (London, 1971); Duncan Tanner, *Political Change and the Labour Party, 1900–1918* (Cambridge, 1990).

16 Tanner, *Political Change,* ch. 1.

17 Roy Douglas, 'Labour in Decline, 1910–1914' in Kenneth D Brown, ed., *Essays in Anti-labour History: Responses to the Rise of Labour in Britain* (London, 1974), pp. 105–125: 125.

18 James Hinton, *The First Shop Stewards' Movement* (London, 1973); J M Winter, *Socialism and the Challenge of War: Ideas and Politics in Britain 1912–18* (London, 1974); Burgess, *The Challenge of Labour,* ch. 5; James E Cronin, *Labour and Society in Britain, 1918–1979* (London, 1984), ch. 2;. Bernard Waites, *A Class Society at War: Britain 1914–1918 (*Leamington Spa, 1987), p. 32, presents a slightly more cautious view, arguing that the war did indeed

strengthen class divisions by consolidating existing tendencies within capitalism, but that the revolutionary implications of this were marginal.

19 Cronin, *Labour and Society,* p. 27.

20 McKibbin, *Evolution of the Labour Party; idem., Classes and Cultures: England 1918–1951* (Oxford, 1998).

21 H C G Matthew, R I McKibbin and J A Kay, 'The Franchise Factor in the Rise of the Labour Party', *English Historical Review,* 91 (1976) pp. 723–752.

22 McKibbin, *The Evolution of the Labour Party; idem.,* 'Why Was There No Marxism in Great Britain?', in *idem., The Ideologies of Class: Social Relations in Britain, 1880–1950* (Oxford, 1990; first published 1983), pp. 1–41.

23 Savage and Miles, *The Remaking of the British Working Class,* ch. 2.

24 Patrick Joyce, *Work, Society and Politics: The Culture of the Factory in Later Victorian England* (Brighton, 1980); Gareth Stedman Jones, 'Working-Class Culture and Working-Class Politics in London, 1870–1900: Notes on the Remaking of a Working Class', in *idem., Languages of Class: Studies in English Working-class History, 1832–1982* (Cambridge, 1983; first published 1974), pp. 179–238: 236–7.

25 Stedman Jones, 'Working-Class Culture', pp. 227–9.

26 Stedman Jones, 'Working-class Culture', pp. 235, 237.

27 Ross McKibbin, 'Work and Hobbies in Britain 1880–1950' in *idem., The Ideologies of Class,* (first published 1983), pp. 139–166; also *idem.,* 'Why Was There No Marxism?', pp. 12–15. McKibbin concludes (p. 296): 'The working class was intensely political but political energies were scattered among a profusion of associations which tended to compete with as much as complement formal political activity.' His findings are borne out by contemporary observations, such as Charles Booth's survey which found that the dominant cultural institutions for the working class were 'not the school, the evening class, the library, the friendly society, the church or the chapel, but the pub, the sporting paper, the race course and the music hall.' Cited in Jay M Winter, 'Trade Unions and the Labour Party in Britain', in Mommsen and Husung, eds, *The Development of Trade Unionism in Great Britain and Germany,* pp. 359–370: 363.

28 Michael Savage, *The Dynamics of Working-class Politics: The Labour Movement in Preston, 1880–1940* (Cambridge, 1987); Tony Jowitt, 'Late Victorian and Edwardian Bradford', in David James, Tony Jowitt and Keith Laybourn, eds, *The Centennial History of the Independent Labour Party* (Halifax, 1992), pp. 95–115: 104.

29 Sidney Pollard, 'Nineteenth Century Co-operation: From Community Building to Shopkeeping', in Asa Briggs and John Saville, eds, *Essays in Labour History, 1886–1923* (London, 1960), pp. 74–112; John Foster, *Class Struggle and the Industrial Revolution: Early Industrial Capitalism in Three English Towns* (London, 1974), pp. 221–2. For the revisionist view of the co-op see Stephen Yeo, ed., *New Views of Co-operation* (London, 1988), and

especially, Peter Gurney, *Co-operative Culture and the Politics of Consumption in England, c.1870–1930* (Manchester, 1996).

30 Gurney, *Co-operative Culture*, p. 11.

31 Rita Rhodes, *An Arsenal for Labour: The Royal Arsenal Co-operative Society and Politics 1896–1996* (Manchester, 1998); Mary Hilson, 'Consumers and Politics: The Co-operative Movement in Plymouth, 1890–1920', *Labour History Review*, 67 (2002), pp. 7–27.

32 G D H Cole, *A Century of Co-operation* (London, 1944), pp. 371–2. This compares to 2 million trade unionists in 1900 (1.2m in TUC-affiliated unions), and 8.3m in 1920 (6.4m). Pelling, *A History of Trade Unionism*, pp. 297–8.

33 Eli F Heckscher, *An Economic History of Sweden*, translated Göran Ohlin (Cambridge, Massachusetts, 1954). The more recent debates are summarised in Bo Gustafsson, 'Sweden', in Mikulás Teich and Roy Porter, eds, *The Industrial Revolution in National Context: Europe and the USA* (Cambridge, 1996), pp. 201–225.

34 Lennart Schön, 'Proto-Industrialisation and Factories: Textiles in Sweden in the Mid-Nineteenth Century', *Scandinavian Economic History Review*, 30 (1982), pp. 57–71; Maths Isacson and Lars Magnusson, *Proto-Industrialisation in Scandinavia: Craft Skills in the Industrial Revolution* (Leamington Spa, 1987).

35 Lennart Schön, *En modern svensk ekonomisk historia. Tillväxt och omvandling under två sekel* (Stockholm, 2000), p. 222.

36 The debate is summarised in Klas Åmark, *Facklig makt och fackligt medlemskap. De svenska fackförbundens medlemsutveckling 1890–1940* (Lund, 1986), pp. 17–20. See in particular Sven Lundkvist, *Folkrörelserna i det svenska samhället, 1850–1920* (Uppsala, 1977).

37 The debate is summarised in Mary Hilson, 'Swedish Approaches to the Rise of Labour: A British Perspective', *Scandinavian Journal of History*, 26 (2001), pp. 103–121, 111–112. As with the comparable generation of historians in Britain, much of this work was informed by a strong, almost polemical, critique of earlier studies and by the historians' own sympathy for radical (usually Marxist) politics.

38 Hans-Olof Ericson, *Vanmakt och styrka. Studier av arbetarrörelsens tillkomst och förutsättningar i Jönköping, Huskvarna och Norrahammar 1880–1909* (Lund, 1987), p. 22. Also Ingemar Johansson, *Strejken som vapen. Fackföreningar och strejker i Norrköping 1870–1910* (Stockholm, 1982); Lars Ekdahl, *Arbete mot kapital. Typografer och ny teknik – studier av Stockholms tryckeriindustri under det industriella genombrottet* (Lund, 1983); Thommy Svensson, *Från ackord till månadslön. En studie av lönpolitiken, fackföreningarna och rationaliseringarna inom svensk varvsindustri under 1900-talet* (Göteborg, 1983); Lars Berggren, *Ångvisslans och brickornas värld. Om arbete och facklig organisering vid Kockums mekaniska verkstad och Carl Lunds fabrik i Malmö 1840–1905* (Lund, 1991); Ulf Magnusson, *Från arbetare till*

arbetarklass. Klassformering och klassrelationer i Fagersta – ett mellansvenskt bruksamhälle ca 1870–1909 (Uppsala, 1996).

39 Åmark, *Facklig makt*, pp. 11, 205–9. Trade union membership suffered a severe setback in the wake of the 1909 general strike, but this did not reverse the underlying trend which meant that Sweden had one of most organised workforces in Europe.

40 Berggren, *Ångvisslans och brickornas värld*, suggests that the remnants of more informal traditions of protest, such as St Monday, initiation and drinking rituals, survived in the Malmö factory which was the subject of his study, but these were gradually rejected as workers came to realise the need for collective discipline. The same point is made by Svensson, *Från ackord till månadslön* and Johansson, *Strejken som vapen*. Cf Geoff Eley, *Forging Democracy: The History of the Left in Europe 1850–2000* (Oxford, 2002), who suggests (p. 81) that the 'small solidarities' in workers' everyday lives – rituals, timewasting, practical jokes – helped to lay the foundations of militancy even if they were not necessarily political acts in themselves.

41 Walter Korpi, *The Working Class in Welfare Capitalism* (London, 1978), p. 74; Anders Kjellberg, *Fackliga organisationer och medlemmar i dagens Sverige* (Lund, 2nd edition 2001; first published 1997), p. 30.

42 For example, Mats Dahlkvist, *Staten, socialdemokratin och socialismen. En inledande analys* (Lund, 1975); C Gynnå and E Mannheimer, *En studie i den svenska arbetarklassens uppkomst* (Lund, 1970); Knut Bäckström, *Arbetarrörelsen i Sverige*, 2 vols. (Stockholm, 1958 and 1963).

43 Edvard Bull, 'Arbeiderbevægelsens stilling i de tre nordiske lande 1914–1920', *Arkiv för studier i arbetarrörelsens historia*, 15/16 (1979), pp. 62–80 (first published 1922); Walter Galenson, ed., *Comparative Labor Movements* (New York, 1952), p. 105; Göran Therborn, et al., 'Sweden Before and After Social Democracy: A First Overview', *Acta Sociologica*, supplement (1978), pp. 37–58: 44.

44 Fulcher, *Labour Movements, Employers and the State*, pp. 46–50.

45 These questions remain under-researched, but see for example Björn Horgby, *Dom där. Främlingsfientligheten och arbetarkulturen i Norrköping 1890–1960* (Stockholm 1996).

46 On masculinity and class consciousness, see for example, Ulla Wikander, *Kvinnors och mäns arbeten. Gustavsberg 1880–1980. Genusarbetsdelning och arbetets degradering vid en porslinsfabrik* (Lund, 1988); Susanne Lundin, *En liten skara äro vi… En studie av typografer vid 1900-talets första decennier* (Stockholm, 1992); Eva Blomberg, *Män i mörker. Arbetsgivare, reformister och syndikalister. Politik och identitet i svensk gruvindustri 1910–1940* (Stockholm, 1995).

47 Lars Magnusson, *Arbetet vid en svensk verkstad. Munktells, 1900–1920* (Lund, 1987); Maths Isacson, *Verkstadsarbete under 1900-talet. Hedemora Verkstäder före 1950* (Lund, 1987); Mats Johansson, 'Paternalism och strej-

ker. En jämförelse mellan sågverken i Båtskärsnäs och Karlsborg i början av 1900-talet', *Arkiv för studier i arbetarrörelsens historia* 88–89 (2003), pp. 23–37.

48 Lars Magnusson, 'Patriarkalism och social kontroll. Några synpunkter på ett problemkomplex', in *Arkiv för studier i arbetarrörelsens historia,* 33 (1986), pp. 46–61.

49 Bo Stråth, *Varvsarbetare i två varvstäder. En historisk studie av verkstadsklubbarna vid varven i Göteborg och Malmö* (Kungälv, 1982); Ulf Magnusson, *Från arbetare till arbetarklass.*

50 Birger Simonson, 'Sweden', in Marcel van der Linden and Jürgen Rojahn, eds, *The Formation of Labour Movements 1870–1914: An International Perspective* (Leiden, 1990), pp. 85–102: 87.

51 Alf Johansson, *Arbetets delning. Stocka sågverk under omvandling 1856–1900* (Lund, 1988; Ulf Eriksson, *Gruva och arbete. Kiirunavaara 1890–1990* (4 vols, Uppsala, 1991); Ella Johansson, *Skogarnas fria söner. Maskulinitet och modernitet i norrländskt skogsarbete* (Kristianstad, 1994). Cf Vagn Wåhlin, 'Omkring studiet af de folklige bevægelser', *Historisk Tidskrift* (S), (1979), pp. 113–151, who suggests that the roots of the nineteenth century popular movements have to be sought in the 'great rural transformation' of the late eighteenth century and afterwards.

52 Lennart K Persson, *Arbete, politik, arbetarrörelse. En studie av stenindustrins Bohuslän 1860–1910* (Gothenburg, 1984). Cf Blomberg, *Män i mörker.*

53 Quoted in Persson, *Arbete, politik, arbetarrörelse,* p. 461.

54 Mats Lindquist, *Klasskamrater. Om industriellt arbete och kulturell formation 1880–1920* (Stockholm, 1994; first published 1987), p. 183.

55 Howell, *British Workers,* p. 6.

56 Stedman Jones, 'Working-Class Culture', p. 236. Peter Clarke, in his own study of Lancashire, described the region as the 'cockpit of Edwardian elections', and impossible to dismiss as precocious or unrepresentative, therefore. Clarke, *Lancashire and the New Liberalism,* p. vii.

57 P J Waller, *Democracy and Sectarianism: A Political and Social History of Liverpool, 1868–1939* (Liverpool, 1981).

58 A M Dawson, 'Politics in Devon and Cornwall, 1900–1931' (unpublished PhD thesis, University of London, 1991); G H Tredidga, 'The Liberal Party in Cornwall, 1918–1939' (unpublished MPhil thesis, University of Exeter, 1991).

59 Sam Davies, *Liverpool Labour: Social and Political Influences on the Development of the Labour Party in Liverpool, 1900–1939* (Keele, 1996), ch. 1.

60 Tanner, *Political Change.*

61 Savage, *The Dynamics of Working-Class Politics.*

62 Gunnar Olofsson, 'Från underklass till arbetarklass. Förändringar i "det arbetande folket" 1870–1930', in *idem., Klass, rörelse, socialdemokrati. Essäer om arbetarrörelsens sociologi* (Lund, 1996; first published 1976), pp. 69–102: 92–94.

63 See Lars Berggren, 'Går det att skriva arbetarhistoriska synteser?' *Historisk Tidskrift* (S), (2003), pp. 181–200.

64 Stephen Yeo, 'A New Life: The Religion of Socialism in Britain, 1883–1896,' *History Workshop Journal,* 4 (1977), pp. 5–56.

65 Harvey Mitchell, 'Labor and the Origins of Social Democracy in Britain, France and Germany, 1890–1914', in Harvey Mitchell and Peter N Stearns, *Workers and Protest: The European Labor Movement, the Working Classes and the Origins of Social Democracy, 1890–1914* (Itasca, 1971), p. 35; McKibbin, 'Why Was There No Marxism?', pp. 17–24; Gregory M Luebbert, *Liberalism, Fascism or Social Democracy: Social Classes and the Political Origins of Regimes in Interwar Europe* (Oxford, 1991), pp. 15–25.

66 Berndt Schiller, 'Years of Crisis', in Steven Koblik, ed., *Sweden's Development From Poverty to Affluence: 1750–1970,* translated Joanne Johnson (Minneapolis, 1975), pp. 197–228: 199.

67 Nils Elvander, *Skandinavisk arbetarrörelse* (Stockholm, 1980), pp. 28–34, concludes that Sweden took a much longer road to democratic reform than either Norway or Denmark.

68 Keir Hardie, 'The Independent Labour Party' in A Reid, ed., *The New Party* London 1895, p. 258; cited in Matthew, Kay and McKibbin, 'The Franchise Factor', p. 724.

69 Torbjörn Vallinder, *I kamp för demokratin. Rösträttsrörelsen i Sverige 1886–1900* (Stockholm, 1962); Rolf Karlbom, *Revolution eller reformer. Studier i SAP:s historia 1889–1902* (Göteborg, 1985).

70 Seppo Hentilä, *Den svenska arbetarklassen och reformismens genombrott* (Helsinki, 1979); Lotta Gröning, *Vägen till makten. SAP:s organisation och dess betydelse för den politiska verksamheten 1900–1933* (Uppsala, 1988).

71 Stig Hadenius, 'Riksdagspartier och rikspartier på 1890-talet', pp. 55–66: 56; and Torsten Henriksson, 'Frisinnade landsföreningen och demokratin', pp. 67–89l; both in Stig Hadenius, ed., *Kring demokratins genombrott i Sverige* (Stockholm, 1966).

72 Heclo, *Modern Social Politics,* p. 40.

73 Martin Pugh, *The Tories and the People, 1880–1935* (Oxford, 1985); Jon Lawrence, 'Class and Gender in the Making of Urban Toryism, 1880–1914,' *English Historical Review,* 108 (1993), pp. 629–653.

74 Hadenius, 'Riksdagspartier och rikspartier', p. 65; also Leif Lewin, *Ideology and Strategy: A Century of Swedish Politics,* translated Victor Kayfetz (Cambridge, 1988).

75 William M Lafferty, *Economic Development and the Response of Labor in Scandinavia: A Multi-Level Analysis* (Oslo, 1971).

76 See Øystein Sørensen and Bo Stråth, 'Introduction' in *idem.,* eds, *The Cultural Construction of* Norden (Oslo, 1997), for a discussion of the symbolic and practical role of the peasant class in nineteenth century Sweden. For a challenge to the 'consensus' view of Swedish political development, see Börje Harnesk, 'Den svenska modellens tidigmoderna rötter?', *Historisk Tidskrift* (S) (2002), pp. 78–90. Most would agree that Sweden lacked a feudal Junker class, though cf. Seymour Martin Lipset, 'Radicalism or

Reformism: The Sources of Working-Class Politics', *American Political Science Review*, 77 (1983), pp. 1–18: 4, who suggests that Sweden was 'the most status-bound society of northern Europe', with a social structure that resembled that of Wilhelmine Germany.

77 Bo Rothstein, 'State Structure and Variations in Corporatism: The Swedish Case', *Scandinavian Political Studies*, 14 (1991), pp. 149–171: 155. This is not to suggest that repressive legislation was entirely absent from Sweden: for example, the '*Åkarpslagen*' of 1889 proscribed picketing and legalised strikebreaking.

78 Rune Bokholm, *Städernas handlingsfrihet. En studie av expansionsskedet 1900–1930* (Lund, 1995). Cf Ira Katznelson's criticism that Britain and America are frequently classified together as the 'Anglo-American weak state', ignoring the presence of intensely local identities within the American federalist system, contrasted with the growth of central government in late nineteenth century Britain. Ira Katznelson, 'Working-Class Formation and the State: Nineteenth Century England in American Perspective', in Evans et al., eds, *Bringing the State Back In*, pp. 257–284: 273–4.

79 Marcel van der Linden, 'The National Integration of European Working Classes (1871–1914): Exploring the Causal Configuration', *International Review of Social History*, 33 (1988), pp. 285–311. Several historians have suggested that Britain – where approximately two thirds of adult men had the right to vote in 1914 – had one of the most restricted franchises in Europe in 1914: Matthew, Kay and McKibbin, 'The Franchise Factor', p. 724; Robert Self, *The Evolution of the British Party System 1885–1940* (Harlow, 2000), p. 14.

80 C Seymour, *Electoral Reform in England and Wales: The Development and Operation of the Parliamentary Franchise 1832–85* (Newton Abbot, 1970; 1st published 1915), pp. 352–8; cited in Ian Machin, *The Rise of Democracy in Britain, 1830–1918* (Basingstoke, 2001); Self, *The Evolution of the British Party System*, p. 14.

81 Dawson, 'Politics in Devon and Cornwall', pp. 85–7.

82 Matthew, Kay and McKibbin, 'The Franchise Factor'; Dror Wahrman, 'The New Political History: A Review Essay', *Social History*, 21 (1996), pp. 343–354, 353.

83 Torbjörn Vallinder, *I kamp för demokratin. Rösträttsrörelsen i Sverige 1886–1900* (Stockholm, 1962).

84 Olle Johansson, 'Socialdemokratins väljare 1911 och 1914. En kvantitativ analys av regional och social gruppering och struktur', *Historisk Tidskrift* (S) (1967), p. 302; cited in Gröning, *Vägen till makten*, p. 23.

85 *Blekinge Folkblad*, 18th September 1911.

86 Peter Essaiasson, *Svenska valkampanjer 1866–1988* (Stockholm, 1990), p. 93.

87 Matthew, Kay and McKibbin, 'The Franchise Factor', pp. 723, 726–731. See Duncan Tanner, 'The Parliamentary Electoral System, the "Fourth" Reform Act and the Rise of Labour in England and Wales', *Bulletin of the*

Institute for Historical Research, 56 (1983), pp. 205–219, for a critique of the thesis that Labour's 'natural' supporters were excluded before 1918.

88 Neal Blewett, *The Peers, the Parties and the People: The General Elections of 1910* (London, 1972), p. 114.

89 Carl Hallendorff, 'Parlamentarism', *Svensk Tidskrift* (1911), pp. 391–401; and Pontus Fahlbeck, *Engelsk parlamentarism contra svensk. Ett stycke nutidshistoria* (Lund, 1916); both cited in Lewin, *Ideology and Politics*, p. 89. Lewin suggests that the Swedish liberals were well aware of the British debate, and both supporters and detractors referred to the British parliamentary system to support their arguments. Cf Torbjörn Nilsson, 'Med historien som ledstjärna. Högern och demokratin 1904–1940', *Scandia*, 68 (2002), pp. 77–107, who shows (p. 78) how the Swedish Right opposed parliamentary democracy as a foreign import and alien to the Swedish traditions of self-government and peasant freedom.

90 Korpi, *The Working Class in Welfare Capitalism*, p. 72.

91 McKibbin, *The Evolution of the Labour Party*, p. 1.

92 Quoted in McKibbin, *The Evolution of the Labour Party*, p. 1. See also Mitchell, 'Labor and the Origins of Social Democracy', pp 36, 41ff; Ralph Miliband, *Parliamentary Socialism: A Study of the Politics of Labour* (London, 1972), pp. 21–22.

93 Donald Sassoon, *One Hundred Years of Socialism: The West European Left in the Twentieth Century* (London, 1996), pp. 15–16.

94 The vagueness of the socialist objective, according to McKibbin, was 'an acceptable formula in a Party where there was otherwise little doctrinal agreement… [It] was thus implanted into the constitution partly as a sop to the professional bourgeoisie: that this was so helps to explain why the trade unions swallowed it as easily as they did.' McKibbin, *The Evolution of the Labour Party*, pp. 96, 97.

95 E P Thompson, 'The Peculiarities of the English', in *idem., The Poverty of Theory and Other Essays* (London, 1978; first published 1965), pp. 245–301: 276–7, 284–5.

96 Kirk Willis, 'The Introduction and Critical Reception of Marxist Thought in Britain, 1850–1900', *The Historical Journal,* 20 (1977), pp. 417–459, 418–20. On the SDF as the sole representative of 'continental' social democracy in Britain, see Graham Johnson, 'Social Democracy and Labour Politics in Britain, 1892–1911', *History*, 85 (2000), pp. 67–87.

97 Egon Wertheimer, *Portrait of the British Labour Party* (London, 1929), p. 47. See also Willis, 'The Introduction of Marxist Thought', p. 457.

98 For this view, see Geoffrey Foote, *The Labour Party's Political Thought: A History* (2nd edn., Beckenham, 1986), p. 17; G D H Cole, *A History of Political Thought 1789–1939* iii/I (London, 1968) p. 143; both cited in Stefan Berger, *The British Labour Party and the German Social Democrats, 1900–1931* (Oxford, 1994), p. 173; Carl Cavanagh Hodge, *The Trammels of Tradition: Social Democracy in Britain, France and Germany* (Westport, Connecticut,

1994), p. 5; Eley, *Forging Democracy,* pp. 27–30; Johnson, 'Social Democracy and Labour Politics', p. 79.

99 Eugenio F Biagini, and Alastair J Reid, eds, *Currents of Radicalism: Popular Radicalism, Organised Labour and Party Politics in Britain, 1850–1914* (Cambridge, 1991).

100 Alastair J Reid, 'Old Unionism Reconsidered: The Radicalism of Robert Knight', in Biagini and Reid, eds, *Currents of Radicalism,* pp. 214–243: 240.

101 Logie Barrow and Ian Bullock, *Democratic Ideas and the British Labour Movement, 1880–1914* (Cambridge, 1996); Andrew Chadwick, *Augmenting Democracy: Political Movements and Constitutional Reform during the Rise of Labour, 1900–1914* (Aldershot, 1999).

102 Eugenio Biagini, *Liberty, Retrenchment and Reform: Popular Liberalism in the Age of Gladstone, 1860–1880* (Cambridge, 1992).

103 Tanner, *Political Change,* p. 242. The debate has frequently been politicised, with many contributors stating their disillusionment with Labour's impotence during the 1980s, and their view that the modern Labour Party needed to develop more self-consciousness of its radical Liberal inheritance. See for example Biagini and Reid, *Currents of Radicalism,* p. 19; Barrow and Bullock, *Democratic Ideas,* pp. 1–5.

104 Gareth Stedman Jones, 'Rethinking Chartism' in *idem., Languages of Class* (first published 1982), pp. 90–178; also Biagini, *Liberty, Retrenchment and Reform,* p. 2.

105 Stedman Jones, 'Rethinking Chartism', p. 107.

106 See especially Joan Wallach Scott, *Gender and the Politics of History* (New York, 1988), p. 59; Sonya O Rose, *Limited Livelihoods: Gender and Class in Nineteenth Century England* (London, 1992); Joanna Bourke, *Working-Class Cultures in Britain 1890–1960: Gender, Class and Ethnicity* (London, 1994), p. 213. For an overview, see Carol E Morgan, *Women Workers and Gender Identities, 1835–1913: The Cotton and Metal industries in England* (London, 2001), ch. 1.

107 Patrick Joyce, *Visions of the People: Industrial England and the Question of Class, 1848–1914* (Cambridge, 1991).

108 John Lindgren, *Det socialdemokratiska arbetarpartiets uppkomst i Sverige 1881–1889* (Stockholm, 1927); G H Nordström, *Sveriges socialdemokratiska arbetareparti under genombrottsåren 1889–1894* (Stockholm, 1938); Herbert Tingsten, *The Swedish Social Democrats: Their Ideological Development,* translated Greta Frankel and Patricia Howard-Rosen (Totowa, New Jersey, 1973).

109 Tingsten, *The Swedish Social Democrats,* p. 712. Because it was one of the first works on the SAP to be translated, Tingsten's study has been immensely influential on the international debate; for example of this see Hamilton, *Democratic Socialism in Britain and Sweden.*

110 The debate is summarised in Lars Björlin, 'De svenska arbetarpartierna. Forskning under 1970- och 1980-talen', in Klaus Misgeld and Klas Åmark,

eds, *Arbetsliv och arbetarrörelse* (Stockholm, 1991), pp. 43–59; also Mary Hilson, 'Swedish Approaches to the Rise of Labour', pp. 106–7.

111 Hentilä, *Den svenska arbetarklassen;* Gröning, *Vägen till makten;* Kjell Östberg, *Byråkrati och reformism. En studie av svensk socialdemokratis politiska och sociala integrering före första världskriget* (Stockholm, 1990); Ingrid Millbourn, 'Swedish Social Democrats' Experiences and Consciousness: A Theory of Learning Processes', *Scandinavian Journal of History,* 22 (1997), pp. 99–119; Hans-Olof Ericson, *Mellan dröm och vardag. Studier av arbetarrörelsens politiska splittring. Jönköping, Huskvarna och Norrahammar 1910–1921* (Lund, 1991).

112 Börje Henningsson, 'Humanism, anarkism och socialism. Varför splittrades det socialdemokratiska vänsterpartiet?', *Arbetarhistoria,* 80–81 (1996–7), pp. 25–36.

113 Karlbom, *Revolution eller reform.*

114 The impact on Swedish historiography is discussed in Henrik Berggren and Lars Trägårdh, 'Historikerna och språket: teoretiska ambitioner och praktiska begränsningar', *Historisk Tidskrift* (S), (1990), pp. 357–375.

115 Susanne Lundin, *En liten skara äro vi,* p. 28. See also Wikander, *Kvinnors och mäns arbeten;* Lena Sommestad, *Från mejerska till mejerist. En studie av mejeriyrkets maskuliniseringsprocess* (Lund, 1992); Johansson, *Skogarnas fria söner;* Blomberg, *Män i mörker.*

116 Björn Horgby, *Egensinne och skötsamhet. Arbetarkulturen i Norrköping 1850–1940* (Stockholm, 1993), pp. 19–20. I am not concerned here with the more explicit attempts to engage with post-structuralist methodology, of which, in fact, there have been relatively few in British labour history.

117 Ronny Ambjörnsson, *Den skötsamme arbetaren. Idéer och ideal i ett norrländskt sågverkssamhälle 1880–1930* (Stockholm, 1998; first published 1988).

118 Olle Josephson, 'Att ta ordet för hundra år sedan', in *idem.,* ed., *Arbetarna tar ordet. Språk och kommunikation i tidig arbetarrörelse* (Stockholm, 1996), pp. 10–43: 15–21.

119 Ambjörnsson, *Den skötsamme arbetaren,* p. 20.

120 Horgby, *Egensinne och skötsamhet,* p. 489; Birgitta Skarin Frykman, 'Arbetarkultur och arbetarkulturforskning', *Arkiv för studier i arbetarrörelsens historia,* 48–49 (1991), pp. 21–46: 31; Josephson, 'Att ta ordet', pp. 37–8.

121 See for example the contributions by Patrick Joyce, James Vernon and others in *Social History,* vols. 18–19 (1993–4); and John Host, *Victorian Labour History: Experience, Identity and the Politics of Representation* (London, 1998), pp. 58–9.

122 Biagini, *Liberty, Retrenchment and Reform,* p. 12. On the importance of democratic ideas in the European labour movement, see also Stefan Berger, 'Democracy and Social Democracy', *European History Quarterly,* 32 (2002), pp. 13–37: 15.

123 Duncan Tanner, 'The Development of British Socialism, 1900–1918', in

E H H Green, ed., *An Age of Transition: British Politics 1880–1914* (Edinburgh, 1997), pp. 48–66: 50.

124 Duncan Tanner, 'Ideological Debate in Edwardian Labour Politics: Radicalism, Revisionism and Socialism', in Biagini and Reid, eds, *Currents of Radicalism,* pp. 271–293: 274–5.

125 Mats Franzén, 'Egensinne och skötsamhet i svensk arbetarkultur. Kommentarer till *Den skötsamme arbetaren* av Ronny Ambjörnsson', *Arkiv för studier i arbetarrörelsens historia,* 48–49 (1991), pp. 3–20: 10; Karlsson, *När industriarbetaren blev historia,* p. 164.

126 Lars Trägårdh, 'Varieties of Volkish Identities', in Bo Stråth, ed., *Language and the Constitution of Class Identities* (Göteborg, 1990), pp. 25–54.

127 Marc Bloch, 'Toward a Comparative History of European Societies', in Frederic C Lane and Jelle C Riermersma, eds, *Enterprise and Secular Change: Readings in Economic History* (Homewood, Illinois, 1953; first published 1928), pp. 494–521: 520.

128 Trägårdh, 'Varieties of Volkish Identities', p. 30.

129 Josephson, 'Att ta ordet', p. 38; see also Jürgen Kocka, 'New Trends in Labour Movement Historiography: A German Perspective', *International Review of Social History,* 42 (1997), pp. 67–78: 71–4; Berggren and Trägårdh, 'Historikerna och språket', pp. 369–372.

130 John Belchem and Neville Kirk, editors' introduction to *idem.,* eds, *Languages of Labour* (Aldershot, 1997), p. 3.

131 Patrick Joyce, *Democratic Subjects: The Self and the Social in Nineteenth Century England* (Cambridge, 1994).

132 The same criticism could be made of the Swedish debate, where the work of ethnologists has done much to illustrate the diversity of working-class life and culture, but has had less impact on our understanding of the SAP.

133 Dror Wahrman, 'The New Political History: A Review Essay', *Social History,* 21, 3 (1996), pp. 343–354, 353. Also Berggren and Trägårdh, 'Historikerna och språket', p. 361.

134 Jon Lawrence, *Speaking for the People: Party, Language and Popular Politics in England, 1867–1914* (Cambridge, 1998), pp. 24–25.

135 See for example the essays in Belchem and Kirk, *Languages of Labour;* also Kocka, 'New Trends in Labour Movement Historiography', pp. 71–4.

136 John Breuilly, (Manchester, 1992), p. 126. To be fair, Joyce has acknowledged the role of custom and a sense of the past in legitimising radical politics.

137 Dick Geary, 'Labour History, the "Linguistic Turn" and Postmodernism', *Contemporary European History,* 9 (2000), pp. 445–462: 452.

138 Geary, 'Labour History and Postmodernism', p. 458.

3. Local and National Politics in the Rise of Labour

1 Andrew August, 'Cultures of Consolidation? Rethinking Politics in Working-Class London, 1870–1914', *Historical Research,* 74 (2001), pp. 193–219: 195–8.

2 Joanna Bourke, *Working-Class Cultures in Britain 1890–1960: Gender, Class and Ethnicity* (London, 1994), p. 213.

3 Richard Price, 'The Future of British Labour History', *International Review of Social History,* 36 (1991), pp. 249–260: 255; Lenard R Berlanstein, 'The Distinctiveness of the Nineteenth-Century French Labor Movement', *Journal of Modern History,* 64 (1992), pp. 660–685: 685; B H Moss, 'Republican Socialism and the Making of the Working Class in Britain, France and the United States: A Critique of Thompsonian Culturalism', *Comparative Studies in Society and History,* 35 (1993), pp. 390–413: 393; Ira Katznelson, 'The "Bourgeois" Dimension: A Provocation About Institutions, Politics and the Future of Labor History', *International Labor and Working-Class History,* 46 (1994), pp. 7–32: 9–11, 15–16; Jürgen Kocka, 'New Trends in Labour Movement Historiography: A German Perspective', *International Review of Social History,* 42 (1997), pp. 67–78: 71–74.

4 Robert Justin Goldstein, 'Political Mobilisation in Nineteenth-Century Europe', *European History Quarterly,* 32 (2002), pp. 233–250: 234.

5 Michael Savage, *The Dynamics of Working-class Politics: The Labour Movement in Preston, 1880–1940* (Cambridge, 1987).

6 Jon Lawrence, *Speaking for the People: Party, Language and Popular Politics in England, 1867–1914* (Cambridge, 1998), p. 36.

7 Lawrence, *Speaking for the People,* p. 61; *idem.,* 'The Dynamics of Urban Politics, 1867–1914', in Jon Lawrence and Miles Taylor, eds, *Party, State and Society: Electoral Behaviour in Britain since 1820* (Aldershot, 1997), pp. 79–105: 84.

8 See also Jon Lawrence, 'Class and Gender in the Making of Urban Toryism, 1880–1914,' *English Historical Review,* 108 (1993), pp. 629–653.

9 Lawrence, *Speaking for the People,* p. 66.

10 Lawrence, 'Class and Gender', p. 632.

11 See also Kocka, 'New Trends in Labour Movement Historiography', p. 74

12 Göran Salmonsson, *Den förståndiga viljan. Svenska Järn- och metallarbetareförbundet 1888–1902* (Uppsala, 1998), p. 15.

13 Salmonsson, *Den förståndiga viljan,* pp. 20, 24.

14 Dror Wahrman, 'The New Political History: A Review Essay', *Social History,* 21 (1996), pp. 343–354, 343–4; Lawrence Black, '"What Kind of People Are You?" Labour, the People and the 'New Political History', pp. 23–38: 23–4; and Alastair J Reid, 'Class and Politics in the Work of Henry Pelling', pp. 101–115: 107–11, both in John Callaghan, Steven Fielding and Steve Ludlam, eds, *Interpreting the Labour Party: New Approaches to Labour Politics and History* (Manchester, 2003).

15 On the influence of liberalism in the Labour Party see the essays in Euge-

nio F Biagini, and Alastair J Reid, eds, *Currents of Radicalism: Popular Radicalism, Organised Labour and Party Politics in Britain, 1850–1914* (Cambridge, 1991); also Andrew Chadwick, *Augmenting Democracy: Political Movements and Constitutional Reform during the Rise of Labour, 1900–1914* (Aldershot, 1999). On the active efforts of British Conservatives to win working-class support, see Martin Pugh, *The Tories and the People, 1880–1935* (Oxford, 1985), esp. ch. 6; E H H Green, 'Radical Conservatism: The Electoral Genesis of Tariff Reform', *Historical Journal,* 28 (1985) 667–692, 686; Lawrence, 'Class and Gender'. See also Katznelson, 'The "Bourgeois" Dimension', pp. 22–24 for discussion of this point.

16 Martin Pugh, 'The Rise of Labour and the Political Culture of Conservatism, 1890–1945', *History,* 87 (2002), pp. 514–537. A similar point, on the formative influence different political parties of right and left had on each other in Sweden is made by Rolf Torstendahl, 'Socialdemokratins roll i industrikapitalismens utveckling', *Arbetarhistoria,* 37–28 (1986), p. 12; cited in Lotta Gröning, *Vägen till makten. SAP:s organisation och dess betydelse för den politiska verksamheten 1900–1933* (Uppsala, 1988), p. 13.

17 Howard Kimeldorf, 'Bringing Unions Back In (or Why We Need a New Old Labor History)', *Labor History,* 32 (1991), pp. 91–103: 91–3, 97–98.

18 James E Cronin, 'Neither Exceptional Nor Peculiar: Towards the Comparative Study of Labor in Advanced Society', *International Review of Social History,* 38 (1993), pp. 59–75: 72–3.

19 Duncan Tanner, *Political Change and the Labour Party, 1900–1918* (Cambridge, 1990), p. xi; also Berggren, 'Går det att skriva arbetarhistoriska synteser?', p. 191.

20 Tanner, *Political Change,* p. 80.

21 See Patricia Lynch, *The Liberal Party in Rural England 1885–1910: Radicalism and Community* (Oxford, 2003), pp. 8–11.

22 Lawrence, *Speaking for the People,* ch. 7. See also Alun Howkins, 'Edwardian Liberalism and Industrial Unrest: A Class View of the Decline of Liberalism', *History Workshop Journal,* 4 (1977), pp. 143–161, which shows that the Liberal Party's rigid adherence to their national reforming strategy during the 1900s left them inflexible and unable to respond to the concerns of agricultural labourers, unlike the Labour Party which had a much looser national party organisation at that time.

23 Ross McKibbin, *The Evolution of the Labour Party, 1910–1924* (Oxford, 1974), p. 1; Andrew Thorpe, *A History of the British Labour Party* (Basingstoke, 1997), p. 13.

24 See Robert Taylor, 'Out of the Bowels of the Movement: The Trade Unions and the Origins of the Labour Party 1900–18', in Brian Brivati and Richard Heffernan, eds, *The Labour Party: A Centenary History* (Basingstoke, 2000), pp. 8–49: 11.

25 James Fulcher, *Labour Movements, Employers and the State: Conflict and Cooperation in Britain and Sweden* (Oxford, 1991), pp. 38–39.

26 Gröning, *Vägen till makten,* p. 29; Rolf Karlbom, *Revolution eller reformer. Studier i SAP:s historia 1889–1902* (Göteborg, 1985), p. 9. For an account which emphasises the contingency of party-trade union relations during the labour movement's early years, see also Bengt Schüllerqvist, *Från kosackval till kohandel. SAP:s väg till makten (1928–33)* (Stockholm, 1992), pp. 41 ff.

27 Salmonsson, *Den förståndiga viljan,* p. 207.

28 Solveig Halvorsen, 'Scandinavian Trade Unions in the 1890s, with Special Reference to the Scandinavian Stonemasons' Union', in *Scandinavian Journal of History,* 13 (1988), pp. 3–21; Martin Grass, 'Från arbetarkongress till samarbetskommitté. Om Skandinaviska samarbetskommitténs bildande', *Arbetarhistoria,* 42 (1987), pp. 5–11.

29 For SAP organisation see Gröning, *Vägen till makten,* from which much of the information here is drawn; also Karlbom, *Revolution eller reformer,* pp. 7–8.

30 Ingrid Millbourn, 'Swedish Social Democrats' Experiences and Consciousness: A Theory of Learning Processes', *Scandinavian Journal of History,* 22 (1997), pp. 99–119: 112–116; Kjell Östberg, *Byråkrati och reformism. En studie av svensk socialdemokratis politiska och sociala integrering före första världskriget* (Stockholm, 1990), pp. 58–9.

31 Sam Davies, *Liverpool Labour: Social and Political Influences on the Development of the Labour Party in Liverpool, 1900–1939* (Keele, 1996), p. 47.

32 Gillian Rose, 'Imagining Poplar in the 1920s: Contested Concepts of Community', *Journal of Historical Geography,* 16 (1990), pp. 425–437: 426; David Gilbert, *Class, Community and Collective Action: Social Change in Two British Coalfields, 1850–1926* (Oxford, 1992), pp. 13–42.

33 David Gilbert, 'Community and Municipalism: Collective Identification in Late-Victorian and Edwardian Mining Towns', *Journal of Historical Geography,* 17 (1991), pp. 257–270: 258.

34 Rose, 'Imagining Poplar', pp. 430–432.

35 Lawrence, 'Class and Gender', p. 647; *idem., Speaking for the People*, p. 229. See also Ira Katznelson, 'Working-Class Formation and the State: Nineteenth Century England in American Perspective', in Peter B Evans, Dietrich Rueschemeyer and Theda Skocpol, eds, *Bringing the State Back In* (Cambridge, 1985), pp. 257–284.

36 Lawrence, *Speaking for the People,* p. 233; Millbourn, 'Swedish Social Democrats' Experiences', p. 112.

37 Rune Bokholm, *Städernas handlingsfrihet. En studie av expansionsskedet 1900–1930* (Lund, 1995).

38 Christine Bellamy, *Administering Central-Local Relations, 1871–1919: The Local Government Board in Its Fiscal and Cultural Context* (Manchester, 1988), pp. 10–12.

39 See also David Kirby, 'What was "Nordic" about the Labour Movement in Europe's Northernmost Regions?', in Pauli Kettunen, ed., *Lokalt och*

internationellt. Dimensioner i den nordiska arbetarrörelsen och arbetarkulturen (Tammerfors, 2002), pp. 13–32: 16–17, 26, for a discussion of this point.

40 Ronald P Formisano, 'The Concept of Political Culture', *Journal of Interdisciplinary History,* 31 (2001), pp. 393–426: 395–6, 419–425.

41 J M Haas, 'Trouble at the Workplace: Industrial Relations in the Royal Dockyards, 1889–1914', *Bulletin of the Institute of Historical Research,* 58 (1985), pp. 210–225: 210.

42 Mary Hilson, 'Labour Politics in a Naval Dockyard: The Case of Karlskrona, Sweden c.1880–1925', *International Review of Social History,* 46 (2001), pp. 341–369: 345.

43 Trevor Harris, 'Government and the Specialised Military Town: The Impact of Defence Policy on Urban Social Structure in the Nineteenth Century', in Michael Bateman and Raymond Riley, eds, *The Geography of Defence* (London, 1987), pp. 100–140: 101; G J Ashworth, *War and the City* (London, 1991), p. 64.

44 See Ann Day, '"Driven from Home": The Closure of Pembroke Dockyard and the Impact on Its Community', *Llafur,* 7 (1996), pp. 78–86.

45 Ashworth, *War and the City,* p. 64; Harris, 'Government and the Specialised Military Town', pp. 101, 105.

46 D K Brown, *A Century of Naval Construction: The History of the Royal Corps of Naval Constructors, 1883–1983* (London, 1983), p. 279.

47 Hans Holmén, *Försvar och samhällsförändring. Avvägningsfrågor i svensk försvarsdebatt, 1880–1925* (Göteborg, 1985).

48 Some historians have suggested that dockyards presented an early example of the problems typical of nationalised industry: William Ashworth, 'Economic Aspects of Late Victorian Naval Administration', *Economic History Review,* 2nd series, 22, (1969), pp. 491–505: 493; Donald Reid, 'The Third Republic as Manager: Labor Policy in the Naval Shipyards, 1892–1902', *International Review of Social History,* 30 (1985), pp. 183–206: 184.

49 There were similar arrangements in the French dockyards: see Reid, 'The Third Republic as Manager'.

50 This was similar to the paternalist schemes adopted by employers in Gothenburg. See Bo Stråth, *Varvsarbetare i två varvstäder. En historisk studie av verkstadsklubbarna vid varven i Göteborg och Malmö* (Kungälv, 1982).

51 For shipbuilding employers' provision for their workers in Göteborg, see Stråth, *Varvsarbetare i två varvsstäder;* for Landskrona, see Magnus Wikdahl, *Varvets tid. Arbetarliv och kulturell förändring i en skeppsbyggarstad* (Stockholm, 1992). Of the British dockyard towns, only the relatively small dockyard at Sheerness was ever associated with any of these features. Cf Malcolm Crook, *Toulon in War and Revolution: From the* Ancien Régime *to the Restoration, 1750–1820* (Manchester, 1991), p. 15, who suggests that the French naval dockyard town of Toulon was a 'forerunner of the celebrated "company towns" of the industrial era'.

52 Kenneth Lunn, 'Labour Culture in Dockyard Towns: A Study of Portsmouth, Plymouth and Chatham, 1900–1950', *Tijdschrift voor Sociale Geschiednis,* 8 (1992), pp. 275–293: 282. Research on the French dockyard towns suggests a similar picture: in Cherbourg, for example, there seems to have been a longstanding rivalry between '*les ouvriers de l'arsenal*' and '*les ouvriers de la ville*'. See Jean Quellien, 'Un milieu ouvrier réformiste: syndicalisme et réformisme à Cherbourg à la «Belle Epoque»', *Mouvement Social,* 127 (1984), pp. 65–88: 67–68.

53 Neil Casey, 'An Early Organisational Hegemony: Methods of Social Control in a Victorian Dockyard', *Social Science Information,* 23 (1984), pp. 677–700: 679–684. On the dockyard schools, see Neil Casey, 'Class Rule: The Hegemonic Role of the Royal Dockyard Schools, 1840–1914', in Kenneth Lunn and Ann Day, eds, *History of Work and Labour Relations in the Royal Dockyards* (London, 1999), pp. 66–86.

54 Tanner, *Political Change,* p. 190. See also Lunn, 'Labour Culture in Dockyard Towns', p. 278.

55 Reid, 'The Third Republic as Manager', p. 202; Quellien, 'Un milieu ouvrier réformiste'.

56 Roger Knight, 'From Impressment to Task Work: Strikes and Disruption in the Royal Dockyards, 1688–1788', pp. 1–20: 9–10; Roger Morriss, 'Government and Continuity: The Changing Context of Labour Relations, 1770–1830', pp. 21–40; both in Kenneth Lunn and Ann Day, eds, *History of Work and Labour Relations in the Royal Dockyards* (London, 1999).

57 Mavis Waters, 'Dockyard and Parliament: A Study of Unskilled Workers in Chatham Yard, 1860–1900', *Southern History,* 6 (1984), pp. 123–138.

58 Peter Galliver, 'Trade Unionism in Portsmouth Dockyard, 1880–1914: Change and Continuity', in Lunn and Day, eds, *History of Work,* pp. 99–126.

59 The cessation of hostilities in 1815, and the long period of peace which followed placed a question mark over the existence of many smaller dockyards in any case, and little effort was made to maintain production capacity in line with new developments in naval architecture. The naval arms race and the First World War postponed closure for many dockyards, but only temporarily. Rochefort dockyard in France closed in 1927 with the loss of 8000 jobs.

60 Galliver, 'Trade Unionism in Portsmouth Dockyard'; Reid, 'The Third Republic as Manager', p. 193.

61 Quellien, 'Un milieu ouvrier réformist', p. 73, n. 34.

62 Lawrence Sondhaus, 'The Imperial German Navy and Social Democracy, 1878–1897', *German Studies Review,* 18 (1995), pp. 51–64: 54–5.

63 Gary E Weir, *Building the Kaiser's Navy: The Imperial Navy Office and German Industry in the von Tirpitz Era, 1890–1919* (Minneapolis, 1992), p. 16.

64 Nils Elvander, *Harald Hjärne och konservatismen. Konservativ idédebatt i Sverige 1865–1922* (Uppsala, 1961), pp. 5–18.

65 There is perhaps a parallel here with the British Conservative Party's defence of the union with Ireland, against Liberal support for Home Rule. In that case the issue was not resolved until after the First World War, but, by provoking an alliance between the Conservatives and the unionist wing of the old Liberal Party, the unionist question played a similar role in reshaping the political right in early twentieth century Britain.

66 See Patrick Salmon, *Scandinavia and the Great Powers 1890–1940* (Cambridge, 1997), pp. 53–55, 71–82.

67 It should be noted, however, that the question of army reform, and the introduction of conscription in 1901, also provoked much political controversy. See Playford V Thorson II, 'The Defense Question in Sweden 1911–1914', (unpublished PhD thesis, University of Minnesota, 1972), pp. 12–13. Conscription was also the object of some nationalist campaigning in Britain, in the wake of the Boer War and concerns about the quality of recruits to the British army. See R J Q Adams and Philip P Poirier, *The Conscription Controversy in Great Britain, 1900–18* (Basingstoke, 1987), pp. 24–5.

68 This type of ship is described as 'a very small, highly manoeuvrable and heavily equipped battleship of about 7000 tons displacement'. Thorson, 'The Defense Question in Sweden', p. 48.

69 Jarl Torbacke, *Försvaret främst. Tre studier till belysning av borggårdskrisens problematik* (Stockholm, 1983), p. 162; Bernt Schiller, 'Years of Crisis', in Steven Koblik ed., *Sweden's Development From Poverty to Affluence,* translated Joanne Johnson (Minneapolis, 1975), pp. 197–228: 217–227.

70 Elvander, *Harald Hjärne och konservatismen*, p. 416.

71 Torbacke, *Försvaret främst*, p. 162; see Patrik Hall, *Den svenskaste historien. Nationalism i Sverige under sex sekler* (Stockholm, 2000), p. 99, for a discussion of this idea in Swedish nationalist discourse. The king was guided partly by his European relatives: Gustav V's consort was cousin of the Kaiser.

72 Torback, *Försvaret främst*, p. 163.

73 Frans Coetzee, *For Party or Country: Nationalism and the Dilemmas of Popular Conservatism in Edwardian England* (Oxford, 1990), p. 44. In Britain these included: Navy League (1895), National Service League (1901), Tariff Reform League (1903). In Sweden: Fosterländska förbundet (1893), Svenska nationalföreningen (1893), Föreningen Sveriges rätt (1893), Sveriges agrar- och lantmannaförbund (1894), Sveriges flaggrörelse (1899).

74 Coetzee, *For Party or Country*, p. 121; Anne Summers, 'The Character of Edwardian Nationalism: Three Popular Leagues,' in Paul Kennedy and Anthony Nicholls, eds, *Nationalist and Racialist Movements in Britain and Germany before 1914* (London, 1981), pp. 98–87: 81, 84.

75 Roy Andersen, 'Ideologiske forutsetningar for den militære opprustningen i Norge 1890–1900', *Historisk Tidskrift* (N) 78 (1999), pp. 48–60: 55.

76 K Lunn and A Thomas, 'Naval Imperialism in Portsmouth, 1905–1914', *Southern History,* 10 (1988) 143–159: 148–9.

77 Paul Ward, *Red Flag and Union Jack: Englishness, Patriotism and the British Left, 1881–1924* (Woodbridge, 1998); Stephen Yeo, 'Socialism, the State and Some Oppositional Englishness', in Robert Colls and Philip Dodd, eds, *Englishness: Politics and Culture, 1880–1920* (London, 1986), pp. 308–369. For accounts which stress the limited possibilities of radical patriotism in the early twentieth century, see Hugh Cunningham, 'The Language of Patriotism, 1750–1914', *History Workshop Journal*, 12 (1981) pp. 8–33; Miles Taylor, 'Patriotism, History and the Left in Twentieth Century Britain', *The Historical Journal*, 33 (1990), pp. 971–987.

78 Ward, *Red Flag and Union Jack*, pp. 102–3, 106, 113, 118.

79 Christer Strahl, *Nationalism och socialism. Fosterlandet i den politiska idédebatten i Sverige 1890–1914* (Lund, 1983), pp. 20–1; Samuel Edquist, *Nyktra svenskar. Godtemplarrörelsen och den nationella identiteten 1879–1918* (Uppsala, 2001).

80 Strahl, *Nationalism och socialism*, p. 42; Bernt Schiller, 'Den skandinaviska arbetarrörelsens internationalism 1870–1914', *Arbetarhistoria*, 42 (1987), pp. 3–4. See also Ward, *Red Flag and Union Jack*, p. 114.

81 Herbert Tingsten, *The Swedish Social Democrats: Their Ideological Development*, translated Greta Frankel and Patricia Howard-Rosen (Totowa, New Jersey, 1973), p. 149; Strahl, *Nationalism and Socialism*, pp. 38–9.

82 Tingsten, *The Swedish Social Democrats*, pp. 489–505; Strahl, *Nationalism och socialism*, p. 44.

83 As Henry Pelling noted, the Plymouth constituencies were instead all marginal seats, where the electorate voted against the outgoing government at almost every opportunity. The exception to this trend, the success of the Liberals in retaining the Devonport seats after 1892, could be attributed to the personal support for the MP in question. Henry Pelling, *Social Geography of British Elections, 1885–1910* (London, 1967), p. 167. See Table 4.1, pp. 319–320.

84 G J Ashworth, *War and the City* (London, 1991), p. 64.

85 Reid, 'The Third Republic as Manager', p. 192.

86 Hilson, 'Labour Politics in a Naval Dockyard', p. 365.

87 For the campaigns surrounding the Contagious Diseases Acts in Plymouth, see Judith Walkowitz, *Prostitution and Victorian Society: Women, Class and the State* (Cambridge, 1980).

88 Lawrence, 'Class and Gender', pp. 643, 647.

89 See Karen J Musolf, *From Plymouth to Parliament: A Rhetorical History of Nancy Astor's 1919 Campaign* (London, 1999), pp. 48–9

90 Crook, Toulon in War and Revolution, p. 4.

91 See Alex Law, 'Neither Colonial nor Historic: Workers' Organisation at Rosyth Dockyard, 1945–95', in Lunn and Day, eds, History of Work, pp. 151–178.

4. The Labour Movement in Plymouth c. 1890–1914

1 Henry Pelling, *Social Geography of British Elections, 1885–1910* (London, 1967), pp. 161–2; A M Dawson, 'Politics in Devon and Cornwall, 1900–1931' (unpublished PhD thesis, University of London, 1991), pp. 338–340.

2 Duncan Tanner, *Political Change and the Labour Party, 1900–1918* (Cambridge, 1990), p. 190.

3 Michael Dawson, 'Liberalism in Devon and Cornwall, 1910–1931: "The Old-Time Religion"', *The Historical Journal*, 38 (1995) pp. 425–437: 428.

4 Dawson, 'Politics in Devon and Cornwall', pp.25–6.

5 Mark Brayshay, 'The Emigration Trade in Nineteenth Century Devon', pp. 108–118; David Starkey, 'The Ports, Seaborne Trade and Shipping Industry of South Devon, 1786–1914'; both in Michael Duffy et al., eds, *The New Maritime History of Devon*, vol. 2 (London, 1994). In 1681 Plymouth had ranked fifth among English ports in tonnage and number of ships entering.

6 Peter Hilditch, 'The Dockyard in the Local Economy', in Duffy et al., eds, *The New Maritime History of Devon*, pp. 215–225.

7 Hilditch, 'The Dockyard in the Local Economy', p. 215.

8 The future of Devonport dockyard was secured when the Admiralty decided that together with Portsmouth and Malta it was to be the site for a new steam yard, and began excavations to extend the existing yard in 1844. The new site was opened in 1853, linked to the older South Yard by means of a tunnel. In 1896 work was begun (under the supervision of future MP Sir John Jackson) to extend the Keyham Yard into a huge fitting-out yard with the facilities and technology for the very largest modern battleships, opened in February 1907. George Dicker, 'A Short History of Devonport Royal Dockyard' (Plymouth, 1969), pp. 7–8.

9 That it dipped to 36% in 1901 must be explained by the absence of Devonport ships and their crews on census night, possibly because of the South African war.

10 PRO ADM 116/1179 (Petitions 1912).

11 Examples of street names with naval links include Drake St, Armada St, Frobisher Terrace, Raleigh St, Grenville Rd. For pub names, see Chris Robinson, *Plymouth Pubs Past and Present*, (Plymouth, 1996 and 1997); for examples of naval imagery in local advertising, see Andy Endacott, *300 Years' Devotion to Duty* (Saltash, 1992). Cf K Lunn and A Thomas, 'Naval Imperialism in Portsmouth, 1905–1914', *Southern History*, 10 (1988), pp. 142–159: 142–3 for the same phenomenon in Portsmouth.

12 See Judith R Walkowitz, *Prostitution and Victorian Society: Women, Class and the State* (Cambridge, 1982; first published 1980), chs. 8–12; V F T Pointon, 'Mid Victorian Plymouth: A Social Geography' (unpublished PhD thesis, Polytechnic South West, 1989), pp. 342–350.

13 Kelly's Directory of Devonshire, 1897, 1919; Eyre's Plymouth Directory, 1882.

14 The UDC was principally responsible for sanitation, highways and, after the abolition of the School Boards in 1902, elementary education.

15 Crispin Gill, *Plymouth: A New History* (Plymouth, 1993), p. 244.

16 *Western Morning News*, 2nd November 1898. WDRO 1648/HW1, Plymouth Housing Committee minutes, 2nd June 1898, minute 1876. WDRO 1069/3, Edgcumbe Family Papers, J G Jackson (Conservative) election address for St Peter's Ward, 1898: 'If this Municipal Contest is to be fought on political grounds, then I ask for your support, with the greatest confidence, because, if there ever was blundering and want of proper management, the policy adopted by the "Liberal Party" is in this respect most marked.' Also Gill, *Plymouth: A New History*, p. 241

17 H B Williams, *History of the Plymouth and District Trades Council from 1892 to 1952* (Plymouth, 1952).

18 Co-operative Union, Co-operative Congress Report, 1906. For the early years of Plymouth Co-operative Society, see Robert Briscoe, *Centenary History: A Hundred Years of Co-operation in Plymouth* (Manchester, 1960).

19 Kelly's Directory of Devonshire, 1906.

20 Board of Trade: Report into Working Class Rents, Housing, Retail Prices and Standard Rates of Wages, (H.C.cd.3864, 1908, cvii.319).

21 Sidney Pollard and Paul Robertson, *The British Shipbuilding Industry, 1870–1914* (Cambridge, Mass, 1979); Keith McClelland and Alastair Reid, 'Wood, Iron and Steel: Technology, Labour and Trade Union Organisation in the Shipbuilding Industry, 1840–1914', in Royden Harrison and Jonathan Zeitlin, eds, *Divisions of Labour: Skilled Workers and Technological Change in Nineteenth Century England*, (Brighton, 1984), pp. 151–184: 158–160.

22 M Waters, 'A Social History of Dockyard Workers at Chatham, Kent, 1860–1914' (unpublished PhD thesis, University of Essex, 1979), pp. 174–7.

23 Neil Casey, 'An Early Organisational Hegemony: Methods of Social Control in a Victorian Dockyard', *Social Science Information*, 23 (1984), pp. 677–700: 679, 682–3.

24 PRO ADM 116/1130 (Case 3012a, revision of regulations for the entry of apprentices, 1911).

25 Regulations for the entry of apprentices list the dockyard trades in order, as follows: shipwrights, engine fitters, electrical fitters, boilermakers, coppersmiths, founders, joiners, painters, patternmakers, plumbers, ropemakers, sailmakers, smiths. PRO ADM 116/1144 (Case 3342, decisions relating to petitions, 1911).

26 The importance attached to the status of different apprenticeships is illustrated by the case of a boy at Pembroke dockyard, whose father wrote to the Admiralty complaining that although his son was very able at mathematical and technical subjects he had not done sufficiently well in the English section of the examination to be considered for any trade other than a joiner's, as his first language was Welsh. In this case, the father's

concern however was not simply that his son was to become a joiner and not a shipwright, but that in becoming a joiner he was deprived of the opportunity of becoming anything else over his working life. PRO ADM 116/1130 (Case 3012a, revision of regulations for the entry of apprentices, 1911).

27 PRO ADM 116/900A (Case 3002, increase of numbers allowed on establishment to 7000, 1899–1902); PRO ADM 116/330 (Case F196, increases of pay, 1890–91).

28 At Devonport in 1904 504 men were granted established status, but the following year this had dropped to 83, and in 1906 and 1907 to only 59 and 30 respectively. Hansard 1909, vol. 11, col. 614; 1914, vol. 63, col. 766.

29 PRO ADM 116/900A (Case 3002, increase in numbers allowed on establishment, 1899–1903).

30 PRO ADM 116/935 (Case 3308, petitions 1902).

31 J M Haas, 'Trouble at the Workplace: Industrial Relations in the Royal Dockyards, 1889–1914', *Bulletin of the Institute of Historical Research,* 58 (1985), pp. 210–225: 224; Trevor Harris, 'Government and the Specialised Military Town: The Impact of Defence Policy on Urban Social Structure in the Nineteenth Century', in Michael Bateman and Raymond Riley, eds, *The Geography of Defence* (London, 1987), pp. 100–140: 119, 136; Kenneth Lunn, 'Labour Culture in Dockyard Towns: A Study of Portsmouth, Plymouth and Chatham, 1900–1950', *Tijdschrift voor Sociale Geschiednis,* 8 (1992), pp. 275–293: 281–2; Waters, 'A Social History of Dockyard Workers', p. 181.

32 Board of Trade Report into rents etc., 1908, p. 745.

33 Mary Hilson, 'Working-Class Politics in Plymouth, c.1890–1920', (unpublished PhD thesis, University of Exeter, 1998), pp. 83–4.

34 WDRO 1472/1–3: Papers of Devonport Dockyard Workmen's Dwellings Co, Ltd. Census 1901: RG 13/2110 (enumeration district no. 8, Devonport).

35 Hilson, 'Working-Class Politics in Plymouth', pp. 73–93; Waters, 'A Social History of Dockyard Workers', p. 181.

36 Waters, 'A Social History of Dockyard Workers', p. 134.

37 Hansard 1905, vol. 146, col 464; vol 148, cols 357–8; Hugh B Peebles, *Warshipbuilding on the Clyde: Naval Orders and the Prosperity of the Clyde Shipbuilding Industry, 1889–1939* (Edinburgh, 1987), pp. 30–32; J M Haas, *A Management Odyssey: The Royal Dockyards, 1714–1914* (London, Maryland, 1994), p. 176.

38 Hansard 1905, vol. 146, col. 464. 2171 men were discharged during 1905 alone. WDRO 2000: Henderson papers, memorandum (20th March 1906).

39 In a memorandum dated 8th November 1904, Henderson set out his vision for the dockyards: 'For the first time in their history the Yards would be placed on a business foundation, with a true state of competition between them, judgment would be given by results, each would strive to secure the

best, and the latent talent within them would be released to this end instead of being made nerveless by over centralised regulations.' WDRO 2000, Henderson papers. See also Haas, *A Management Odyssey,* p. 172.

40 WDRO 2000, Henderson papers: newspaper cuttings relating to Devonport Dockyard, 1900–05. The greatest source of resentment was that, through being discharged as inefficient, the men in question would have difficulties in finding alternative employment. Less sympathetic commentators concurred with Henderson's findings that dockyard efficiency was hindered by 'the mass of the workmen who by every possible means try to evade doing their full share of the work.'

41 PRO ADM 116/1101 (Petitions: abstracts and comments, 1905).

42 PRO ADM 116/874 (Abstract of petitions, 1892–3); Waters, 'A Social History of Dockyard Workers', pp. 233–235.

43 Waters, 'A Social History of Dockyard Workers', p. 232. The official line was that they were 'perfectly prepared… to hear representations on behalf of trade unions generally, but that the workmen who might be responsible for preparing the Navy for instant action which was necessary in war should all be affiliated with a trade union, which might influence their action at a critical moment, was not a position that the Admiralty could accept.' Hansard, vol. 149 (1905) col. 494.

44 The roots of the petitioning system as the central plank of dockyard industrial relations stretch back much further, however. See Ken Lunn and Ann Day, 'Deference and Defiance: The Changing Nature of Petitioning in British Naval Dockyards', *International Review of Social History,* 46 (2001), Supplement, pp. 131–150: 134–5.

45 Mavis Waters, 'The Dockyardmen Speak Out: Petition and Tradition in Chatham Dockyard, 1860–1906', in Kenneth Lunn and Ann Day, eds, *History of Work and Labour Relations in the Royal Dockyards* (London, 1999), pp. 87–98.

46 PRO ADM 116/1137 (Case 3335: petitions 1911, vol 2); PRO ADM 116/1173 (Minutes of evidence).

47 *Western Morning News,* 9th September 1903.

48 PRO ADM 116/1137 (Case 3335, minutes of evidence, vol 2, 1911); PRO ADM 116/1029 (Case 3310: petitions, documents commenting on petitions, 1906). The Admiralty was generally reluctant to accede to such requests. Responding to the request of the skilled labourers employed as iron caulkers to be recognised as a trade, the Director of Dockyards commented that '[i]f you comply with their request and make them a trade you will create an injustice upon other workmen who are made to qualify through apprenticeship.' PRO ADM 116/874 (Abstract of petitions, evidence and proposals, 1892).

49 Plymouth Central Library: *South-Western Labour Journal,* August 1903, p. 3.

50 Hansard 1905, vol. 142, col. 1271.

51 Hansard 1913, vol. 53, cols. 977–8.

52 PRO ADM 116/1011 (Case 3309, petitions, abstracts and comments, 1905); Lunn and Day, 'Deference and Defiance', p. 147.

53 ADM 116/1129A (Case 3011, Method for obtaining redress of grievances, 1911).

54 PRO ADM 116/1142 (Case 3339, petitions, detailed recommendations, 1911).

55 PRO ADM 116/1129A (Case 3011, Method for obtaining redress of grievances, 1911).

56 See below, pp. 106–107.

57 PRO ADM 116/1137 (Case 3335, petitions vol 2, 1911).

58 Other groups also adopted this tactic: examples include the sailmakers' petition of 1911, and the skilled labourers employed as iron caulkers, and seeking recognition as a trade. PRO ADM 116/1139 (Case 3335, petitions vol. 4, 1911).

59 PRO ADM 116/1101 (Petitions 1905; abstracts and comments).

60 PRO ADM 116/1129A (Case 3011, Method for Obtaining Redress of Grievances, 1911).

61 PRO ADM 116/1142 (Case 3339, petitions, detailed recommendations, 1911).

62 Mavis Waters, 'Dockyard and Parliament: A Study of Unskilled Workers in Chatham Yard, 1860–1900', *Southern History*, 6 (1984), pp. 123–138: 137.

63 Hansard, 1905, vol. 142, col. 483.

64 Pelling, *Social Geography of British Elections*, p. 167; Dawson, 'Politics in Devon and Cornwall', p. 59.

65 H E Kearley (Viscount Devonport), *The Travelled Road: Some Memories of a Busy Life*, (Rochester, 1934), p. 113.

66 Dawson, 'Politics in Devon and Cornwall', p. 31.

67 Unionist election address for Devonport, *Western Morning News*, 5th January 1910.

68 *Western Daily Mercury*, 15th June 1904.

69 Conservative election advertisement in *South-Western Labour Journal*, January 1906, p. 339: 'Remember that German Naval Expenditure has risen since 1890 from about 4 Millions to nearly 11 Millions, and the Naval Expenditure of every one of the Great Powers has risen in the same manner. BEWARE or the Efficiency of your splendid Navy will be injured and your first line of Defence weakened. Don't allow this to happen!'

70 Similar swings against the Liberal government were also recorded in Chatham and Woolwich. Neal Blewett, *The Peers, the Parties and the People: The General Elections of 1910* (London, 1972), p. 410.

71 *Western Morning News*, 5th January 1910.

72 *Western Morning News*, 6th January 1910; 12th January 1910; Frans Coetzee, *For Party or Country: Nationalism and the Dilemmas of Popular Conservatism in Edwardian England* (Oxford, 1990), pp. 122, 141–2.

73 Lunn and Thomas, 'Naval Imperialism in Portsmouth', pp. 147–8.

74 *Western Morning News*, 5th January 1910.

75 *Western Morning News,* 6th January 1910.

76 *Western Morning News,* 4th January 1910.

77 *Western Morning News,* 8th January 1910.

78 *Western Morning News,* 8th January 1910.

79 *Western Morning News,* 4th January 1910.

80 'Think for a minute of Drake, in view of the dangers that menaced this empire, consenting to a reduction of the navy, and refusing, when he was warned, to make the necessary provision for the defence, not only of the State, but of their lives and liberties.' *Western Morning News,* 14th January 1910.

81 *Western Morning News,* 15th January 1910.

82 *Western Morning News,* 5th January 1910.

83 Kelly's Directory of Devonshire, 1910, p. 479.

84 Robert H MacDonald, *The Language of Empire: Myths and Metaphors of Popular Imperialism, 1880–1918* (Manchester, 1994), p. 67.

85 This was the theme of a number of famous literary works, including for example Charles Kingsley's novel *Westward Ho!* (1855), which was incidentally the set text for the English literature component of the dockyard apprentices' entrance exam in 1913. Henry Newbolt's poem 'Drake's Drum' (1897) has the image of Francis Drake buried at sea in the Caribbean, but 'dreamin' arl the time o' Plymouth Hoe.' Tennyson's 'The *Revenge*: A Ballad of the Fleet' (1878) refers to the courage of the 'Men of Bideford in Devon'.

86 Two such events are analysed here in detail, firstly the visit of the King and Queen in March 1902 to take part in two ceremonies concerning ships named in their honour. These were the launch of *HMS Queen,* and the laying down of the keel plate for one of the largest ships of the pre-Dreadnought era, *HMS King Edward VII.* The second ceremony took place in July 1903, when the Prince and Princess of Wales returned to Devonport to launch *HMS King Edward VII.* Details of both events are taken from reports in the local newspapers: *Western Daily Mercury,* 8th March, 10th March 1902; 24th July 1903; *Western Morning News,* 23rd July, 24th July 1903.

87 *Western Daily Mercury,* 24th July 1903.

88 *Western Daily Mercury,* 10th March 1902.

89 Kelly's Directory of Devonshire, 1910.

90 Hansard, 1905, vol. 142, cols. 485, 1271.

91 Hansard, 1905, vol. 148, cols. 552, 576. The *South-Western Labour Journal* (May 1905), p. 253, commented in similar vein: 'They [the Admiralty] ought to have known that the Dockyards were the only large centres of employment in the district they were taking the men to, and that their policy of taking possession of practically the whole of the available space and sea frontage is the reason why there are not existing in the towns factories or manufacturing establishments.'

92 Hansard, 1905, vol. 148, col. 581.

93 Leader column, *Western Daily Mercury,* 22nd February 1907.

94 Devonport Liberal Association meeting, reported in *Western Morning News,* 20th February 1907.

95 Profile in *South-Western Labour Journal,* October 1903, p. 24. Proctor was later selected as Labour candidate for Grimsby.

96 Williams, *History of the Plymouth and District Trades Council,* p. 9. In the same year, two dockyard organisations, the Devonport Ship Constructive Association and the Dockyard and Keyham Labour Federation, combined to support two 'working men candidates' in the municipal elections, and were successful in one ward. *Western Morning News,* 2nd November 1892.

97 Labour Party archives, LRC 1/333, incoming correspondence from A Macry, 27th April 1900; Williams, *History of the Plymouth and District Trades Council,* p. 9.

98 Labour Party archives, LRC 23/68, A H Orchard to LRC, 26th April 1905.

99 Labour Party archives, LP.GC 1/263, Tom Proctor to Ramsay MacDonald, 14th February 1906; 2/167, R Benallack to Ramsay MacDonald, 30th March 1906; 3/233/1–2, R Benallack to Ramsay MacDonald, 29th April 1906; 4/331, R Benallack to Ramsay MacDonald, 7th May 1906. See Ross McKibbin, *The Evolution of the Labour Party, 1910–1924* (Oxford, 1974), pp. 33–39, who suggests that these local disputes between trade councils and other Labour bodies were a fairly common problem during the early years.

100 Known affiliates of the LRA which had at least some dockyard members include the Amalgamated Society of Carpenters and Joiners, Amalgamated Society of Engineers, Steam Engine Makers, Associated Society of Enginemen, Government Labourers' Union, Hammermen, Iron Founders, Painters, Pattern Makers, Plumbers, Associated Shipwrights' Society. At the 1903 municipal elections the LRA candidates were Tom Proctor, engine fitter (ASE); A Stroud, engine fitter (ASE); R D Monk, Chief Constructor's department (GLU). *South-Western Labour Journal,* October 1903, p. 24.

101 *Western Morning News,* 2nd November 1893, 2nd November 1898; *Western Daily Mercury,* 2nd November 1906, 2nd November 1907, 2nd November 1909.

102 *South-Western Labour Journal,* January 1904, p. 65; June 1905, p. 265; July 1905, p. 277; August 1905, p. 289.

103 Hansard, 1910, vol. 17, cols. 237–8, 1459.

104 LRC.LB 1/54 (J McNeill (LRC) to W Rutter, 6th October 1902); LRC.LB 1/57–8 (J McNeill to Secretary, Devonport LRC, 6th October 1902).

105 LRC 5/5 (Lewington to LRC, 7th October 1902).

106 LRC.LB 5/119 (Bell to LRC, 14th October 1902); LRC.LB 5/321 (Pickles to McNeill, 12th October 1902).

107 See below, pp. 112–113. There was a further attempt to secure a Labour candidature for Plymouth in 1910, this time with the support of the Indepen-

dent Labour Party (ILP), but the matter had to be dropped when the ILP's National Administrative Council (NAC) refused to assist with either funds or organisation. *Western Morning News,* 21st October 1909; 8th December 1909.

108 Pointon, 'Mid-Victorian Plymouth', pp. 108, 210, 212.

109 Percentages of the population recorded as overcrowded (defined as more than two people living in one room) in the 1901 census were as follows: Plymouth 20.19%; Devonport 17.38%, Stonehouse 24.32%. The average for England and Wales was 8.9%, and in Portsmouth, similar in population size to Plymouth, only 1.19% of population was overcrowded. It is clear, therefore, that the problem was unusually severe in Plymouth, although the town was by no means unique. See Richard Rodger, *Housing in Urban Britain 1780–1914* (London, 1989), p. 53.

110 This finding it attributed to the accommodation of much of the working-class population in large old townhouses subdivided into tenements, similar to the conditions in central London and Dublin, but essentially different from conditions in most English industrial towns. Board of Trade report into rents, etc. 1908, pp. 370–1.

111 WDRO 1648/HW 1–3, Plymouth Borough Council, Minutes of the Housing of the Working Classes Committee, 1893–1914; WDRO 1814/69, Devonport Borough Council, Minutes of the Housing of the Working Classes Committee, 1897–1913.

112 Gill, *Plymouth: A New History,* p. 241.

113 *Western Morning News,* 2nd November 1893; WDRO 1069/2a, Edgcumbe family papers: Conservative election address for 1896.

114 The surviving municipal election literature suggests that housing and the rates formed the main point on most municipal election programmes around the turn of the century. *Western Morning News,* 3rd November 1891, 2nd November 1894, 1898; *Western Daily Mercury,* 2nd November 1896; WDRO 1069/3, Edgcumbe family papers: J G Jackson, election address for St Peter's ward, Plymouth, 1898; WDRO 1069/7: S Edgcumbe, election address for St Peter's ward, Plymouth, 1900.

115 *Western Daily Mercury,* 14th March 1900. The housing issue had been a prominent one for the SDF nationally since its foundation in the 1880s. See David Englander, *Landlord and Tenant in Urban Britain, 1838–1918* (Oxford, 1983), pp. 104–5.

116 WDRO 1814/69, Devonport Borough Council, Minutes of the Housing of the Working Classes Committee, 5th February 1901.

117 WDRO 1814/15–6, Devonport Borough Council minutes, 11th March 1901.

118 Housing Association Annual Meeting, 21st April 1904; reported in *South-Western Labour Journal,* May 1904, p. 107.

119 'The Housing Question in Devonport – A Chat with the Labour Councillor (R D Monk)', *South-Western Labour Journal,* August 1903, p. 2.

120 *Justice,* 1st October 1904.

121 WDRO 470/18, Plymouth SDF papers: Grindley, 'The Future of the SDF in Plymouth', MS (n.d.).

122 For this conflict in more detail see Mary Hilson, 'Consumers and Politics: The Co-operative Movement in Plymouth, 1890–1920', *Labour History Review*, 67 (2002), pp. 7–27: 11–12.

123 Michael J Winstanley, *The Shopkeeper's World 1830–1914* (Manchester, 1983), pp. 79, 101.

124 *Plymouth Co-operative Record*, February 1903, p. 180.

125 *Record*, December 1900, pp. 132–3.

126 *Record*, December 1900, p. 133.

127 *Record*, December 1900, p. 133.

128 *Record*, April 1903, p. 206.

129 *Record*, December 1903, p. 133.

130 *Record*, September 1900, p. 106.

131 *South-Western Labour Journal*, October 1904, p. 166.

132 LRC.LB 5/259: R D Monk to LRC, n.d.

133 LRC.LB 5/119: Richard Bell to LRC, 14th October 1902.

134 *South-Western Labour Journal*, July 1904, p. 135.

135 *Western Daily Mercury*, 15th June 1904.

136 LRC.LB 15/87–90, 115; 16/30, 364, 382, 385, 420, 435.

137 LRC.LB 15/206: LRC to Proctor, 20th June 1904.

138 *South-Western Labour Journal*, November 1903, pp. 39–40.

139 *South-Western Labour Journal*, September 1906, p. 408; special supplement, 15th September 1906.

140 *South-Western Labour Journal*, October 1903, p. 27.

141 *Western Daily Mercury*, 14th March 1900.

142 *South-Western Labour Journal*, August 1903, p. 7; Plymouth Central Library, SDF papers (F W Ireland, SDF election bill, November 1905).

143 In the words of one speaker: 'Personally, he was in favour of extending to others the same privilege he had himself, that of buying a house by means of the Society's capital. He certainly should not feel the same sense of security if the walls only were his… It was his ambition to do something towards solving the old age question by his house, and he believed this was so generally.' *Record*, July 1902, p. 79.

144 Plymouth Central Library, Housing Association papers: pamphlet, 'Warrens of the Poor', 1906, p. 26. The *South-Western Labour Journal* also felt that it was 'much to be regretted' that the Plymouth Co-operative Society had not followed the example of other co-operative mutual ownership schemes: 'Individual ownership is chiefly beneficial to those who are well able to look after themselves; collective ownership is the thing for the mass of the people.' *South-Western Labour Journal*, May 1905, p. 249.

145 *Record*, July 1902, p. 78.

146 WDRO 1648/HW1–3: Plymouth Borough Council, Minutes of the Housing of the Working Classes Committee, 19th September 1905.

147 Housing Association papers: pamphlets, 'The Housing Question', n.d. (1903?), and 'Warrens of the Poor', 1906.

148 Plymouth Central Library, SDF papers: *The Social-Democrat*, vol. V, no. 3, March 1901.

149 The title of the Housing Association's 1906 pamphlet, 'Warrens of the Poor', alluded to these concerns (from a work by Tennyson): 'There among the gloomy alleys Progress halts on palsied feet,/Crime and hunger cast our maidens by the thousand on the street./There the master scrimps his haggard sempstress of her daily bread,/There a single sordid attic holds the living and the dead./There the smouldering fire of fever creeps across the rotted floor,/And the crowded couch of incest in the warrens of the poor.

150 Warrens of the Poor, pp. 4, 17.

151 *Western Morning News*, 14th March 1906, 15th March 1906.

152 *Record*, July 1894, p. 66.

153 *Record*, July 1894, p. 64.

154 *Record*, January 1910, p. 302.

155 *Record*, November 1907, pp. 561–2.

156 *Record*, October 1910, pp. 420–1.

157 W J G 'Education: Co-operative and Otherwise', *Record*, December 1904, pp. 141–2.

158 WDRO 470/18, SDF papers. The *Labour Journal* teased the SDF for organising a concert: 'Just fancy, people with an economic basis like the SDF going in for concerts! Whoever heard of Karl Marx composing a cantata, or of Hyndman taking part in a duet? The idea is preposterous.' *South-Western Labour Journal*, April 1906, p. 363.

159 *South-Western Labour Journal*, March 1906, p. 351.

160 *South-Western Labour Journal*, June 1906, p. 377.

161 WDRO 470/18, SDF papers.

162 A new branch of the SDF was founded in Devonport in 1905, but it failed to make any impact at all, and had ceased to exist by 1909. *Justice* 15th June 1905. In 1906 the SDF candidate was only 9 votes behind the winning Liberal candidate in Sutton. The party claimed that it would have demanded a recount but was unable to raise the necessary funds. *Western Morning News*, 2nd November 1906.

163 *Justice*, 25th August 1906.

164 *Justice*, passim, 15th July – 29th September 1906.

165 *Justice*, May 26th 1906.

166 When the Plymouth School Board was wound up in 1901, Arthur Grindley reflected ruefully of his year as an SDF representative: 'I haven't succeeded very much in my work. I am just a man of amendments and minorities.' WDRO 470/18: Plymouth SDF papers.

167 *South-Western Labour Journal*, November 1905, p. 314.

168 *South-Western Labour Journal*, July 1904, p. 137.

169 *South-Western Labour Journal*, October 1904, p. 166.

170 *South-Western Labour Journal,* July 1904, p. 137.

171 *South-Western Labour Journal,* October 1905, p. 307.

172 *Record,* April 1903, pp. 211–2.

173 Co-operative Congress Report, 1910, p. 34, cited in Peter Gurney, *Co-operative Culture and the Politics of Consumption in England, c1870–1930* (Manchester, 1996), p. 54.

174 LRA programme for Guardians election, *South-Western Labour Journal,* May 1906, p. 369.

175 *South-Western Labour Journal,* March 1904, p. 90.

176 *South-Western Labour Journal,* June 1904, p. 118.

177 *South-Western Labour Journal,* June 1904, p. 118; WDRO 1472/12–13: W H Welsford papers.

178 *South-Western Labour Journal,* October 1903, p. 23.

179 *South-Western Labour Journal,* June 1904, p. 118.

180 *South-Western Labour Journal,* May 1906, p. 369.

181 See Philip MacDougall, 'The Changing Nature of the Dockyard Dispute, 1790–1840', in Lunn and Day, eds, *History of Work and Labour Relations,* pp. 41–65: 55–7; n. 56.

182 *South-Western Labour Journal,* January 1904, June 1904. Unfortunately, no records relating to this or other dockyard societies seem to have survived.

5. Plymouth during World War I and after

1 Keith Burgess, *The Challenge of Labour: Shaping British Society* (London, 1980); James E Cronin, *Labour and Society in Britain, 1918–1979* (London, 1984).

2 Duncan Tanner, *Political Change and the Labour Party, 1900–1918* (Cambridge, 1990).

3 Hansard 1914–15, vol. 69, col. 1023; vol. 72, col. 267; vol. 73, cols. 453–4, 1663. Time rates were increased from October 1914; new overtime rates were adopted in March 1915. By September 1915 adult male employees were earning an extra four shillings a week in war supplements. On the issue of badges: Hansard 1914–15, vol. 70, col. 1734; also H Wolfe, *Labour Supply and Regulation* (Oxford, 1923), p. 24. By the end of July 1915 the Admiralty had issued 400,000 badges (including to those employed by its contractors).

4 Hansard 1914–15, vol. 72, col. 267.

5 PRO ADM 116/1541 (Case 11247: Dilution of Labour in HM Dockyards, 1916).

6 Hansard 1916, vol. 86, col. 1096.

7 Hansard 1917–18, vol. 91, col. 1060.

8 Burgess, *The Challenge of Labour,* pp. 161–4; Wolfe, *Labour Supply and Regulation,* pp 21–27.

9 PRO ADM 116/1541 (Case 11247: Memo from Adm Supt at Devonport, 15th February 1916).

10 PRO ADM 116/1541 (Case 11247: Minute from Director of Dockyards, 17th March 1916. See also Kenneth Lunn and Ann Day, 'Continuity and Change: Labour Relations in the Royal Dockyards, 1914–50', in Kenneth Lunn and Ann Day, eds, *History of Work and Labour Relations in the Royal Dockyards* (London, 1999), pp. 127–150: 136.

11 PRO ADM 116/1541 (Case 11247: Sheerness ASE to Senior Officer, Sheerness Dockyard, 12th April 1916).

12 PRO ADM 116/1541 (Case 11247: Memo from Financial Secretary, 15th June 1916).

13 PRO ADM 116/1541 (Case 11247: Portsmouth ASE to Electrical Engineer, Portsmouth Dockyard, 12th April 1916).

14 Hansard 1918, vol. 105, col. 370.

15 Lunn and Day, 'Continuity and Change', p. 133.

16 Hansard 1918, vol. 105, cols. 987–9, 1858–9.

17 Lunn and Day, 'Continuity and Change', p. 134.

18 Lunn and Day, 'Continuity and Change', p. 140.

19 Co-operative Union archive: T W Mercer, 'The Late Mr W H Watkins: Guildsman and Co-operator', National Co-operative Men's Guild printed paper no. 51, August 1924.

20 Joyce M Bellamy and John Saville, eds, *Dictionary of Labour Biography,* vol. 1 (London, 1972), pp. 238–9; 338–9.

21 *Co-operative News,* 3rd October 1914.

22 *Plymouth Co-operative Record,* November 1914.

23 Percy Redfern, *The New History of the CWS* (London, 1938), p. 130. For a discussion of the tension between this position and the co-operative movement's commitment to internationalism, see Peter Gurney, *Co-operative Culture and the Politics of Consumption in England, c1870–1930* (Manchester, 1996), pp. 105–110.

24 For a discussion of the profiteering issue see Jonathan S Boswell and Bruce R Johns, 'Patriots or Profiteers? British Businessmen and the First World War', *Journal of European Economic History* 11 (1982), pp. 423–445: 423–5; Bernard Waites, *A Class Society at War: Britain 1914–1918* (Leamington Spa, 1987), p. 68.

25 The Joint Parliamentary Committee made no attempt to justify their acceptance of the tax on fiscal grounds, but instead spoke emotively of 'the nation's need', arguing that, 'the fact that any trading or business organisation which is showing a larger benefit to its proprietors than it did before the war can at least afford to contribute something less that one-half of the surplus to the aid of the community in its greatest peril.' Co-operative Congress Report, 1916: Reports of the Central Board of the Co-operative Union: Joint Parliamentary Committee.

26 Quarterly meeting report, *Plymouth Co-operative Record,* January 1916, p. 21.

27 The Plymouth Co-operative Society's principal argument against the tax

was put by counsel thus: 'The society was in fact a distributing agency which returned to its members, by what it chose to call dividend, the difference between the price paid by the members at the time of purchase, and what was actually found to be the actual cost of the article, plus the cost of distribution, originally paid by the society.' *Plymouth Co-operative Record,* January 1917, p. 17.

28 *Plymouth Co-operative Record,* January 1916.

29 *Plymouth Co-operative Record,* August 1916; *The Co-operator,* 17th February 1917.

30 *The Co-operator,* 3rd February 1917.

31 For a discussion of this debate, see Mary Hilson, 'Consumers and Politics: The Co-operative Movement in Plymouth, 1890–1920', *Labour History Review,* 67 (2002), pp. 7–27: 8–9.

32 Quarterly meeting report, *Plymouth Co-operative Record,* January 1916, p. 20.

33 Special meeting of the Central Board at Lancaster Co-operative Congress, 1916, to consider Joint Parliamentary's Committee's report on Excess Profits Tax; Co-operative Congress Report 1916.

34 *Plymouth Co-operative Record,* January 1916.

35 One estimate suggests that the price index for basic foodstuffs stood at 168 in October 1916, where July 1914 = 100. Peter Dewey, 'Nutrition and Living Standards in Wartime Britain', in Richard Wall and Jay Winter, eds, *The Upheaval of War: Family, Work and Welfare in Europe, 1914–1918* (Cambridge, 1988), pp. 197–220: 201.

36 *Plymouth Co-operative Record,* March 1917, pp. 29–30.

37 *The Co-operator,* 7th April 1917.

38 *Plymouth Co-operative Record,* July 1917, p. 192.

39 *The Co-operator,* 21st April 1917.

40 According to W H Watkins in 1918, 184,000 ration books were issued by the Plymouth Food Control Committee. This compared with the 183 000 people registered with Plymouth Co-operative Society for potatoes, 121 000 for sugar, 50 000 for butter, 84 000 for lard, 72 000 for tea, 46 000 for meat and 37 000 for bacon. *Plymouth Co-operative Record,* November 1918, p. 243. For the government response to the food problem, see José Harris, 'Bureaucrats and Businessmen in British Food Control, 1916–1919', in Kathleen Burk, ed., *War and the State: The Transformation of British Government 1914–1919* (London, 1982), pp. 135–156.

41 *The Co-operator,* September 1917, *passim.,* 5th October 1917; *Plymouth Co-operative Record,* September 1917.

42 *The Co-operator,* 6th October 1917.

43 *The Co-operator,* 13th October 1917, 17th October 1917.

44 *The Co-operator,* 19th January 1918.

45 *Plymouth Co-operative Record,* October 1917.

46 *The Co-operator,* 13th October 1917.

47 *The Co-operator,* 19th January 1918.

48 *Plymouth Co-operative Record,* November 1918, p. 242.

49 *The Co-operator,* 23rd February 1918.

50 *The Co-operator,* 9th February 1918.

51 *Plymouth Co-operative Record,* February 1918, p. 41.

52 *The Co-operator,* 19th January 1918.

53 *The Co-operator,* 23rd February 1918.

54 *Plymouth Co-operative Record,* June 1917, p. 152.

55 *The Co-operator,* 28th April 1917.

56 *Plymouth Co-operative Record,* December 1917, p. 313.

57 H B Williams, *History of the Plymouth and District Trades Council from 1892 to 1952* (Plymouth, 1952), p. 18.

58 Williams, *History of the Plymouth Trades Council,* p. 18.

59 *Plymouth Co-operative Record,* July 1918, pp. 161–2.

60 *Plymouth Co-operative Record,* November 1917, pp. 280–1.

61 Report of special meetings to discuss LCRA, *Plymouth Co-operative Record,* June 1917, pp. 116–8.

62 *Plymouth Co-operative Record,* April 1917, p. 116.

63 *The Co-operator,* 7th July 1917.

64 *Plymouth Co-operative Record,* December 1917, p. 313; *The Co-operator,* 15th December 1917.

65 Labour Party archives: National Executive Committee minutes, 26th September 1917; Re-organisation sub-committee minutes, 13th November 1917.

66 Re-organisation sub-committee minutes, 13th November 1917; National Executive Committee minutes, 15th November 1917.

67 National Executive Committee minutes, 12th December 1917.

68 *Plymouth Co-operative Record,* April 1916.

69 *Plymouth Co-operative Record,* August 1918.

70 *Plymouth Co-operative Record,* September 1918, p. 199.

71 *Plymouth Co-operative Record,* September 1918.

72 *Plymouth Co-operative Record,* September 1918.

73 Editorial, *Plymouth Co-operative Record,* July 1917.

74 G Scott, '"The Working-class Women's Most Active and Democratic Movement": The Women's Co-operative Guild from 1883 to 1950' (unpublished DPhil thesis, University of Sussex, 1988), pp. 67–70.

75 *Plymouth Co-operative Record,* May 1916, p. 159.

76 See also Karen Hunt, 'Negotiating the Boundaries of the Domestic: British Socialist Women and the Politics of Consumption', *Women's History Review,* 9 (2000), pp. 389–410, for a discussion of this point.

77 *Plymouth Co-operative Record,* January 1916, p. 20; March 1916, p. 93.

78 *Plymouth Co-operative Record,* February 1917, p. 30.

79 *Western Morning News,* 6th November 1918. See also John Turner, *British Politics and the Great War: Coalition and Conflict 1915–1918* (London, 1992), pp. 308–318.

80 *The Co-operator,* 21st December 1918.

81 *Western Daily Mercury,* 19th November 1918.

82 *The Co-operator,* 4th January 1919.

83 *Western Daily Mercury,* 30th November 1918.

84 *Western Morning News,* 27th November 1918.

85 *The Co-operator,* 14th December 1918.

86 *Western Daily Mercury,* 12th December 1918; *The Co-operator,* 21st December 1918.

87 *Western Daily Mercury,* 4th December 1918; *Western Morning News,* 26th December 1918.

88 Karen J Musolf, *From Plymouth to Parliament: A Rhetorical History of Nancy Astor's 1919 Campaign* (London, 1999), pp. 13–14; Martin Pugh, *The Tories and the People, 1880–1935* (Oxford, 1985), p. 99.

89 *Western Morning News,* 22nd November 1918, 26th November 1918, 13th December 1918.

90 *Western Morning News,* 7th December 1918.

91 A M Dawson, 'Politics in Devon and Cornwall, 1900–1931' (unpublished PhD thesis, University of London, 1991), p. 284.

92 *Western Morning News,* 22nd November 1918; *Western Daily Mercury,* 21st November 1918.

93 *Western Daily Mercury,* 2nd December 1918.

94 *Western Daily Mercury,* 13th December 1918.

95 *The Co-operator,* 14th December 1918.

96 *The Co-operator,* 30th November 1918; also *Western Daily Mercury,* 30th November 1918.

97 *Western Daily Mercury,* 20th November 1918.

98 *Western Daily Mercury,* 7th December 1918.

99 *Western Daily Mercury,* 12th December 1918.

100 *Western Morning News,* 7th December 1918.

101 *Western Daily Mercury,* 28th November 1918.

102 *Western Morning News,* 27th November 1918.

103 *Western Daily Mercury,* 2nd December 1918. There was an ILP branch in Plymouth but little is known about its activities.

104 *Western Daily Mercury,* 2nd December 1918, 6th December 1918: 'What was a Pacifist? A man who believed in peace. Did anyone to-day believe in war? To show they had been fed up with it they had jubilated when the armistice was signed.'

105 *Western Daily Mercury,* 9th December 1918.

106 *Western Daily Mercury,* 2nd December 1918, 9th December 1918.

107 *Western Daily Mercury,* 19th November 1918.

108 *Western Daily Mercury,* 5th December 1918.

109 *Western Daily Mercury,* 26th November 1918, 30th November 1918.

110 Labour Party manifesto, printed in *The Co-operator,* 7th December 1918.

111 *Co-operative News,* 7th December, quoted in *The Co-operator,* 14th December 1918.

112 *Western Daily Mercury,* 2nd December 1918.

113 *Western Daily Mercury,* 30th November 1918.

114 *Western Morning News,* 11th December 1918.

115 *Western Morning News,* 26th November 1918.

116 *The Co-operator,* 14th December 1918.

117 *The Co-operator,* 4th January 1919.

118 T W Mercer, 'The Fight for Sutton', *The Co-operator,* 21st December 1918.

119 LCRA meeting, 29th December 1918; reported in *Plymouth Co-operative Record,* January 1919.

120 Mercer, 'Election Reflections', *Plymouth Co-operative Record,* December 1918, p. 268.

121 Those against raised the question of whether the use of the society's car, 'for anything other than the Society's business purposes' was legitimate, but were defeated. *Plymouth Co-operative Record,* January 1919.

122 *Plymouth Co-operative Record,* February 1919.

123 'Mr Carling said he was returned at the head of the poll as evidence of the gratitude of the membership for his stand against wasting the people's money in insane political adventures.' *Plymouth Co-operative Record,* June 1919.

124 *Plymouth Co-operative Record,* June 1919.

125 They cited rule 4, which stated that: 'The objects of this Society are to carry on the trades or businesses of general dealers, manufacturers, builders and insurers of property against risk of every description, and shall also include dealings of every description with land. The Society shall have full power to do all things necessary or expedient for the accomplishment of all objects specified in its rules, and to agree with any other Society for a profit-sharing or other working agreement.' The President said that his reading of rule 4 was that the assertion that the objects of the Society did not include political action was indeed the case. The resolution was defeated by a majority of 365 to 100. *Plymouth Co-operative Record,* June 1919.

126 *Plymouth Co-operative Record,* September 1919.

127 *Plymouth Co-operative Record,* October 1919.

128 *Plymouth Co-operative Record,* November 1919.

129 *Plymouth Co-operative Record,* October 1919.

130 *Plymouth Co-operative Record,* June 1919.

131 *Plymouth Co-operative Record,* February 1919.

132 At Nancy's selection meeting Waldorf promised that he would make every attempt to be back before the electors very shortly in his own right and Nancy herself endorsed this hope. *Western Daily Mercury,* 4th November 1919.

133 *Western Morning News,* 31st October 1919.

134 Gay was adopted at a mass Labour meeting on 2nd November. Labour Party archive: National Executive Committee minutes, 12th November 1919.

135 *Western Morning News,* 4th November 1919.

136 National Executive Committee minutes, 8th December 1919.

137 Liberal eve-of-poll rally, *Western Daily Mercury*, 15th November 1919. Foot's election address was the same: '<u>If you wish to:</u> Stop Waste, Clear out Dilly & Dally, Demobilise the Limpets, Get out of Russia, Regain your Liberties, Kill Conscription, Lower Prices, Speed up Housing, Restore the Authority of Parliament and Secure Fair Play for all, VOTE FOR FOOT.'

138 *Western Daily Mercury*, 31st October 1919. In a campaign speech, Foot also referred to the 1832 parliamentary reform: 'The constituency has got great political traditions. When the Reform Act was refused they closed the shops and went into mourning in Plymouth, and when it was passed there was great rejoicing in Plymouth. They thought politics a serious matter in those days, but matters are more serious to-day.' *Western Morning News*, 7th November 1919.

139 Meeting for women voters, *Western Morning News*, 5th November 1919.

140 Editorial, *Western Morning News*, 29th November 1919.

141 Musolf, *From Plymouth to Parliament*, pp. 51, 63.

142 WDRO 186/18/3: Astor papers, press cuttings file, 31st October–15th November 1919: *Western Dispatch*, 9th November 1919. The *Western Morning News* commented in an editorial (7th November 1919), that, 'Lady Astor is receiving many promises of support from women who have not been associated with the Unionist party, the fact being that in this election, with such a personality as her ladyship before the constituency, the ordinary barriers of party are quite broken down.'

143 Astor press cuttings: *Morning Post*, 12th November 1919; Pugh, *The Tories and the People*, p. 180. The *Western Morning News*, 17th November 1919, reported that there were 600 volunteers working for the Unionists, and that the constituency was 'uniquely well canvassed'.

144 *Western Morning News*, 4th November 1919; *Western Daily Mercury*, 12th November 1919.

145 *Western Morning News*, 10th November 1919.

146 Astor press cuttings: *Observer*, 9th November 1919. One such meeting was reported thus: 'This evening's gathering was in a girls' school, outside which the usual crowd of Devon women had assembled before the little scholars were liberated from their lessons. They filed out and grouped in mass to greet Lady Astor, who is immensely popular with them. A shrill infantile cheer gave those within the first indication of the candidate's arrival. It was a packed audience sitting at the desks in the big schoolroom, the many mothers bringing their babies. Earlier speakers had elevated themselves on chairs; Lady Astor stood on the headmistress's table, and from there talked to the women in a homely fashion.' *Daily Telegraph*, 11th November 1919.

147 Astor press cuttings: *Observer*, 2nd November 1919. Astor's charity work included a Girls' Club offering singing, drill, painting, drawing and sewing for the slumdwellers of Vintry district; Homes for Invalid Children; the Civic Guild of Help, the Three Towns Nursing Association and the Low-

er Deck Benevolent Association. *Western Morning News,* 10th November 1919; Musolf, *From Plymouth to Parliament,* p. 14.

148 *Western Morning News,* 3rd November 1919; *Western Daily Mercury,* 5th November 1919.

149 *Western Daily Mercury,* 4th November 1919.

150 Astor press cuttings: *Morning Post,* 5th November 1919.

151 *Western Morning News,* 3rd November 1919.

152 *Western Daily Mercury,* 8th November 1919; *Western Independent,* 9th November 1919.

153 Astor press cuttings: *Westminster Gazette,* 4th November 1919.

154 *Western Daily Mercury,* 11th November 1919.

155 *Western Morning News,* 7th November 1919; *Western Evening Herald,* 12th November 1919.

156 *Western Daily Mercury,* 14th November 1919.

157 *Western Morning News,* 3rd November 1919.

158 *Western Daily Mercury,* 8th November 1919.

159 H.C.Cmd.581 (1920) xxi, 635. Report of the Colwyn Committee (utilisation of the Royal Dockyards for construction of merchant ships).

160 Hansard 1919, vol. 121, col. 1449.

161 *Western Morning News,* 29th November 1919.

162 Labour Party archives: National Executive Committee minutes, 8th September 1920.

163 The NEC endorsed the candidature of J Gorman of the Amalgamated Engineering Union (AEU) for Plymouth Drake in 1922, and sanctioned the withdrawal of W H Watkins, who was adopted instead for another Devon borough, Torquay. That Watkins did not remain in Plymouth, where he was well known, must be attributed to a serious rift between the Coop and the labour movement. Labour Party archives: NEC minutes 7th February 1922; 5th April 1922.

6. The Labour Movement in Karlskrona c. 1890–1911

1 Ann Hörsell, 'Från segel och trä till ånga och stål 1866–1910', pp. 7–80; Björn Gäfvert, 'Kontinuitet i föränderlig omvärld', pp. 81–134; both in Erik Norberg, ed., *Karlskronavarvets historia,* vol. 2, 1866–1992 (Karlskrona, 1993).

2 Rune Hillbom, *Karlskrona 300 år,* vol. II (Karlskrona, 1982), pp. 45–54.

3 Hillbom, *Karlskrona 300 år,* p. 54.

4 Janvik Bromé, *Karlskrona stads historia,* vol. III, 1862–1930 (Karlskrona, 1930), pp. 81–2.

5 The Seamens Corps (*Sjömanskåren*) alone, made up of regulars and conscripts doing their military service, numbered 4000 men in 1908. Bromé, *Karlskrona stads historia,* p. 404.

6 See chapter 7, p. 223.

7 Sveriges officiella statistik.

8 Erik Palmstierna, *Ett brytningsskede. Minnen och dagboks anteckningar av Erik Palmstierna* (Stockholm, 1951), p. 21.

9 Hillbom, *Karlskrona 300 år*, p. 4; Palmstierna, *Ett brytningsskede*, p. 21.

10 Thommy Svensson, *Från ackord till månadslön. En studie av lönpolitiken, fackföreningarna och rationaliseringarna inom svensk varvsindustri under 1900-talet* (Göteborg, 1983), p. 25.

11 Björn Gäfvert, 'Kontinuitet i föränderlig omvärld', pp. 106–107.

12 Ann Hörsell, 'Från segel och trä till ånga och stål', p. 68.

13 This last category was also a declining group within the yard. Prisoners had been used since the seventeenth century for performing heavier manual work, such as in the anchor smithy, and for unskilled tasks such as coaling and cleaning. Fifty-three prisoners were employed in the dockyard in 1868, but the use of penal labour was phased out by the beginning of the twentieth century.

14 Krigsarkivet: Reglemente för Marinen, del I (1915 edition), Kap I, §§ 14, 15.

15 Reglemente för Marinen, del I (1907) § 57:2.

16 Reglemente för Marinen, del I (1915) Bil 46, 'Bestämmelser för varvsarbetare vid flottan', §§ 1:1, 4:2.

17 Karlskrona arbetarekommun, *Människor och händelser – ett axplock. Karlskrona arbetarekommun 100 år 1896–1996* (Karlskrona, 1996). C A Nyström, the first chairman of the dockyard union's executive committee, implied that dockyard workers were prevented by the terms of their contract from using the strike weapon. Kaj Björk, *Försvarsverkens civila personals förbund 1917–1942* (Stockholm, 1943), p. 36. See pp. 222–223.

18 Paul Ericson, *Från fyrkvälde till folkmakt. En kort krönika om blekingsk arbetrrörelse* (Karlskrona, 1957), pp. 5–8.

19 Marinmusei arkiv, Karlskrona: Statsanställdas förbund avd 2136 arkiv, Karlskrona Varvsarbetarnas Förening (KVAF) minutes 28th April 1900.

20 KVAF minutes 28th June 1901, 23rd August 1901, 6th June 1907. The wages petition was abandoned when it was established that the majority of workers were satisfied with their wages.

21 Reglemente för Marinen, del I (1915) bil § 12:1, a,b; Folkrörelsearkiv i Blekinge län, 1984/67: KVAF, 1900–1920. Report of committee set up to inquire into sickness benefit fund, 8th February 1901.

22 KVAF minutes, 4th September 1903.

23 KVAF minutes, 20th May 1904, 10th June 1904.

24 KVAF minutes, n.d. (August 1904).

25 KVAF minutes, 15th May 1903, 4th September 1903. Also Thorvald Pettersson, *Historik över Försvarsverkens civila personals förbunds avdelning 36 verksamhet under den förflutna 15:års perioden, samt en överblick av det organisatoriska arbetet inom varvsarbetarekåren för tiden 1900–1921* (Karlskrona, 1936), p. 4.

26 Pettersson, *Historik över FCPF:s avdelning 36*, p. 3; KVAF minutes, 1st

November 1901, 15th November 1901. One member disagreed, arguing that "those who turned up and worked at the bazaar needed a drink, so it wasn't too much to ask."

27 The so-called 'spritstrejken' was short-lived, however. Notices were circulated asking members to sign up in support, but the matter was dropped when the executive pulled out of organising further action. KVAF minutes, 6th March 1903, 20th February 1904.

28 Palmstierna, *Ett brytningsskede*, p. 21.

29 J A Henricsson, *Tid som flytt eller några pänndrag ur minnet från socialismens första kampår* (Karlskrona, 1923), pp. 75- 76.

30 The grain scheme later had to be abandoned for lack of support. KVAF minutes 4th July 1902, 28th May 1906. Folkrörelsearkiv i Blekinge län, 1984/67: KVAF annual report, 1900

31 KVAF minutes, 28th April 1900.

32 There were two main groups of woodworkers employed in the dockyard: *timmermän* and *snickare*. The *timmermän* were responsible for the heavy construction, including laying down the keel plate and the ribs of the hull. Before the advent of iron and steel shipbuilding, their trade would certainly have corresponded to that of the English shipwrights, but given the special use of this term in the British dockyards, I have avoided translating *timmerman* as shipwright. The *snickare* were responsible for the finer woodwork. Neither trade was specific to shipbuilding, and both *timmermän* and *snickare* were both found in the construction industry. For a discussion of the division of labour in Swedish shipbuilding, see Jan Bohlin, *Svensk varvsindustri 1920–1975. Lönsamhet, finansiering och arbetsmarknad* (Göteborg, 1989), pp. 224–7; Magnus Wikdahl, *Varvets tid. Arbetarliv och kulturell förändring i en skeppsbyggarstad* (Stockholm, 1992), p. 31.

33 Gunnar Berg, *Karlskrona Grovarbetarefackförening 40 år 1902–1942. Några glimtar ur verksamheten* (Karlskrona, 1942). There are also isolated references to organisations of dockyard woodworkers and painters, but no formal records: Arbetarekommun minutes, 8th January 1908; *Blekinge Folkblad*, 14th April 1908, 13th June 1908.

34 *Svenska metallindustriarbetareförbundet avdelning 96 i Karlskrona. En jubileumsskrift* (Karlskrona, 1976).

35 Ericson, *Från fyrkvälde till folkmakt;* Karlskrona arbetarekommun, *Människor och händelser.*

36 Ericson, *Från fyrkvälde till folkmakt,* pp. 10–11. It is significant that this account ignores the existence of earlier labour organisations such as Karlskrona Labour Society (*arbetarförening*), founded in 1872 with the liberal aim of promoting conciliation between workers and their employers, and Karlskrona Typographical Society, founded in 1873. See Karlskrona arbetarförening, *En kortfattad historik över Karlskrona arbetarförenings verksamhet* (Karlskrona, 1933); Ragnar Fors, *Karlskrona arbetarförening 1872–1972* (Karlskrona, 1972); Dag Magnus Hermfelt, *Arbetareföreningens*

bibliotek i Karlskrona 1877–1900 (Borås, 1983); Hillbom, *Karlskrona 300 år*, p. 141.

37 Solveig Halvorsen, 'Scandinavian Trade Unions in the 1890s, with Special Reference to the Scandinavian Stonemasons' Union', *Scandinavian Journal of History*, 13 (1988), pp. 3–21: 6, 8, 15.

38 Ericson, *Från fyrkvälde till folkmakt*, p. 18.

39 Ericson, *Från fyrkvälde till folkmakt*, pp. 18–19; Torbjörn Vallinder, *I kamp för demokratin. Rösträttsrörelsen i Sverige 1886–1900* (Stockholm, 1962), pp. 88–91. The social democratic candidate topped the poll, with 327 votes against 96 for his nearest rival. The unexpected victory was attributed to the split in the liberal vote, as two liberal candidates stood.

40 Arbetarekommun minutes, 15th September 1896. The unions represented on this occasion included the shoemakers, tailors, bricklayers, painters, tobacco workers, cabinet makers and the stove-builders.

41 Ericson, *Från fyrkvälde till folkmakt*, p. 19.

42 1862 was a year of municipal reform in Karlskrona as in the rest of Sweden, which was to lay the foundations of a modern system of municipal government. Under the new arrangements, municipal government was to be based on an elected, decision-making legislature, the town council or *stadsfullmäktige*; and an administrative committee, the *drätselkammare*, elected by the council. The administrative tasks of the *drätselkammare* were shared by various boards and committees, and from 1886 by an administrative committee, or *beredningsutskott*. The first municipal elections in Karlskrona took place in December 1862, and 36 councillors were elected to the new *stadsfullmäktige*, increased to 42 during the 1890s.

43 Cf Bromé, *Karlskrona stads historia*, p. 3, who suggests that municipal politics was dominated by the military.

44 The 1862 laws regulated the actions of local authorities in areas such as law and order, fire fighting, building, public health, poor relief and education. See Rune Bokholm, *Städernas handlingsfrihet. En studie av expansionsskedet 1900–1930* (Lund, 1995).

45 R Nylander, *Karlskrona föreläsningsförening 1903–1938* (Karlskrona, 1938).

46 *Blekinge Läns Tidning*, 1st April 1905.

47 Palmstierna, *Ett brytningsskede*, pp. 21–22. Sweden had a nominally secret ballot at this time; Palmstierna is referring to the practice of taking the ballot paper for the preferred party when entering the polling booth to vote.

48 Arbetarekommun minutes, 12th June 1902.

49 *Blekinge Folkblad*, 2nd December 1904.

50 Arbetarekommun minutes, 29th June 1905.

51 *Blekinge Folkblad*, 1st September 1905.

52 *Blekinge Folkblad*, 15th September 1905.

53 Hillbom, *Karlskrona 300 år*, pp. 81–2. Speaking at a debating society meeting on employers and labour organisation, Palmstierna was reported to have

said that, '[i]t would be in the interest of the workers of our country to distance their organisations from socialist and anti-religious tendencies, as is the case in several European countries, so that every worker could join them, whatever religious view he has, or political colour he belongs to.' *Blekinge Läns Tidning,* 17th March 1905.

54 *Blekinge Folkblad,* 12th September 1905; Arbetarekommun minutes, 25th October 1905.

55 Arbetarekommun minutes, 26th October 1905, 31st January 1907; Arbetarekommun styrelsen minutes 11th September 1906, 7th November 1906.

56 Arbetarekommun minutes, 20th July 1908; *Blekinge Folkblad,* 6th August 1908.

57 *Blekinge Folkblad,* 8th August 1908.

58 *Blekinge Folkblad,* 15th August 1908.

59 *Blekinge Folkblad,* 25th July 1908, 20th August 1908.

60 Arbetarekommun minutes, 8th September 1908.

61 *Blekinge Folkblad,* 10th September 1908.

62 *Blekinge Folkblad,* 26th September 1908.

63 Arbetarekommun minutes 15th October 1906; 3rd December 1911.

64 The development of the political right in Karlskrona is discussed in chapter 7.

65 See Sven-Eric Liedman, 'Liberalism in the Nordic Context', in Ilkka K Lakaniemi, Anna Rotkirch and Henrik Stenius, eds, *Liberalism in the Nordic Context* (Helsinki, 1995), pp. 33–48.

66 The Swedish Academy's definition of *frisinnad* is as follows: 'om person: som besitter [eller] karakteriseras av frisinne, fördomsfri (motsatt: trångbröstad, fördomsfull, bigott), i sht på det politiska området: framstegsvänlig; som omfattar [eller] gillar de åsikter [eller] reformer för vilka de framstegsvänliga politiska partierna kämpa [eller] som tillhör ngt av dessa partier;' *Frisinnad* could also have a more specific political meaning: 'liberal (närmast motsatt: konservativ); i pl. i substantivisk anv. de frisinnade, benämning på olika politiska mellanpartier med framstegsvänlig karaktär, i Sv. efter 1923 särskildt på den kvarvarande huvuddelen av den detta år splittrade frisinnade landsföreningen: liberala folkpartiet.' In other words, this implies that it was not until after the First World War that *frisinnad* took on a more specific political meaning. Svenska Akademiens ordbok, http://g3.spraakdata.gu.se/saob/index.html (accessed 21st September 2004).

67 *Blekinge Folkblad,* 15th August 1908.

68 *Blekinge Folkblad,* 2nd December 1904.

69 Arbetarekommun minutes, 25th June 1899. A suffrage society (*rösträttsförening*) was one of the organisations which was involved in the foundation of the *arbetarekommun* in 1896. It was the view of some *kommun* members that such a society was not necessary once the SAP had adopted uni-

versal suffrage as one of the main points in their party programme: Arbetarekommun minutes, 14th June 1898.

70 *Blekinge Folkblad,* 8th September 1905.

71 *Blekinge Folkblad,* 30th July 1908.

72 Arbetarekommun minutes, 15th October 1906; *Blekinge Folkblad,* 12th
March 1907.

73 Arbetarekommun minutes, 18th March 1910.

74 *Blekinge Folkblad,* 23rd May 1910.

75 *Blekinge Folkblad,* 30th March 1910.

76 *Blekinge Folkblad,* 2nd September 1911.

77 *Blekinge Folkblad,* 4th September 1911.

78 *Blekinge Folkblad,* 5th August 1911.

79 Lotta Gröning, *Vägen till makten. SAP:s organisation och dess betydelse för
den politiska verksamheten 1900–1933* (Uppsala, 1988), p. 31.

80 Ericson, *Från fyrkvälde till folkmakt,* p. 29.

81 Ericson, *Från fyrkvälde till folkmakt,* pp. 29–30.

82 Arbetarekommun styrelsen minutes, 14th February 1904, 16th November
1905. See Stig Hadenius, Jan-Olof Seveborg and Lennart Weibull,
Socialdemokratisk press och presspolitik 1899–1909 (Stockholm, 1968), p. 75.

83 Ericsson, *Från fyrkvälde till folkmakt,* pp. 29–30.

84 This figure fell to 2300 in 1909, however, as a result of the unsuccessful
general strike. See pp. 202–203.

85 Gröning, *Vägen till makten,* p. 31.

86 Arbetarekommun minutes, 12th April 1901, 15th April 1901.

87 Arbetarekommun minutes, 12th April 1901. In the event the *kommun* organised a demonstration for 12th May, following the party's lead.

88 Arbetarekommun styrelsen minutes, 12th May 1902; Arbetarekommun
minutes, 13th May 1902.

89 Arbetarekommun styrelsen minutes, 14th May 1905, 15th May 1905, 16th
May 1905. The *kommun* also held a demonstration in response to the
national executive's call for action following the Russian revolution in 1905.

90 Arbetarekommun minutes, 5th April 1901.

91 Arbetarekommun styrelsen minutes, 16th November 1905.

92 Arbetarekommun minutes, 2nd March 1904.

93 Arbetarekommun styrelsen minutes, 21st December 1905.

94 Arbetarekommun minutes, 4th January 1906; *Blekinge Folkblad,* 5th January 1906.

95 Arbetarekommun minutes, 27th November 1906; *Blekinge Folkblad,* 30th
November 1906.

96 Arbetarekommun styrelsen minutes, 9th January 1907, 6th February 1907,
20th March 1907. 702 members took part in the voting, of which 593
voted *yes* and 102 *no.*

97 Arbetarekommun styrelsen minutes, 25th June 1908.

98 Arbetarekommun minutes, 30th June 1908.

99 Arbetarekommun minutes, 23rd August 1911; Arbetarekommun styrelsen minutes, 8th June 1911, 25th September 1911.
100 Arbetarekommun minutes, 25th October 1896, 14th February 1897, 4th April 1899.
101 Arbetarekommun minutes 18th July 1898.
102 Arbetarekommun minutes, 7th February 1899.
103 Arbetarekommun minutes, 8th May 1900, 5th July 1900.
104 Arbetarekommun minutes 3rd May 1902, 25th May 1902. It was reported that negotiations between workers and employers had broken down, but that the sweeps were seeking the approval of the *kommun* betore going ahead with their strike. This was agreed, and arrangements were made to set up a strike fund. A few weeks later, it was reported that the strike was over and the conflict had been settled satisfactorily with a new agreement on pay, conditions and working hours.
105 Arbetarekommun minutes, 24th March 1907; Arbetarekommun styrelsen minutes, 3rd April 1907, 2nd May 1907.
106 Ericsson, *Från fyrkvälde till folkmakt*, p. 33.
107 Arbetarekommun minutes, 24th September 1909; Arbetarekommun styrelsen minutes, 20th December 1909.
108 The Metalworkers' Union had a very successful year in 1907, when its membership rose from 63 in 1906 to 381, mainly due to its success recruiting in the dockyard. Following the failure of its wage negotiations, membership fell back to 87 in 1908, and this was more than halved after the strike in 1909. *Metall avdelning 96 jubileumsskrift.*
109 Berg, *Karlskrona Grovarbetarefackförening.*
110 Arbetarekommun minutes, 17th February 1908; Arbetarekommun styrelsen minutes, 4th March 1908, 1st March 1909.
111 Arbetarekommun styrelsen minutes, 10th January 1911.
112 Arbetarekommun minutes, 6th October 1910, Arbetarekommun styrelsen minutes, 10th January 1912.
113 Arbetarekommun minutes, 16th June 1913.
114 Arbetarekommun minutes, 14th June 1898, 4th September 1902; Arbetarekommun styrelsen minutes, 30th July 1902.
115 Arbetarekommun minutes, 15th September 1903; Arbetarekommun styrelsen minutes, 13th November 1903, 29th December 1903.
116 Arbetarekommun minutes, 20th April 1902.
117 See chapter 7, p. 207.
118 *Blekinge Läns Tidning,* 4th May 1896. C J Björklund, *Första maj och första maj demonstrationerna* (Stockholm, 1996), p. 44.
119 Arbetarekommun styrelsen minutes, 23rd March 1903.
120 Björklund, *Första maj,* p. 112.
121 Arbetarekommun styrelsen minutes, 2nd April 1903.
122 Folkrörelsearkiv i Blekinge län, Folkets Hus arkiv: samlingsvolym 1899–1963.

123 Arbetarekommun minutes, 8th October 1896, 24th May 1897.

124 Arbetarekommun minutes, 7th October 1898; 10th September 1901, 19th June 1903. It was reported in June 1903 that the boycott had not been as effective as was hoped, but it was decided to continue it anyway.

125 Arbetarekommun minutes, 10th September 1901.

126 *Blekinge Folkblad,* 26th August 1904, 2nd September 1904, 16th September 1904.

127 KVAF minutes, 10th September 1900, 29th March 1900, 29th March 1901, 15th April 1901, 3rd January 1902.

128 KVAF minutes, 16th May 1902.

129 KVAF minutes, 17th October 1902.

130 *Blekinge Folkblad,* 1st September 1905, 26th September 1905.

131 *Blekinge Folkblad,* 29th September 1908; *Karlskrona Weckoblad,* 27th September 1908. Emphasis in the original.

7. Naval Politics in Karlskrona c. 1911–1921

1 For the interest in Karl XII, the Karolinska Förbundet and the commemoration of the 200th anniversary of the Battle of Poltava, see Nils Elvander, *Harald Hjärne och konservatismen. Konservativ idédebatt i Sverige 1865–1922* (Uppsala, 1961), pp. 419ff.

2 For example, *Karlskrona Weckoblad,* 21st June 1894 described the launch of the minesweeper *Gudur,* in the presence of 'the naval minister, the commander-in-chief, and many officers of all ranks together with a large number of other interested parties.'

3 Förening Gamla Carlscrona, *1:a maj-reveljen i Karlskrona: ett 20-årigt perspektiv* (Karlskrona, 2000).

4 *Karlskrona-Tidningen,* 2nd May 1914.

5 *Karlskrona-Tidningen,* 6th September 1911.

6 *Karlskrona-Tidningen,* 6th September 1911, 8th September 1911.

7 *Blekinge Läns Tidning,* 9th September 1911.

8 *Blekinge Folkblad,* 9th September 1911.

9 *Karlskrona Weckoblad,* 14th September 1905.

10 See pp. 188–189.

11 *Karlskrona Weckoblad,* 2nd September 1908.

12 *Blekinge Folkblad,* 1st September 1905, 26th September 1905.

13 *Blekinge Läns Tidning,* October 1908, *passim.* A new poll was held in December 1908, and the original winner, the Liberal Ulrik Leander, increased his majority.

14 *Karlskrona Weckoblad,* 2nd September 1908.

15 *Karlskrona Weckoblad,* 22nd September 1908. A correspondent to the newspaper wrote that, 'every grant towards [defence], and all the money which is used for it, benefits our community, and is useful to its citizens, trade and business, and consequently any potential riksdagsman must see it as his foremost duty to work for something of vital necessity to this com-

munity, and not concern himself with such unimportant, not to say unnecessary questions such as introducing absolute veto and votes for women.'

16 *Karlskrona Weckoblad,* 22nd September 1908.

17 Ulrik Leander, *En fängelsedirektörs minnen* (Stockholm, 1936), p. 298.

18 *Karlskrona Weckoblad,* 25th September 1908.

19 *Karlskrona Weckoblad,* 2nd September 1908.

20 *Karlskrona Weckoblad,* 2nd September 1908, 9th September 1908, 11th September 1908. Leander later sought to justify his actions in his memoirs. 'In connection with the question of [state] pensions (*den allmänna folkpensioneringen*),' he wrote, 'I expressed my opinion that the state ought to show especial consideration to those who were directly employed in its service. By this I meant above all the large group of dockyard workers in Karlskrona, but also others who worked for the state. A few days' annual leave for dockyard workers depending on length of service would not be out of place either, I thought. But I should have kept this to myself. By doing this I had bent myself to the dockyard workers, thrown blue dust in their eyes and dragged their votes from them. At election time people grab the arguments... that they find closest to hand in order to defeat their political opponents... At all events, I considered that I had the right to say what I thought about the dockyard workers' pensions, since I was entirely serious in what I said.' Leander, *En fängelsedirektörs minnen,* p. 310.

21 *Blekinge Folkblad,* 7th November 1907.

22 *Blekinge Folkblad,* 22nd March 1913.

23 *Blekinge Folkblad,* 10th January 1914.

24 Announcement placed by SAP Blekinge district *styrelsen,* in *Blekinge Folkblad,* 28th January 1914.

25 *Blekinge Folkblad,* 9th February 1914.

26 *Karlskrona-Tidningen* (6th March 1914) reported on a Liberal meeting in Stockholm under the headline 'Cheers for republicanism at Staaff demonstration.'

27 Peter Essaiasson, *Svenska valkampanjer 1866–1988* (Stockholm, 1990), pp. 114, 116.

28 In Karlskrona these included the Women's Union for Sweden's Naval Defence (*Kvinnoförbundet för Sveriges sjöförsvar*), with 125 members; the Association of Independent Defence Supporters (*Föreningen frisinnade försvarsvänner*), campaigning to keep politics out of the defence question; Young Sweden Union (*Ungsvenska förbundet*) and Peasants' March Defence Union (*Bondetågets försvarsförbund*). *Karlskrona-Tidningen,* 4th March 1914, 14th March 1914, 17th March 1914, 21st March 1914.

29 *Karlskrona-Tidningen,* 4th September 1914.

30 *Blekinge Folkblad,* 5th September 1914.

31 *Blekinge Läns Tidning,* 2nd September 1914.

32 *Karlskrona-Tidningen,* 18th August 1914.

33 Ann Hörsell, 'Från segel och trä till ånga och stål', in Erik Norberg, ed., *Karlskronavarvets historia,* vol. 2, 1866–1992 (Karlskrona, 1993), pp. 7–80: 53, 64.

34 Björn Gäfvert, 'Kontinuitet i föränderlig omvärld', in Norberg, ed., *Karlskronavarvets historia,* pp. 81–134: 81.

35 Gäfvert, 'Kontinuitet i föränderlig omvärld', p. 87.

36 Right party election leaflet, issued with *Karlskrona-Tidningen,* 28th March 1914. The address asked, 'What influence would the Staaff programme have for Karlskrona and its environs? It would be the ruin of our community.' Emphasis in original.

37 Right party election leaflet, *Karlskrona-Tidningen,* 28th March 1914.

38 *Blekinge Läns Tidning,* 26th March 1914.

39 *Karlskrona-Tidningen,* 27th March 1914.

40 *Karlskrona-Tidningen,* 9th March 1914; *Blekinge Läns Tidning,* 10th March 1914.

41 *Blekinge Läns Tidning,* 10th March 1914, 13th March 1914, 21st March 1914.

42 *Blekinge Läns Tidning,* 17th March 1914.

43 *Blekinge Läns Tidning,* 28th March 1914.

44 *Karlskrona-Tidningen,* 29th March 1914.

45 *Blekinge Läns Tidning,* 24th March 1914.

46 Marinmusei arkiv, Karlskrona, Statsanställdas förbund avd 2136 arkiv, MVAF minutes, 12th March 1914.

47 MVAF minutes, 6th March 1915.

48 MVAF minutes, 6th March 1915.

49 Folkrörelsearkiv i Blekinge län, FCPF incoming correspondence, Dockyard departments to varvschefen, n.d. (early 1916).

50 Varvschefen to KMF, 24th November 1914.

51 Head of Engineering Department to varvschefen, 28th July 1914.

52 Head of Buildings Department to varvschefen, 3rd February 1916.

53 *Blekinge Folkblad,* 21st June 1915.

54 MVAF minutes, 6th March 1916, 16th October 1916.

55 Varvschefen to KMF, 31st March 1916.

56 MVAF minutes, 29th April 1917.

57 Krigsarkivet, KÖV, Varvschefens kansli, serie F VII b, Handlingar ang arbetares löner, volym I: Kungl. Maj:t to KMF, 16th May 1917 (copy).

58 MVAF minutes, 4th January 1918.

59 FCPF outgoing correspondence, Karlskrona branch to Kungl Maj:t 25th August 1921; ARAB: FCPF Medlemsbladet, March 1922; Thorvald Pettersson, *Historik över Försvarsverkens civila personals förbunds avdelning 36* (Karlskrona, 1936), p. 11.

60 Marinmusei arkiv, Statsanställdas förbund avd 2136: Medlemsmatrikel Serie E I a: 2 (1913–1918).

61 MVAF minutes, 7th March 1913. Different representatives were elected for the following: fitters' shop, machine shop, plating shop, smithy, new docks,

electrical shop, slips, machine department, torpedo shop, mine shop, tailors' shop, shoemakers' shop, boatbuilders' shop, old docks, foundry, buildings office, and the armoury.

62 Kaj Björk, *Försvarsverkens civila personals förbund 1917–1942* (Stockholm, 1943), p. 49.

63 MVAF minutes, 8th September 1916.

64 MVAF minutes, 12th October 1918, 13th September 1919.

65 FCPF incoming correspondence, Nyström to Karlskrona branch, 8th April 1917. In an editorial article in the members' newsletter, written in 1925, Edoff Andersson condemned the existence of 'local patriotism' within the trade union movement, which meant that, through their misplaced loyalty to their local branches, members were apt to misunderstand the wider implications of the federation and the movement. Medlemsbladet, October 1925.

66 Folkrörelsearkiv i Blekinge län, Statsanställdas Förbund avd 2136: Serie A I:2, Torped departementets verkstadsklubb protokollsbok, 1915–20.

67 Medlemsbladet, November 1925.

68 FCPF outgoing correspondence: report on branch membership 14th February 1929.

69 The question of LO affiliation was first discussed by the branch in 1917. The meeting agreed to investigate the rules for membership, but to take no further action for the present. MVAF minutes, 12th January 1917.

70 Edoff Andersson, *Försvarsverkens civila personals förbund 10 år* (Stockholm, 1927), p. 11.

71 MVAF minutes: möte med samtliga Warvets arbetare, 14th February 1913. Although the KVAF and MVAF minutes were archived together, there is a gap between 1910 and 1913.

72 Magnus Wikdahl, *Varvets tid. Arbetarliv och kulturell förändring i en skeppsbyggarstad* (Stockholm, 1992).

73 As one local historian has remarked, 'It is a good question whether any other place in our country was affected so tangibly by the outbreak of war as Karlskrona.' Hillbom, *Karlskrona 300 år*, p. 7.

74 *Blekinge Läns Tidning*, 3rd August 1914.

75 *Blekinge Läns Tidning*, 5th August 1914.

76 *Blekinge Läns Tidning*, 6th August 1914, 11th August 1914; *Blekinge Folkblad*, 6th August 1914.

77 *Blekinge Folkblad*, 6th August 1914.

78 Citizens were asked to leave the town, 'and thereby avoid burdening the town's food supply, which would of course be requisitioned due to the strengthened garrison.' *Blekinge Folkblad*, 6th August 1914.

79 *Blekinge Folkblad*, 8th August 1914.

80 Rune Bokholm, *Städernas handlingsfrihet. En studie av expansionsskedet 1900–1930* (Lund, 1995), p. 212.

81 Hillbom, *Karlskrona 300 år*, p. 7.

82 Arbetarekommun minutes, 13th February 1917.
83 Carl Göran Andræ, 'The Swedish Labor Movement and the 1917–1918 Revolution' in Steven Koblik, *Sweden's Development from Poverty to Affluence, 1750–1970*, translated Joanne Johnson (Minneapolis, 1975), pp. 232–253: 232; *Blekinge Folkblad*, March 1917, *passim*.
84 SAP district executive committee call to demonstrate, printed in *Blekinge Folkblad*, 25th April 1917.
85 Arbetarekommun call to demonstrate, printed in *Blekinge Folkblad*, 2nd April 1917.
86 SAP district executive committee call to demonstrate *Blekinge Folkblad*, 25th April 1917.
87 *Blekinge Folkblad*, 23rd April 1917.
88 *Blekinge Folkblad*, 28th April 1917.
89 *Blekinge Folkblad*, 28th April 1917.
90 Arbetarekommun minutes, 26th April 1917.
91 *Blekinge Folkblad*, 30th April 1917.
92 *Blekinge Folkblad*, 30th April 1917, 3rd May 1917; MVAF minutes, 11th May 1917.
93 *Blekinge Folkblad*, 3rd May 1917.
94 *Blekinge Folkblad*, 3rd May 1917.
95 A Påhlman and W Sjölin, *Kooperationen i Karlskrona, 1869–1939*, (Stockholm, 1940).
96 *Blekinge Folkblad*, 3rd February 1915.
97 Other slogans were 'Bread to the people' and 'For peace and brotherhood'. *Blekinge Folkblad*, 3rd May 1915.
98 Arbetarekommun minutes, 13th February 1917, 28th June 1917, 21st December 1918.
99 *Blekinge Folkblad*, 22nd November 1915.
100 *Blekinge Folkblad*, 11th October 1915.
101 *Blekinge Folkblad*, 19th July 1915.
102 Arbetarekommun minutes, 21st December 1918; MVAF minutes, 31st January 1916, 8th December 1916.
103 *Blekinge Folkblad*, 19th July 1915, 11th October 1915; Arbetarekommun minutes, 25th January 1917, 13th February 1917.
104 Arbetarekommun styrelsen minutes, 7th August 1917.
105 Arbetarekommun minutes, 9th August 1917, 19th February 1918; Arbetarekommun styrelsen minutes, 7th August 1918, 3rd February 1918.
106 Arbetarekommun minutes, 6th July 1914.
107 Börje Henningsson, 'Humanism, anarkism och socialism. Varför splittrades det socialdemokratiska vänsterpartiet?', in *Arbetarhistoria*, 80–81 (1996–7), pp. 25–36; Carl Göran Andræ, *Revolt eller reform. Sverige inför revolutionerna i Europa 1917–1918* (Stockholm, 1998).
108 Ericson, *Från fyrkvälde till folkmakt*, p. 49.
109 Arbetarekommun minutes, 18th January 1917.

110 One speaker suggested that differences had been overemphasised because 'academics had come into the party for the sake of provocation.' Arbetarekommun minutes, 18th January 1917.
111 Arbetarekommun styrelsen minutes, 28th March 1917.
112 Arbetarekommun minutes, 31st July 1917.
113 Arbetarekommun styrelsen minutes, 7th February 1918, 13th February 1918, 14th August 1918, 16th August 1918, 20th August 1918.
114 *Blekinge Folkblad*, 2nd May 1918.
115 Arbetarekommun styrelsen minutes, 22nd January 1919.
116 Arbetarekommun styrelsen minutes, 2nd February 1919, 4th February 1919.
117 Folkrörelsearkiv i Blekinge län: Blekinge distrikt av Svenska demokratiska vänstern. Protokoll book 1918–1926: vänsterkommun minutes, 15th November 1925.
118 Vänsterkommun minutes, 24th January 1926.
119 Vänsterkommun minutes, 25th April 1926.
120 *Blekinge Folkblad*, 2nd May 1918.
121 Medlemsbladet, March 1920.
122 The union leadership also opposed an attempt to found a Defence Workers' Social Democratic Club in Stockholm, stating that they had nothing against workers' political engagement, but felt that there were already enough political organisations outside the workplace, and they emphasised again the need to keep trade and politics separate. Medlemsbladet, May 1923.
123 MVAF minutes, 18th June 1913.
124 MVAF minutes, 8th October 1914.
125 MVAF minutes, 19th July 1915.
126 MVAF minutes, 16th March 1916.
127 MVAF minutes, 13th April 1917, 26th April 1917, 10th August 1917, 28th August 1917.
128 Arbetarekommun minutes, 26th January 1918; Arbetarekommun styrelsen minutes, 27th February 1918.
129 MVAF minutes, 8th March 1918.
130 *Blekinge Folkblad*, 25th March 1918.
131 Folkrörelsearkiv 1984/67: Upprop till varvets arbetare, 1917; MVAF minutes, 10th August 1917.
132 Gäfvert, 'Kontinuitet i föränderlig omvärld', p. 82.
133 Gäfvert, 'Kontinuitet i föränderlig omvärld', p. 87.
134 *Blekinge Folkblad*, 31st January 1916.
135 Karlskrona kommunarkiv: Kommittéen utsedd att följa Örlogsvarvets verksamhet: Protokoll med handlingar, 1919–1920, stadsfullmäktige meeting, 19th July 1919, § 13.
136 Gäfvert, 'Kontinuitet i föränderlig omvärld', pp. 83–84.
137 Gäfvert, 'Kontinuitet i föränderlig omvärld', p. 86.

138 Folkrörelsearkiv i Blekinge län: Socialdemokratiska fullmäktigegruppen, Karlskrona, Protokoll, 1919–1934: 2nd April 1919.

139 This provoked angry allegations of unfair competition from the Swedish Shipbuilding Association (Sveriges Varvsindustriförening). The naval authorities denied this, arguing that they were taking on private work for military ends, principally the need to maintain a competent workforce in readiness for military goals. Gäfvert, 'Kontinuitet i föränderlig omvärld', p. 89.

140 Folkrörelsearkiv i Blekinge län: Socialdemokratiska fullmäktigegruppen, Karlskrona, protokoll: 9th December 1924.

141 Marinmusei arkiv: Statsanställdas förbund avd 2136: Medlemsmatrikel 1913–1918.

8. Conclusion

1 Peter Baldwin, 'Comparing and Generalizing: Why All History is Comparative, Yet No History is Sociology', in Deborah Cohen and Maura O'Connor, eds, *Comparison and History: Europe in Cross-National Perspective* (New York and Abingdon, 2004), pp. 1–22: 1–2.

2 Marc Bloch, 'Toward a Comparative History of European Societies', in Frederic C Lane and Jelle C Riermersma, eds, *Enterprise and Secular Change: Readings in Economic History* (Homewood, Illinois, 1953; first published 1928), pp. 494–521; for an attempt to develop such a method for labour history see Marcel van der Linden, 'Doing Comparative Labour History: Some Preliminaries', in *idem., Transnational Labour History: Explorations* (Aldershot, 2003), pp. 173–196.

3 Deborah Cohen and Maura O'Connor, 'Comparative History, Cross-National History, Transnational History – Definitions', in *idem*, eds, *Comparison and History*, pp. ix–xxiv: xii.

4 Patrick Joyce, *Visions of the People: Industrial England and the Question of Class, 1848–1914* (Cambridge, 1991); James Vernon, *Politics and the People: A Study in English Political Culture, c. 1815–1867* (Cambridge, 1993).

5 Eugenio F Biagini, and Alastair J Reid, eds, *Currents of Radicalism: Popular Radicalism, Organised Labour and Party Politics in Britain, 1850–1914* (Cambridge, 1991); Eugenio Biagini, *Liberty, Retrenchment and Reform: Popular Liberalism in the Age of Gladstone, 1860–1880* (Cambridge, 1992).

6 Andrew Chadwick, *Augmenting Democracy: Political Movements and Constitutional Reform during the Rise of Labour, 1900–1914* (Aldershot, 1999). Logie Barrow and Ian Bullock, *Democratic Ideas and the British Labour Movement, 1880–1914* (Cambridge, 1996).

7 This also has contemporary political resonances, with the architects of New Labour arguing for the importance of Liberalism in the political inheritance of the Labour Party. See Steven Fielding, 'New Labour and the Past', in Duncan Tanner, Pat Thane and Nick Tiratsoo, eds, *Labour's First Century* (Cambridge, 2000), pp. 367–392: 375–6.

8 See for example Øystein Sørensen and Bo Stråth, eds, *The Cultural Construction of* Norden (Oslo, 1997).

9 Eric Hobsbawm, *Interesting Times: A Twentieth-Century Life* (London, 2002), p. 294, cited in Lars Berggren, 'Går det att skriva arbetarhistoriska synteser?', *Historisk Tidskrift* (S) (2003), pp. 181–200: 182–3.

10 Aristide R Zolberg, 'How Many Exceptionalisms?' in Ira Katznelson and Aristide R Zolberg, eds, *Working-Class Formation: Nineteenth-Century Patterns in Western Europe and the United States* (Princeton, New Jersey, 1986), pp. 397–455.

11 These terms are difficult to translate. The dictionary translation of *egensinne* is indeed wilfulness, but the term implies lack of control over oneself or self-discipline. *Skötsamhet* is translated by Ronny Ambjörnsson as 'conscientiousness' which does indeed convey some of the meaning, but I find the term rather cumbersome. The nineteenth century British equivalent of Ambjörnsson's *skötsamme arbetaren* is undoubtedly the 'respectable artisan'. In English the dichotomy is best summed up as the distinction between rough culture and respectability.

12 See Lars Edgren, *Lärling – gesäll – mästare: hantverk och hantverkare i Malmö 1750–1847* (Lund, 1987); Lars Magnusson, *Den bråkiga kulturen: förläggare och smideshantverkare i Eskilstuna 1800–1850* (Stockholm, 1988).

13 Lars Berggren, *Ångvisslans och brickornas värld. Om arbete och facklig organisering vid Kockums mekaniska verkstad och Carl Lunds fabrik i Malmö 1840–1905* (Lund, 1991); Björn Horgby, *Egensinne och skötsamhet. Arbetarkulturen i Norrköping 1850–1940* (Stockholm, 1993). For respectability among British workers see Keith McClelland, 'Time to Work, Time to Live: Some Aspects of Work and the Re-Formation of Class in Britain, 1850–1880', in Patrick Joyce, ed., *The Historical Meanings of Work* (Cambridge, 1987), pp. 180–209.

14 Ronny Ambjörnsson, *Den skötsamme arbetaren. Idéer och ideal i ett norrländskt sågverkssamhälle 1880–1930* (Stockholm, 1998; first published 1988).

15 Horgby, *Egensinne och skötsamhet*; Mats Franzén, 'Egensinne och skötsamhet i svensk arbetakultur. Kommentarer till *Den skötsamme arbetaren* av Ronny Ambjörnsson', *Arkiv för studier i arbetarrörelsens historia*, 48–49 (1991), pp. 3–20: 10, 12–13; Birgitta Skarin Frykman, 'Arbetarkultur och arbetarkulturforskning', *Arkiv för studier i arbetarrörelsens historia*, 48–49 (1991), pp. 21–46: 27.

16 See though Jon Lawrence's analysis of the addresses of labour activists in Wolverhampton, which suggests that Labour politicians were under-represented in the most solidly working-class wards. Jon Lawrence, *Speaking for the People: Party, Language and Popular Politics in England, 1867–1914* (Cambridge, 1998), pp. 132–133.

17 The former Liberal *riksdagsman* Ulrik Leander wrote of his time as Karlskrona prison director that he had noticed that a large number of tramps visited the town. When he asked one of these men why he had come all

313

the way to Karlskrona, in this case all the way from Dalarna, the response was, "Where should a poor wanderer wend his way if not to Karlskrona, town of dreams? For there a man can get the strongest drink, the largest drink and the cheapest drink in the whole of the Swedish kingdom." Ulrik Leander, *En fångelsedirektörs minnen* (Stockholm, 1936), p. 282.

18 Göran Salmonsson, *Den förståndiga viljan. Svenska Järn- och metallarbetareförbundet 1888–1902* (Uppsala, 1998).

19 Frank Trentmann, 'Bread, Milk and Democracy: Consumption and Citizenship in Twentieth-Century Britain', in Martin Daunton and Matthew Hilton, eds, *The Politics of Consumption: Material Culture and Citizenship in Europe and America* (Oxford, 2001), pp. 129–163: 130, 134–5, 139.

20 Belinda Davis, 'Food Scarcity and the Empowerment of the Female Consumer in World War I Berlin', in Victoria de Grazia with Ellen Furlough, eds, *The Sex of Things: Gender and Consumption in Historical Perspective* (Berkeley, LA, 1996), pp. 287–310: 289.

21 Samuel Edquist, *Nyktra svenskar. Godtemplarrörelsen och den nationella identiteten 1879–1918* (Uppsala, 2001); Paul Ward, Red Flag and Union Jack: Englishness, Patriotism and the British Left, 1881–1924 (Woodbridge, 1998).

Maps

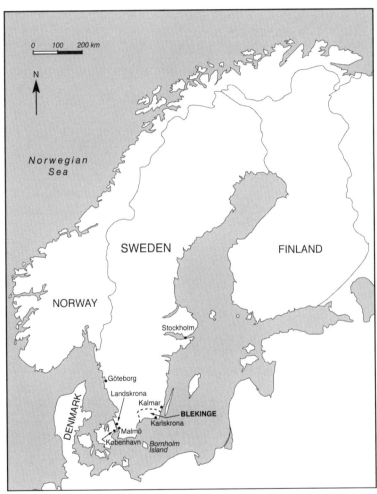

Map 1. Karlskrona, the Baltic and some major Swedish industrial towns, c. 1900.

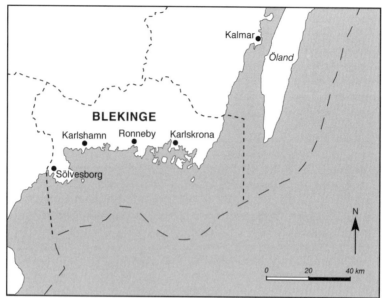

Map 2. Karlskrona and Blekinge.

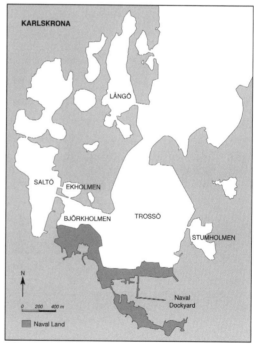

Map 3. Karlskrona.

Map 4. British naval dockyard towns.

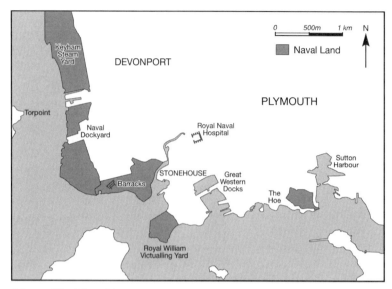

Map 5. The Three Towns.

Tables

TABLE 4.1. *Parliamentary Election Results, Plymouth and Devonport, 1892–1910.*

PLYMOUTH, 1892–1910 (2 MEMBERS ELECTED)

Date	Candidate	Party	Votes	% of vote	Electors	Turnout
1892	Sir E G Clarke	Con	5 081	25.5	12 431	81.1
	Sir W G Pearce Bt	Con	5 081	25.5		
	C Harrison	Lib	4 921	24.6		
	G Lidgett	Lib	4 861	24.4		
1895	Sir E G Clarke*	Con	5 575	25.6	13 460	81.8
	C Harrison	Lib	5 482	25.1		
	Hon E Hubbard	Con	5 456	25.0		
	S F Mendl	Lib	5 298	24.3		
1898 (by-election)	S F Mendl	Lib	5 966	50.7	13 223	89.0
	Hon I C Guest	Con	5 802	49.3		
1900 (by-election)	Hon I C Guest	Con	unopp-osed			
1900	H E Duke	Con	6 009	26.4	13 566	84.8
	Hon I C Guest*	Con	6 005	26.4		
	S F Mendl*	Lib	5 460	24.0		
	H de R Walker	Lib	5 264	23.2		
1906	T W Dobson	Lib	9 021	29.4	18 196	85.3
	C E Mallet	Lib	8 914	29.0		
	H E Duke*	Con	6 547	21.3		
	H G Smith	Con	6 234	20.3		
1910 (Jan)	C E Mallet*	Lib	8 091	25.8	18 085	87.9
	A Williams	Lib	7 961	25.5		
	W W Astor	Con	7 650	24.5		
	Rt Hon Sir H M Durand	Con	7 556	24.2		
1910 (Dec)	W W Astor	Con	8 113	26.4	18 085	85.5
	A S Benn	Con	7 942	25.9		
	C E Mallet*	Lib	7 379	24.0		
	A Williams*	Lib	7 260	23.7		

DEVONPORT, 1892–1910 (2 MEMBERS ELECTED)						
Date	Candidate	Party	Votes	% of vote	Electors	Turnout
1892	H E Kearley	Lib	3 354	26.4	7 692	83.6
	E J C Morton	Lib	3 325	26.3		
	G E Price	Con	3 012	23.8		
	R Harvey	Con	2 972	23.5		
1895	H E Kearley*	Lib	3 570	26.2	7 911	86.9
	E J C Morton*	Lib	3 511	25.7		
	P H P Wippell	Con	3 303	24.2		
	T U Thynne	Con	3 263	23.9		
1900	H E Kearley*	Lib	3 626	25.9	8 351	85.1
	E J C Morton*	Lib	3 538	25.2		
	J Lockie	Con	3 458	24.7		
	F E McCormick-Goodhart	Con	3 394	24.2		
1902 (by-election)	J Lockie	Con	3 785	50.2	8 946	84.3
	Hon T A Brassey	Lib	3 757	49.8		
1904 (by-election)	J W Benn	Lib	6 219	54.6	14 379	79.3
	Sir J Jackson	Con	5 179	45.4		
1906	H E Kearley*	Lib	6 923	29.1	14 978	81.4
	J W Benn*	Lib	6 527	27.5		
	Sir J Jackson	Con	5 239	22.0		
	F Holme-Sumner	Con	5 080	21.4		
1910 (Jan)	Sir J Jackson	Con	5 658	26.7	12 125	89.2
	Sir C Kinloch-Cooke	Con	5 286	24.9		
	Sir J W Benn*	Lib	5 146	24.2		
	S Lithgow	Lib	5 140	24.2		
1910 (Dec)	Sir J Jackson*	Con	5 170	26.0	12 125	83.0
	Sir C Kinloch-Cooke*	Con	5 111	25.7		
	S Lithgow	Lib	4 841	24.3		
	G Baring	Lib	4 782	24.0		

Members elected shown in **bold**. *denotes retiring member.

SOURCE: F W S Craig, *British Parliamentary Election Results 1885–1918* (London, 1974).

TABLE 4.2. *Political Affiliation of Plymouth Borough Council Members, 1896–1913.*

NO. OF ALDERMEN AND COUNCILLORS, BY PARTY						
Year	Con	Lib	Ind	Lab	SDF	RA
1896	14	21	4			
1897	11	24	4			
1898	18	17	4			
1899	29	25	2			
1900	26	28	2			
1901	24	31	1			
1902	24	31	1			
1903	23	32	1			
1904	21	32	2	1		
1905	22	29	3	1	1	
1906	21	28	3	1	1	2
1907	17	27	5	1	6	
1908	14	27	8		7	
1909	14	28	8		6	
1910	15	29	8		4	
1911	21	27	4		4	
1912	22	25	5		4	
1913	23	25	4		4	

Key
Con = Conservative/Unionist
Lib = Liberal
Ind = Independent
Lab = Labour Representation Association
SDF = Social Democratic Federation
RA = Ratepayers' Association
Note: The figures for 1896–98 do not include aldermen.

SOURCE: *Western Morning News* and *Western Daily Mercury,* 1896–1913.

TABLE 4.3. *Political Affiliation of Devonport Borough Council Members, 1895–1913.*

NO. OF ALDERMEN AND COUNCILLORS, BY PARTY				
Year	Con	Lib	Ind	Lab
1895	25	23		
1896	24	24		
1897	21	27	0	
1898	17	31	0	
1899	21	27	0	
1900	32	28	0	
1901	32	28	0	
1902	30	24	5	1
1903	26	32	0	2
1905	14	23	6	2
1906	18	39	1	2
1907	20	36	1	3
1908	24	24	0	2
1909	30	28	0	2
1909	35	24	0	1
1910	32	18	0	1
1911	36	24	0	
1912	35	24	1	
1913	36	23	1	

Key
Con = Conservative/Unionist
Lib = Liberal
Ind = Independent
Lab = Labour Representation Association
Note: The figures for 1904 and 1910 do not include aldermen.

SOURCE: *Western Morning News* and *Western Daily Mercury,* 1895–1913.

TABLE 5.1. *Parliamentary Election Results in the Three Plymouth Constituencies, 1918.*

Candidate	Party	Votes	% share of vote
Plymouth Sutton (turnout 59.6%)			
Hon W Astor*	Coalition Conservative	17 091	65.9
W T Gay	Labour and Co-operative	5 334	20.6
S Ransom	Liberal	3 488	13.5
Plymouth Devonport (turnout 67.2%)			
Sir K Kinloch-Cooke*	Coalition Conservative	13 240	62.2
F Bramley	Labour	4 115	19.3
S Lithgow	Liberal	3 930	18.5
Plymouth Drake (turnout 54.7%)			
Sir A S Benn*	Coalition Conservative	17 188	73.4
T W Dobson	Liberal	6 225	26.6
*denotes retiring member			

SOURCE: F W S Craig, *British Parliamentary Election Results, 1918–1949* (Glasgow, 1969).

TABLE 5.2. *Result of Plymouth Sutton By-Election, 15th November, 1919.*

Candidate	Party	Votes	% share of vote
Viscountess Astor	Coalition Conservative	14 495	33.3
W T Gay	Labour and Co-operative	9 292	20.6
I Foot	Liberal	4 239	14.8
Turnout 72.5%			

SOURCE: F W S Craig, *British Parliamentary Election Results, 1918–1949* (Glasgow, 1969).

TABLE 5.3. *Political Affiliation of Council Members, 1914–1924.*
Amalgamated Council, incorporating Plymouth and Devonport Borough Councils, and Stonehouse District Council.

Year	Conservative	Liberal	Labour and Co-operative	Independent	Citizens Ass.
1914	48	30	1	1	0
1919	44	24	10	1	1
1920	43	21	12	2	2
1921	48	15	11	6	0
1922	55	16	4	5	0
1923	53	16	7	4	0

SOURCE: *Western Morning News* and *Western Daily Mercury*, 1914, 1919–1923.

TABLE 6.8. Organisations affiliated to Karlskrona arbetarekommun, 1897–1914. SOURCE: Karlskrona arbetarekommun protokoll, passim.

	1897	1898	1899	1900	1901	1902	1903	1904	1905	1906	1907	1908	1909	1910	1911	1912	1913	1914
Shoemakers' union	48	48	55	55	55	55	53	43	32	48	42	37	28	29	24	29		31
Tobacco workers' union	21	27	33	20	15	15	15	15	32	70	49	63	45	26	29		43	
Painters' union	24	20	21	29	34	42	45	50	60	70	74	71	65	52	42	25		
Tilemakers' union	16	25	26	27	25	32	39	42	51	54	53	51	27	29	28	23	27	
Bricklayers' union	30	30	25	25	34	32	80	56	38	28	43	29	18					
Joiners' union					19	24	17	19	20	21	26	24	17	17	16	13	13	
Bakery workers' union					32	36	32	33	35	30	37	41	38					
Tailors' union					31	45	44	40	45	54	46	35	33	42	34	38	30	35
Tanners' union					12	15	15	15	15	15	15	15	15	15	15			
Tinsmiths' union					17	12	17	17	14	24	19	18	14	5	5	5	5	5
Carpenters' union					23	18	21	19	15	15	17	22	16	5	5			
Hatmakers' union					24	28	27	26	14	36	26			14				
Bookbinders' union					4	5	5	6										
Iron and metal-workers' union					16	26	25	30	15	61	381	87	41	38	40	48	60	51
Chimney sweeps' union					7	7	7	8	7	9	9	9	8	8	8	48		
Labourers' union						17	4	14	11	96	280	90	26					
Transport workers' union								72	38	39								
Foundry workers' union								8	7	17	25							
Textile workers' union									37	26	106	50						
Woodworkers' (construction workers) union										159	128	58	55	45	46	30	29	34
Decorators' union										17	12	13	7	8	8			
Sawmill workers' union										26	39	16	8					
Womens' club											28	15	5					
Harbour workers' union											50	23						
Dustmen's union												10						
Warehousemen's union																		
Leatherworkers' union																10	9	9
Other																1	2	
TOTAL	139	150	160	156	348	409	446	513	472	893	1515	803	458	320	287	230	266	165
Individual members	5	7	6	7	10	18	26	38	40	44	46	46						

TABLE 6.9. *Members of the* riksdag *(Second Chamber) for Karlskrona, 1887–1908.*

Year	Name	Occupation
1887	Carl Gilius Frick	Former naval lieutenant
1888	Carl Gilius Frick	Former naval lieutenant
1891	Edvard Svensson	Naval warrant officer
1894	Edvard Svensson	Naval warrant officer
1897	Edvard Svensson	Under lieutenant
1900	Baron Fredrik Wilhelm von Otter	Former cabinet minister, vice admiral
1902 (by election)	Gustaf Wilhelm Alexander Roos	County secretary
1903	Gustaf Wilhelm Alexander Roos	County secretary
1905	Gustaf Wilhelm Alexander Roos	County secretary
1908	Ulrik Leander	Prison director

SOURCE: Sveriges officiella statistik.

TABLE 7.2. *Distribution of votes in Second Chamber Elections 1914, Blekinge län.*

District	Social Democrats		Liberals		Right	
	Spring	Autumn	Spring	Autumn	Spring	Autumn
Eastern district rural division	400	585	1 012	726	946	883
Medelstad rural division	1 092	1 348	979	772	1 684	1486
Bräkne rural division	747	733	464	369	1 314	1 222
Lister rural division	612	739	879	711	1 365	1 315
Ronneby	158	150	88	93	209	191
Sölvesborg	146	162	135	123	117	121
Karlshamn	250	262	244	201	354	340
Karlskrona	667	720	954	790	1 581	1 589
Whole of Blekinge	4 078	4 701	4 753	3 797	7 570	7 151

SOURCE: *Blekinge Folkblad,* 4th April 1914, 12th September 1914.

Bibliography

Primary Sources (Plymouth)

Parliamentary Papers

Census of the population, 1891, 1901, 1911

H.C. cd.2861, p.3 (1906) lxx.77. Changes in H.M. Dockyards

H.C. cd.3864 (1908) cvii.319. Report by Board of Trade into working class rents, housing, retail prices and standard rates of wages.

H.C. cd.581 (1920) xxi, 635. Report of the Colwyn Committee (utilisation of Royal Dockyards for construction of merchant ships).

Hansard: vols. 89–199 H.C. Deb 4th series (1901–1908); vols. 1–121 H.C. Deb 5th series (1909–1919).

Admiralty Records, Public Record Office

ADM 1/8332 Civil Engineer's Department document, August 1913

ADM 116/330 Case F196, increases of pay (1890–91)

ADM 116/874 Abstract of petitions, evidence and proposals (1892)

ADM 116/900A Case 3002, increase in numbers allowed on establishment (1899–1903)

ADM 116/935 Case 3308, abstracts of petitions (1902)

ADM 116/1011 Case 3309, petitions, abstracts and comments (1905)

ADM 116/1027 Case 3006, working hours in home yards (1906)

ADM 116/1029 Case 3310, petitions, documents commenting on petitions (1906)

ADM 116/1043A Case 3312, petitions, minutes of evidence (1907)

ADM 116/1129A Case 3011, method for obtaining redress for grievances (1911)

ADM 116/1130 Case 3012a, revision of regulations for the entry of apprentices (1911)

ADM 116/1133, 1137, 1138, 1139 Case 3335, petitions, vols. 1–4 (1911)

ADM 116/1141, 1142, 1144 Case 3339, petitions, detailed recommendations (1911)

ADM 116/1170 petitions (1912–13)

ADM 116/1171 petitions miscellaneous papers (1912)

ADM 116/1173 Case 3371, petitions and minutes of evidence (1912)

ADM 116/1179 petitions; rates of wages of unskilled labourers (1912)

ADM 116/1216 Case 3013, conditions of employment, employees' representations (1913)

ADM 116/1218 Case 3019, establishment of workmen (1913)

ADM 116/1541 Case 11247, dilution of labour (1916)

ADM 116/1743 Case 3246, skilled labourers: introduction of titular descriptions with rates of pay (1917)

West Devon Record Office, Plymouth

WDRO 1648/HW1–3. Plymouth County Council, Minutes of the Housing of the Working Classes Committee, 1893–1914.

WDRO 1814/69. Devonport County Council, Minutes of the Housing of the Working Classes Committee, 1897–1913.

WDRO 1540. Petition presented to Devonport County Council (1902).

WDRO 1069, Edgcumbe family papers.

WDRO 470/18, Plymouth SDF papers.

WDRO 186/18/3 Astor press cuttings file, 31st October – 15th November 1919.

WDRO 2000, Henderson papers. Microfilm of National Maritime Museum MS.55/071 HEN/9/1–9.

WDRO 1472, Devonport Dockyard Workman's Dwellings Co. papers.

Plymouth Central Library

South West Labour Journal, no. 1 (August 1903) – no. 41 (October 1906)

Western Morning News, 1891–1920.

Western Daily Mercury, 1891–1920.

Plymouth SDF papers and press cuttings.

Three Towns Association for the Better Housing of the Working Classes, annual reports, 1903–4, 1907–9, 1911.

A T Grindley, 'The Housing Question', Plymouth: Housing Association, n.d.

A T Grindley, 'The Warrens of the Poor', Plymouth: Housing Association, 1906.

Plymouth and South Devon Co-operative Society archives, Plymouth

The Co-operator, 1917–1919.

Plymouth Co-operative Record, 1894–1920.

Co-operative Union archives, Manchester

Co-operative Congress Reports, 1897–1920.

The Co-operative News

T W Mercer, 'The Co-operative Movement in Politics: A Statement of the Case For and Against the Proposed Co-operative Political Alliance', Manchester: Co-operative Union, 1920.

T W Mercer, 'The Relation of Co-operative Education and Co-operative Politics', Manchester: Co-operative Union, 1921.

T W Mercer, 'The Late Mr W H Watkins: Guildsman and Co-operator', National Co-operative Men's Guild printed papers no. 51, August 1924 (Co-operative Union Library, Manchester).

W H Watkins, 'The Co-operative Party: Its Aim and Work', Manchester: Co-operative Union, 1921.

Labour Party Archive, Manchester

LRC correspondence, Labour Party general correspondence, Labour Party archive, Manchester.
Labour Party/LRC annual conference reports, 1900–1920.

Devonport Dockyard Museum

Devonport dockyard letters and other papers (uncatalogued).

Other published sources

SPD News, 1910–11.
Justice, 1899–1906, 1909.
Kelly's Directory of Devonshire, 1897, 1906, 1910.
H E Kearley, (Viscount Devonport) *The Travelled Road: Some Memories of a Busy Life* (Rochester, 1934).

Primary sources – Karlskrona

Arbetarrörelsens arkiv och bibliotek, Stockholm

Försvarsverkens Civila Personals Förbund (FCPF), *Medlemsblad,* 1922–1929.

Marinmusei arkiv, Karlskrona

Statsanställdas förbund avd 2136, Karlskrona: Protokollsbok för KVAF, 1900–1906, Serie A 1:2
Statsanställdas förbund avd 2136, Karlskrona: VAF styrelsen protokoll, 1900–1910, serie A 1:2
Statsanställdas förbund avd 2136, Karlskrona: Protokollsbok för KVAF, 1913–1917, Serie A 1:2
Statsanställdas förbund avd 2136, Karlskrona: Protokollsbok för KVAF, 1917–1920, Serie A 1:2
Statsanställdas förbund avd 2136, Karlskrona: Torped departementets verkstadsklubb protokoll, 1915–1920, Serie A 1:2
Statsanställdas förbund avd 2136, Karlskrona: Cirkulär, Protokoll, Insatsbevis, 1906–1938, Serie A 1:1
Medlemsmatrikel för Karlskrona Varvsarbetareförbund, 1913–1918

Folkrörelsearkivet i Blekinge

1984/67, Karlskrona varvsarbetareförening, protokoll böcker 1900–1920.
1984/67, Försvarsverkens civila personalförbund, avd 36, Karlskrona. Ankomna skrivelser, 1913–1925, 1931–34.
1984/67, Försvarsverkens civila personalförbund, avd 36, Karlskrona. Outgoing correspondence, 1928–36.
Blekinge distrikt av Socialdemokratiska vänstern, protokoll 1918–1926.

Allmänna nykterhetskommittén i Karlskrona. Samlingsvolym 1888–1927.
Socialdemokratiska ungdomsklubben i Karlskrona, samlingsvolym, 1909–1945.
Folkets Hus Karlskrona. Samlingsvolym 1899–1963.
1992/6 Socialdemokratiska kvinnoklubben Karlskrona, årsberättelser
Karlskrona arbetarekommun protokoll, 1896–1925
Karlskrona arbetarekommun års- och revisionsberättelser
Socialdemokratiska fullmäktigegruppen, Karlskrona, protokoll, 1919-

Krigsarkivet, Stockholm

Karlskrona Örlogsvarv, Varvschefens kansli, serie F VII b. Handlingar ang arbe-
tares löner, volym 1 (1917–1946)
Karlskrona Örlogsvarv, Varvschefens militärexpedition. Journaler 1911–1939. Serie
DI: vol 9–11.
Karlskrona Örlogsvarv, Varvschefens militärexpedition. Journal över uppgifter
beträffande varfsdriften 1898–1910, Serie DI: vol 8–9.

Karlskrona kommunarkiv

Kommittéen utsedd att följa Örlogsvarvets verksamhet, A 1:1 Protokoll med
handlingar, 1919–1920.

Printed sources

Blekinge Folkblad, 1903–1921
Blekinge Läns Tidning, 1896-passim
Karlskrona Weckoblad, 1905–1908
Karlskrona-Tidningen, 1911-passim
Edoff Andersson, *Försvarverkens civila personals förbund 10 år* (Stockholm, 1927).
J A Henricsson, *Tid som flytt eller några pänndrag ur minnet från socialismens
första kampår* (Karlskrona, 1923).
Ulrik Leander, *En fängelsedirektörs minnen* (Stockholm, 1936).
Erik Palmstierna, *Ett brytningsskede. Minnen och dagboks anteckningar av Erik
Palmstierna* (Stockholm, 1951).

Secondary Sources

*(Note: the bibliography is listed according to Swedish alphabetical order, i.e. names
beginning with å, ä, and ö are listed after those beginning with z).*

Tony Adams, 'The Formation of the Co-operative Party Reconsidered', *International Review of Social History,* 32 (1987), pp. 48–68.
R J Q Adams and Philip P Poirier, *The Conscription Controversy in Great Britain,
1900–18* (Basingstoke, 1987).
Roy Andersen, 'Ideologiske forutsetninger for den militære opprustningen i Norge 1890–1900', *Historisk Tidskrift* (N), (1999), pp. 48–60.

Ronny Ambjörnsson, *Den skötsamme arbetaren. Idéer och ideal i ett norrländskt sågverkssamhälle 1880–1930* (Stockholm, 1998; first published 1988).

Perry Anderson, 'Origins of the Present Crisis', *New Left Review,* 23 (1964), pp. 26–53.

Carl-Göran Andræ, 'The Swedish Labor Movement and the 1917–1918 Revolution;, in Steven Koblik, ed., *Sweden's Development from Poverty to Affluence 1750–1970,* translated Joanne Johnson (Minneapolis, 1975), pp. 232–253.

Carl-Göran Andræ, *Revolt eller reform. Sverige inför revolutionerna i Europa 1917–1918* (Stockholm, 1998).

Carl-Göran Andræ and Sven Lundkvist, 'Folkrörelserna och den svenska demokratiseringsprocessen', *Historisk Tidskrift* (S), (1969), pp. 197–214.

David Armitage, 'Greater Britain: A Useful Category of Historical Analysis', *American History Review,* 104 (1999), pp. 427–445.

G J Ashworth, *War and the City* (London, 1991).

William Ashworth, 'Economic Aspects of Late Victorian Naval Administration', *Economic History Review,* 2nd series, 22, (1969), pp. 491–505.

Andrew August, 'Cultures of Consolidation? Rethinking Politics in Working-Class London, 1870–1914', *Historical Research,* 74 (2001), pp. 193–219.

Peter Baldwin, 'Comparing and Generalizing: Why All History is Comparative, Yet No History is Sociology', in Deborah Cohen and Maura O'Connor, eds, *Comparison and History: Europe in Cross-National Perspective* (New York and Abingdon, 2004), pp. 1–22.

Logie Barrow and Ian Bullock, *Democratic Ideas and the British Labour Movement, 1880–1914* (Cambridge, 1996).

John Belchem and Neville Kirk, eds, *Languages of Labour* (Aldershot, 1997).

Christine Bellamy, *Administering Central-Local Relations, 1871–1919: The Local Government Board in Its Fiscal and Cultural Context* (Manchester, 1988).

Stefan Berger, *The British Labour Party and the German Social Democrats, 1900–1931* (Oxford, 1994).

Stefan Berger, 'Labour in Comparative Perspective', in Duncan Tanner, Pat Thane and Nick Tiratsoo, eds, *Labour's First Century* (Cambridge, 2000), pp. 309–340.

Stefan Berger, 'Working-class Culture and the Labour Movement in the South Wales and the Ruhr Coalfields 1850–2000: A Comparison', *Llafur,* 8 (2001), pp. 5–40.

Stefan Berger, 'Democracy and Social Democracy', *European History Quarterly,* 32 (2002), pp. 13–37.

Stefan Berger, 'Comparative History', in Stefan Berger, Heiko Feldner and Kevin Passmore, eds, *Writing History: Theory and Practice* (London, 2003), pp. 161–179.

Stefan Berger with Mark Donovan and Kevin Passmore, 'Apologias for the Nation-State in Western Europe since 1800', in Stefan Berger, Mark Donovan and Kevin Passmore, eds, *Writing National Histories: Western Europe since 1800* (London, 1999), pp. 3–14.

Gunnar Berg, *Karlskrona Grovarbetarefackförening 40 år 1902–1942. Några glimtar ur verksamheten* (Karlskrona, 1942).

Henrik Berggren and Lars Trägårdh, 'Historikerna och språket: teoretiska ambitioner och praktiska begränsningar', *Historisk Tidskrift* (S), (1990), pp. 357–375.

Lars Berggren, *Ångvisslans och brickornas värld. Om arbete och facklig organisering vid Kockums mekaniska verkstad och Carl Lunds fabrik i Malmö 1840–1905* (Lund, 1991).

Lars Berggren, 'Går det att skriva arbetarhistoriska synteser?', *Historisk Tidskrift* (S) (2003), pp. 181–200.

Lenard R Berlanstein, 'The Distinctiveness of the Nineteenth-Century French Labor Movement', *Journal of Modern History*, 64 (1992), pp. 660–685.

Sheri Berman, *The Social Democratic Moment: Ideas and Politics in the Making of Interwar Europe* (Cambridge (Massachusetts), 1998).

Richard Bessel, 'Workers, Politics and Power in Modern German History: Some Recent Writing on the German Labour Movement and the German Working Class in the Nineteenth and Twentieth Centuries', *The Historical Journal*, 33 (1990), pp. 211–226.

Eugenio Biagini, *Liberty, Retrenchment and Reform: Popular Liberalism in the Age of Gladstone, 1860–1880* (Cambridge, 1992).

Eugenio F Biagini and Alastair J Reid, eds, *Currents of Radicalism: Popular Radicalism, Organised Labour and Party Politics in Britain, 1850–1914* (Cambridge, 1991).

Pierre Birnbaum, *States and Collective Action: The European Experience* (Cambridge, 1988).

Kaj Björk, *Försvarsverkens civila personals förbund 1917–1942* (Stockholm, 1943).

C J Björklund, *Första maj och första maj demonstrationerna* (Stockholm, 1996).

Lars Björlin, 'De svenska arbetarpartierna. Forskning under 1970- och 1980-talen', in Klaus Misgeld och Klas Åmark, eds, *Arbetsliv och arbetarrörelse. Modern historisk forskning i Sverige* (Stockholm, 1991), pp. 43–59

Lawrence Black, '"What Kind of People Are You?" Labour, the People and the 'New Political History', in John Callaghan, Steven Fielding and Steve Ludlam, eds, *Interpreting the Labour Party: New Approaches to Labour Politics and History* (Manchester, 2003), pp. 23–38.

David Blackbourn and Geoff Eley, *The Peculiarities of German History: Bourgeois Society and Politics in Nineteenth Century Germany* (Oxford, 1984).

Neal Blewett, *The Peers, the Parties and the People: The General Elections of 1910* (London, 1972).

Marc Bloch, 'Toward a Comparative History of European Societies', in Frederic C Lane and Jelle C Riermersma, eds, *Enterprise and Secular Change: Readings in Economic History* (Homewood, Illinois, 1953; first published 1928), pp. 494–521.

Eva Blomberg, *Män i mörker. Arbetsgivare, reformister och syndikalister. Politik och identitet i svensk gruvindustri 1910–1940* (Stockholm, 1995).

Jan Bohlin, *Svensk varvsindustri 1920–1975. Lönsamhet, finansiering och arbets-marknad* (Göteborg, 1989).

Rune Bokholm, *Städernas handlingsfrihet. En studie av expansionsskedet 1900–1930* (Lund, 1995).

Jonathan S Boswell and Bruce R Johns, 'Patriots or Profiteers? British Business-men and the First World War', *Journal of European Economic History* 11 (1982), pp. 423–445.

Joanna Bourke, *Working-Class Cultures in Britain 1890–1960: Gender, Class and Ethnicity* (London, 1994).

Mark Brayshay, 'The Emigration Trade in Nineteenth Century Devon', in Michael Duffy et al., eds, *The New Maritime History of Devon*, vol. 2 (London, 1994), pp. 108–118.

John Breuilly, *Labour and Liberalism in Nineteenth Century Europe: Essays in Comparative History* (Manchester, 1992).

Robert Briscoe, *Centenary History: A Hundred Years of Co-operation in Plymouth* (Manchester, 1960).

Frank Broeze, 'Militancy and Pragmatism: An International Perspective on Maritime Labour 1870–1914', *International Review of Social History*, 36 (1991), pp. 165–200.

Janvik Bromé, *Karlskrona stads historia*, vol. III, 1862–1930 (Karlskrona, 1930).

D K Brown, *A Century of Naval Construction: The History of the Royal Corps of Naval Constructors, 1883–1983* (London, 1983).

Gunnar Brånsted, *Organisation och utveckling. Blekinge socialdemokratiska par-tidistrikts verksamhet 1907–1977* (Karlskrona, 1977).

Edvard Bull, 'Arbeiderbevægelsens stilling i de tre nordiske lande 1914–1920', *Arkiv för studier i arbetarrörelsens historia*, 15/16 (1979; first published 1922), pp. 62–80.

Keith Burgess, *The Challenge of Labour: Shaping British Society 1850–1930* (London, 1980).

Knut Bäckström, *Arbetarrörelsen i Sverige*, 2 vols (Stockholm, 1958 and 1963).

Neil Casey, 'An Early Organisational Hegemony: Methods of Social Control in a Victorian Dockyard', *Social Science Information*, 23 (1984), pp. 677–700.

Neil Casey, 'Class Rule: The Hegemonic Role of the Royal Dockyard Schools, 1840–1914', in Kenneth Lunn and Ann Day, *History of Work and Labour Rela-tions in the Royal Dockyards* (London, 1999), pp. 66–86.

Marina Cattaruzza, '"Organisieter Konflikt" und "direkte Aktion". Zwei For-men des Arbeiterkampfes am Beispiel der Werftarbeiterstreiks in Hamburg und Triest (1880–1914)', *Archiv für Sozialgeschichter*, 20 (1980), pp. 325–355.

Andrew Chadwick, *Augmenting Democracy: Political Movements and Constitu-tional Reform during the Rise of Labour, 1900–1914* (Aldershot, 1999).

P F Clarke, *Lancashire and the New Liberalism* (London, 1971).

Frans Coetzee, *For Party or Country: Nationalism and the Dilemmas of Popular Conservatism in Edwardian England* (Oxford, 1990).

Deborah Cohen and Maura O'Connor, 'Comparative History, Cross-Nation-al History, Transnational History – Definitions', in *idem*, eds, *Comparison and History: Europe in Cross-National Perspective* (New York and Abingdon, 2004), pp. ix–xxiv.

G D H Cole, *A Century of Co-operation* (London, 1944).

Martin Crick, *The History of the Social Democratic Federation* (Keele, 1994).

Malcolm Crook, *Toulon in War and Revolution: From the* ancien régime *to the Restoration, 1750–1820* (Manchester, 1991).

James E Cronin, *Labour and Society in Britain, 1918–1979* (London, 1984).

James E Cronin, 'Neither Exceptional Nor Peculiar: Towards the Comparative Study of Labor in Advanced Society', *International Review of Social History,* 38 (1993), pp. 59–75.

Hugh Cunningham, 'The Language of Patriotism, 1750–1914', *History Workshop Journal,* 12 (1981), pp. 8–33.

Mats Dahlkvist, *Staten, socialdemokratin och socialismen. En inledande analys* (Lund, 1975).

Sam Davies, *Liverpool Labour: Social and Political Influences on the Development of the Labour Party in Liverpool, 1900–1939* (Keele, 1996).

Sam Davies, et al., eds, *Dock Workers: International Explorations in Comparative Labour History, 1790–1970* (Aldershot, 2000).

Belinda Davis, 'Food Scarcity and the Empowerment of the Female Consumer in World War I Berlin', in Victoria de Grazia with Ellen Furlough, eds, *The Sex of Things: Gender and Consumption in Historical Perspective* (Berkeley, 1996), pp. 287–310.

A M Dawson, 'Politics in Devon and Cornwall, 1900–1931' (unpublished PhD thesis, University of London, 1991).

Michael Dawson, 'Liberalism in Devon and Cornwall, 1910–1931: "The Old-Time Religion"', *The Historical Journal,* 38 (1995), pp. 425–437.

Ann Day, '"Driven from Home": The Closure of Pembroke Dockyard and the Impact on Its Community', *Llafur,* 7 (1996), pp. 78–86.

Peter Dewey, 'Nutrition and Living Standards in Wartime Britain', in Richard Wall and Jay Winter, eds, *The Upheaval of War: Family, Work and Welfare in Europe, 1914–1918* (Cambridge, 1988), pp. 197–220.

George Dicker, *A Short History of Devonport Royal Dockyard* (Plymouth, 1969).

Roy Douglas, 'Labour in Decline, 1910–1914', in Kenneth D Brown, ed., *Essays in Anti-Labour History: Responses to the Rise of Labour in Britain* (London, 1974), pp. 105–125.

Lars Edgren, *Lärling – gesäll – mästare: hantverk och hantverkare i Malmö 1750–1847* (Lund, 1987).

Samuel Edquist, *Nyktra svenskar. Godtemplarrörelsen och den nationella identiteten 1879–1918* (Uppsala, 2001).

Christiane Eisenberg, 'The Comparative View in Labour History: Old and New Interpretations of the English and German Labour Movements before 1914', *International Review of Social History,* 34 (1989), pp. 403–432.

Lars Ekdahl, *Arbete mot kapital. Typografer och ny teknik – studier av Stockholms tryckeriindustri under det industriella genombrottet* (Lund, 1983).

Geoff Eley, *Forging Democracy: The History of the Left in Europe 1850–2000* (Oxford, 2002).

Nils Elvander, *Harald Hjärne och konservatismen. Konservativ idédebatt i Sverige 1865–1922* (Uppsala, 1961).

Nils Elvander, *Skandinavisk arbetarrörelse* (Stockholm, 1980).

David Englander, *Landlord and Tenant in Urban Britain, 1838–1918* (Oxford, 1983).

Hans-Olof Ericson, *Vanmakt och styrka. Studier av arbetarrörelsens tillkomst och förutsättningar i Jönköping, Huskvarna och Norrahammar 1880–1909* (Lund, 1987).

Hans-Olof Ericson, *Mellan dröm och vardag. Studier av arbetarrörelsens politiska splittring. Jönköping, Huskvarna och Norrahammar 1910–1921* (Lund, 1991).

Paul Ericson, *Från fyrkvälde till folkmakt. Ett kort krönika om blekingsk arbetarrörelse* (Karlskrona, 1957).

Ulf Eriksson, *Gruva och arbete. Kiirunavaara 1890–1990* (4 vols, Uppsala, 1991).

Peter Essaiasson, *Svenska valkampanjer 1866–1988* (Stockholm, 1990).

Roger Fagge, *Power, Culture and Conflict in the Coalfields: West Virginia and South Wales, 1900–1922* (Manchester, 1996).

Ilaria Favretto, *The Long Search for a Third Way: The British Labour Party and the Italian Left since 1945* (Basingstoke, 2002).

Steven Fielding, 'New Labour and the Past', in Duncan Tanner, Pat Thane and Nick Tiratsoo, eds, *Labour's First Century* (Cambridge, 2000), pp. 367–392.

Eric Foner, 'Why Is There No Socialism in the United States?' *History Workshop Journal*, 17 (1984), pp. 55–80.

Ronald P Formisano, 'The Concept of Political Culture', *Journal of Interdisciplinary History*, 31 (2001), pp. 393–426.

Ragnar Fors, *Karlskrona arbetareförening 1872–1972* (Karlskrona, 1972).

John Foster, *Class Struggle and the Industrial Revolution: Early Industrial Capitalism in Three English Towns* (London, 1974).

Mats Franzén, 'Egensinne och skötsamhet i svensk arbetakultur. Kommentarer till *Den skötsamme arbetaren av Ronny Ambjörnsson*', *Arkiv för studier i arbetarrörelsens historia*, 48–49 (1991), pp. 3–20.

Katarina Friberg, *The Workings of Co-operation: A Comparative Study of Consumer Co-operation Organisation in Britain and Sweden 1860 to 1970* (Växjö, 2005).

Gerald Friedman, *State-Making and Labor Movements: France and the United States, 1876–1914* (Ithaca, 1998).

Birgitta Skarin Frykman, 'Arbetarkultur och arbetarkulturforskning', *Arkiv för studier i arbetarrörelsens historia*, 48–49 (1991), pp. 21–46.

Mary Fulbrook, 'Introduction: States, Nations and the Development of Europe', in idem., ed., *National Histories and European History* (London, 1993), pp. 1–17.

James Fulcher, *Labour Movements, Employers and the State: Conflict and Co-operation in Britain and Sweden* (Oxford, 1991).

Förening Gamla Carlscrona, *1:a maj-reveljen i Karlskrona: ett 20-årigt perspektiv* (Karlskrona, 2000).

Walter Galenson, *Labor in Norway* (Cambridge, Massachusetts, 1948).

Walter Galenson, 'Scandinavia', in *idem.*, ed., *Comparative Labor Movements* (New York, 1952), pp. 104–172.

Peter Galliver, 'Trade unionism in Portsmouth Dockyard, 1880–1914: Change and Continuity', in Kenneth Lunn and Ann Day, eds, *History of Work and Labour Relations in the Royal Dockyards* (London, 1999), pp. 99–126.

Dick Geary, 'Labour History, the "Linguistic Turn" and Postmodernism', *Contemporary European History*, 9 (2000), pp. 445–462.

David Gilbert, 'Community and Municipalism: Collective Identification in Late-Victorian and Edwardian Mining Towns', *Journal of Historical Geography*, 17 (1991), pp. 257–270.

David Gilbert, *Class, Community and Collective Action: Social Change in Two British Coalfields, 1850–1926* (Oxford, 1992).

Crispin Gill, *Plymouth: A New History* (Plymouth, 1993).

Robert Justin Goldstein, 'Political Mobilisation in Nineteenth-Century Europe', *European History Quarterly*, 32 (2002), pp. 233–250.

Martin Grass, 'Från arbetarkongress till samarbetskommitté. Om Skandinaviska samarbetskommitténs bildande', *Arbetarhistoria*, 42 (1987), pp. 5–11.

E H H Green, 'Radical Conservatism: The Electoral Genesis of Tariff Reform', *Historical Journal*, 28 (1985), pp. 667–692.

Lotta Gröning, *Vägen till makten. SAP:s organisation och dess betydelse för den politiska verksamheten 1900–1933* (Uppsala, 1988).

Peter Gurney, *Co-operative Culture and the Politics of Consumption in England, c1870–1930* (Manchester, 1996).

Bo Gustafsson, 'Sweden', in Mikulás Teich and Roy Porter, eds, *The Industrial Revolution in National Context: Europe and the USA* (Cambridge, 1996), pp. 201–225.

Björn Gäfvert, 'Kontinuitet i föränderlig omvärld', in Erik Norberg, ed., *Karlskronavarvets historia*, vol. 2, 1866–1992 (Karlskrona, 1993), pp. 81–134.

J M Haas, 'Trouble at the Workplace: Industrial Relations in the Royal Dockyards, 1889–1914', *Bulletin of the Institute of Historical Research*, 58 (1985), pp. 210–225.

J M Haas, *A Management Odyssey: The Royal Dockyards, 1714–1914* (London, Maryland, 1994).

Stig Hadenius, 'Riksdagspartier och rikspartier på 1890-talet', in Stig Hadenius, ed., *Kring demokratins genombrott i Sverige* (Stockholm, 1966) pp. 55–66.

Stig Hadenius, Jan-Olof Seveborg and Lennart Weibull, *Socialdemokratisk press och presspolitik 1899–1909* (Stockholm, 1968).

Stig Hadenius, Jan-Olof Seveborg and Lennart Weibull, *Partipress. Socialdemokratisk press och presspolitik 1910–1920* (Stockholm, 1970).

Patrik Hall, *Den svenskaste historien. Nationalism i Sverige under sex sekler* (Stockholm, 2000).

Rick Halpern and Jonathan Morris, 'The Persistence of Exceptionalism: Class Formation and the Comparative Method', in *idem.*, eds, *American Exceptionalism? US Working-Class Formation in an International Context* (Basingstoke, 1997), pp. 1–13.

Solveig Halvorsen, 'Scandinavian Trade Unions in the 1890s, with Special Reference to the Scandinavian Stonemasons' Union', in *Scandinavian Journal of History*, 13 (1988), pp. 3–21.

Malcolm B Hamilton, *Democratic Socialism in Britain and Sweden* (Basingstoke, 1989).

Börje Harnesk, 'Den svenska modellens tidigmoderna rötter?', *Historisk Tidskrift* (S) (2002), pp. 78–90.

José Harris, 'Bureaucrats and Businessmen in British Food Control, 1916–1919', in Kathleen Burk, ed., *War and the State: The Transformation of British Government, 1914–1919* (London, 1982), pp. 135–156.

Trevor Harris, 'Government and the Specialised Military Town: The Impact of Defence Policy on Urban Social Structure in the Nineteenth Century', in Michael Bateman and Raymond Riley, eds, *The Geography of Defence* (London, 1987), pp. 100–140.

Eli F Heckscher, *An Economic History of Sweden*, translated Göran Ohlin (Cambridge, Massachusetts, 1954).

Hugh Heclo, *Modern Social Politics in Britain and Sweden: From Relief to Income Maintenance* (New Haven, 1974).

Börje Henningsson, 'Humanism, anarkism och socialism. Varför splittrades det socialdemokratiska vänsterpartiet?', in *Arbetarhistoria*, 80–81 (1996–7), pp. 25–36.

Torsten Henriksson, 'Frisinnade landsföreningen och demokratin', in Stig Hadenius, ed., *Kring demokratins genombrott* (Stockholm, 1966), pp. 67–89.

Seppo Hentilä, *Den svenska arbetarklassen och reformismens genombrott* (Helsinki, 1979).

Dag Magnus Hermfelt, *Arbetareföreningens bibliotek i Karlskrona 1877–1900* (Borås, 1983).

Peter Hilditch, 'The Dockyard in the Local Economy', in Michael Duffy et al., eds, *The New Maritime History of Devon*, vol. 2 (London, 1994), pp. 215–225.

Rune Hillbom, *Karlskrona 300 år*, del II (Karlskrona, 1982).

Mary Hilson, 'Working-Class Politics in Plymouth, c.1890–1920', (unpublished PhD thesis, University of Exeter, 1998).

Mary Hilson, 'Swedish Approaches to the Rise of Labour: A British Perspective', *Scandinavian Journal of History*, 26 (2001), pp. 103–121.

Mary Hilson, 'Labour Politics in a Naval Dockyard: The Case of Karlskrona, Sweden c.1880–1925', *International Review of Social History*, 46 (2001), pp. 341–369.

Mary Hilson, 'Consumers and Politics: The Co-operative Movement in Plymouth, 1890–1920', *Labour History Review*, 67 (2002), pp. 7–27.

James Hinton, *The First Shop Stewards' Movement* (London, 1973).

Eric Hobsbawm, 'The Labour Aristocracy in Nineteenth Century Britain', in *idem., Labouring Men* (London, 1964), pp. 272–315.

Eric J Hobsbawm, 'The "New Unionism" Reconsidered', in Wolfgang J Mommsen and Hans-Gerhard Husung, eds, *The Development of Trade Unionism in Great Britain and Germany, 1880–1914* (London, 1985), pp. 13–31.

Hanna Hodacs, *Converging World Views: The European Expansion and Early Nineteenth Century Anglo-Swedish Contacts* (Uppsala, 2003).

Carl Cavanagh Hodge, *The Trammels of Tradition: Social Democracy in Britain, France and Germany* (Westport, Connecticut, 1994).

Hans Holmén, *Försvar och samhällsförändring. Avvägningsfrågor i svensk försvarsdebatt, 1880–1925* (Göteborg, 1985).

Björn Horgby, *Egensinne och skötsamhet. Arbetarkulturen i Norrköping 1850–1940* (Stockholm, 1993).

John N Horne, *Labour at War: France and Britain, 1914–1918* (Oxford, 1991).

John Host, *Victorian Labour History: Experience, Identity and the Politics of Representation* (London, 1998).

David Howell, *British Workers and the Independent Labour Party, 1888–1906* (Manchester, 1983).

Alun Howkins, 'Edwardian Liberalism and Industrial Unrest: A Class View of the Decline of Liberalism', *History Workshop Journal*, 4 (1977), pp. 143–161.

Madeleine Hurd, *Public Spheres, Public Mores and Democracy: Hamburg and Stockholm 1870–1914* (Ann Arbor, 2000).

Karen Hunt, 'Negotiating the Boundaries of the Domestic: British Socialist Women and the Politics of Consumption', *Women's History Review*, 9 (2000), pp. 389–410.

Ann Hörsell, 'Från segel och trä till ånga och stål 1866–1910', in Erik Norberg, ed., *Karlskronavarvets historia*, vol. 2, 1866–1992 (Karlskrona, 1993), pp. 7–80.

Maths Isacson and Lars Magnusson, *Proto-Industrialisation in Scandinavia: Craft Skills in the Industrial Revolution* (Leamington Spa, 1987).

Alf Johansson, *Arbetets delning. Stocka sågverk under omvandling 1856–1900* (Lund, 1988).

Alf O Johansson and Joseph Melling, 'The Roots of Consensus: Bargaining Attitudes and Political Commitment among Swedish and British Workers c.1920–1950', *Economic and Industrial Democracy*, 16 (1995), pp. 353–397.

Ella Johansson, *Skogarnas fria söner. Maskulinitet och modernitet i norrländskt skogsarbete* (Kristianstad, 1994).

Ingemar Johansson, *Strejken som vapen. Fackföreningar och strejker i Norrköping 1870–1910* (Stockholm, 1982).

Mats Johansson, 'Paternalism och strejker. En jämförelse mellan sågverken i Båtskärsnäs och Karlsborg i början av 1900-talet', *Arkiv för studier i arbetarrörelsens historia*, 88–89 (2003), pp. 23–37.

Graham Johnson, 'Social Democracy and Labour Politics in Britain, 1892–1911', *History*, 85 (2000), pp. 67–87.

Gareth Stedman Jones, 'Working-Class Culture and Working-Class Politics in London, 1870–1900: Notes on the Remaking of a Working Class', in *idem., Languages of Class: Studies in English Working-class History, 1832–1982* (Cambridge, 1983; first published 1974), pp. 179–238.

Gareth Stedman Jones, 'Rethinking Chartism' in *idem., Languages of Class: Studies in English Working-class History, 1832–1982* (Cambridge, 1983; first published 1982), pp. 90–178.

Olle Josephson, 'Att ta ordet för hundra år sedan', in *idem.*, ed., *Arbetarna tar ordet. Språk och kommunikation i tidig arbetarrörelse* (Stockholm, 1996), pp. 10–43.

Tony Jowitt, 'Late Victorian and Edwardian Bradford', in David James, Tony Jowitt and Keith Laybourn, eds, *The Centennial History of the Independent Labour Party* (Halifax, 1992), pp. 95–115.

Patrick Joyce, *Work, Society and Politics: The Culture of the Factory in Later Victorian England* (Brighton, 1980).

Patrick Joyce, *Visions of the People: Industrial England and the Question of Class, 1848–1914* (Cambridge, 1991).

Patrick Joyce, *Democratic Subjects: The Self and the Social in Nineteenth Century England* (Cambridge, 1994).

Rolf Karlbom, *Revolution eller reformer. Studier i SAP:s historia 1889–1902* (Göteborg, 1985).

Karlskrona arbetareförening, *En kortfattad historik över Karlskrona arbetareförenings verksamhet* (Karlskrona, 1933).

Sten Karlsson, *När industriarbetaren blev historia. Studier i svensk arbetarhistoria 1965–1995* (Lund, 1998).

Ira Katznelson, 'Working-Class Formation and the State: Nineteenth Century England in American Perspective', in Peter B Evans, Dietrich Rueschemeyer and Theda Skocpol, eds, *Bringing the State Back In* (Cambridge, 1985), pp. 257–284.

Ira Katznelson, 'Working-Class Formation: Constructing Cases and Comparisons', in Ira Katznelson and Aristide R Zolberg, eds, *Working-Class Formation: Nineteenth-Century Patterns in Western Europe and the United States* (Princeton, New Jersey, 1986), pp. 3–41.

Ira Katznelson, 'The "Bourgeois" Dimension: A Provocation About Institutions, Politics and the Future of Labor History', *International Labor and Working-Class History*, 46 (1994), pp. 7–32.

Howard Kimeldorf, 'Bringing Unions Back In (or Why We Need a New Old Labor History)', *Labor History*, 32 (1991), pp. 91–103.

David Kirby, 'What was "Nordic" about the Labour Movement in Europe's Northernmost Regions?', in Pauli Kettunen, ed., *Lokalt och internationellt. Dimensioner i den nordiska arbetarrörelsen och arbetarkulturen* (Tammerfors, 2002), pp. 13–32.

Neville Kirk, *Change, Continuity and Class: Labour in British Society, 1850–1920* (Manchester, 1998).

Neville Kirk, *Comrades and Cousins: Globalization, Workers and Labour Movements in Britain, the USA and Australia from the 1880s to 1914* (London, 2003).

Anders Kjellberg, *Fackliga organisationer och medlemmar i dagens Sverige* (Lund, 2001; first published 1997).

Roger Knight, 'From Impressment to Task Work: Strikes and Disruption in the Royal Dockyards, 1688–1788', in Kenneth Lunn and Ann Day, eds, *History of Work and Labour Relations in the Royal Dockyards* (London, 1999), pp. 1–20.

Jürgen Kocka, 'Probleme einer europäischen Geschichte in komparativer Absicht', in *idem., Geschichte und Aufklärung* (Göttingen, 1989), pp. 21–28

Jürgen Kocka, 'Comparative Historical Research: German Examples', *International Review of Social History*, 38 (1993), pp. 369–379.

Jürgen Kocka, 'New Trends in Labour Movement Historiography: A German Perspective', *International Review of Social History*, 42 (1997), pp. 67–78.

Walter Korpi, *The Working Class in Welfare Capitalism* (London, 1978).

William M Lafferty, *Economic Development and the Response of Labor in Scandinavia: A Multi-Level Analysis* (Oslo, 1971).

Bill Lancaster, *Radicalism, Co-operation and Socialism: Leicester Working-class Politics, 1860–1906* (Leicester, 1987).

John H M Laslett, *Colliers Across the Sea: A Comparative Study of Class Formation in Scotland and the American Midwest, 1830–1924* (Urbana and Chicago, 2000).

Alex Law, 'Neither Colonial Nor Historic: Workers' Organisation at Rosyth Dockyard, 1945–95', in in Kenneth Lunn and Ann Day, eds, *History of Work and Labour Relations in the Royal Dockyards* (London, 1999), pp. 151–178.

Jon Lawrence, 'Popular Politics and the Limitations of Party: Wolverhampton, 1867–1900', in Eugenio F Biagini and Alastair J Reid, eds, *Currents of Radicalism: Popular Radicalism, Organised Labour and Party Politics in Britain, 1850–1914* (Cambridge, 1991).

Jon Lawrence, 'Class and Gender in the Making of Urban Toryism, 1880–1914', *English Historical Review*, 108 (1993) 629–653.

Jon Lawrence, 'The Dynamics of Urban Politics, 1867–1914', in Jon Lawrence and Miles Taylor, eds, *Party, State and Society: Electoral Behaviour in Britain since 1820* (Aldershot, 1997), pp. 79–105.

Jon Lawrence, *Speaking for the People: Party, Language and Popular Politics in England, 1867–1914* (Cambridge, 1998).

Friedrich Lenger, 'Beyond Exceptionalism: Notes on the Artisanal Phase of the Labour Movement in France, England, German and the United States', *International Review of Social History*, 36 (1991), pp. 1–23.

Leif Lewin, *Ideology and Strategy: A Century of Swedish Politics*, translated Victor Kayfetz (Cambridge, 1988).

Sven-Eric Liedman, 'Liberalism in the Nordic Context', in Ilkka K Lakaniemi, Anna Rotkirch and Henrik Stenius, eds, *Liberalism in the Nordic Context* (Helsinki, 1995), pp. 33–48.

Marcel van der Linden, 'The National Integration of European Working Classes (1871–1914): Exploring the Causal Configuration', *International Review of Social History*, 33 (1988), pp. 285–311.

Marcel van der Linden, *Transnational Labour History: Explorations* (Aldershot, 2003).

Marcel van der Linden and Jürgen Rojahn, 'Introduction', in *idem.*, eds, *The Formation of Labour Movements, 1870–1914: An International Perspective*, vol. 1 (Leiden, 1990), pp. ix-xvii.

Marcel van der Linden and Lex Heerma van Voss, 'Introduction', in *idem.*, eds, *Class and Other Identities: Gender, Religion and Ethnicity in the Writing of European Labour History* (New York, 2002), pp. 1–39.

John Lindgren, *Det socialdemokratiska arbetarpartiets uppkomst i Sverige 1881–1889* (Stockholm, 1927).

Mats Lindquist, *Klasskamrater. Om industriellt arbete och kulturell formation 1880–1920* (Stockholm, 1994; first published 1987).

Seymour Martin Lipset, 'Radicalism or Reformism: The Sources of Working-Class Politics', *American Political Science Review*, 77 (1983), pp. 1–18.

Seymour Martin Lipset and Stein Rokkan, 'Cleavage Structures, Party Systems and Voter Alignments: An Introduction', in *idem.*, eds, *Party Systems and Voter Alignments: Cross-National Perspectives* (New York, 1967), pp. 1–64.

Edward H Lorenz, 'Two Patterns of Development: The Labour Process in the British and French Shipbuilding Industries 1880 to 1930', *Journal of European Economic History*, 13 (1984), pp. 599–634.

Gregory M Luebbert, *Liberalism, Fascism or Social Democracy: Social Classes and the Political Origins of Regimes in Interwar Europe* (Oxford, 1991).

Susanne Lundin, *En liten skara äro vi... En studie av typografer vid 1900-talets första decennier* (Stockholm, 1992).

Sven Lundkvist, *Folkrörelserna i det svenska samhället, 1850–1920* (Uppsala, 1977).

Kenneth Lunn, 'Labour Culture in Dockyard Towns: A Study of Portsmouth, Plymouth and Chatham, 1900–1950', *Tijdschrift voor Sociale Geschiednis*, 8 (1992), pp. 275–293.

Kenneth Lunn and Ann Day, 'Continuity and Change: Labour Relations in the Royal Dockyards, 1914–50', in *idem.*, eds, *History of Work and Labour Relations in the Royal Dockyards* (London, 1999), pp. 127–150.

Ken Lunn and Ann Day, 'Deference and Defiance: The Changing Nature of Petitioning in British Naval Dockyards', *International Review of Social History*, 46 (2001), Supplement, pp. 131–150.

K Lunn and A Thomas, 'Naval Imperialism in Portsmouth, 1905–1914', *Southern History*, 10 (1988), pp. 142–159.

Patricia Lynch, *The Liberal Party in Rural England 1885–1910: Radicalism and Community* (Oxford, 2003).

Robert H MacDonald, *The Language of Empire: Myths and Metaphors of Popular Imperialism, 1880–1918* (Manchester, 1994).

Philip MacDougall, 'The Changing Nature of the Dockyard Dispute, 1790–1840', in Kenneth Lunn and Ann Day, eds, *History of Work and Labour Relations in the Royal Dockyards* (London, 1999), pp. 41–65.

Ian Machin, *The Rise of Democracy in Britain, 1830–1918* (Basingstoke, 2001).

Lars Magnusson, 'Patriarkalism och social kontroll. Några synpunkter på ett problemkomplex', in *Arkiv för studier i arbetarrörelsens historia*, 33 (1986), pp. 46–61.

Lars Magnusson, *Arbetet vid en svensk verkstad. Munktells, 1900–1920* (Lund, 1987).

Lars Magnusson, *Den bråkiga kulturen: förläggare och smideshantverkare i Eskilstuna 1800–1850* (Stockholm, 1988).

Ulf Magnusson, *Från arbetare till arbetarklass. Klassformering och klassrelationer i Fagersta – ett mellansvenskt brukssamhälle ca 1870–1909* (Uppsala, 1996).

Gary Marks, *Unions in Politics: Britain, Germany and the United States in the Nineteenth and Early Twentieth Centuries* (Princeton, 1989).

H C G Matthew, R I McKibbin and J A Kay, 'The Franchise Factor in the Rise of the Labour Party', *English Historical Review*, 91 (1976), pp. 723–752.

Derek Matthews, '1889 and All That: New Views on the New Unionism', *International Review of Social History*, 36 (1991), pp. 24–58.

Keith McClelland, 'Time to Work, Time to Live: Some Aspects of Work and the Re-Formation of Class in Britain, 1850–1880', in Patrick Joyce, ed., *The Historical Meanings of Work* (Cambridge, 1987), pp. 180–209.

Keith McClelland and Alastair Reid, 'Wood, Iron and Steel: Technology, Labour and Trade Union Organisation in the Shipbuilding Industry, 1840–1914', in Royden Harrison and Jonathan Zeitlin, eds, *Divisions of Labour: Skilled Workers and Technological Change in Nineteenth Century England* (Brighton, 1984), pp. 151–184.

Ross McKibbin, *The Evolution of the Labour Party, 1910–1924* (Oxford, 1974).

Ross McKibbin, 'Work and Hobbies in Britain, 1880–1950', in *idem., The Ideologies of Class: Social Relations in Britain, 1880–1950* (Oxford, 1990; first published 1983), pp. 139–166.

Ross McKibbin, 'Why Was There No Marxism in Great Britain?', in *idem., The Ideologies of Class: Social Relations in Britain, 1880–1950* (Oxford, 1990; first published 1984), pp. 1–41.

Ross McKibbin, *Classes and Cultures: England 1918–1951* (Oxford, 1998).

Flemming Mikkelsen, 'Fra proletarisering til klassesamfund. Industrialisering, urbanisering og fremvæksten af en arbejderklasse og arbejderbevægelse i Skandinavia ca 1750–1900', *Arbejderhistorie*, 30 (1988), pp. 2–20.

Ralph Miliband, *Parliamentary Socialism: A Study of the Politics of Labour* (London, 1972).

Ingrid Millbourn, 'Swedish Social Democrats' Experiences and Consciousness: A Theory of Learning Processes', *Scandinavian Journal of History*, 22 (1997), pp. 99–119.

Harvey Mitchell, 'Labor and the Origins of Social Democracy in Britain, France and Germany, 1890–1914', in Harvey Mitchell and Peter N Stearns, *Workers and Protest: The European Labor Movement, the Working Classes and the Origins of Social Democracy, 1890–1914* (Itasca, 1971).

Carol E Morgan, *Women Workers and Gender Identities, 1835–1913: The Cotton and Metal industries in England* (London, 2001).

Roger Morriss, 'Government and Continuity: The Changing Context of Labour Relations, 1770–1830', in Kenneth Lunn and Ann Day, eds, *History of Work and Labour Relations in the Royal Dockyards* (London, 1999), pp. 21–40.

B H Moss, 'Republican Socialism and the Making of the Working Class in Britain, France and the United States: A Critique of Thompsonian Culturalism', *Comparative Studies in Society and History*, 35 (1993), pp. 390–413.

Karen J Musolf, *From Plymouth to Parliament: A Rhetorical History of Nancy Astor's 1919 Campaign* (London, 1999).

Människor och händelser – ett axplock. Karlskrona arbetarekommun 100 år 1896–1996 (Karlskrona, 1996).

Tom Nairn, 'The British Political Elite', *New Left Review*, 23 (1964), pp. 19–25.

Torbjörn Nilsson, 'Med historien som ledstjärna. Högern och demokratin 1904–1940', *Scandia*, 68 (2002), pp. 77–107.

G H Nordström, *Sveriges socialdemokratiska arbetareparti under genombrottsåren 1889–1894* (Stockholm, 1938).

R Nylander, *Karlskrona föreläsningsförening 1903–1938* (Karlskrona, 1938).

Gunnar Olofsson, 'Från underklass till arbetarklass. Förändringar i "det arbetande folket" 1870–1930', in idem., *Klass, rörelse, socialdemokrati. Essäer om arbetarrörelsens sociologi* (Lund, 1996; first published 1976), pp. 69–102.

Gunnar Olofsson, 'Den svenska socialdemokratin. Syntes om den svenska arbetarrörelsen', in idem., *Klass, rörelse, socialdemokrati. Essäer om arbetarrörelsens sociologi* (Lund, 1996; first published 1984), pp. 103–122.

Hugh B Peebles, *Warshipbuilding on the Clyde: Naval Orders and the Prosperity of the Clyde Shipbuilding Industry, 1889–1939* (Edinburgh, 1987).

Henry Pelling, *The Origins of the Labour Party, 1880–1906* (London, 1954).

Henry Pelling, *A History of British Trade Unionism*, (Harmondsworth, 1987; first published 1963).

Henry Pelling, *Social Geography of British Elections, 1885–1910* (London, 1967).

Lennart K Persson, *Arbete, politik, arbetarrörelse. En studie av stenindustrins Bohuslän 1860–1910* (Gothenburg, 1984).

Thorvald Pettersson, *Historik över Försvarsverkens civila personals förbunds avdelning 36 verksamhet under den förflutna 15:års perioden, samt en överblick av det organisatoriska arbetet inom varvsarbetarekåren för tiden 1900–1921* (Karlskrona, 1936).

J G A Pocock, 'History and Sovereignty: The Historiographical Response to Europeanization in Two British Cultures', *Journal of British Studies*, 31 (1992), pp. 358–389.

V F T Pointon, 'Mid Victorian Plymouth: A Social Geography' (unpublished PhD thesis, Polytechnic South West, 1989).

Sidney Pollard, 'Nineteenth Century Co-operation: From Community Building to Shopkeeping', in Asa Briggs and John Saville, eds, *Essays in Labour History, 1886–1923* (London, 1960), pp. 74–112.

Sidney Pollard and Paul Robertson, *The British Shipbuilding Industry, 1870–1914* (Cambridge, Mass, 1979).

Richard Price, 'The Future of British Labour History', *International Review of Social History,* 36 (1991), pp. 249–260.

Martin Pugh, *The Tories and the People, 1880–1935* (Oxford, 1985).

Martin Pugh, 'The Rise of Labour and the Political Culture of Conservatism, 1890–1945', *History,* 87 (2002), pp. 514–537.

Martin Purvis, 'The Development of Co-operative Retailing in England and Wales, 1851–1901: A Geographical Study', *Journal of Historical Geography,* 16 (1990), pp. 314–331.

A Påhlman and W Sjölin, *Kooperationen i Karlskrona, 1869–1939,* (Stockholm, 1940).

Jean Quellien, 'Un milieu ouvrier réformiste: syndicalisme et réformisme à Cherbourg à la «Belle Epoque»', *Mouvement Social,* 127 (1984), pp. 65–88.

Percy Redfern, *The New History of the CWS* (London, 1938).

Alastair Reid, 'The Division of Labour and Politics in Britain, 1880–1920', in Wolfgang J Mommsen and Hans-Gerhard Husung, eds, *The Development of Trade Unionism in Great Britain and Germany, 1880–1914* (London, 1985), pp. 150–165.

Alastair J Reid, 'Old Unionism Reconsidered: The Radicalism of Robert Knight', in Eugenio F Biagini and Alastair J Reid, eds, *Currents of Radicalism: Popular Radicalism, Organised Labour and Party Politics in Britain, 1850–1914* (Cambridge, 1991), pp. 214–243.

Alastair J Reid, 'Class and Politics in the Work of Henry Pelling', in John Callaghan, Steven Fielding and Steve Ludlam, eds, *Interpreting the Labour Party: New Approaches to Labour Politics and History* (Manchester, 2003), pp. 101–115.

Donald Reid, 'The Third Republic as Manager: Labor Policy in the Naval Shipyards, 1892–1902', *International Review of Social History,* 30 (1985), pp. 183–206.

Rita Rhodes, *An Arsenal for Labour: The Royal Arsenal Co-operative Society and Politics 1896–1996* (Manchester, 1998).

Richard Rodger, *Housing in Urban Britain 1780–1914* (London, 1989).

Gillian Rose, 'Imagining Poplar in the 1920s: Contested Concepts of Community', *Journal of Historical Geography,* 16 (1990), pp. 425–437.

Sonya O Rose, 'Gender Antagonism and Class Conflict: Exclusionary Strategies of Male Trade Unionists in Nineteenth Century Britain', *Social History,* 13 (1988), pp. 191–208.

Sonya O Rose, *Limited Livelihoods: Gender and Class in Nineteenth Century England* (London, 1992).

Bo Rothstein, 'State Structure and Variations in Corporatism: The Swedish Case', *Scandinavian Political Studies,* 14 (1991), pp. 149–171.

Patrick Salmon, *Scandinavia and the Great Powers, 1890–1940* (Cambridge, 1997).

Göran Salmonsson, *Den förståndiga viljan. Svenska Järn- och metallarbetareförbundet 1888–1902* (Uppsala, 1998).

Donald Sassoon, *One Hundred Years of Socialism: The West European Left in the Twentieth Century* (London, 1996).

Michael Savage, *The Dynamics of Working-Class Politics: The Labour Movement in Preston, 1880–1940* (Cambridge, 1987).

Mike Savage and Andrew Miles, *The Remaking of the British Working Class, 1840–1940* (London, 1994).

John Saville, 'Trade Unions and Free Labour: the Background to the Taff Vale Decision', in Asa Briggs and John Saville, eds, *Essays in Labour History in Memory of G D H Cole* (London, 1960), pp. 317–350.

Berndt Schiller, 'Den skandinaviska arbetarrörelsens internationalism 1870–1914', *Arbetarhistoria*, 42 (1987), pp. 3–4.

Berndt Schiller, 'Years of Crisis', in Steven Koblik ed., *Sweden's Development from Poverty to Affluence: 1750–1970*, translated Joanne Johnson (Minneapolis, 1975), pp. 197–228.

Lennart Schön, *En modern svensk ekonomisk historia. Tillväxt och omvandling under två sekel* (Stockholm, 2000).

G Scott, '"The Working-class Woman's Most Active and Democratic Movement": The Women's Co-operative Guild from 1883 to 1950' (unpublished DPhil thesis, University of Sussex, 1988).

Joan Wallach Scott, *Gender and the Politics of History* (New York, 1988).

Bengt Schüllerqvist, *Från kosackval till kohandel. SAP:s väg till makten (1928–33)* (Stockholm, 1992).

Lennart Schön, 'Proto-Industrialisation and Factories: Textiles in Sweden in the Mid-Nineteenth Century', *Scandinavian Economic History Review*, 30 (1982), pp. 57–71.

Robert Self, *The Evolution of the British Party System 1885–1940* (Harlow, 2000).

Theda Skocpol, 'Bringing the State Back In: Strategies of Analysis in Current Research', in Peter B Evans, Dietrich Rueschemeyer and Theda Skocpol, eds, *Bringing the State Back In* (Cambridge, 1985), pp. 3–37.

Birger Simonson, *Socialdemokratin och maktövertagandet. SAP:s politiska strategier 1889–1911* (Göteborg, 1985).

Birger Simonson, 'Sweden', in Marcel van der Linden and Jürgen Rojahn, eds, *The Formation of Labour Movements 1870–1914: An International Perspective* (Leiden, 1990), pp. 85–102.

Margaret Ramsay Somers, 'Workers of the World, Compare!', *Contemporary Sociology*, 18 (1989), pp. 325–329.

Lena Sommestad, *Från mejerska till mejerist. En studie av mejeriyrkets maskuliniseringsprocess* (Lund, 1992).

Lawrence Sondhaus, 'The Imperial German Navy and Social Democracy, 1878–1897', *German Studies Review*, 18 (1995), pp. 51–64.

David Starkey, 'The Ports, Seaborne Trade and Shipping Industry of South

Devon, 1786–1914', in Michael Duffy et al., eds, *The New Maritime History of Devon*, vol. 2 (London, 1994).

Peter N Stearns, 'The European Labour Movement and the Working Classes 1890–1914', in Harvey Mitchell and Peter N Stearns, *Workers and Protest: The European Labor Movement, the Working Classes and the Origins of Social Democracy, 1890–1914* (Itasca, 1971).

Christer Strahl, *Nationalism och socialism. Fosterlandet i den politiska idédebatten i Sverige 1890–1914* (Lund, 1983).

Bo Stråth, *Varvsarbetare i två varvstäder. En historisk studie av verkstadsklubbarna vid varven i Göteborg och Malmö* (Kungälv, 1982).

Bo Stråth, 'Workers' Radicalism in Theory and Practice: A Study of the Shipyard Workers and Industrial Development in Gothenburg, Malmö and Bremen', *Scandinavian Journal of History*, 8 (1983), pp. 261–291.

Benedikt Stuchtey, 'Literature, Liberty and Life of the Nation: British Historiography from Macaulay to Trevelyan', in Stefan Berger, Mark Donovan and Kevin Passmore, eds, *Writing National Histories: Western Europe since 1800* (London, 1999), pp. 30–48.

Anne Summers, 'The Character of Edwardian Nationalism: Three Popular Leagues,' in Paul Kennedy and Anthony Nicholls, eds, *Nationalist and Racialist Movements in Britain and Germany before 1914* (London, 1981), pp. 98–87.

Svenska metallindustriarbetareförbundet avdelning 96 I Karlskrona. En jubileumsskrift (Karlskrona, 1976).

Thommy Svensson, *Från ackord till månadslön. En studie av lönpolitiken, fackföreningarna och rationaliseringarna inom svensk varvsindustri under 1900-talet* (Göteborg, 1983).

Øystein Sørensen and Bo Stråth, eds, *The Cultural Construction of Norden* (Oslo, 1997).

Duncan Tanner, 'The Parliamentary Electoral System, the "Fourth" Reform Act and the Rise of Labour in England and Wales', *Bulletin of the Institute for Historical Research*, 56 (1983), pp. 205–219.

Duncan Tanner, *Political Change and the Labour Party, 1900–1918* (Cambridge, 1990).

Duncan Tanner, 'Ideological Debate in Edwardian Labour Politics: Radicalism, Revisionism and Socialism', in Eugenio F Biagini and Alastair J Reid, eds, *Currents of Radicalism: Popular Radicalism, Organised Labour and Party Politics in Britain, 1850–1914* (Cambridge, 1991), pp. 271–293.

Duncan Tanner, 'The Development of British Socialism, 1900–1918', in E H H Green, ed., *An Age of Transition: British Politics 1880–1914* (Edinburgh, 1997), pp. 48–66.

Miles Taylor, 'Patriotism, History and the Left in Twentieth Century Britain', *The Historical Journal*, 33 (1990), pp. 971–987.

Robert Taylor, 'Out of the Bowels of the Movement: The Trade Unions and the Origins of the Labour Party 1900–18', in Brian Brivati and Richard Heffernan, eds, *The Labour Party: A Centenary History* (Basingstoke, 2000), pp. 8–49.

Göran Therborn, Anders Kjellberg, Staffan Marklund and Ulf Öhlund, 'Sweden Before and After Social Democracy: A First Overview', *Acta Sociologica*, (1978), Supplement, pp. 37–58.

E P Thompson, *The Making of the English Working Class* (Harmondsworth, 1968; first published 1963).

E P Thompson, 'The Peculiarities of the English', reprinted in *idem., The Poverty of Theory and Other Essays* (London, 1978; first published 1965), pp. 245–301.

Paul Thompson, *Socialists, Liberals and Labour: The Struggle for London, 1885–1914* (London, 1967).

Andrew Thorpe, *A History of the British Labour Party* (Basingstoke, 1997).

Playford V Thorson II, 'The Defense Question in Sweden 1911–1914', (unpublished PhD thesis, University of Minnesota, 1972).

Yngve Tidman, *Spräng Amalthea! Arbete, facklig kamp och strejkbryteri i nordvästeuropeiska hamnar 1870–1914* (Lund, 1998).

Herbert Tingsten, *The Swedish Social Democrats: Their Ideological Development*, translated Greta Frankel and Patricia Howard-Rosen (Totowa, New Jersey, 1973).

Charles Tilly, *Big Structures, Large Processes, Huge Comparisons* (New York, 1984).

Jarl Torbacke, *Försvaret främst. Tre studier till belysning av borggårdskrisens problematik* (Stockholm, 1983).

G H Tredidga, 'The Liberal Party in Cornwall, 1918–1939' (unpublished MPhil thesis, University of Exeter, 1991).

Frank Trentmann, 'Bread, Milk and Democracy: Consumption and Citizenship in Twentieth-Century Britain', in Martin Daunton and Matthew Hilton, eds, *The Politics of Consumption: Material Culture and Citizenship in Europe and America* (Oxford, 2001), pp. 129–163.

Lars Trägårdh, 'Varieties of Volkish Identities', in Bo Stråth, ed., *Language and the Constitution of Class Identities* (Göteborg, 1990), pp. 25–54.

John Turner, *British Politics and the Great War: Coalition and Conflict, 1915–1918* (London, 1992).

Patricia R Turner, 'Hostile Participants? Working-Class Militancy, Associational Life, and the "Distinctiveness" of the Prewar French Labor Movement', *The Journal of Modern History*, 71 (1999), pp. 28–55.

Natasha Vall, 'Explorations in Comparative History: Economy and Society in Malmö and Newcastle since 1945', (unpublished PhD thesis, Northumbria University, 2000).

Torbjörn Vallinder, *I kamp för demokratin. Rösträttsrörelsen i Sverige 1886–1900* (Stockholm, 1962).

Antonio Varsoni, 'Is Britain Part of Europe? The Myth of British Difference', in Cyril Buffet and Beatrice Heuser, eds, *Haunted by History: Myths in International Relations* (Providence, 1998), pp. 135–156.

James Vernon, *Politics and the People: A Study in English Political Culture, c. 1815–1867* (Cambridge, 1993).

Dror Wahrman, 'The New Political History: A Review Essay', *Social History,* 21 (1996), pp. 343–354.

Bernard Waites, *A Class Society at War: Britain 1914–1918* (Leamington Spa, 1987).

Judith R Walkowitz, *Prostitution and Victorian Society: Women, Class and the State* (Cambridge, 1982; first published 1980).

P J Waller, *Democracy and Sectarianism: A Political and Social History of Liverpool, 1868–1939* (Liverpool, 1981).

Paul Ward, *Red Flag and Union Jack: Englishness, Patriotism and the British Left, 1881–1924* (Woodbridge, 1998).

M Waters, 'A Social History of Dockyard Workers at Chatham, Kent, 1860–1914' (unpublished PhD thesis, University of Essex, 1979).

Mavis Waters, 'Dockyard and Parliament: A Study of Unskilled Workers in Chatham Yard, 1860–1900', *Southern History,* 6 (1984), pp. 123–138.

Mavis Waters, 'The Dockyardmen Speak Out: Petition and Tradition in Chatham Dockyard, 1860–1906', in Kenneth Lunn and Ann Day, eds, *History of Work and Labour Relations in the Royal Dockyards* (London, 1999), pp. 87–98.

Gary E Weir, *Building the Kaiser's Navy: The Imperial Navy Office and German Industry in the von Tirpitz Era, 1890–1919* (Minneapolis, 1992).

Margaret Weir and Theda Skocpol, 'State Structures and the Possibilities for "Keynesian" Responses to the Great Depression in Sweden, Britain and the United States', in Peter B Evans, Dietrich Rueschemeyer and Theda Skocpol, eds, *Bringing the State Back In* (Cambridge, 1985), pp. 107–163.

Egon Wertheimer, *Portrait of the British Labour Party* (London, 1929).

Ulla Wikander, *Kvinnors och mäns arbeten. Gustavsberg 1880–1980: Genusarbetsdelning och arbetets degradering vid en porslinsfabrik* (Lund, 1988).

Magnus Wikdahl, *Varvets tid. Arbetarliv och kulturell förändring i en skeppsbyggarstad* (Stockholm, 1992).

Sean Wilentz, 'Against Exceptionalism: Class Consciousness and the American Labor Movement', *International Labor and Working-Class History,* 26 (1984), pp. 1–24.

H B Williams, *History of the Plymouth and District Trades Council from 1892 to 1952* (Plymouth, 1952).

Kirk Willis, 'The Introduction and Critical Reception of Marxist Thought in Britain, 1850–1900', *The Historical Journal,* 20 (1977), pp. 417–459.

Michael J Winstanley, *The Shopkeeper's World 1830–1914* (Manchester, 1983).

J M Winter, *Socialism and the Challenge of War: Ideas and Politics in Britain 1912–18* (London, 1974).

Jay M Winter, 'Trade Unions and the Labour Party in Britain', in Wolfgang J Mommsen and Hans-Gerhard Husung, eds, *The Development of Trade Unionism in Great Britain and Germany, 1880–1914* (London, 1985), pp. 359–370.

H Wolfe, *Labour Supply and Regulation* (Oxford, 1923).

Vagn Wåhlin, 'Omkring studiet af de folklige bevægelser', *Historisk Tidskrift* (S) (1979), pp. 113–151.

Stephen Yeo, 'A New Life: The Religion of Socialism in Britain, 1883–1896', *History Workshop Journal,* 4 (1977), pp. 5–56.

Stephen Yeo, 'Socialism, the State and Some Oppositional Englishness', in Robert Colls and Philip Dodd, *Englishness: Politics and Culture, 1880–1920* (London, 1986), pp. 308–369.

Stephen Yeo, ed., *New Views of Co-operation* (London, 1988).

Jonathan Zeitlin, 'Industrial Structure, Employer Strategy and the Diffusion of Job Control in Britain, 1880–1920', in Wolfgang J Mommsen and Hans-Gerhard Husung, eds, *The Development of Trade Unionism in Great Britain and Germany, 1880–1914* (London, 1985), pp. 325–337.

Aristide R Zolberg, 'How Many Exceptionalisms?', in Ira Katznelson and Aristide R Zolberg, eds, *Working-Class Formation: Nineteenth-Century Patterns in Western Europe and the United States* (Princeton, 1986), pp. 397–455.

Klas Åmark, *Facklig makt och fackligt medlemskap. De svenska fackförbundens medlemsutveckling 1890–1940* (Lund, 1986).

Kjell Östberg, *Byråkrati och reformism. En studie av svensk socialdemokratis politiska och sociala integrering före första världskriget* (Stockholm, 1990).

Index